May | 2007
No 737

Monthly Digest of Statistics

D1796713

Editor: Dilys Rosen

Office for National Statistics

palgrave
macmillan

ISBN 978-0-230-52604-4

ISSN 0308–6666

Contact points

For enquiries about this publication, contact

the Editor

Tel: 01633 655850

E-mail: monthly.digest@ons.gsi.gov.uk

For general enquiries, contact the National Statistics

Customer Contact Centre on: 0845 601 3034

(minicom: 01633 812399)

E-mail: info@statistics.gsi.gov.uk

Fax: 01633 652747

Post: Room 1015, Government Buildings,

Cardiff Road, Newport NP10 8XG

You can also find National Statistics on the Internet at:
www.statistics.gov.uk

Subscriptions

To subscribe to this publication, contact Palgrave Macmillan at:
www.palgrave.com/ons or on 01256 357893.

About the Office for National Statistics

The Office for National Statistics (ONS) is the government agency responsible for compiling, analysing and disseminating many of the United Kingdom's economic, social and demographic statistics, including the retail prices index, trade figures and labour market data, as well as the periodic census of the population and health statistics. It is also the agency that administers the statutory registration of births, marriages and deaths in England and Wales. The Director of ONS is also the National Statistician and the Registrar General for England and Wales.

A National Statistics publication

National Statistics are produced to high professional standards set out in the National Statistics Code of Practice. They undergo regular quality assurance reviews to ensure that they meet customer needs. They are produced free from any political influence.

Contents

Contents

Contents

Units of Measurement

Length

1 millimetre (mm)		= 0.03937 inch
1 centimetre (cm)	= 10 millimetres	= 0.3937 inch
1 metre (m)	= 1,000 millimetres	= 1.094 yards
1 kilometre (km)	= 1,000 metres	= 0.6214 mile
1 inch (in.)		= 25.40 millimetres or 2.540 centimetres
1 foot (ft.)	= 12 inches	= 0.3048 metre
1 yard (yd.)	= 3 feet	= 0.9144 metre
1 mile	= 1,760 yards	= 1.609 kilometres

Area

1 square millimetre (mm²)		= 0.001550 square inch
1 square metre (m²)		= 1.196 square yards
1 hectare (ha)	= 10,000 square metres	= 2.471 acres
1 square kilometre (km²)		= 247.1 acres
1 square inch (sq. in.)		= 645.2 square millimetres or 6.452 square centimetres
1 square foot (sq. ft.)	= 144 square inches	= 0.09290 square metre or 929.0 square centimetres
1 square yard (sq. yd.)	= 9 square feet	= 0.8361 square metre
1 acre	= 4,840 square yards	4,046 square metres or 0.4047 hectare
1 square mile (sq. mile)	= 640 acres	= 2.590 square kilometres or 259.0 hectares

Volume

1 cubic centimetre (cm³)		= 0.06102 cubic inch
1 cubic decimetre (dm³)	= 1,000 cubic centimetres	= 0.03531 cubic foot
1 cubic metre (m³)		= 1.308 cubic yards
1 cubic inch (cu.in.)		=16.39 cubic centimetres
1 cubic foot (cu. ft.)	= 1,728 cubic inches	= 0.02832 cubic metre or 28.32 cubic decimetres
1 cubic yard (cu. yd.)	= 27 cubic feet	= 0.7646 cubic metre

Capacity

1 litre (l)	= 1 cubic decimetre	= 0.2200 gallon
1 hectolitre (hl)	= 100 litres	= 22.00 gallons
1 pint		= 0.5682 litre
1 quart	= 2 pints	= 1.137 litres
1 gallon	= 8 pints	= 4.546 litres
1 bulk barrel	= 36 gallons (gal.)	= 1.637 hectolitres

Weight

1 gram (g)		= 0.03527 ounce avoirdupois
1 hectogram (hg)	= 100 grams	= 3.527 ounces or 0.2205 pound
1 kilogram (kg)	= 1,000 grams or 10 hectograms	= 2.205 pounds
1 tonne (t)	= 1,000 kilograms	= 1.102 short tons or 0.9842 long ton
1 ounce avoirdupois (oz.)	= 437.5 grains	= 28.35 grams
1 pound avoirdupois (lb.)	= 16 ounces	= 0.4536 kilogram
1 hundredweight (cwt.)	= 112 pounds	= 50.80 kilograms
1 short ton	= 2,000 pounds	= 907.2 kilograms or 0.9072 tonne
1 long ton (referred to as ton)	= 2,240 pounds	= 1,016 kilograms or 1.016 tonnes
1 ounce troy	= 480 grains	= 31.10 grams

Energy

British thermal unit (Btu)	= 0.2520 kilocalorie	(kcal) = 1.055 kilojoule (kj)
Therm	= 10^5 British thermal	units = 25,200 kcal = 105,506 kj
Megawatt hour (MWh)	= 10^6 watt hours (Wh)	
Gigawatt hour (GWh)	= 10^6 kilowatt hours = 34,121 therms	

Food and drink

Butter	23,310 litres milk	= 1 tonne butter (average)
Cheese	10,070 litres milk	= 1 tonne cheese
Condensed milk	2,550 litres milk	= 1 tonne full cream condensed milk
	2,953 litres skimmed milk	= 1 tonne skimmed condensed milk
Milk	1 million litres	= 1,030 tonnes
Milk powder	8,054 litres milk	= 1 tonne full cream milk powder
	10,740 litres skimmed milk	= 1 tonne skimmed milk powder
Eggs	17,126 eggs	= 1 tonne (approximate)
Sugar	100 tonnes sugar beet	= 92 tonnes refined sugar
	100 tonnes cane sugar	= 96 tonnes refined sugar

Shipping

Gross tonnage	= total volume of all the enclosed spaces of a vessel, the unit of measurement being a 'ton' of 100 cubic feet.
Deadweight tonnage	= Deadweighttonnage is the total weight in tons of 2,240 lb. that a ship can legally carry, that is the total weight of cargo, bunkers, stores and crew.

Introduction

This publication has been prepared by the Office for National Statistics (ONS) in collaboration with a number of government departments and other organisations. The assistance provided by them is gratefully acknowledged.

The name of the department or organisation providing the statistics is shown under each table, additionally, on some tables this is followed by a contact telephone number.

All the data series published in the *Monthly Digest* are contained on an ONS database, and nearly all are stored with a four letter identification code (e.g. ABMZ). These codes appear at the start of columns or rows so that they can be quoted if you contact us requiring any further information.

The latest Annual Supplement to *Monthly Digest* was published in the January 2007 edition. This gives detailed definitions and explanatory notes and includes an index of sources.

Definitions and classifications

The following general definitions should be noted in using the *Digest*:

Area covered. Except where otherwise stated, all statistics relate to the United Kingdom of Great Britain and Northern Ireland.

Seasonality. Except where otherwise stated, all statistics are not adjusted to take account of seasonal factors.

The UK Standard Industrial Classification 1992 is used in a number of tables in this digest to split economic activity. Full details are available from *UK Standard Industrial Classification of Economic Activities 1992*, and *Indexes to the UK Standard Industrial Classification of Economic Activities 1992*, both available from Palgrave Macmillan.

Regional classification is based on the Government Office Regions.

Symbols and conventions used

Change of basis. Where consecutive figures have been compiled on different bases and are not strictly comparable, a footnote is added indicating the nature of the difference. Also, a line may be drawn across a column between two consecutive figures indicating that the figures above and below the line have been compiled on different bases.

Units of measurement. The various units of measurement used in this digest are listed on the opposite page.

Symbols. The following symbols have been used throughout:

.. = not available (also information suppressed to avoid disclosure)

- = nil or less than half the final digit shown

† = indicates that the data have been revised

p = provisional data

since the last edition: the period marked is the earliest in the table to have been revised

Also, some tables have symbols specific to them. These will be explained in the footnotes to those tables.

Rounding of figures. In tables where figures have been rounded to the nearest final digit, there may be a slight discrepancy between the sum of the constituent items and the total as shown.

Provisional data

Some figures are provisional and may be subject to revision in later editions. This applies par ticularly to data for the most recent time periods. Where data has been revised a dagger symbol, as previously mentioned, will appear.

National Statistics Online: www.statistics.gov.uk

Web-based access to time series, cross sectional data and metadata from across the Government Statistical Service (GSS), available using the site search and index functions from the homepage. Download many datasets, in whole or in part, or consult directory information for all GSS statistical resources, including censuses, surveys, periodicals and enquiry services. Information is posted as PDF electronic documents or in XLS and CSV formats, compatible with most spreadsheet packages.

Time Series Data

Access to around 40,000 time series, of primarily macro-economic data, drawn from the main tables in a range of our major economic and labour market publications. Download complete releases, or view and download your own customised selection of individual time series.

Complete copies of this publication are available to download free of charge on the following web page. www.statistics.gov. uk/monthlydigest

Web: www.palgrave.com/ons, email: ons@palgrave.com

Acknowledgements

Contributors

The Editor wishes to thank all her colleagues in ONS, the rest of the Government Statistical Service and all contributors in other organisations for their generous support and helpful comments.

1 National accounts

1.1 Gross domestic product and gross national income

£ million

	At current prices					Chained volume measures			
	Gross national income at market prices	Net income from abroad[1]	Gross domestic product at market prices	less Basic price adjust- ment[2]	Gross value added at basic prices	Gross domestic product at market prices	less Basic price adjust- ment[1]	Gross value added at basic prices	Gross value added at factor cost
	ABMZ	CAES	YBHA	NTAP	ABML	ABMI	NTAO	ABMM	YBHH
1997	811 797	603	811 194	90 570	720 624	936 717	103 014	833 944	820 939
1998	869 706	8 910	860 796	97 116	763 680	968 040	105 165	863 147	849 467
1999	904 737	−1 830	906 567	105 956	800 611	997 295	107 873	889 722	875 372
2000	954 004	777	953 227	112 248	840 979	1 035 295	112 020	923 583	908 587
2001	1 005 313	8 326	996 987	114 234	882 753	1 059 648	116 584	943 186	927 875
2002	1 069 839	21 072	1 048 767	118 470	930 297	1 081 469	121 657	959 811	943 960
2003	1 132 938	22 642	1 110 296	124 738	985 558	1 110 296	124 738	985 558	969 067
2004	1 202 075	25 548	1 176 527	132 362	1 044 165	1 146 523	128 660	1 017 863	1 000 888
2005	1 252 406	26 428	1 225 978	137 472	1 088 506	1 168 674	130 561	1 038 113	1 020 696
2006	1 311 752	21 763	1 289 989	144 822	1 145 167	1 200 960	134 366	1 066 594	1 048 471
Seasonally adjusted									
1997 Q2	202 256	1 293	200 963	22 245	178 718	233 166	25 664	207 562	204 322
Q3	205 717	947	204 770	23 165	181 605	235 045	26 028	209 079	205 785
Q4	206 698	−1 069	207 767	23 746	184 021	237 150	26 036	211 175	207 846
1998 Q1	211 244	662	210 582	24 040	186 542	239 311	26 041	213 337	209 945
Q2	214 567	1 207	213 360	23 971	189 389	240 634	26 162	214 540	211 148
Q3	221 773	4 353	217 420	24 341	193 079	243 161	26 396	216 833	213 402
Q4	222 122	2 688	219 434	24 764	194 670	244 934	26 566	218 437	214 972
1999 Q1	220 523	−976	221 499	25 385	196 114	245 774	26 682	219 157	215 658
Q2	224 191	−905	225 096	25 813	199 283	247 398	26 642	220 839	217 255
Q3	228 802	−79	228 881	26 913	201 968	250 676	27 005	223 752	220 145
Q4	231 221	130	231 091	27 845	203 246	253 447	27 544	225 974	222 314
2000 Q1	235 382	735	234 647	27 659	206 988	256 262	27 989	228 340	224 648
Q2	236 889	−330	237 219	28 227	208 992	258 132	27 954	230 250	226 534
Q3	240 987	1 314	239 673	28 160	211 513	259 667	27 877	231 881	228 111
Q4	240 746	−942	241 688	28 202	213 486	261 234	28 200	233 112	229 294
2001 Q1	248 119	1 774	246 345	28 373	217 972	263 631	28 568	235 130	231 322
Q2	250 036	1 978	248 058	28 696	219 362	263 935	28 828	235 149	231 338
Q3	252 418	2 971	249 447	28 492	220 955	265 519	29 323	236 213	232 374
Q4	254 740	1 603	253 137	28 673	224 464	266 563	29 865	236 694	232 841
2002 Q1	261 806	4 438	257 368	29 317	228 051	267 948	29 957	237 993	234 098
Q2	264 279	3 251	261 028	29 402	231 626	269 392	30 346	239 044	235 077
Q3	271 124	7 075	264 049	29 733	234 316	271 368	30 620	240 747	236 737
Q4	272 630	6 308	266 322	30 018	236 304	272 761	30 734	242 027	238 048
2003 Q1	278 360	7 442	270 918	30 341	240 577	274 119	30 740	243 381	239 321
Q2	279 619	4 489	275 130	30 692	244 438	275 712	31 096	244 616	240 522
Q3	284 071	4 047	280 024	31 504	248 520	278 748	31 396	247 351	243 211
Q4	290 888	6 664	284 224	32 201	252 023	281 717	31 506	250 210	246 013
2004 Q1	292 547	5 573	286 975	32 806	254 169	283 725	31 832	251 893	247 727
Q2	299 293	6 173	293 120	32 972	260 148	286 307	32 148	254 159	249 919
Q3	300 666	4 668	295 998	33 209	262 789	287 400	32 311	255 089	250 813
Q4	309 569	9 134	300 434	33 375	267 059	289 091	32 369	256 722	252 429
2005 Q1	308 536	6 741	301 795	33 913	267 882	289 945	32 340	257 605	253 304
Q2	314 076	9 331	304 745	34 140	270 605	291 297	32 526	258 771	254 424
Q3	313 251	6 315	306 936	34 908	272 028	292 813	32 812	260 001	255 634
Q4	316 543	4 041	312 502	34 511	277 991	294 619	32 883	261 736	257 334
2006 Q1	321 014	5 882	315 133	35 216	279 917	297 004	33 159	263 845	259 397
Q2	327 987	8 641	319 346	36 008	283 338	299 295	33 481	265 814	261 278
Q3	329 904	4 491	325 413	36 641	288 772	301 316	33 771	267 545	262 991
Q4	332 847	2 749	330 097	36 957	293 140	303 345	33 955	269 390	264 805
2007 Q1	..	..	..	..	..	305 468	..	271 276	..

3

1.1 Gross domestic product and gross national income

continued

2003 = 100

	Value indices at current prices		Chained volume indices			Implied deflators[3]		
	Gross domestic product at market prices	Gross value added at basic prices	Gross domestic product at market prices	Gross value added at basic prices	Gross national disposable income at market prices	Gross domestic final expenditure	Gross domestic product at market prices	Gross value added at basic prices
	YBEU	YBEX	YBEZ	CGCE	YBFP	YBFV	YBGB	CGBV
1997	73.1	73.1	84.4	84.6	82.0	88.1	86.6	86.4
1998	77.5	77.5	87.2	87.6	85.9	89.9	88.9	88.5
1999	81.7	81.2	89.8	90.3	87.7	91.6	90.9	90.0
2000	85.9	85.3	93.2	93.7	90.8	93.0	92.1	91.1
2001	89.8	89.6	95.4	95.7	93.8	95.2	94.1	93.6
2002	94.5	94.4	97.4	97.4	97.2	97.3	97.0	96.9
2003	100.0	100.0	100.0	100.0	100.0	100.0	100.0	100.0
2004	106.0	105.9	103.3	103.3	103.4	102.4	102.6	102.6
2005	110.4	110.4	105.3	105.3	104.5	105.4	104.9	104.9
2006	116.2	116.2	108.2	108.2	106.6	108.2	107.4	107.4
Seasonally adusted								
1997 Q2	72.4	72.5	84.0	84.2	82.2	87.6	86.2	86.1
Q3	73.8	73.7	84.7	84.9	82.6	88.7	87.1	86.9
Q4	74.9	74.7	85.4	85.7	82.9	89.0	87.6	87.1
1998 Q1	75.9	75.7	86.2	86.6	83.9	89.3	88.0	87.4
Q2	76.9	76.9	86.7	87.1	85.3	89.6	88.7	88.3
Q3	78.3	78.4	87.6	88.0	87.4	90.0	89.4	89.0
Q4	79.1	79.0	88.2	88.7	86.9	90.5	89.6	89.1
1999 Q1	79.8	79.6	88.5	88.9	86.1	90.9	90.1	89.5
Q2	81.1	80.9	89.1	89.6	87.2	91.5	91.0	90.2
Q3	82.5	82.0	90.3	90.8	88.4	91.9	91.3	90.3
Q4	83.3	82.5	91.3	91.7	89.0	92.2	91.2	89.9
2000 Q1	84.5	84.0	92.3	92.7	90.2	92.5	91.6	90.6
Q2	85.5	84.8	93.0	93.4	90.6	92.7	91.9	90.8
Q3	86.3	85.8	93.5	94.1	91.7	93.2	92.3	91.2
Q4	87.1	86.6	94.1	94.6	90.8	93.8	92.5	91.6
2001 Q1	88.7	88.5	95.0	95.4	93.2	94.5	93.4	92.7
Q2	89.4	89.0	95.1	95.4	93.4	94.8	94.0	93.3
Q3	89.9	89.7	95.7	95.9	94.5	95.5	93.9	93.5
Q4	91.2	91.1	96.0	96.1	94.2	95.8	95.0	94.8
2002 Q1	92.7	92.6	96.5	96.6	95.9	96.6	96.1	95.8
Q2	94.0	94.0	97.1	97.0	96.3	97.1	96.9	96.9
Q3	95.1	95.1	97.8	97.7	98.4	97.5	97.3	97.3
Q4	95.9	95.9	98.3	98.2	98.3	98.0	97.6	97.6
2003 Q1	97.6	97.6	98.8	98.8	99.4	98.8	98.8	98.8
Q2	99.1	99.2	99.3	99.3	98.9	99.8	99.8	99.9
Q3	100.9	100.9	100.4	100.4	100.0	100.4	100.5	100.5
Q4	102.4	102.3	101.5	101.6	101.7	101.0	100.9	100.7
2004 Q1	103.4	103.2	102.2	102.2	101.9	101.0	101.1	100.9
Q2	105.6	105.6	103.1	103.2	103.2	102.3	102.4	102.4
Q3	106.6	106.7	103.5	103.5	103.0	102.8	103.0	103.0
Q4	108.2	108.4	104.1	104.2	105.4	103.4	103.9	104.0
2005 Q1	108.7	108.7	104.5	104.6	104.2	104.0	104.1	104.0
Q2	109.8	109.8	104.9	105.0	105.6	104.8	104.6	104.6
Q3	110.6	110.4	105.5	105.5	103.9	106.1	104.8	104.6
Q4	112.6	112.8	106.1	106.2	104.4	106.8	106.1	106.2
2006 Q1	113.5	113.6	107.0	107.1	105.3	107.2	106.1	106.1
Q2	115.0	115.0	107.8	107.9	107.0	107.8	106.7	106.6
Q3	117.2	117.2	108.6	108.6	107.0	108.6	108.0	107.9
Q4	118.9	119.0	109.3	109.3	107.1	109.2	108.8	108.8
2007 Q1	..	..	110.0	110.1	..	..	..	..

1 Includes employment, entrepreneurial and property income.
2 Taxes on products *less* subsidies on products.
3 Derived from expenditure components.

Source: Office for National Statistics: 020 7533 6031

1.2 Gross domestic product: by category of expenditure

£ million[1]

| | | Domestic expenditure on goods and services at market prices | | | | | | | | | | Statis-tical discre-pancy (expen-diture) | Gross domestic product at market prices |
| | Final consumption expenditure | | | Gross capital formation | | | | | | | | | |
	House-holds	Non-profit instit-utions [2]	General government	Gross fixed capital formation	Change in inven-tories[3]	Acquisi-tions less disposals of valuables	Total	Total exports	Total final expend-iture	less Total imports		
At current prices													
	ABPB	ABNV	NMRK	NPQX	ABMP	NPJO	YBIJ	KTMW	ABMD	KTMX	GIXM	YBHA
1997	501 290	19 372	150 554	133 620	4 621	−27	809 430	234 019	1 043 449	232 255	–	811 194
1998	534 153	20 837	156 409	151 083	5 026	429	867 937	232 034	1 099 971	239 175	–	860 796
1999	567 994	21 874	169 520	156 344	6 060	229	922 021	239 782	1 161 803	255 236	–	906 567
2000	600 826	23 169	181 851	161 468	5 271	3	972 588	267 602	1 240 190	286 963	–	953 227
2001	632 496	24 720	194 503	165 472	6 189	396	1 023 776	273 140	1 296 916	299 929	–	996 987
2002	664 562	25 968	212 464	173 525	2 909	214	1 079 642	276 511	1 356 153	307 386	–	1 048 767
2003	697 160	27 185	232 699	178 751	3 983	−37	1 139 741	285 397	1 425 138	314 842	–	1 110 296
2004	732 531	28 953	250 708	194 491	4 856	−37	1 211 502	298 694	1 510 196	333 669	–	1 176 527
2005	760 032	31 588	269 491	205 891	4 071	−377	1 270 696	325 946	1 596 642	370 420	−244	1 225 978
2006	793 322	33 312	287 635	223 682	5 510	45	1 343 506	370 103	1 713 609	424 189	569	1 289 989
Unadjusted													
2002 Q3	168 281	6 517	53 530	42 995	2 690	75	274 088	71 145	345 233	79 523		
Q4	174 355	6 596	54 117	46 657	−2 634	13	279 104	67 694	346 798	75 754		
2003 Q1	164 428	6 679	56 739	45 416	2 612	−15	275 859	70 334	346 193	76 165		
Q2	171 826	6 731	58 158	41 917	−1 079	105	277 658	70 387	348 045	77 433		
Q3	177 152	6 837	58 449	43 719	3 700	−75	289 782	71 728	361 510	81 178		
Q4	183 754	6 938	59 353	47 699	−1 250	−52	296 442	72 948	369 390	80 066		
2004 Q1	173 338	7 101	61 166	48 625	3 383	107	293 720	69 837	363 557	77 865		
Q2	180 921	7 193	62 020	46 193	239	−80	296 486	73 410	369 896	82 348		
Q3	185 550	7 279	63 028	48 959	2 084	−104	306 796	76 089	382 885	86 802		
Q4	192 722	7 380	64 494	50 714	−850	40	314 500	79 358	393 858	86 654		
2005 Q1	179 889	7 746	65 457	51 160	2 071	−171	306 152	74 404	380 556	84 170		
Q2	187 211	7 848	66 835	48 222	−334	101	309 883	81 384	391 267	91 386		
Q3	192 264	7 950	68 298	52 183	3 413	−224	323 884	82 385	406 269	97 775		
Q4	200 668	8 044	68 901	54 326	−1 079	−83	330 777	87 773	418 550	97 089		
2006 Q1	187 043	8 193	71 281	55 320	2 890	−155	324 572	94 955	419 527	108 614		
Q2	195 189	8 284	71 164	53 090	7	254	327 988	100 792	428 780	115 383		
Q3	200 541	8 350	72 199	55 855	4 011	−46	340 910	87 580	428 490	102 673		
Q4	210 549	8 485	72 991	59 417	−1 398	−8	350 036	86 776	436 812	97 519		
Seasonally adjusted													
	ABJQ	HAYE	NMRP	NPQS	CAEX	NPJQ	YBIL	IKBH	ABMF	IKBI		
2002 Q3	166 634	6 517	53 589	43 779	692	75	271 286	69 926	341 212	77 163	–	264 049
Q4	168 609	6 596	54 190	45 374	384	13	275 166	67 002	342 168	75 846	–	266 322
2003 Q1	170 937	6 679	56 026	43 973	−550	−15	277 050	72 531	349 581	78 663	–	270 918
Q2	173 555	6 731	57 776	44 100	−555	105	281 712	70 700	352 412	77 282	–	275 130
Q3	175 502	6 837	58 818	44 304	2 238	−75	287 624	70 821	358 445	78 421	–	280 024
Q4	177 166	6 938	60 079	46 374	2 850	−52	293 355	71 345	364 700	80 476	–	284 224
2004 Q1	180 057	7 101	60 824	47 112	−159	107	295 042	71 906	366 948	79 973	–	286 975
Q2	182 611	7 193	62 189	48 619	995	−80	301 527	74 030	375 557	82 437	–	293 120
Q3	184 131	7 279	63 183	49 363	1 182	−104	305 034	75 188	380 222	84 224	–	295 998
Q4	185 732	7 380	64 512	49 397	2 838	40	309 899	77 570	387 469	87 035	–	300 434
2005 Q1	187 423	7 746	65 023	49 937	2 187	−171	312 145	76 555	388 700	86 827	−78	301 795
Q2	188 508	7 848	66 737	50 287	690	101	314 171	80 066	394 237	89 414	−78	304 745
Q3	191 012	7 950	68 381	52 719	652	−224	320 490	81 754	402 244	95 247	−61	306 936
Q4	193 089	8 044	69 350	52 948	542	−83	323 890	87 571	411 461	98 932	−27	312 502
2006 Q1	194 011	8 193	70 781	54 086	1 898	−155	328 814	95 915	424 729	109 690	94	315 133
Q2	197 137	8 284	71 098	55 464	2 365	254	334 602	97 873	432 475	113 263	134	319 346
Q3	199 591	8 350	72 291	56 257	1 524	−46	337 967	88 701	426 668	101 417	162	325 413
Q4	202 583	8 485	73 465	57 875	−277	−8	342 123	87 614	429 737	99 819	179	330 097

1.2 Gross domestic product: by category of expenditure
continued

£ million[1]

| | Domestic expenditure on goods and services at market prices | | | | | | | | | | Statistical discrepancy (expenditure) | Gross domestic product at market prices |
| | Final consumption expenditure | | | Gross capital formation | | | | | | | | |
	Households	Non-profit institutions[2]	General government	Gross fixed capital formation	Changes in inventories[3]	Acquisitions less disposals of valuables	Total	Total exports	Gross final expenditure	less Total imports		
Chained volume indices												
	ABPF	ABNU	NMRU	NPQR	ABMQ	NPJP	YBIK	KTMZ	ABME	KTNB	GIXS	ABMI
1997	558 064	23 391	196 353	139 064	3 394	-35	918 661	231 494	1 150 396	218 613	–	936 717
1998	579 342	25 092	198 592	158 525	4 291	30	965 970	238 344	1 203 987	238 834	–	968 040
1999	606 648	25 023	205 853	163 039	5 803	–	1 006 378	247 289	1 253 258	257 809	–	997 295
2000	633 662	27 177	212 265	167 486	4 648	-28	1 045 373	269 830	1 315 374	281 081	–	1 035 295
2001	653 326	27 155	217 359	171 639	5 577	342	1 075 760	277 694	1 353 632	294 449	–	1 059 648
2002	676 833	27 130	224 868	178 066	2 289	183	1 109 596	280 593	1 390 217	308 706	–	1 081 469
2003	697 160	27 185	232 699	178 751	3 982	-37	1 139 741	285 397	1 425 138	314 842	–	1 110 296
2004	721 434	27 327	240 129	189 492	4 597	-42	1 182 937	299 289	1 482 225	335 703	–	1 146 523
2005	731 274	28 119	247 412	195 107	3 611	-354	1 205 170	322 869	1 528 039	359 132	-233	1 168 674
2006	744 933	29 883	253 235	207 704	5 501	66	1 241 320	360 440	1 601 760	401 331	529	1 200 960
Unadjusted												
2002 Q3	171 224	6 793	56 241	43 845	2 642	62	281 010	72 412	353 470	79 914		
Q4	176 748	6 819	56 901	47 463	-2 601	7	285 438	69 143	354 527	76 886		
2003 Q1	165 903	6 843	58 099	46 880	2 644	-8	280 509	70 460	350 960	76 806		
Q2	172 040	6 779	57 436	42 110	-1 247	-12	277 848	70 218	348 072	77 276		
Q3	176 448	6 790	58 001	43 129	3 793	-14	287 655	71 428	359 081	80 246		
Q4	182 769	6 773	59 163	46 632	-1 208	-3	293 729	73 291	367 025	80 514		
2004 Q1	171 913	6 830	60 335	48 601	3 248	112	291 040	71 101	362 141	79 844		
Q2	178 308	6 805	59 021	45 087	-154	-90	288 976	73 901	362 877	83 080		
Q3	182 480	6 826	59 766	47 333	2 385	-96	298 695	76 134	374 829	86 480		
Q4	188 733	6 866	61 007	48 471	-882	32	304 226	78 153	382 378	86 299		
2005 Q1	175 117	6 996	61 219	49 254	1 934	-158	294 362	73 468	367 830	83 342		
Q2	180 573	6 975	61 548	45 982	-373	86	294 791	80 543	375 334	89 377		
Q3	183 988	7 028	62 192	48 954	3 232	-201	305 193	82 860	388 053	93 395		
Q4	191 596	7 120	62 453	50 917	-1 182	-81	310 824	85 998	396 822	93 018		
2006 Q1	177 287	7 325	62 573	51 791	3 130	-128	301 978	93 037	395 015	103 021		
Q2	183 719	7 415	62 663	49 165	153	233	303 348	99 373	402 721	109 286		
Q3	187 445	7 508	63 771	51 758	3 980	-29	314 433	84 049	398 482	95 937		
Q4	196 482	7 635	64 228	54 990	-1 762	-10	321 561	83 981	405 542	93 087		
Seasonally adjusted												
	ABJR	HAYO	NMRY	NPQT	CAFU	NPJR	YBIM	IKBK	ABMG	IKBL		
2002 Q4	170 727	6 819	56 395	46 393	346	7	280 820	68 564	349 337	76 624	–	272 761
2003 Q1	171 828	6 843	57 099	44 934	-571	-8	280 285	72 662	352 958	78 836	–	274 119
Q2	174 146	6 779	57 684	44 161	-644	94	282 367	70 611	352 971	77 283	–	275 712
Q3	175 140	6 790	58 445	43 924	2 264	-68	286 503	70 334	356 830	78 089	–	278 748
Q4	176 046	6 773	59 471	45 732	2 934	-55	290 586	71 790	362 379	80 634	–	281 717
2004 Q1	178 197	6 830	59 969	47 256	-381	112	291 983	73 389	365 373	81 648	–	283 725
Q2	180 362	6 805	59 530	47 102	1 050	-90	294 759	74 861	369 620	83 313	–	286 307
Q3	181 032	6 826	60 002	47 813	1 025	-96	296 603	75 097	371 700	84 300	–	287 400
Q4	181 843	6 866	60 628	47 321	2 903	32	299 592	75 942	375 532	86 442	–	289 091
2005 Q1	182 197	6 996	60 908	48 106	2 029	-158	300 079	75 533	375 611	85 591	-75	289 945
Q2	182 206	6 975	61 792	47 937	678	86	299 673	79 293	378 967	87 595	-75	291 297
Q3	182 998	7 028	62 272	49 524	474	-201	302 095	82 167	384 262	91 391	-58	292 813
Q4	183 873	7 120	62 440	49 540	430	-81	303 323	85 876	389 199	94 555	-25	294 619
2006 Q1	183 907	7 325	62 705	50 616	2 173	-128	306 599	93 903	400 502	103 587	89	297 004
Q2	185 998	7 415	63 106	51 207	2 407	233	310 366	96 086	406 451	107 282	126	299 295
Q3	186 543	7 508	63 495	52 273	1 310	-29	311 100	85 409	396 509	95 344	150	301 316
Q4	188 485	7 635	63 929	53 608	-389	-10	313 257	85 042	398 300	95 118	164	303 345
2007 Q1	..	..	..	..	..	..	..	..	..	..	..	305 468

1 Estimates given to nearest million but cannot be regarded as accurate to that degree.
2 Non-profit institutions serving households.
3 Quarterly alignment adjustment included in this series.

Source: Office for National Statistics: 020 7533 6031

1.3 Gross domestic product: by category of income

£ million[1]

		Gross operating surplus of corporations						Taxes on production		Gross
	Compen-	Non-financial corporations		Financial			Gross value	*less*	Statistical	domestic
	sation of			corporations	Total	Other income[3]	added at	subsidies	discrepancy	product at
	employees	Public	Private[2]				factor cost		(income)	market prices
At current prices										
	HAEA	NRJT	NRJK	NQNV	CGBY	CGBW	CGCA	GCSC	GIXQ	YBHA
1997	429 967	7 249	171 338	17 385	195 972	80 449	706 388	104 806	–	811 194
1998	466 080	7 754	174 846	18 430	201 030	81 806	748 916	111 880	–	860 796
1999	495 793	7 678	178 939	15 976	202 593	86 723	785 109	121 458	–	906 567
2000	532 179	7 188	185 198	12 398	204 784	87 842	824 805	128 422	–	953 227
2001	564 194	6 892	185 942	12 052	204 886	97 352	866 432	130 555	–	996 987
2002	587 396	6 657	189 906	32 230	228 793	97 468	913 657	135 110	–	1 048 767
2003	616 893	7 265	202 479	39 936	249 680	102 494	969 067	141 229	–	1 110 296
2004	648 717	6 653	219 738	46 020	272 411	106 183	1 027 311	149 216	–	1 176 527
2005	685 345	7 833	228 054	37 512	273 399	114 551	1 073 295	152 606	77	1 225 978
2006	717 665	8 339	241 966	42 179	292 484	118 475	1 128 624	161 092	273	1 289 989
Unadjusted										
2002 Q3	144 964	1 704	45 857	11 023	58 584	22 656	226 204	34 225		
Q4	149 508	1 469	52 186	8 815	62 470	24 401	236 379	34 810		
2003 Q1	155 541	1 888	47 530	12 109	61 527	22 576	239 644	33 231		
Q2	151 315	1 788	48 831	8 838	59 457	28 255	239 027	34 747		
Q3	153 142	1 721	50 917	10 974	63 612	23 983	240 737	35 704		
Q4	156 895	1 868	55 201	8 015	65 084	27 680	249 659	37 547		
2004 Q1	165 466	1 992	53 583	10 950	66 525	25 143	257 134	35 868		
Q2	159 003	1 514	53 952	10 554	66 020	28 258	253 281	36 907		
Q3	159 427	1 476	54 708	12 563	68 747	25 953	254 127	37 619		
Q4	164 821	1 671	57 495	11 953	71 119	26 829	262 769	38 822		
2005 Q1	174 596	1 832	54 777	9 884	66 493	27 158	268 247	36 066		
Q2	167 622	1 750	56 830	8 792	67 372	30 269	265 263	37 899		
Q3	168 826	2 146	56 669	8 815	67 630	27 953	264 409	39 060		
Q4	174 301	2 105	59 778	10 021	71 904	29 171	275 376	39 581		
2006 Q1	185 117	1 981	57 524	9 386	68 891	28 228	282 236	37 474		
Q2	175 314	2 150	59 981	8 635	70 766	32 120	278 200	40 069		
Q3	175 912	2 013	59 758	12 675	74 446	28 452	278 810	40 961		
Q4	181 322	2 195	64 703	11 483	78 381	29 675	289 378	42 588		
Seasonally adjusted										
	DTWM	CAEQ	CAER	NHCZ	CGBZ	CGBX	CGCB	CMVL		
2002 Q3	147 571	1 759	47 615	9 032	58 406	24 201	230 178	33 871	–	264 049
Q4	149 755	1 468	47 060	9 806	58 334	24 077	232 166	34 156	–	266 322
2003 Q1	150 812	1 855	48 689	10 938	61 482	24 127	236 421	34 497	–	270 918
Q2	152 768	1 807	49 468	10 029	61 304	26 243	240 315	34 815	–	275 130
Q3	155 699	1 802	52 340	9 437	63 579	25 128	244 406	35 618	–	280 024
Q4	157 614	1 801	51 982	9 532	63 315	26 996	247 925	36 299	–	284 224
2004 Q1	159 239	1 813	52 656	9 624	64 093	26 712	250 044	36 931	–	286 975
Q2	160 899	1 524	55 385	11 667	68 576	26 509	255 984	37 136	–	293 120
Q3	162 653	1 593	55 940	11 163	68 696	27 199	258 548	37 450	–	295 998
Q4	165 926	1 723	55 757	13 566	71 046	25 763	262 735	37 699	–	300 434
2005 Q1	167 833	1 883	56 969	9 208	68 060	28 259	264 152	37 635	8	301 795
Q2	170 023	1 830	56 380	10 543	68 753	28 085	266 861	37 869	15	304 745
Q3	172 737	2 006	56 830	7 321	66 157	29 279	268 173	38 741	22	306 936
Q4	174 752	2 114	57 875	10 440	70 429	28 928	274 109	38 361	32	312 502
2006 Q1	177 401	2 050	58 377	8 715	69 142	29 337	275 880	39 196	57	315 133
Q2	177 960	2 104	58 765	10 216	71 085	30 164	279 209	40 071	66	319 346
Q3	180 356	2 086	61 284	11 258	74 628	29 617	284 601	40 739	73	325 413
Q4	181 948	2 099	63 540	11 990	77 629	29 357	288 934	41 086	77	330 097

1 Estimates given to the nearest million but cannot be regarded as accurate to that degree
2 Quarterly alignment adjustment included in this series.
3 Includes mixed income and the operating surplus of non-corporate sector less the adjustment for financial intermediation services indirectly measured (FISIM)

Source: Office for National Statistics: 020 7533 6031

1.4 Index numbers: gross domestic product, chained volume indices at basic prices: by industry of output

2003 = 100

| | Output at basic prices[1] | | | | | | | | |
| | | | | Service industries | | | | | |
	Agriculture, hunting forestry and fishing	Total production industries[2]	Construc-tion	Distribu-tion, hotels and catering; repairs	Transport, storage and communi-cation	Business services and finance	Government and other services	Total services	Gross domestic product[3]
2003 weights[1,4]	10	186	61	153	78	277	235	744	1000
	GDQA	CKYW	GDQB	GDQE	GDQH	GDQN	GDQU	GDQS	YBEZ
1999	101.1	101.9	89.8	86.3	83.4	85.8	91.0	87.2	89.8
2000	100.3	103.8	90.2	89.1	92.9	90.7	93.1	91.3	93.2
2001	90.9	102.3	92.2	92.1	97.0	94.4	95.3	94.5	95.4
2002	102.1	100.3	95.5	96.4	98.2	96.3	97.7	96.9	97.4
2003	100.0	100.0	100.0	100.0	100.0	100.0	100.0	100.0	100.0
2004	99.0	100.8	104.0	105.2	102.5	105.1	102.0	103.9	103.3
2005	101.4	98.9	105.6	106.4	107.0	109.5	104.1	106.9	105.3
2006	99.6	99.0	106.8	109.9	110.3	115.4	106.1	110.8	108.2
Seasonally adjusted									
1997 Q4	96.2	99.6	90.0	82.4	71.2	78.0	89.1	81.4	85.4
1998 Q1	98.3	100.5	92.6	82.7	73.4	78.7	89.7	82.2	86.2
Q2	99.3	100.6	88.5	82.9	74.9	80.8	89.5	83.1	86.7
Q3	97.2	100.6	88.6	83.8	77.3	82.2	90.4	84.4	87.6
Q4	96.7	100.4	89.0	84.9	79.2	83.3	90.8	85.4	88.2
1999 Q1	101.0	100.7	89.9	85.1	80.1	84.2	90.3	85.7	88.5
Q2	101.0	101.0	88.6	85.9	82.5	85.2	90.5	86.6	89.1
Q3	100.7	102.8	90.5	86.8	84.8	86.0	91.2	87.6	90.3
Q4	101.8	103.1	90.3	87.6	86.3	87.6	91.9	88.8	91.3
2000 Q1	101.1	103.6	92.1	88.2	89.1	88.6	92.7	89.8	92.3
Q2	100.6	104.1	89.8	88.6	92.2	90.1	92.9	90.9	93.0
Q3	101.6	103.7	88.8	89.5	94.6	91.6	93.3	92.0	93.5
Q4	98.0	104.0	89.9	89.9	95.6	92.4	93.5	92.5	94.1
2001 Q1	91.6	104.0	91.5	91.2	97.2	93.5	94.3	93.7	95.0
Q2	90.2	102.5	91.7	91.3	97.2	94.2	94.9	94.1	95.1
Q3	89.8	102.4	92.3	92.4	96.5	94.9	95.5	94.7	95.7
Q4	92.1	100.5	93.3	93.6	97.1	95.1	96.4	95.4	96.0
2002 Q1	101.0	100.5	94.8	95.3	98.0	94.7	96.9	95.9	96.5
Q2	102.6	100.5	94.4	95.5	96.9	96.1	97.5	96.5	97.1
Q3	102.8	100.2	95.8	96.7	98.4	97.0	97.9	97.4	97.8
Q4	102.0	100.2	97.0	98.0	99.3	97.3	98.3	98.0	98.3
2003 Q1	99.7	99.9	97.0	98.2	99.2	98.5	98.8	98.6	98.8
Q2	99.3	99.4	98.9	99.4	99.8	98.9	99.5	99.3	99.3
Q3	100.1	100.0	101.7	100.6	100.3	100.4	100.3	100.4	100.4
Q4	100.9	100.8	102.4	101.8	100.7	102.2	101.3	101.7	101.5
2004 Q1	99.1	100.9	102.8	103.6	100.7	103.4	101.4	102.5	102.2
Q2	98.3	101.3	103.4	105.2	102.2	104.3	102.2	103.6	103.1
Q3	99.3	100.3	104.4	106.0	103.1	105.6	102.0	104.3	103.5
Q4	99.2	100.6	105.4	105.9	104.1	106.9	102.5	105.0	104.1
2005 Q1	100.9	99.6	106.0	105.8	105.7	107.6	103.1	105.6	104.5
Q2	102.3	99.3	106.4	105.8	106.1	108.8	103.7	106.3	104.9
Q3	101.2	98.6	105.0	106.4	107.1	110.0	104.6	107.3	105.5
Q4	101.0	98.0	104.8	107.6	108.9	111.7	104.9	108.4	106.1
2006 Q1	100.3	98.9	105.9	108.7	109.3	112.9	105.6	109.3	107.0
Q2	99.4	99.0	106.3	109.7	110.0	114.8	105.8	110.4	107.8
Q3	99.5	99.2	107.0	109.9	110.2	116.4	106.4	111.2	108.6
Q4	99.0	99.0	107.9	111.2	111.7	117.6	106.8	112.2	109.3
2007 Q1	99.6	99.1	108.8	111.8	113.6	118.8	107.2	113.2	110.0

1 Components of output are valued at basic prices, which excludes taxes *less* subsidies on products, whereas GDP is valued at market prices.

2 The latest data for the index of production (series CKYW) are presented in Table 7.1. The figures given in this table are consistent with the figures for gross value added .

3 Includes an implicit discrepancy compared with the sum of the previous columns because the GDP aggregate takes account of other information based on incomes and expenditures.

4 The weights shown are in proportion to total gross value added (GVA) in 2003 and are used to combine the industry output indices to calculate the totals for 2004 and 2005. For 2003 and earlier, totals are calculated using the equivalent weights for the previous year (eg total for 2002 use 2001 weights).

Source: Office for National Statistics: 020 7533 6031

1.5 Households sector[1]: allocation of primary income account

£ million

	RESOURCES					USES			
	Gross operating surplus including gross mixed income	Wages and salaries	Employers' social contributions	Property Income received	Total resources	Property Income paid	Balance of primary incomes, gross	Total uses	Households' share of gross national income[2]
	RVGJ	QWLW	QWLX	QWME	QWMF	QWMI	QWMJ	QWMF	RVGG
1997	94 187	374 510	55 540	118 339	642 576	42 078	600 498	642 576	74.0
1998	100 465	406 548	59 522	124 863	691 398	51 435	639 963	691 398	73.7
1999	106 929	431 795	64 199	120 966	723 889	47 649	676 240	723 889	74.8
2000	111 765	462 505	69 824	128 800	772 894	53 090	719 804	772 894	75.5
2001	121 204	491 044	73 216	132 918	818 382	52 356	766 026	818 382	76.2
2002	128 315	508 681	78 782	119 736	835 514	51 729	783 785	835 514	73.3
2003	137 057	527 689	89 263	120 914	874 923	53 796	821 127	874 923	72.5
2004	144 667	550 654	98 134	127 180	920 635	62 901	857 734	920 635	71.4
2005	153 792	577 048	108 362	146 506	985 708	71 315	914 393	985 708	73.0
2006	161 135	603 203	114 520	152 999	1 031 857	75 277	956 580	1 031 857	72.9
Unadjusted									
2002 Q1	31 538	127 957	20 237	28 570	208 302	12 650	195 652	208 302	74.9
Q2	31 888	125 928	18 738	32 004	208 558	12 670	195 888	208 558	75.3
Q3	32 251	126 065	19 003	29 176	206 495	13 009	193 486	206 495	71.1
Q4	32 638	128 731	20 804	29 986	212 159	13 400	198 759	212 159	71.9
2003 Q1	33 249	133 142	22 310	27 438	216 139	13 340	202 799	216 139	72.4
Q2	34 137	130 600	20 754	33 397	218 888	13 264	205 624	218 888	74.8
Q3	34 577	131 180	22 053	29 536	217 346	13 417	203 929	217 346	71.5
Q4	35 094	132 767	24 146	30 543	222 550	13 775	208 775	222 550	71.3
2004 Q1	35 556	139 478	25 893	28 277	229 204	14 367	214 837	229 204	72.5
Q2	35 901	135 934	23 117	32 250	227 202	15 019	212 183	227 202	72.4
Q3	36 353	136 101	23 428	32 804	228 686	16 396	212 290	228 686	70.8
Q4	36 857	139 141	25 696	33 849	235 543	17 119	218 424	235 543	69.8
2005 Q1	37 535	146 836	27 646	33 870	245 887	17 627	228 260	245 887	74.4
Q2	38 214	142 616	25 055	38 127	244 012	17 628	226 384	244 012	72.9
Q3	38 762	142 589	26 345	37 924	245 620	18 034	227 586	245 620	72.5
Q4	39 281	145 007	29 316	36 585	250 189	18 026	232 163	250 189	72.2
2006 Q1	39 640	153 510	31 490	35 996	260 636	18 172	242 464	260 636	75.6
Q2	40 031	149 154	26 203	39 284	254 672	18 103	236 569	254 672	72.9
Q3	40 506	148 907	27 106	39 963	256 482	19 083	237 399	256 482	72.2
Q4	40 958	151 632	29 721	37 756	260 067	19 919	240 148	260 067	71.1
Seasonally adjusted									
	NRJN	ROYJ	ROYK	ROYL	ROYR	ROYT	ROYS	ROYR	NRJH
2002 Q1	31 538	124 971	19 019	30 312	205 840	12 671	193 169	205 840	73.8
Q2	31 888	126 664	19 443	30 405	208 400	12 823	195 577	208 400	74.0
Q3	32 251	127 816	19 778	29 795	209 640	12 970	196 670	209 640	72.5
Q4	32 638	129 230	20 542	29 224	211 634	13 265	198 369	211 634	72.8
2003 Q1	33 358	129 933	20 894	29 701	213 886	13 292	200 594	213 886	72.1
Q2	33 938	131 181	21 610	31 556	218 285	13 422	204 863	218 285	73.3
Q3	34 479	132 790	22 920	29 360	219 549	13 328	206 221	219 549	72.6
Q4	35 282	133 785	23 839	30 297	223 203	13 754	209 449	223 203	72.0
2004 Q1	35 556	134 980	24 274	30 521	225 331	14 319	211 012	225 331	72.1
Q2	35 901	136 807	24 124	30 570	227 402	15 200	212 202	227 402	70.9
Q3	36 353	138 323	24 347	32 422	231 445	16 289	215 156	231 445	71.6
Q4	36 857	140 544	25 389	33 667	236 457	17 093	219 364	236 457	70.9
2005 Q1	37 535	142 247	25 593	35 766	241 141	17 581	223 560	241 141	72.5
Q2	38 214	143 431	26 621	36 659	244 925	17 840	227 085	244 925	72.3
Q3	38 762	144 999	27 755	37 197	248 713	17 984	230 729	248 713	73.7
Q4	39 281	146 371	28 393	36 884	250 929	17 910	233 019	250 929	73.6
2006 Q1	39 640	148 404	29 001	37 919	254 964	18 114	236 850	254 964	73.8
Q2	40 031	149 983	28 001	37 818	255 833	18 334	237 499	255 833	72.4
Q3	40 506	151 670	28 694	38 923	259 793	19 029	240 764	259 793	73.0
Q4	40 958	153 146	28 824	38 339	261 267	19 800	241 467	261 267	72.5

1 This sector includes households and non-profit institutions serving households

2 The balance of gross primary incomes of the households and non-profit institutions serving households sector as a percentage of gross national income.

Source: Office for National Statistics: 020 7533 6031

1.6 Households sector[1]: secondary distribution of income account

£ million

	RESOURCES					USES						
	Gross balance of primary incomes	Social contributi-ons	Social benefits other than social transfers in kind	Other current transfers	Total resources	Current taxes on incomes etc.	Social contributi-ons	Social benefits other than social transfers in kind	Other current transfers	Gross disposable income	Total uses	Real households' disposable income
	QWMJ	RVFH	QWML	QWMO	QWMP	QWMS	QWMY	QWMZ	QWNC	QWND	QWMP	RVGK
1997	600 498	410	150 844	34 521	786 273	91 208	110 848	880	23 396	559 941	786 273	625 184
1998	639 963	478	154 438	36 405	831 284	106 566	116 012	950	24 966	582 790	831 284	634 508
1999	676 240	450	157 647	38 154	872 491	115 186	123 516	922	23 879	608 988	872 491	652 060
2000	719 804	476	162 833	43 670	926 783	124 726	130 679	948	27 015	643 415	926 783	681 249
2001	766 026	502	171 814	44 687	983 029	133 054	135 998	977	26 688	686 312	983 029	710 531
2002	783 785	530	182 673	50 218	1 017 206	134 959	143 558	1 006	28 635	709 048	1 017 206	722 823
2003	821 127	505	193 596	49 511	1 064 739	138 261	158 348	987	26 754	740 389	1 064 739	740 389
2004	857 734	495	202 074	51 778	1 112 081	147 134	170 437	984	27 843	765 683	1 112 081	752 890
2005	914 393	500	214 367	55 741	1 185 001	159 422	187 600	994	31 203	804 778	1 185 001	772 016
2006	956 580	508	223 341	57 690	1 238 119	169 833	..	1 004	32 766	834 240	1 238 119	781 945
Unadjusted												
2002 Q1	195 652	132	44 006	13 175	252 965	44 162	36 616	251	6 948	164 988	252 965	169 321
Q2	195 888	132	44 904	12 086	253 010	28 065	35 491	251	6 790	182 413	253 010	185 919
Q3	193 486	133	45 665	12 604	251 888	33 621	35 297	252	7 395	175 323	251 888	178 554
Q4	198 759	133	48 098	12 353	259 343	29 111	36 154	252	7 502	186 324	259 343	189 029
2003 Q1	202 799	129	46 491	12 406	261 825	44 396	39 244	249	6 649	171 287	261 825	172 922
Q2	205 624	128	47 224	12 360	265 336	29 351	38 188	248	6 728	190 821	265 336	191 102
Q3	203 929	125	48 544	12 254	264 852	34 429	40 199	246	7 100	182 878	264 852	182 136
Q4	208 775	123	51 337	12 491	272 726	30 085	40 717	244	6 277	195 403	272 726	194 229
2004 Q1	214 837	123	48 626	12 786	276 372	46 462	44 785	245	6 955	177 925	276 372	176 256
Q2	212 183	124	49 977	12 954	275 238	30 540	41 067	246	7 209	196 176	275 238	193 050
Q3	212 290	124	50 522	13 553	276 489	37 117	41 171	246	7 089	190 866	276 489	187 382
Q4	218 424	124	52 949	12 485	283 982	33 015	43 414	247	6 590	200 716	283 982	196 202
2005 Q1	228 260	125	50 466	13 985	292 836	50 716	47 937	248	7 996	185 290	292 836	179 846
Q2	226 384	125	52 606	14 646	293 761	34 076	45 598	248	8 472	205 601	293 761	197 694
Q3	227 586	125	53 993	14 024	295 728	40 422	46 290	249	8 070	200 407	295 728	191 210
Q4	232 163	125	57 302	13 086	302 676	34 208	47 775	249	6 665	213 480	302 676	203 266
2006 Q1	242 464	127	53 404	13 158	309 153	53 899	54 875	251	7 643	193 622	309 153	183 083
Q2	236 569	127	54 561	14 842	306 099	35 999	..	251	8 634	213 320	306 099	200 381
Q3	237 399	127	56 782	14 914	309 222	43 011	..	251	8 179	209 413	309 222	195 437
Q4	240 148	127	58 594	14 776	313 645	36 924	..	251	8 310	217 885	313 645	203 044
Seasonally adjusted												
	ROYS		RPHL	RPHM	RPHP	RPHR	RPHU	RPIA	RPIB	RPHQ	RPHP	NRJR
2002 Q1	193 169	132	45 060	12 939	251 300	33 921	35 252	251	6 712	175 164	251 300	179 363
Q2	195 577	132	45 510	12 050	253 269	33 463	35 635	251	6 754	177 166	253 269	180 917
Q3	196 670	133	45 831	12 471	255 105	33 804	35 961	252	7 262	177 826	255 105	181 266
Q4	198 369	133	46 272	12 758	257 532	33 771	36 710	252	7 907	178 892	257 532	181 277
2003 Q1	200 594	129	47 778	12 121	260 622	33 808	37 125	249	6 364	183 076	260 622	184 156
Q2	204 863	128	47 783	12 237	265 011	34 897	38 697	248	6 605	184 564	265 011	185 216
Q3	206 221	125	48 613	12 152	267 111	34 263	41 102	246	6 998	184 502	267 111	184 087
Q4	209 449	123	49 422	13 001	271 995	35 293	41 424	244	6 787	188 247	271 995	186 930
2004 Q1	211 012	123	50 048	12 565	273 748	34 979	42 135	245	6 734	189 655	273 748	187 493
Q2	212 202	124	50 428	12 794	275 548	36 312	41 825	246	7 049	190 116	275 548	187 472
Q3	215 156	124	50 578	13 399	279 257	37 285	42 176	246	6 935	192 615	279 257	189 038
Q4	219 364	124	51 020	13 020	283 528	38 558	44 301	247	7 125	193 297	283 528	188 887
2005 Q1	223 560	125	51 718	13 892	289 295	39 164	45 277	248	7 903	196 703	289 295	190 687
Q2	227 085	125	53 408	14 267	294 885	40 012	46 614	248	8 093	199 918	294 885	192 620
Q3	230 729	125	54 337	13 924	299 115	40 426	48 197	249	7 970	202 273	299 115	193 196
Q4	233 019	125	54 904	13 658	301 706	39 820	48 516	249	7 237	205 884	301 706	195 513
2006 Q1	236 850	127	54 636	13 075	304 688	41 380	49 818	251	7 560	205 679	304 688	194 511
Q2	237 499	127	55 214	14 307	307 147	42 240	49 293	251	8 099	207 264	307 147	195 141
Q3	240 764	127	56 970	14 767	312 628	43 240	50 196	251	8 032	210 909	312 628	196 813
Q4	241 467	127	56 521	15 541	313 656	42 973	50 969	251	9 075	210 388	313 656	195 480

1 This sector includes households and non-profit institutions serving house-holds.

Source: Office for National Statistics: 020 7533 6031

1.7 Households sector[1]: use of disposable income account

£ million

	RESOURCES			USES			
	Gross disposable income	Adjustment for the change in net equity of households in pension funds	Total resources	Individual consumption expenditure	Gross saving	Total uses	Households' saving ratio[2]
	QWND	NSSE	NSSF	NSSG	NSSH	NSSF	RVGL
1997	559 941	15 111	575 052	520 662	54 390	575 052	9.5
1998	582 790	14 044	596 834	554 990	41 844	596 834	7.0
1999	608 988	14 016	623 004	589 868	33 136	623 004	5.3
2000	643 415	14 164	657 579	623 995	33 584	657 579	5.1
2001	686 312	16 041	702 353	657 216	45 137	702 353	6.4
2002	709 048	17 783	726 831	690 530	36 301	726 831	5.0
2003	740 389	21 377	761 766	724 345	37 421	761 766	4.9
2004	765 683	25 108	790 791	761 484	29 307	790 791	3.7
2005	804 778	31 210	835 988	791 620	44 368	835 988	5.3
2006	834 240	35 307	869 547	826 634	42 913	869 547	4.9
Unadjusted							
2002 Q1	164 988	4 550	169 538	164 176	5 362	169 538	3.2
Q2	182 413	4 774	187 187	170 605	16 582	187 187	8.9
Q3	175 323	4 242	179 565	174 798	4 767	179 565	2.7
Q4	186 324	4 217	190 541	180 951	9 590	190 541	5.0
2003 Q1	171 287	5 998	177 285	171 107	6 178	177 285	3.5
Q2	190 821	4 228	195 049	178 557	16 492	195 049	8.5
Q3	182 878	5 570	188 448	183 989	4 459	188 448	2.4
Q4	195 403	5 581	200 984	190 692	10 292	200 984	5.1
2004 Q1	177 925	7 516	185 441	180 439	5 002	185 441	2.7
Q2	196 176	5 766	201 942	188 114	13 828	201 942	6.8
Q3	190 866	5 346	196 212	192 829	3 383	196 212	1.7
Q4	200 716	6 480	207 196	200 102	7 094	207 196	3.4
2005 Q1	185 290	8 955	194 245	187 635	6 610	194 245	3.4
Q2	205 601	6 619	212 220	195 059	17 161	212 220	8.1
Q3	200 407	7 204	207 611	200 214	7 397	207 611	3.6
Q4	213 480	8 432	221 912	208 712	13 200	221 912	5.9
2006 Q1	193 622	11 441	205 063	195 236	9 827	205 063	4.8
Q2	213 320	7 925	221 245	203 473	17 772	221 245	8.0
Q3	209 413	7 567	216 980	208 891	8 089	216 980	3.7
Q4	217 885	8 374	226 259	219 034	7 225	226 259	3.2
Seasonally adjusted							
	RPHQ	RPQJ	RPQK	RPQM	RPQL	RPQK	NRJS
2002 Q1	175 164	4 144	179 308	170 261	9 047	179 308	5.0
Q2	177 166	4 126	181 292	171 913	9 379	181 292	5.2
Q3	177 826	4 706	182 532	173 151	9 381	182 532	5.1
Q4	178 892	4 807	183 699	175 205	8 494	183 699	4.6
2003 Q1	183 076	5 107	188 183	177 616	10 567	188 183	5.6
Q2	184 564	4 035	188 599	180 286	8 313	188 599	4.4
Q3	184 502	6 086	190 588	182 339	8 249	190 588	4.3
Q4	188 247	6 149	194 396	184 104	10 292	194 396	5.3
2004 Q1	189 655	6 273	195 928	187 158	8 770	195 928	4.5
Q2	190 116	5 788	195 904	189 804	6 100	195 904	3.1
Q3	192 615	5 892	198 507	191 410	7 097	198 507	3.6
Q4	193 297	7 155	200 452	193 112	7 340	200 452	3.7
2005 Q1	196 703	7 245	203 948	195 169	8 779	203 948	4.3
Q2	199 918	7 148	207 066	196 356	10 710	207 066	5.2
Q3	202 273	8 259	210 532	198 962	11 570	210 532	5.5
Q4	205 884	8 558	214 442	201 133	13 309	214 442	6.2
2006 Q1	205 679	9 276	214 955	202 204	12 751	214 955	5.9
Q2	207 264	8 572	215 836	205 421	10 415	215 836	4.8
Q3	210 909	8 766	219 675	207 941	11 734	219 675	5.3
Q4	210 388	8 693	219 081	211 068	8 013	219 081	3.7

1 This sector includes households and non-profit institutions serving households.

2 Households' and non-profit institutions serving households' gross saving as a percentage of total resources.

Source: Office for National Statistics: 020 7533 6031

1.8 Household final consumption expenditure[1]

£ million

| | | | | | | | | UK National[2] | | | | | | | |
| | | | | | | | | UK Domestic[3] | | | | | | | |
	Total	Net tourism	Total	Food & Drink	Alcohol & tobacco[4]	Clothing & footwear	Housing	Household goods & services	Health	Transport[4]	Communication	Recreation & culture	Education	Restaurants & hotels[4]	Miscellaneous
COICOP	-	-	0	01	02	03	04	05	06	07	08	09	10	11	12

At current prices

	ABPB	ABTE	ABQI	ABZV	ADFL	ADFP	ADFS	ADFY	ADGP	ADGT	ADGX	ADGY	ADIE	ADIF	ADII
1997	501 290	905	500 385	53 787	21 553	30 901	91 977	29 492	7 757	77 204	9 984	58 012	7 440	57 164	55 114
1998	534 153	2 369	531 784	55 162	22 459	31 947	98 114	31 002	8 306	82 506	10 902	63 246	7 814	61 807	58 519
1999	567 994	5 378	562 616	57 040	24 458	33 375	103 193	32 846	8 775	87 237	12 005	67 481	8 943	64 387	62 876
2000	600 826	6 941	593 885	58 628	24 617	35 479	108 050	35 675	9 208	93 052	13 356	70 154	9 534	68 557	67 575
2001	632 496	9 524	622 972	59 804	25 158	36 822	115 905	37 974	9 976	96 435	14 157	73 452	9 409	71 620	72 260
2002	664 562	10 563	653 999	61 310	25 966	39 092	121 238	40 448	10 778	100 147	14 675	79 122	9 381	76 426	75 416
2003	697 160	12 158	685 002	63 174	27 297	41 155	129 051	42 466	11 335	104 569	15 654	84 386	9 610	78 902	77 403
2004	732 531	12 041	720 490	65 521	27 713	42 792	138 040	44 029	11 932	109 213	16 448	91 057	9 990	83 595	80 160
2005	760 032	12 049	747 983	67 539	28 009	43 813	146 663	43 445	12 003	112 938	16 800	94 118	10 409	88 937	83 309
2006	793 322	11 862	781 460	70 809	28 522	45 947	158 739	45 061	12 501	116 505	16 911	97 768	10 998	91 918	85 781

Percentage change, year on previous year

1997	6.0		5.9	1.4	5.5	4.6	4.9	6.2	4.4	9.7	6.7	8.3	13.3	3.8	6.9
1998	6.6		6.3	2.6	4.2	3.4	6.7	5.1	7.1	6.9	9.2	9.0	5.0	8.1	6.2
1999	6.3		5.8	3.4	8.9	4.5	5.2	5.9	5.6	5.7	10.1	6.7	14.4	4.2	7.4
2000	5.8		5.6	2.8	0.7	6.3	4.7	8.6	4.9	6.7	11.3	4.0	6.6	6.5	7.5
2001	5.3		4.9	2.0	2.2	3.8	7.3	6.4	8.3	3.6	6.0	4.7	−1.3	4.5	6.9
2002	5.1		5.0	2.5	3.2	6.2	4.6	6.5	8.0	3.8	3.7	7.7	−0.3	6.7	4.4
2003	4.9		4.7	3.0	5.1	5.3	6.4	5.0	5.2	4.4	6.7	6.7	2.4	3.2	2.6
2004	5.1		5.2	3.7	1.5	4.0	7.0	3.7	5.3	4.4	5.1	7.9	4.0	5.9	3.6
2005	3.8		3.8	3.1	1.1	2.4	6.2	−1.3	0.6	3.4	2.1	3.4	4.2	6.4	3.9
2006	4.4		4.5	4.8	1.8	4.9	8.2	3.7	4.1	3.2	0.7	3.9	5.7	3.4	3.0

Not seasonally adjusted

2003 Q4	183 754	1 787	181 967	16 471	7 618	12 922	33 896	11 750	3 007	23 806	4 210	24 113	2 451	20 754	20 969
2004 Q1	173 338	2 364	170 974	16 171	6 496	9 075	35 251	10 292	2 881	26 485	4 070	20 878	2 470	18 299	18 606
Q2	180 921	3 214	177 707	16 298	6 832	10 242	33 609	10 871	2 990	26 904	4 024	22 666	2 487	20 980	19 804
Q3	185 550	4 680	180 870	15 665	6 745	10 224	33 148	10 933	2 973	30 377	4 089	22 034	2 501	22 492	19 689
Q4	192 722	1 783	190 939	17 387	7 640	13 251	36 032	11 933	3 088	25 447	4 265	25 479	2 532	21 824	22 061
2005 Q1	179 889	2 481	177 408	16 421	6 541	9 267	37 000	10 409	2 907	27 486	4 145	21 877	2 558	19 521	19 276
Q2	187 211	3 126	184 085	17 031	6 876	10 382	35 573	10 673	2 921	28 320	4 127	22 840	2 592	22 501	20 249
Q3	192 264	4 902	187 362	16 179	6 806	10 396	35 311	10 173	3 005	31 210	4 109	22 728	2 617	23 910	20 918
Q4	200 668	1 540	199 128	17 908	7 786	13 768	38 779	12 190	3 170	25 922	4 419	26 673	2 642	23 005	22 866
2006 Q1	187 043	2 517	184 526	16 769	6 550	9 354	40 071	10 461	3 081	28 650	4 241	22 425	2 673	19 989	20 262
Q2	195 189	3 369	191 820	17 551	6 962	10 860	38 374	11 039	3 127	29 006	4 150	24 079	2 711	23 185	20 776
Q3	200 541	4 441	196 100	17 290	7 020	11 009	38 190	10 934	3 101	32 175	4 110	23 764	2 771	24 903	20 833
Q4	210 549	1 535	209 014	19 199	7 990	14 724	42 104	12 627	3 192	26 674	4 410	27 500	2 843	23 841	23 910

Seasonally adjusted

	ABJQ	ABTF	ZAKV	ZWUM	ZAKX	ZAKZ	ZAVN	ZAVV	ZAWB	ZAWL	ZAWV	ZAWZ	ZWUS	ZAXR	ZAYF
2003 Q4	177 166	2 923	174 243	15 761	6 941	10 399	33 227	10 840	2 903	26 282	4 028	21 738	2 451	20 170	19 503
2004 Q1	180 057	2 975	177 082	16 381	6 926	10 617	33 870	10 671	2 925	26 806	4 101	22 150	2 470	20 527	19 638
Q2	182 611	2 905	179 706	16 211	6 925	10 736	34 287	11 083	3 030	26 991	4 083	23 052	2 487	20 827	19 994
Q3	184 131	3 121	181 010	16 285	6 918	10 734	34 668	11 294	2 995	27 407	4 166	22 936	2 501	20 999	20 107
Q4	185 732	3 040	182 692	16 644	6 944	10 705	35 215	10 981	2 982	28 009	4 098	22 919	2 532	21 242	20 421
2005 Q1	187 423	3 084	184 339	16 718	6 989	10 910	35 559	10 991	2 957	28 016	4 170	23 266	2 558	21 981	20 224
Q2	188 508	2 829	185 679	16 920	6 989	10 909	36 323	10 718	2 947	28 184	4 201	23 138	2 592	22 215	20 543
Q3	191 012	3 262	187 750	16 834	6 978	10 943	36 904	10 761	3 030	28 178	4 197	23 630	2 617	22 300	21 378
Q4	193 089	2 874	190 215	17 067	7 053	11 051	37 877	10 975	3 069	28 560	4 232	24 084	2 642	22 441	21 164
2006 Q1	194 011	3 089	190 922	17 087	7 002	11 066	38 352	10 973	3 131	28 933	4 259	23 812	2 673	22 474	21 160
Q2	197 137	3 048	194 089	17 422	7 082	11 419	39 311	11 273	3 151	29 067	4 217	24 390	2 711	22 896	21 150
Q3	199 591	2 840	196 751	17 932	7 197	11 634	40 189	11 379	3 126	29 148	4 205	24 724	2 771	23 173	21 273
Q4	202 583	2 885	199 698	18 368	7 241	11 828	40 887	11 436	3 093	29 357	4 230	24 842	2 843	23 375	22 198

1.8 Household final consumption expenditure[1]
continued

	Total	Net tourism	Total	Food & Drink	Alcohol & tobacco[4]	Clothing & footwear	Housing	Household goods & services	Health	Transport[4]	Communication	Recreation & culture	Education	Restaurants & hotels[4]	Miscellaneous
						UK National[2]									
						UK Domestic[3]									
COICOP	-	-	0	01	02	03	04	05	06	07	08	09	10	11	12

Chained volume measures

	ABPF	ABTG	ABQJ	ADIP	ADIS	ADIW	ADIZ	ADJF	ADJM	ADJQ	ADJU	ADJV	ADMJ	ADMK	ADMN
1997	558 064	−319	558 122	57 261	27 125	25 696	121 226	30 248	10 531	85 325	8 698	52 550	10 582	71 229	64 600
1998	579 342	2 074	576 994	58 058	26 829	26 736	122 959	31 443	10 472	89 008	9 644	57 871	10 530	73 811	65 059
1999	606 648	5 868	600 627	59 904	27 623	28 689	123 662	33 130	10 362	92 969	10 948	63 601	11 394	74 191	67 867
2000	633 662	8 151	625 437	61 944	26 704	31 744	125 299	36 305	10 421	96 209	12 698	68 038	11 489	76 252	70 524
2001	653 326	10 733	642 595	61 048	26 497	34 485	126 749	38 310	10 697	98 485	14 452	72 552	10 692	76 434	73 239
2002	676 833	12 084	664 790	62 143	26 884	38 499	127 979	40 552	10 980	101 621	14 796	77 597	10 091	78 303	75 715
2003	697 160	12 158	685 002	63 174	27 297	41 155	129 051	42 466	11 335	104 569	15 654	84 386	9 610	78 902	77 403
2004	721 434	12 770	708 664	65 181	27 444	44 087	131 490	43 577	11 609	106 610	16 361	92 889	9 541	81 796	78 079
2005	731 274	11 593	719 681	66 230	27 258	46 197	131 640	42 743	11 534	107 305	17 150	98 594	9 475	83 882	77 673
2006	744 933	11 309	733 624	67 861	27 007	48 890	133 587	43 868	11 822	107 841	17 339	104 252	9 480	83 560	78 117

Percentage change, year on previous year

1997	3.5		2.9	1.7	1.2	3.7	1.1	5.1	−1.3	3.8	9.5	7.0	7.8	–	2.8
1998	3.8		3.4	1.4	−1.1	4.0	1.4	4.0	−0.6	4.3	10.9	10.1	−0.5	3.6	0.7
1999	4.7		4.1	3.2	3.0	7.3	0.6	5.4	−1.1	4.5	13.5	9.9	8.2	0.5	4.3
2000	4.5		4.1	3.4	−3.3	10.6	1.3	9.6	0.6	3.5	16.0	7.0	0.8	2.8	3.9
2001	3.1		2.7	−1.4	−0.8	8.6	1.2	5.5	2.6	2.4	13.8	6.6	−6.9	0.2	3.8
2002	3.6		3.5	1.8	1.5	11.6	1.0	5.9	2.6	3.2	2.4	7.0	−5.6	2.4	3.4
2003	3.0		3.0	1.7	1.5	6.9	0.8	4.7	3.2	2.9	5.8	8.7	−4.8	0.8	2.2
2004	3.5		3.5	3.2	0.5	7.1	1.9	2.6	2.4	2.0	4.5	10.1	−0.7	3.7	0.9
2005	1.4		1.6	1.6	−0.7	4.8	0.1	−1.9	−0.6	0.7	4.8	6.1	−0.7	2.6	−0.5
2006	1.9		1.9	2.5	−0.9	5.8	1.5	2.6	2.5	0.5	1.1	5.7	0.1	−0.4	0.6

Not seasonally adjusted

2003 Q4	182 769	1 741	180 953	16 328	7 561	12 871	33 187	11 696	2 951	23 639	4 197	24 368	2 411	20 673	20 951
2004 Q1	171 913	2 630	169 283	16 006	6 451	9 303	34 090	10 271	2 831	26 231	4 034	21 221	2 401	18 117	18 327
Q2	178 308	3 388	174 920	16 177	6 776	10 469	32 195	10 700	2 908	26 500	3 949	22 943	2 389	20 596	19 318
Q3	182 480	4 911	177 569	15 721	6 648	10 696	31 512	10 886	2 883	29 355	4 084	22 420	2 380	21 950	19 034
Q4	188 733	1 841	186 892	17 277	7 569	13 619	33 693	11 720	2 987	24 524	4 294	26 305	2 371	21 133	21 400
2005 Q1	175 117	2 593	172 524	16 108	6 411	9 795	33 966	10 393	2 802	26 683	4 195	22 661	2 371	18 722	18 417
Q2	180 573	3 044	177 529	16 638	6 698	10 866	32 170	10 483	2 807	27 311	4 200	23 537	2 371	21 305	19 143
Q3	183 988	4 498	179 490	15 956	6 599	11 109	31 565	10 019	2 882	29 252	4 208	23 807	2 371	22 422	19 300
Q4	191 596	1 458	190 138	17 528	7 550	14 427	33 939	11 848	3 043	24 059	4 547	28 589	2 362	21 433	20 813
2006 Q1	177 287	2 403	174 884	16 355	6 269	10 077	34 420	10 320	2 936	26 973	4 294	23 753	2 365	18 462	18 660
Q2	183 719	3 106	180 613	17 005	6 620	11 466	32 678	10 756	2 963	26 862	4 245	25 311	2 369	21 155	19 183
Q3	187 445	4 139	183 306	16 514	6 571	11 853	32 320	10 653	2 925	29 446	4 247	25 164	2 379	22 522	18 712
Q4	196 482	1 661	194 821	17 987	7 547	15 494	34 169	12 139	2 998	24 560	4 553	30 024	2 367	21 421	21 562

Seasonally adjusted

	ABJR	ABTH	ZAKW	ZWUN	ZAKY	ZALA	ZAVO	ZAVW	ZAWC	ZAWM	ZAWW	ZAXA	ZWUT	ZAXS	ZAYG
2003 Q4	176 046	2 803	173 236	15 590	6 870	10 507	32 491	10 841	2 848	26 142	4 020	21 894	2 411	20 085	19 514
2004 Q1	178 197	3 141	175 056	16 262	6 869	10 769	32 750	10 587	2 870	26 324	4 065	22 500	2 401	20 321	19 338
Q2	180 362	3 165	177 197	16 153	6 877	11 047	32 902	10 950	2 950	26 391	4 008	23 490	2 389	20 460	19 580
Q3	181 032	3 310	177 722	16 239	6 837	11 108	32 881	11 207	2 908	26 738	4 162	23 396	2 380	20 464	19 402
Q4	181 843	3 154	178 689	16 527	6 861	11 163	32 957	10 833	2 881	27 157	4 126	23 503	2 371	20 551	19 759
2005 Q1	182 197	3 091	179 106	16 407	6 848	11 406	32 692	10 897	2 845	26 914	4 230	24 064	2 371	21 090	19 342
Q2	182 206	2 781	179 425	16 556	6 809	11 486	32 875	10 569	2 836	27 036	4 285	24 118	2 371	21 054	19 430
Q3	182 998	3 043	179 955	16 527	6 794	11 566	32 817	10 542	2 908	26 619	4 296	24 925	2 371	20 881	19 709
Q4	183 873	2 678	181 195	16 740	6 807	11 739	33 256	10 735	2 945	26 736	4 339	25 487	2 362	20 857	19 192
2006 Q1	183 907	2 811	181 096	16 673	6 709	11 780	33 132	10 753	2 979	26 913	4 329	25 160	2 365	20 762	19 541
Q2	185 998	2 833	183 165	16 894	6 738	12 121	33 397	11 020	2 992	26 785	4 332	26 061	2 369	20 887	19 569
Q3	186 543	2 734	183 809	17 058	6 769	12 384	33 531	11 054	2 950	26 854	4 343	26 423	2 379	20 948	19 116
Q4	188 485	2 931	185 554	17 236	6 791	12 605	33 527	11 041	2 901	27 289	4 335	26 608	2 367	20 963	19 891

1 Until September 2001, Household Expenditure was published and broken down into 13 main headings according to existing UK National Accounts convention. From September 2001 it has been reclassified so as to conform to the European System of Accounts 1995 (ESA 95) COICOP (Classification Of Individual Consumption by Purpose).
2 Final consumption expenditure by UK households in the UK and abroad.
3 Final expenditure consumption in the UK by UK and foreign households.

4 Following reclassification to COICOP, alcohol consumed on the premises has been transferred from the "alcohol and tobacco" heading to "restaurants and hotels". Similarly, under reclassification, transport now includes purchase of bicycles.

Source: Office for National Statistics: 020 7533 6031

1.9 Change in inventories at chained volume measures

£ million[1]

	Mining and quarrying	Manufacturing industries				Electricity, gas and water supply	Distributive trades		Other industries[3]	Change in inventories
		Materials and fuel	Work in progress	Finished goods	Total		Wholesale[2]	Retail[2]		
Value of stocks held at end-December 2005	984	16 220	16 052	19 787	52 059	1 833	28 486	24 786	54 056	162 204
	FADO	FBID	FBIE	FBIF	DHBH	FADP	FAJM	FBYH	DLWV	ABMQ
1997	72	254	−1 413	295	−864	54	1 703	979	1 713	3 394
1998	367	537	−703	317	151	−163	666	1 186	2 636	4 291
1999	−325	503	−259	−430	−186	−167	1 743	1 722	3 464	5 803
2000	−263	543	358	418	1 319	202	1 939	1 480	−283	4 648
2001	87	−513	369	160	16	16	887	1 113	3 458	5 577
2002	−37	−496	−149	−372	−1 017	−132	788	1 716	971	2 289
2003	−66	−198	−650	−138	−986	−13	407	1 241	3 399	3 982
2004	−46	7	−614	−296	−903	8	304	1 000	4 234	4 597
2005	−47	−179	863	56	740	586	978	−412	1 766	3 611
2006	−74	−362	742	−147	233	197	340	470	4 333	5 501
Unadjusted										
2002 Q3	−16	212	577	−489	300	4	1 093	664	597	2 642
Q4	−31	−495	−715	−1 048	−2 258	−187	−1 145	−348	1 368	−2 601
2003 Q1	−33	342	124	822	1 288	35	508	−409	1 255	2 644
Q2	56	86	519	−363	242	−4	−614	778	−1 705	−1 247
Q3	−89	−313	−55	113	−255	22	786	1 054	2 275	3 793
Q4	−	−313	−1 238	−710	−2 261	−66	−273	−182	1 574	−1 208
2004 Q1	−28	−512	625	−61	52	117	629	691	1 787	3 248
Q2	12	−7	−345	160	−192	−116	325	−349	166	−154
Q3	−29	551	−70	190	671	105	−177	305	1 510	2 385
Q4	−1	−25	−824	−585	−1 434	−98	−473	353	771	−882
2005 Q1	−	207	248	763	1 218	−150	−696	−966	2 528	1 934
Q2	−29	−300	372	−434	−362	228	1 100	−883	−427	−373
Q3	−11	36	219	7	262	198	666	1 525	592	3 232
Q4	−7	−122	24	−280	−378	310	−92	−88	−927	−1 182
2006 Q1	−80	−43	846	469	1 272	−299	−906	−67	3 210	3 130
Q2	18	−168	427	−566	−307	226	818	−343	−258	153
Q3	−17	212	221	−59	374	273	731	1 578	1 040	3 980
Q4	5	−363	−752	9	−1 106	−3	−303	−698	341	−1 762
Seasonally adjusted										
	FAEA	FBNF	FBNG	FBNH	DHBM	FAEB	FAJX	FBYN	DLWX	CAFU
2002 Q3	−22	−141	305	−265	−101	−74	475	−50	283	511
Q4	−29	−339	−259	−590	−1 188	−119	−598	−68	2 348	346
2003 Q1	−28	482	−29	−236	217	77	108	−156	−789	−571
Q2	55	−8	306	−31	267	−33	−370	894	−1 457	−644
Q3	−99	−557	−243	273	−527	−44	291	445	2 198	2 264
Q4	6	−115	−684	−144	−943	−13	378	58	3 448	2 934
2004 Q1	−27	−435	420	−1 177	−1 192	159	270	927	−518	−381
Q2	12	−76	−547	580	−43	−145	436	−128	918	1 050
Q3	−35	355	−199	283	439	39	−582	−362	1 526	1 025
Q4	4	163	−288	18	−107	−45	180	563	2 308	2 903
2005 Q1	4	246	197	57	500	−106	110	−352	1 873	2 029
Q2	−28	−186	151	−125	−160	188	496	−631	813	678
Q3	−19	−219	103	7	−109	133	157	712	−400	474
Q4	−4	−20	412	117	509	371	215	−141	−520	430
2006 Q1	−70	−63	444	30	411	−250	−347	563	1 866	2 173
Q2	15	6	113	−89	30	180	540	64	1 578	2 407
Q3	−21	−7	−10	−332	−349	190	325	393	772	1 310
Q4	4	−298	195	244	141	77	−178	−550	117	−389

1 Estimates are given to the nearest £ million but cannot be regarded as accurate to this degree.
2 Wholesaling and retailing estimates exclude the motor trades.
3 Quarterly alignment adjustment included in this series. For description see notes.

Source: Office for National Statistics: 0207 533 5934

1.10 Gross fixed capital formation by sector and type of asset

£ million

| | | | Analysis by sector | | | | | | Analysis by asset | | | | |
	Business invest-ment[2]	General govern-ment[3]	Public corporations[1] Dwellings	Existing buildings and dwellings[4]	Private sector Dwellings	Existing buildings and dwellings[4]	Total	Transport equipment	Other machinery and equipment	Dwellings	Other buildings and struct-ures	Intang-ible fixed assets	Total
At current prices													
	NPEM	NNBF	DEER	DLXQ	DFDF	EQBY	NPQX	DLWZ	DLXI	DFDK	EQEC	DLXP	NPQX
1997	92 801	10 487	1 623	−1 009	22 017	7 701	133 620	12 580	51 465	23 928	41 398	4 249	133 620
1998	107 882	11 910	1 632	−1 162	23 317	7 504	151 083	16 113	58 915	25 222	46 286	4 547	151 083
1999	110 417	12 599	1 529	−1 906	23 921	9 784	156 344	14 683	60 670	25 700	50 646	4 645	156 344
2000	113 213	12 227	1 421	−2 171	25 604	11 174	161 468	13 577	63 535	27 394	51 996	4 966	161 468
2001	112 024	13 533	2 387	−2 254	27 085	12 697	165 472	14 656	60 929	29 806	55 065	5 016	165 472
2002	111 146	15 452	2 837	−2 764	31 455	15 399	173 525	16 314	57 152	34 499	59 972	5 588	173 525
2003	109 218	20 509	3 509	−5 674	34 804	16 385	178 751	15 592	54 441	38 462	64 355	5 901	178 751
2004	111 811	23 206	3 235	−5 440	40 927	20 752	194 491	14 939	57 053	44 299	71 805	6 395	194 491
2005	132 088	7 661	3 574	−2 675	44 618	20 625	205 891	14 948	57 036	48 263	78 869	6 775	205 891
2006	124 950	24 054	4 117	−2 562	51 914	21 209	223 682	15 494	59 815	56 037	85 033	7 303	223 682
Unadjusted													
2002 Q3	26 951	3 732	522	−648	8 058	4 380	42 995	4 092	14 036	8 656	14 796	1 415	42 995
Q4	29 640	3 539	890	−791	9 064	4 315	46 657	3 619	15 365	10 014	16 186	1 473	46 657
2003 Q1	27 135	7 017	1 478	−2 121	7 457	4 450	45 416	3 953	14 245	8 955	16 824	1 439	45 416
Q2	26 717	3 658	479	−1 123	8 724	3 462	41 917	4 134	12 519	9 231	14 578	1 455	41 917
Q3	26 515	4 591	721	−1 124	8 835	4 181	43 719	3 941	12 818	9 608	15 866	1 486	43 719
Q4	28 851	5 243	831	−1 306	9 788	4 292	47 699	3 564	14 859	10 668	17 087	1 521	47 699
2004 Q1	27 823	7 250	1 157	−1 923	8 957	5 361	48 625	3 727	14 144	10 140	19 063	1 551	48 625
Q2	26 832	4 710	520	−1 149	10 404	4 876	46 193	4 202	13 123	10 952	16 332	1 584	46 193
Q3	28 242	5 233	708	−1 211	10 247	5 740	48 959	3 721	14 446	11 005	18 172	1 615	48 959
Q4	28 914	6 013	850	−1 157	11 319	4 775	50 714	3 289	15 340	12 202	18 238	1 645	50 714
2005 Q1	28 552	8 086	1 237	−1 080	9 600	4 765	51 160	3 578	14 544	10 893	20 482	1 663	51 160
Q2	44 088	−11 794	525	−581	11 178	4 806	48 222	4 111	13 200	11 706	17 522	1 683	48 222
Q3	29 205	5 678	860	−501	11 434	5 507	52 183	3 899	13 861	12 301	20 420	1 702	52 183
Q4	30 243	5 691	952	−513	12 406	5 547	54 326	3 360	15 431	13 363	20 445	1 727	54 326
2006 Q1	29 418	8 416	1 632	−946	10 743	6 057	55 320	3 263	15 041	12 377	22 886	1 753	55 320
Q2	30 105	4 508	586	−453	13 395	4 949	53 090	4 390	13 498	13 985	19 435	1 782	53 090
Q3	31 506	5 619	935	−553	13 404	4 944	55 855	3 895	14 857	14 339	20 906	1 858	55 855
Q4	33 921	5 511	964	−610	14 372	5 259	59 417	3 946	16 419	15 336	21 806	1 910	59 417
Seasonally adjusted													
	NPEK	RPZG	DKQG	TLNI	GGAG	TLOP	NPQS	TLPX	TLPW	GGAE	EQED	TLPK	NPQS
2002 Q3	27 426	4 112	647	−819	8 183	4 230	43 779	4 165	14 393	8 910	14 896	1 415	43 779
Q4	28 796	3 710	915	−844	8 500	4 297	45 374	4 040	14 197	9 470	16 194	1 473	45 374
2003 Q1	27 054	5 291	985	−1 685	8 150	4 178	43 973	4 059	14 146	9 155	15 174	1 439	43 973
Q2	27 439	4 658	802	−1 303	8 586	3 918	44 100	3 641	13 478	9 416	16 110	1 455	44 100
Q3	26 840	5 073	885	−1 308	8 896	3 918	44 304	3 923	13 188	9 833	15 874	1 486	44 304
Q4	27 885	5 487	837	−1 378	9 172	4 371	46 374	3 969	13 629	10 058	17 197	1 521	46 374
2004 Q1	27 739	5 345	757	−1 453	9 805	4 919	47 112	3 847	13 989	10 588	17 137	1 551	47 112
Q2	27 555	5 771	840	−1 353	10 231	5 575	48 619	3 755	14 063	11 099	18 118	1 584	48 619
Q3	28 439	5 811	818	−1 392	10 278	5 409	49 363	3 683	14 688	11 146	18 231	1 615	49 363
Q4	28 078	6 279	820	−1 242	10 613	4 849	49 397	3 654	14 313	11 466	18 319	1 645	49 397
2005 Q1	28 776	6 009	781	−722	10 714	4 379	49 937	3 759	14 450	11 551	18 514	1 663	49 937
Q2	44 730	−10 662	861	−777	10 866	5 269	50 287	3 621	14 121	11 730	19 132	1 683	50 287
Q3	29 349	6 233	974	−634	11 390	5 407	52 719	3 883	14 102	12 371	20 661	1 702	52 719
Q4	29 233	6 081	958	−542	11 648	5 570	52 948	3 685	14 363	12 611	20 562	1 727	52 948
2006 Q1	29 754	6 124	1 062	−589	12 013	5 722	54 086	3 533	14 991	13 077	20 732	1 753	54 086
Q2	30 729	5 902	986	−655	13 029	5 473	55 464	3 815	14 478	14 019	21 370	1 782	55 464
Q3	31 567	6 175	1 067	−680	13 351	4 777	56 257	3 863	15 046	14 418	21 072	1 858	56 257
Q4	32 900	5 853	1 002	−638	13 521	5 237	57 875	4 283	15 300	14 523	21 859	1 910	57 875

1.10 Gross fixed capital formation by sector and type of asset

continued

£ million

| | Analysis by sector | | | | | | | Analysis by asset | | | | | |
| | | | Public corporations[1] | | Private sector | | | | | | Other new | | |
	Business invest-ment[2]	General govern-ment[3]	Dwellings	Existing buildings and dwellings[4]	Dwellings	Existing buildings and dwellings[4]	Total	Transport equipment	Other machinery and equipment	Dwellings	buildings and struct-ures	Intang-ible fixed assets	Total
Chained volume measures													
	NPEN	EQDN	DEEW	EQDF	DFDP	EQCY	NPQR	DLWJ	DLWM	DFDV	DLWQ	EQDT	NPQR
1997	83 481	11 140	2 032	−2 215	31 610	18 197	139 064	12 960	38 200	33 942	54 092	4 950	139 064
1998	100 225	12 218	1 974	−2 284	31 971	15 614	158 525	16 279	47 919	34 201	58 200	4 982	158 525
1999	104 205	13 059	1 747	−3 141	30 928	16 821	163 039	14 602	51 650	32 863	59 956	4 956	163 039
2000	108 933	12 665	1 552	−3 093	31 041	16 293	167 486	13 489	55 766	32 888	58 736	5 172	167 486
2001	110 390	13 980	2 521	−2 825	31 318	16 173	171 639	14 698	56 779	34 172	59 527	5 129	171 639
2002	111 678	15 740	2 898	−3 092	33 748	17 369	178 066	16 414	55 968	36 839	62 088	5 676	178 066
2003	109 218	20 509	3 509	−5 674	34 804	16 385	178 751	15 592	54 441	38 462	64 355	5 901	178 751
2004	111 765	22 266	3 161	−5 561	38 245	19 616	189 492	14 706	58 817	41 541	68 135	6 294	189 492
2005	130 941	6 495	3 423	−2 896	39 102	18 043	195 107	14 899	58 867	42 594	72 174	6 573	195 107
2006	124 765	21 737	3 876	−2 147	42 081	17 392	207 704	15 459	63 310	45 963	75 981	6 991	207 704
Unadjusted													
2002 Q3	27 116	3 790	531	−694	8 547	4 759	43 845	4 121	13 750	9 135	15 142	1 433	43 845
Q4	29 863	3 609	898	−791	9 543	4 330	47 463	3 642	15 098	10 502	16 422	1 488	47 463
2003 Q1	27 246	7 542	1 491	−2 284	7 834	4 859	46 880	4 101	13 996	9 377	17 816	1 449	46 880
Q2	26 764	3 530	479	−1 177	8 639	3 770	42 110	4 089	12 255	9 127	15 069	1 458	42 110
Q3	26 453	4 426	717	−1 038	8 724	3 893	43 129	3 900	13 063	9 486	15 203	1 483	43 129
Q4	28 755	5 011	822	−1 175	9 607	3 863	46 632	3 502	15 127	10 472	16 267	1 511	46 632
2004 Q1	27 727	7 430	1 140	−2 187	8 761	5 730	48 601	3 755	14 580	9 927	18 805	1 534	48 601
Q2	26 939	4 545	509	−904	9 584	4 414	45 087	4 151	13 633	10 121	15 618	1 563	45 087
Q3	28 259	4 925	689	−857	9 476	4 841	47 333	3 663	14 888	10 214	16 982	1 587	47 333
Q4	28 840	5 366	823	−1 613	10 424	4 631	48 471	3 137	15 716	11 279	16 730	1 610	48 471
2005 Q1	28 407	7 595	1 197	−651	8 794	3 912	49 254	3 512	14 881	10 045	19 195	1 622	49 254
Q2	43 534	−11 435	503	−627	9 658	4 349	45 982	4 139	13 743	10 164	16 299	1 637	45 982
Q3	28 915	5 222	821	−747	9 954	4 789	48 954	3 905	14 240	10 782	18 377	1 649	48 954
Q4	30 085	5 113	902	−871	10 696	4 993	50 917	3 343	16 003	11 603	18 303	1 665	50 917
2006 Q1	29 391	7 430	1 543	−624	9 257	4 794	51 791	3 324	15 694	10 802	20 284	1 687	51 791
Q2	29 895	4 287	550	−364	10 735	4 063	49 165	4 372	14 349	11 289	17 444	1 711	49 165
Q3	31 487	5 078	878	−534	10 742	4 107	51 758	3 869	15 737	11 620	18 757	1 775	51 758
Q4	33 992	4 942	905	−625	11 347	4 428	54 990	3 894	17 530	12 252	19 496	1 818	54 990
Seasonally adjusted													
	NPEL	DLWF	DKQH	DLWH	DFEA	DLWI	NPQT	DLWL	DLWO	DFEG	DLWT	EQDO	NPQT
2002 Q3	27 574	4 259	660	−894	8 669	4 613	44 765	4 269	14 253	9 400	15 363	1 433	44 765
Q4	28 980	3 875	925	−863	8 954	4 582	46 393	4 213	14 201	9 943	16 569	1 492	46 393
2003 Q1	27 111	5 673	994	−1 833	8 452	4 517	44 934	4 049	13 815	9 467	16 148	1 450	44 934
Q2	27 395	4 507	804	−1 378	8 695	4 145	44 161	3 726	13 165	9 536	16 287	1 463	44 161
Q3	26 712	4 999	882	−1 243	8 812	3 772	43 924	3 896	13 392	9 752	15 405	1 482	43 924
Q4	28 000	5 330	829	−1 220	8 845	3 951	45 732	3 921	14 069	9 707	16 515	1 506	45 732
2004 Q1	27 166	5 970	746	−1 598	9 421	5 551	47 256	3 771	14 083	10 193	17 675	1 534	47 256
Q2	27 757	5 360	824	−1 174	9 578	4 757	47 102	3 760	14 627	10 430	16 722	1 563	47 102
Q3	28 634	5 311	797	−1 186	9 524	4 733	47 813	3 635	15 299	10 370	16 922	1 587	47 813
Q4	28 208	5 625	794	−1 603	9 722	4 575	47 321	3 540	14 808	10 548	16 816	1 610	47 321
2005 Q1	28 580	5 675	756	−145	9 569	3 671	48 106	3 658	14 644	10 379	17 804	1 622	48 106
Q2	44 247	−10 517	827	−907	9 599	4 688	47 937	3 718	14 740	10 429	17 412	1 637	47 937
Q3	29 067	5 761	931	−971	9 946	4 790	49 524	3 863	14 559	10 884	18 569	1 649	49 524
Q4	29 047	5 576	909	−873	9 988	4 894	49 540	3 660	14 924	10 902	18 389	1 665	49 540
2006 Q1	29 679	5 437	1 005	−134	10 104	4 525	50 616	3 490	15 475	11 111	18 854	1 687	50 616
Q2	30 582	5 313	929	−659	10 658	4 384	51 207	3 902	15 416	11 591	18 587	1 711	51 207
Q3	31 543	5 619	1 002	−756	10 725	4 140	52 273	3 816	16 021	11 727	18 934	1 775	52 273
Q4	32 961	5 368	940	−598	10 594	4 343	53 608	4 251	16 398	11 534	19 606	1 818	53 608

1 Remaining investment by public corporations included within business investment.

2 Not including dwellings and purchases less sales of land and existing buildings.

3 Please note that the data in the second quarter of 2005 is due to the transfer of nuclear reactors. In April 2005 British Nuclear Fuels (BNFL) transferred to the Nuclear Decommissioning Authority (NDA) nuclear reactors that were reaching the ends of their productive lives. BNFL is classified as a public corporation in the National Accounts and the NDA as central government. This transfer does not affect whole economy gross fixed capital formation (GFCF) since it is an acquisition by one sector and a disposal by another. The value of the transfer was -£15.6 billion. The negative value reflects the fact that the reactors are at the end of their productive lives and have large decommissioning and clean-up liabilities.

4 Including costs associated with the transfer of ownership of buildings, dwellings, and non-produced assets.

Source: Office for National Statistics: 0207 533 5934

1.11 Business Investment[1] by Industry, Chained volume measures

Reference year 2003, £ million[2]

| | Manufacturing | | | Non-manufacturing | | | | | | | Total |
| | | | | Private Sector [3] | | | | | | | |
	Private [3] Sector	Public Corporations [5]	Total	Other [4] Production	Construction	Distribution Services	Other Services	Public Corporations	Total		Total Business Investment
2003	13 138	309	13 447	11 853	3 296	12 109	64 800	3 713	95 771		109 218
2004	12 222	262	12 484	11 783	3 646	12 088	68 628	3 136	99 281		111 765
2005	13 976	15 332	29 308	10 780	2 621	13 468	70 792	3 972	101 633		130 941
2006	13 736	11	13 747	13 762	3 096	12 724	77 579	3 857	111 018		124 765

Not seasonally adjusted

	INKL	APIA	APIL	IOCQ	KWOC	IOYO	JZKH	APII	APIP		NPEN
2003 Q1	3 233	92	3 325	3 214	816	3 096	15 263	1 527	23 919		27 246
Q2	2 999	68	3 067	2 872	553	2 828	16 727	723	23 695		26 764
Q3	3 138	67	3 205	2 891	880	2 800	15 936	741	23 251		26 453
Q4	3 768	82	3 850	2 876	1 047	3 385	16 874	722	24 906		28 755
2004 Q1	2 541	77	2 618	3 033	845	3 177	17 234	820	25 109		27 727
Q2	3 007	55	3 062	2 811	1 001	2 402	16 917	746	23 877		26 939
Q3	3 034	55	3 089	2 998	880	3 149	17 378	765	25 170		28 259
Q4	3 640	75	3 715	2 941	920	3 360	17 099	805	25 125		28 840
2005 Q1	2 996	74	3 070	2 871	563	3 822	17 129	952	25 337		28 407
Q2	3 400	15 255	18 655	2 667	636	2 892	17 704	980	24 879		43 534
Q3	3 525	1	3 526	2 679	711	3 303	17 653	1 043	25 389		28 915
Q4	4 055	2	4 057	2 563	711	3 451	18 306	997	26 028		30 085
2006 Q1	3 210	2	3 212	3 136	764	3 128	18 113	1 038	26 179		29 391
Q2	3 167	4	3 171	3 079	811	2 821	19 107	906	26 724		29 895
Q3	3 389	2	3 391	3 592	756	3 220	19 515	1 013	28 096		31 487
Q4	3 970	3	3 973	3 955	765	3 555	20 844	900	30 019		33 992

Percentage change, latest quarter on previous quarter

2006 Q4	17.1	50.0	17.2	10.1	1.2	10.4	6.8	−11.2	6.8		8.0

Percentage change, latest quarter on corresponding quarter of previous year

2006 Q4	−2.1	50.0	−2.1	54.3	7.6	3.0	13.9	−9.7	15.3		13.0

Seasonally adjusted

	INLN	APIE	APIN	IOCR	KWOE	IOYQ	JZKI	APIK	APIT		NPEL
2003 Q1	3 535	62	3 595	3 063	833	3 036	15 298	1 341	23 576		27 111
Q2	3 116	77	3 194	2 988	598	3 213	16 520	844	24 135		27 395
Q3	3 099	85	3 186	2 897	887	2 842	16 004	812	23 466		26 712
Q4	3 388	85	3 472	2 905	978	3 018	16 978	716	24 594		28 000
2004 Q1	2 788	40	2 828	2 886	892	3 047	16 777	736	24 338		27 166
Q2	3 130	63	3 193	2 897	1 053	2 799	16 981	834	24 564		27 757
Q3	3 029	77	3 106	3 010	861	3 178	17 678	801	25 528		28 634
Q4	3 275	82	3 357	2 990	840	3 064	17 192	765	24 851		28 208
2005 Q1	3 282	48	3 330	2 745	609	3 668	17 380	848	25 250		28 580
Q2	3 596	15 263	18 859	2 777	654	3 363	17 539	1 055	25 388		44 247
Q3	3 513	11	3 524	2 686	702	3 295	17 799	1 061	25 543		29 067
Q4	3 585	10	3 595	2 572	656	3 142	18 074	1 008	25 452		29 047
2006 Q1	3 512	4	3 516	2 974	838	3 015	18 385	951	26 163		29 679
Q2	3 345	4	3 349	3 204	820	3 255	18 991	963	27 233		30 582
Q3	3 388	2	3 390	3 568	738	3 209	19 614	1 024	28 153		31 543
Q4	3 491	1	3 492	4 016	700	3 245	20 589	919	29 469		32 961

Percentage change, latest quarter on previous quarter

2006 Q4	3.0	−50.0	3.0	12.6	−5.1	1.1	5.0	−10.3	4.7		4.5

Percentage change, latest quarter on corresponding quarter of previous year

2006 Q4	−2.6	−90.0	−2.9	56.1	6.7	3.3	13.9	−8.8	15.8		13.5

1 All figures are exclusive of expenditure on land and existing buildings.
2 Estimates are shown to the nearest £ million but should not be regarded as accurate to this degree.
3 All private sector figures are exclusive of expenditure on dwellings.
4 Includes Agricultural Contractors.
5 Please note that the data in the second quarter of 2005 is due to the transfer of nuclear reactors. In April 2005 British Nuclear Fuels (BNFL) transferred to the Nuclear Decommissioning Authority (NDA) nuclear reactors that were reaching the end of their productive lives. BNFL is classified as a public corporation in the National Accounts and the NDA as central government. This transfer does not affect whole economy gross fixed capital formation (GFCF) since it is an acquisition by one sector and a disposal by another. The value of the transfer was -£15.6 billion. The negative value reflects the fact that the reactors are at the end of their productive lives and have large decommissioning and clean-up liabilities.

Source: Office for National Statistics: 020 7533 5934

1.12 Business Investment[1] by Industry at Current Prices

£ million[2]

| | Manufacturing | | | Non-manufacturing | | | | | | | Total Business Investment |
| | | | | Private Sector [3] | | | | | | | |
	Private [3] Sector	Public Corporations [5]	Total	Other [4] Production	Construction	Distribution Services	Other Services	Public Corporations	Total		
2003	13 138	309	13 447	11 853	3 296	12 109	64 800	3 713	95 771		109 218
2004	12 141	275	12 416	11 854	3 633	12 145	68 573	3 190	99 395		111 811
2005	13 953	15 664	29 617	11 692	2 653	13 699	70 248	4 179	102 471		132 088
2006	13 789	11	13 800	14 508	3 160	12 985	76 361	4 136	111 150		124 950

Not seasonally adjusted

	INJJ	APGG	APGZ	IOCP	KWOD	IOYP	JZKF	APGS	APHR		NPEM
2003 Q1	3 221	90	3 311	3 178	816	3 089	15 215	1 526	23 824		27 135
Q2	2 994	68	3 062	2 875	552	2 827	16 678	723	23 655		26 717
Q3	3 144	67	3 211	2 907	881	2 802	15 974	740	23 304		26 515
Q4	3 779	84	3 863	2 893	1 047	3 391	16 933	724	24 988		28 851
2004 Q1	2 538	79	2 617	3 019	844	3 189	17 332	822	25 206		27 823
Q2	2 974	58	3 032	2 805	994	2 392	16 850	759	23 800		26 832
Q3	3 013	58	3 071	3 017	875	3 162	17 337	780	25 171		28 242
Q4	3 616	80	3 696	3 013	920	3 402	17 054	829	25 218		28 914
2005 Q1	2 978	79	3 057	3 012	560	3 871	17 062	990	25 495		28 552
Q2	3 389	15 582	18 971	2 893	643	2 935	17 615	1 031	25 117		44 088
Q3	3 520	1	3 521	2 953	723	3 367	17 545	1 096	25 684		29 205
Q4	4 066	2	4 068	2 834	727	3 526	18 026	1 062	26 175		30 243
2006 Q1	3 230	2	3 232	3 399	781	3 197	17 702	1 107	26 186		29 418
Q2	3 190	4	3 194	3 306	830	2 882	18 911	982	26 911		30 105
Q3	3 392	2	3 394	3 751	771	3 284	19 229	1 077	28 112		31 506
Q4	3 977	3	3 980	4 052	778	3 622	20 519	970	29 941		33 921

Percentage change, latest quarter on previous quarter

| 2006 Q4 | 17.2 | 50.0 | 17.3 | 8.0 | 0.9 | 10.3 | 6.7 | −9.9 | 6.5 | | 7.7 |

Percentage change, latest quarter on corresponding quarter of previous year

| 2006 Q4 | −2.2 | 50.0 | −2.2 | 43.0 | 7.0 | 2.7 | 13.8 | −8.7 | 14.4 | | 12.2 |

Seasonally adjusted

	IOBN	APID	APIF	IOBM	IOYV	IOYW	JZKG	APIJ	APIO		NPEK
2003 Q1	3 523	64	3 587	3 037	832	3 023	15 233	1 342	23 467		27 054
Q2	3 124	78	3 202	2 985	598	3 219	16 592	843	24 237		27 439
Q3	3 094	86	3 180	2 909	891	2 846	16 203	811	23 660		26 840
Q4	3 397	81	3 478	2 922	975	3 021	16 772	717	24 407		27 885
2004 Q1	2 786	42	2 828	2 887	890	3 052	17 343	739	24 911		27 739
Q2	3 125	64	3 189	2 894	1 048	2 799	16 777	848	24 366		27 555
Q3	2 991	81	3 072	3 021	858	3 195	17 476	817	25 367		28 439
Q4	3 239	88	3 327	3 052	837	3 099	16 977	786	24 751		28 078
2005 Q1	3 267	44	3 311	2 870	608	3 746	17 357	884	25 465		28 776
Q2	3 577	15 592	19 169	2 981	660	3 390	17 425	1 105	25 561		44 730
Q3	3 516	14	3 530	2 956	715	3 362	17 667	1 119	25 819		29 349
Q4	3 593	14	3 607	2 885	670	3 201	17 799	1 071	25 626		29 233
2006 Q1	3 536	5	3 541	3 219	859	3 071	18 047	1 017	26 213		29 754
Q2	3 361	4	3 365	3 431	837	3 331	18 726	1 039	27 364		30 729
Q3	3 392	1	3 393	3 743	752	3 275	19 311	1 093	28 174		31 567
Q4	3 500	1	3 501	4 115	712	3 308	20 277	987	29 399		32 900

Percentage change, latest quarter on previous quarter

| 2006 Q4 | 3.2 | − | 3.2 | 9.9 | −5.3 | 1.0 | 5.0 | −9.7 | 4.3 | | 4.2 |

Percentage change, latest quarter on corresponding quarter of previous year

| 2006 Q4 | −2.6 | −92.9 | −2.9 | 42.6 | 6.3 | 3.3 | 13.9 | −7.8 | 14.7 | | 12.5 |

1 All figures are exclusive of expenditure on land and existing buildings.
2 Estimates are shown to the nearest £ million but should not be regarded as accurate to this degree.
3 All private sector figures are exclusive of expenditure on dwellings.
4 Includes Agricultural Contractors.
5 The data in the second quarter of 2005 is due to the transfer of nuclear reactors. In April 2005 British Nuclear Fuels (BNFL) transferred to the Nuclear Decommissioning Authority (NDA) nuclear reactors that were reaching the ends of their productive lives. BNFL is classified as a public corporation in the National Accounts and the NDA as central government. This transfer does not affect whole economy gross fixed capital formation (GFCF) since it is an acquisition by one sector and a disposal by another. The value of the transfer was -£15.6 billion. The negative value reflects the fact that the reactors are at the end of their productive lives and have large decommissioning and clean-up liabilities.

Source: Office for National Statistics: 020 7533 5934

1.13 Private Sector[1] Manufacturing Business Investment[2] by Industry, Chained volume measures

Reference year 2003, £ million[3]

	Solid & nuclear fuels, oil refining	Metals & metal goods	Chemicals and man made fibres	Engineering and vehicles	Food, drink and tobacco	Textiles, clothing, leather and footwear	Other manufacturing	Total all manufacturing
			Analysis by industry group					
2003	418	1 159	1 885	3 155	2 357	243	3 921	13 138
2004	355	1 114	1 912	3 523	1 994	148	3 176	12 222
2005	341	1 263	1 793	4 061	2 233	188	4 097	13 976
2006	497	1 361	1 758	3 726	2 288	146	3 960	13 736
Not seasonally adjusted								
	INJX	INKA	INJY	INJO	INJT	INJU	JZKL	INKL
2003 Q1	90	296	450	813	554	68	963	3 233
Q2	87	262	415	722	577	45	893	2 999
Q3	119	276	485	780	546	57	873	3 138
Q4	122	325	535	840	680	73	1 192	3 768
2004 Q1	65	211	395	664	430	40	736	2 541
Q2	70	247	443	967	498	40	742	3 007
Q3	88	327	505	781	542	37	754	3 034
Q4	132	329	569	1 111	524	31	944	3 640
2005 Q1	68	258	408	839	491	56	876	2 996
Q2	71	275	421	1 074	534	48	977	3 400
Q3	78	307	438	1 006	580	44	1 072	3 525
Q4	124	423	526	1 142	628	40	1 172	4 055
2006 Q1	119	319	375	928	527	34	908	3 210
Q2	134	362	366	761	574	43	927	3 167
Q3	119	327	431	931	550	26	1 005	3 389
Q4	125	353	586	1 106	637	43	1 120	3 970
Percentage change, latest quarter on previous quarter								
2006 Q4	5.0	8.0	36.0	18.8	15.8	65.4	11.4	17.1
Percentage change, latest quarter on corresponding quarter of previous year								
2006 Q4	0.8	−16.5	11.4	−3.2	1.4	7.5	−4.4	−2.1
Seasonally adjusted								
	INKZ	INLC	INLA	INKQ	INKV	INKW	JZKM	INLN
2003 Q1	107	314	542	891	599	68	1 013	3 535
Q2	102	278	427	745	589	45	931	3 116
Q3	117	274	483	777	528	57	862	3 099
Q4	92	293	433	742	641	73	1 115	3 388
2004 Q1	78	228	467	742	461	40	772	2 788
Q2	85	268	468	983	507	40	779	3 130
Q3	91	325	505	798	525	37	748	3 029
Q4	101	293	472	1 000	501	31	877	3 275
2005 Q1	84	291	471	926	534	56	920	3 282
Q2	82	293	462	1 138	542	48	1 031	3 596
Q3	78	308	436	999	574	44	1 074	3 513
Q4	97	371	424	998	583	40	1 072	3 585
2006 Q1	141	358	434	1 020	572	34	953	3 512
Q2	148	376	412	799	582	43	985	3 345
Q3	115	323	436	936	545	26	1 007	3 388
Q4	93	304	476	971	589	43	1 015	3 491
Percentage change, latest quarter on previous quarter								
2006 Q4	−19.1	−5.9	9.2	3.7	8.1	65.4	0.8	3.0
Percentage change, latest quarter on corresponding quarter of previous year								
2006 Q4	−4.1	−18.1	12.3	−2.7	1.0	7.5	−5.3	−2.6

1 All private sector figures are exclusive of expenditure on dwellings.
2 All figures are exclusive of expenditure on land and existing buildings.
3 Estimates are shown to the nearest £ million but should not be regarded as accurate to this degree.

Source: Office for National Statistics: 020 7533 5934

1.14 Private Sector[1] Manufacturing Business Investment[2] by Industry at Current Prices

£ million[3]

	Solid & nuclear fuels, oil refining	Metals & metal goods	Chemicals and man made fibres	Engineering and vehicles	Food, drink and tobacco	Textiles, clothing, leather and footwear	Other manufacturing	Total all manufacturing
			Analysis by industry group					
2003	418	1 159	1 885	3 155	2 357	243	3 921	13 138
2004	360	1 108	1 907	3 501	1 955	150	3 160	12 141
2005	341	1 268	1 774	4 055	2 223	189	4 103	13 953
2006	497	1 381	1 745	3 722	2 316	148	3 980	13 789
Not seasonally adjusted								
	INIV	INIY	INIW	INIM	INIR	INIS	JZKJ	INJJ
2003 Q1	90	295	450	810	547	68	961	3 221
Q2	87	261	414	718	576	45	893	2 994
Q3	119	277	485	784	550	57	872	3 144
Q4	122	326	536	843	684	73	1 195	3 779
2004 Q1	65	210	397	664	426	40	736	2 538
Q2	71	244	441	957	483	42	736	2 974
Q3	90	325	504	776	530	37	751	3 013
Q4	134	329	565	1 104	516	31	937	3 616
2005 Q1	68	257	403	834	486	56	874	2 978
Q2	71	275	417	1 074	527	48	977	3 389
Q3	78	308	432	1 006	580	44	1 072	3 520
Q4	124	428	522	1 141	630	41	1 180	4 066
2006 Q1	119	323	373	931	533	34	917	3 230
Q2	134	369	363	761	582	45	936	3 190
Q3	119	331	427	927	557	26	1 005	3 392
Q4	125	358	582	1 103	644	43	1 122	3 977
Percentage change, latest quarter on previous quarter								
2006 Q4	5.0	8.2	36.3	19.0	15.6	65.4	11.6	17.2
Percentage change, latest quarter on corresponding quarter of previous year								
2006 Q4	0.8	−16.4	11.5	−3.3	2.2	4.9	−4.9	−2.2
Seasonally adjusted								
	IOAZ	IOBC	IOBA	IOAQ	IOAV	IOAW	JZKK	IOBN
2003 Q1	107	314	543	887	591	68	1 013	3 523
Q2	103	277	426	748	593	45	932	3 124
Q3	116	275	482	780	530	57	854	3 094
Q4	92	293	434	740	643	73	1 122	3 397
2004 Q1	78	227	469	744	456	40	772	2 786
Q2	86	265	466	994	498	42	774	3 125
Q3	92	323	503	787	510	37	739	2 991
Q4	104	293	469	976	491	31	875	3 239
2005 Q1	85	291	465	924	529	56	917	3 267
Q2	83	293	458	1 127	536	48	1 032	3 577
Q3	78	309	431	1 005	574	44	1 075	3 516
Q4	95	375	420	999	584	41	1 079	3 593
2006 Q1	142	364	431	1 027	578	34	960	3 536
Q2	148	383	409	790	592	45	994	3 361
Q3	114	328	432	932	552	26	1 008	3 392
Q4	93	306	473	973	594	43	1 018	3 500
Percentage change, latest quarter on previous quarter								
2006 Q4	−18.4	−6.7	9.5	4.4	7.6	65.4	1.0	3.2
Percentage change, latest quarter on corresponding quarter of previous year								
2006 Q4	−2.1	−18.4	12.6	−2.6	1.7	4.9	−5.7	−2.6

1 All private sector figures are exclusive of expenditure on dwellings.
2 All figures are exclusive of expenditure on land and existing buildings.
3 Estimates are shown to the nearest £ million but should not be regarded as accurate to this degree.

Source: Office for National Statistics: 020 7533 5934

1.15 Private Sector[1] Manufacturing Business Investment[2] by Asset

£ million[3]

| | Chained volume measures, reference year 2003 | | | | Current prices | | | |
| | Analysis by asset | | | | Analysis by asset | | | |
	New Building Work	Vehicles	Other Capital Equipment	Total all manufacturing	New Building Work	Vehicles	Other Capital Equipment	Total all manufacturing
2003	1 471	551	11 116	13 138	1 471	551	11 116	13 138
2004	1 272	480	10 470	12 222	1 304	481	10 356	12 141
2005	1 635	643	11 698	13 976	1 676	647	11 630	13 953
2006	1 636	524	11 576	13 736	1 684	529	11 576	13 789
Not seasonally adjusted								
	IMGV	IMSG	INDR	INKL	IMDA	IMOL	IMZW	INJJ
2003 Q1	371	162	2 742	3 233	371	162	2 688	3 221
Q2	348	131	2 526	2 999	347	131	2 516	2 994
Q3	324	140	2 657	3 138	324	140	2 680	3 144
Q4	428	118	3 191	3 768	429	118	3 232	3 779
2004 Q1	242	118	2 181	2 541	247	118	2 173	2 538
Q2	312	113	2 582	3 007	322	113	2 539	2 974
Q3	325	122	2 587	3 034	332	123	2 558	3 013
Q4	393	127	3 120	3 640	403	127	3 086	3 616
2005 Q1	303	139	2 554	2 996	309	139	2 530	2 978
Q2	379	214	2 807	3 400	389	216	2 784	3 389
Q3	469	139	2 917	3 525	481	140	2 899	3 520
Q4	484	151	3 420	4 055	497	152	3 417	4 066
2006 Q1	405	110	2 695	3 210	413	111	2 706	3 230
Q2	392	121	2 654	3 167	408	123	2 659	3 190
Q3	387	150	2 852	3 389	397	151	2 844	3 392
Q4	452	143	3 375	3 970	466	144	3 367	3 977
Percentage change, latest quarter on previous quarter								
2006 Q4	16.8	−4.7	18.3	17.1	17.4	−4.6	18.4	17.2
Percentage change, latest quarter on corresponding quarter of previous year								
2006 Q4	−6.6	−5.3	−1.3	−2.1	−6.2	−5.3	−1.5	−2.2
Seasonally adjusted								
	IMKQ	IMWB	INHM	INLN	INSA	INVV	INZQ	IOBN
2003 Q1	413	162	3 003	3 535	413	161	2 949	3 523
Q2	339	135	2 646	3 116	352	134	2 638	3 124
Q3	295	133	2 652	3 099	314	134	2 646	3 094
Q4	424	121	2 815	3 388	392	122	2 883	3 397
2004 Q1	273	121	2 394	2 788	280	120	2 386	2 786
Q2	303	114	2 713	3 130	328	113	2 684	3 125
Q3	308	116	2 605	3 029	326	118	2 547	2 991
Q4	388	129	2 758	3 275	370	130	2 739	3 239
2005 Q1	334	142	2 806	3 282	351	142	2 774	3 267
Q2	395	220	2 981	3 596	400	222	2 955	3 577
Q3	450	131	2 932	3 513	479	132	2 905	3 516
Q4	456	150	2 979	3 585	446	151	2 996	3 593
2006 Q1	446	114	2 952	3 512	465	115	2 956	3 536
Q2	405	124	2 816	3 345	415	126	2 820	3 361
Q3	370	143	2 875	3 388	392	144	2 856	3 392
Q4	415	143	2 933	3 491	412	144	2 944	3 500
Percentage change, latest quarter on previous quarter								
2006 Q4	12.2	–	2.0	3.0	5.1	–	3.1	3.2
Percentage change, latest quarter on corresponding quarter of previous year								
2006 Q4	−9.0	−4.7	−1.5	−2.6	−7.6	−4.6	−1.7	−2.6

1 All private sector figures are exclusive of expenditure on dwellings.
2 All figures are exclusive of expenditure on land and existing buildings.
3 Estimates are shown to the nearest £ million but shown not be regarded as accurate to this degree.

Source: Office for National Statistics: 020 7533 5934

2 Population and vital statistics

2.1 Mid-year estimates of resident population

Thousands

	England and Wales			Scotland			Northern Ireland			United Kingdom		
	Males	Females	Persons	Males	Females	Persons	Males	Females	Persons	Males	Females	Persons
	BBAE	BBAF	BBAD	BBAH	BBAI	BBAG	BBAK	BBAL	BBAJ	BBAB	BBAC	DYAY
1984	24 185	25 528	49 713	2 475	2 664	5 139	761	796	1 557	27 421	28 989	56 409
1985	24 254	25 606	49 861	2 470	2 658	5 128	765	800	1 565	27 489	29 065	56 554
1986	24 311	25 687	49 999	2 462	2 649	5 112	768	805	1 574	27 542	29 142	56 684
1987	24 371	25 752	50 123	2 455	2 644	5 099	773	809	1 582	27 599	29 205	56 804
1988	24 434	25 820	50 254	2 444	2 633	5 077	774	812	1 585	27 652	29 265	56 916
1989	24 510	25 898	50 408	2 443	2 635	5 078	776	814	1 590	27 729	29 348	57 076
1990	24 597	25 964	50 561	2 444	2 637	5 081	778	818	1 596	27 819	29 419	57 237
1991	24 681	26 067	50 748	2 445	2 639	5 083	783	824	1 607	27 909	29 530	57 439
1992	24 739	26 136	50 876	2 445	2 640	5 086	792	831	1 623	27 977	29 608	57 585
1993	24 793	26 193	50 986	2 448	2 644	5 092	798	837	1 636	28 039	29 675	57 714
1994	24 853	26 263	51 116	2 453	2 649	5 102	802	842	1 644	28 108	29 754	57 862
1995	24 946	26 326	51 272	2 453	2 650	5 104	804	845	1 649	28 204	29 821	58 025
1996	25 030	26 381	51 410	2 447	2 645	5 092	810	851	1 662	28 287	29 877	58 164
1997	25 113	26 446	51 560	2 442	2 641	5 083	816	856	1 671	28 371	29 943	58 314
1998	25 201	26 519	51 720	2 439	2 638	5 077	819	859	1 678	28 458	30 017	58 475
1999	25 323	26 610	51 933	2 437	2 635	5 072	818	861	1 679	28 578	30 106	58 684
2000	25 438	26 702	52 140	2 432	2 631	5 063	820	862	1 683	28 690	30 196	58 886
2001	25 574	26 786	52 360	2 434	2 630	5 064	824	865	1 689	28 832	30 281	59 113
2002	25 702	26 868	52 570	2 432	2 623	5 055	829	868	1 697	28 963	30 359	59 322
2003	25 841	26 953	52 794	2 435	2 623	5 057	833	870	1 703	29 108	30 446	59 554
2004	25 988	27 057	53 046	2 446	2 632	5 078	836	874	1 710	29 271	30 563	59 834
2005	26 179	27 211	53 390	2 456	2 639	5 095	844	880	1 724	29 479	30 730	60 209

Sources: Office for National Statistics;
General Register Office (Scotland);
Northern Ireland Statistics and Research Agency

2.2 Age distribution of estimated resident population at 30 June 2005

Thousands

	Resident population										
	England and Wales[1]		Wales		Scotland		Northern Ireland		United Kingdom[1]		
	Males	Females	Males	Females	Males	Females	Males	Females	Males	Females	Persons
0-4	1 564	1 489	82	77	136	130	57	54	1 756	1 672	3 428
5-9	1 616	1 541	90	85	146	139	61	58	1 823	1 737	3 560
10-14	1 736	1 644	99	94	161	154	64	62	1 962	1 859	3 821
15-19	1 802	1 703	103	97	168	159	68	64	2 038	1 927	3 965
20-24	1 751	1 703	96	94	167	164	62	59	1 980	1 926	3 906
25-29	1 664	1 663	79	80	149	149	54	55	1 867	1 867	3 735
30-34	1 848	1 864	86	92	159	171	59	61	2 066	2 096	4 162
35-39	2 054	2 071	100	107	187	202	64	66	2 305	2 338	4 643
40-44	2 016	2 054	105	110	195	209	63	66	2 274	2 329	4 602
45-49	1 765	1 793	95	99	180	190	56	58	2 001	2 041	4 042
50-54	1 602	1 637	92	96	163	168	50	50	1 815	1 855	3 670
55-59	1 715	1 760	103	105	168	173	47	49	1 929	1 982	3 912
60-64	1 347	1 410	84	88	131	142	41	43	1 519	1 595	3 114
65-69	1 158	1 238	71	75	115	131	33	37	1 306	1 406	2 711
70-74	963	1 104	59	67	94	118	26	32	1 083	1 254	2 337
75-79	751	981	45	59	69	99	20	29	839	1 108	1 947
80-84	508	817	31	50	43	75	13	22	564	914	1 477
85-89	225	456	13	28	18	41	5	11	248	508	756
90 and over	94	285	5	16	7	25	2	7	103	316	419
0-14	4 916	4 673	270	257	443	422	182	173	5 541	5 269	10 809
15-64	17 564	17 658	942	968	1 668	1 729	563	570	19 795	19 956	39 751
65 and over	3 699	4 880	225	296	345	488	99	137	4 143	5 505	9 649
All ages	26 179	27 211	1 438	1 521	2 456	2 639	844	880	29 479	30 730	60 209

Sources: Office for National Statistics;
General Register Office (Scotland);
Northern Ireland Statistics and Research Agency

2.3 Births[1] and marriages

Thousands

	Live births[2]						Marriages					
	England and Wales			Scotland	Northern Ireland[3]	United Kingdom[3]	England and Wales			Scotland	Northern Ireland	United Kingdom
	Total	England	Wales				Total	England	Wales			
	BBCB	G8ZT	BBCC	BBCD	BBCE	BBCA	BBCG	G8ZU	BBCH	BBCI	BBCJ	BBCF
2001	594.6	563.7	30.6	52.5	22.0	669.1	249.2	236.2	13.0	29.6	7.3	286.1
2002	596.1	565.7	30.2	51.3	21.4	668.8	255.6	242.1	13.5	29.8	7.6	293.0
2003	621.5	589.9	31.4	52.4	21.6	695.6	270.1	255.6	14.5	30.8	7.8	308.6
2004	639.7	607.2	32.3	54.0	22.3	716.0	270.7	255.9	14.8	32.2	8.3	311.2
2005	645.8	613.0	32.6	54.4	22.3	722.6	..	..	..	30.9	..	..
2003 Q1	147.4	139.9	7.5	12.8	5.4	165.6	34.0	32.3	1.7	3.7	0.8	38.2
Q2	155.1	147.3	7.8	12.9	5.4	173.4	75.2	71.2	4.0	8.4	2.2	85.9
Q3	162.9	154.4	8.3	13.8	5.6	182.2	111.9	105.6	6.2	12.3	3.3	127.0
Q4	156.0	148.2	7.8	13.0	5.3	174.3	49.1	46.5	2.6	6.3	1.4	56.1
2004 Q1	155.2	147.3	7.8	13.5	5.7	174.3	35.0	33.3	1.7	3.9	0.8	39.7
Q2	157.4	149.6	7.8	13.3	5.4	176.2	75.0	71.0	4.0	8.7	2.4	86.1
Q3	165.4	156.9	8.4	13.8	5.8	185.1	113.2	106.8	6.4	12.7	3.5	129.4
Q4	161.7	153.3	8.3	13.3	5.4	180.4	49.9	47.2	2.7	6.8	1.6	58.4
2005 Q1	154.3	146.4	7.8	13.4	5.5[4]	173.2[4]	30.1[4]	28.5[4]	1.6[4]	3.8[4]	0.9[4]	34.9[4]
Q2	159.8	151.8	7.9	13.6	5.7[4]	179.0[4]	67.8[4]	63.9[4]	3.9[4]	8.6[4]	2.2[4]	78.7[4]
Q3	170.2	161.4	8.7	14.2	5.9[4]	190.3[4]	103.9[4]	97.9[4]	6.0[4]	12.3[4]	3.5[4]	119.7[4]
Q4	161.7	153.4	8.2	13.2	5.2[4]	180.1[4]	42.9[4]	40.4[4]	2.5[4]	6.1[4]	1.4[4]	50.5[4]
2006 Q1	159.5[4]	151.3[4]	8.1[4]	13.6[4]	5.8[4]	178.9[4]	..	..	..	3.5[4]	..	..
Q2	165.9[4]	157.6[4]	8.3[4]	14.0[4]	5.8[4]	185.7[4]	..	..	..	8.3[4]	..	..
Q3	173.5[4]	164.7[4]	8.7[4]	14.2[4]	6.1[4]	190.3[4]	..	..	..	12.2[4]	..	..

Note: Figures may not add exactly due to rounding.
1 Excluding stillbirths.
2 Birth figures for England and also for Wales each exclude events for persons usually resident outside England and Wales. These events are however, included in the totals for England and Wales combined, and for the United Kingdom.

3 For England and Wales, figures relate to numbers occurring in a period; for Scotland and Northern Ireland, figures relate to those registered in a period.
4 Provisional.

Sources: Office for National Statistics;
General Register Office for Scotland;;
Northern Ireland Statistics & Research Agency.

2.4 Deaths registered

Thousands

	Total					Infants aged under one year				
	England and Wales		Scotland	Northern Ireland	United Kingdom	England and Wales		Scotland	Northern Ireland	United Kingdom
	Total	Wales				Total	Wales			
	BBDB	BBDC	BBDD	BBDE	BBDA	BBDG	BBDH	BBDI	BBDJ	BBDF
2001	532.5	33.2	57.4	14.5	604.4	3.27	0.17	0.29	0.13	3.69
2002	535.4	33.3	58.1	14.6	608.0	3.20	0.10	0.30	0.10	3.50
2003	539.2	33.8	58.4	14.5	612.0	3.30	0.13	0.27	0.12	3.69
2004	514.3	32.3	56.2	14.4	584.8	3.27	0.16	0.27	0.12	3.66
2005	513.0	32.2	55.7	14.2	583.0	3.25	0.14	0.28	0.14	3.67
2002 Q4	137.7	8.5	15.2	3.7	156.5	0.83	0.04	0.07	0.03	0.92
2003 Q1	143.1	9.0	15.7	3.9	162.6	0.83	0.04	0.07	0.03	0.93
Q2	129.2	8.3	14.1	3.4	146.7	0.79	0.03	0.06	0.02	0.87
Q3	124.3	7.7	13.3	3.5	141.0	0.80	0.04	0.07	0.04	0.91
Q4	142.6	8.9	15.3	3.7	161.7	0.87	0.02	0.07	0.03	0.97
2004 Q1	142.0	8.9	15.3	3.9	161.1	0.86	0.05	0.06	0.03	0.96
Q2	122.5	7.7	13.6	3.6	139.7	0.78	0.04	0.07	0.03	0.88
Q3	119.0	7.5	13.1	3.4	135.5	0.81	0.05	0.07	0.04	0.92
Q4	130.6	8.2	14.2	3.5	148.3	0.82	0.03	0.06	0.02	0.91
2005 Q1	145.3	9.2	15.6	3.8	164.7	0.82	0.03	0.07	0.03	0.91
Q2	125.9	8.0	13.7	3.7	143.3	0.83	0.04	0.07	0.04	0.94
Q3	115.4	7.2	12.8	3.4	131.6	0.80	0.03	0.08	0.04	0.92
Q4	126.2	7.8	13.6	3.4	143.3	0.80	0.04	0.07	0.03	0.90
2006 Q1[1]	140.8	8.7	14.9	4.0	159.7	0.82	0.03	0.05	0.03	0.90
Q2[1]	123.6	7.6	13.9	3.6	141.1	0.84	0.03	0.07	0.03	0.93

1 Provisional.

Sources: Office for National Statistics;
General Register Office (Scotland);
Northern Ireland Statistics and Research Agency

3 Labour market

3.1 Labour market activity
United Kingdom

Thousands, seasonally adjusted[1]

	Employment categories					Unemployment	Total economically active	Economically inactive	Total aged 16 and over	Employment rate: aged 16 - 59/64[2] %
	Employees	Self employed	Unpaid family workers	Government training and employment programmes	Total employment					
	MGRN	MGRQ	MGRT	MGRW	MGRZ	MGSC	MGSF	MGSI	MGSL	MGSU
2003 Q4	24 402	3 655	99	107	28 263	1 453	29 716	17 467	47 183	74.6
2004 Q1	24 558	3 623	104	116	28 402	1 432	29 834	17 434	47 268	74.8
Q2	24 514	3 676	98	123	28 412	1 433	29 844	17 508	47 352	74.7
Q3	24 649	3 583	89	129	28 450	1 400	29 850	17 593	47 443	74.7
Q4	24 738	3 637	97	125	28 597	1 411	30 008	17 538	47 547	74.9
2005 Q1	24 823	3 622	105	126	28 676	1 411	30 087	17 563	47 650	74.9
Q2	24 848	3 630	101	114	28 693	1 433	30 126	17 628	47 753	74.7
Q3	24 936	3 661	90	107	28 794	1 447	30 242	17 611	47 853	74.8
Q4	24 861	3 699	90	108	28 758	1 554	30 312	17 634	47 946	74.5
2006 Q1	24 966	3 740	88	93	28 887	1 599	30 486	17 552	48 038	74.6
Q2	25 023	3 719	93	94	28 930	1 683	30 613	17 518	48 131	74.6
Q3	25 026	3 759	104	97	28 986	1 711	30 696	17 527	48 224	74.5
Q4	25 039	3 794	101	102	29 036	1 687	30 723	17 593	48 316	74.5

1 Seasonally adjusted estimates are subject to periodic revision.
2 The employment rate equals those in employment aged 16-64 (male) and 16-59 (female), as a percentage of all in these age groups.

Source: Labour Force Survey, Office for National Statistics: 020 7533 6094

3.2 Distribution of the workforce[1,2]
United Kingdom

Thousands

	Not seasonally adjusted						Seasonally adjusted		
		Employee jobs			Self-employment jobs (with or without employees)[3]	HM Forces[4]	Workforce jobs	Employee jobs	Self-employment jobs
	Workforce jobs	Males	Females	Total					
At June									
	DYDA	BCAE	BCAF	BCAD	BCAG	BCAH	DYDC	BCAJ	DYZN
2002	30 065	13 088	12 992	26 081	3 684	214	30 071	26 102	3 664
2003	30 352	13 183	12 963	26 146	3 896	223	30 366	26 169	3 882
2004	30 663	13 215	13 143	26 358	3 982	218	30 690	26 389	3 974
2005	31 010	13 374	13 373	26 747	3 961	210	31 042	26 779	3 957
2006	31 372	13 601	13 434	27 035	4 072	204	31 409	27 067	4 073
2004 Q1	30 532	13 123	13 115	26 238	3 969	220	30 636	26 340	3 974
Q2	30 663	13 215	13 143	26 358	3 982	218	30 690	26 389	3 974
Q3	30 681	13 273	13 151	26 423	3 942	215	30 689	26 429	3 942
Q4	30 990	13 433	13 300	26 733	3 940	215	30 868	26 596	3 957
2005 Q1	30 912	13 329	13 325	26 654	3 941	213	31 007	26 750	3 944
Q2	31 010	13 374	13 373	26 747	3 961	210	31 042	26 779	3 957
Q3	31 125	13 467	13 364	26 831	3 992	207	31 142	26 846	3 993
Q4	31 407	13 569	13 496	27 065	4 046	206	31 277	26 924	4 060
2006 Q1	31 232	13 497	13 365	26 861	4 084	206	31 322	26 955	4 085
Q2	31 372	13 601	13 434	27 035	4 072	204	31 409	27 067	4 073
Q3	31 479	13 658	13 415	27 073	4 150	202	31 494	27 090	4 146
Q4	31 744	13 752	13 546	27 298	4 187	202	31 583	27 155	4 171

1 The data in this table include revised figures for self-employment. For more information please see: http://www.statistics.gov.uk/StatBase/Product.asp?vlnk=9765
2 Estimates for employee jobs and workforce jobs for Great Britain use the Annual Business Inquiry as a benchmark on which the quarterly movements are based.

3 Estimates of the self-employed are based on the results of the Labour Force Survey. The estimates given in the table are unadjusted.
4 HM Forces figures, provided by the Ministry of Defence, represent the total number of UK service personnel, male and female, in HM Regular Forces wherever serving and including those on release leave. The numbers are not subject to seasonal adjustment.

Sources: Office for National Statistics;
Department of Economic Development (Northern Ireland)

3.3 Employee jobs: all industries[1,2]
Great Britain
Not seasonally adjusted

Thousands

SIC 1992 Divisions or Classes	All employee jobs	Employee jobs		Manufact-uring indus-tries; all jobs	Production indus-tries; all jobs	Production and constru-ction; all jobs	Production and constru-ction; male	Production and constru-ction; female	Service industries; all jobs
		male	female						
	A-O			D	C-E	C-F			G-O
	LMAB	DYCA	DYCB	LMAD	LMAF	LMAH	LMBL	LMBM	LMAJ
2005	26 053	13 038	13 015	3 013	3 163	4 331	3 340	990	21 497
2006	26 335	13 262	13 073	2 913	3 066	4 315	3 342	974	21 805
2005 Q3	26 136	13 131	13 005	2 982	3 133	4 346	3 365	981	21 571
Q4	26 362	13 230	13 133	2 944	3 093	4 309	3 343	967	21 839
2006 Q1	26 162	13 158	13 004	2 919	3 068	4 287	3 325	962	21 665
Q2	26 335	13 262	13 073	2 913	3 066	4 315	3 342	974	21 805
Q3	26 369	13 317	13 052	2 907	3 063	4 340	3 369	972	21 799
Q4	26 585	13 408	13 177	2 887	3 045	4 323	3 356	967	22 019
2006 Mar	..	..	..	2 919	3 068	..	..	..	..
Apr	..	..	..	2 915	3 065	..	..	..	..
May	..	..	..	2 910	3 061	..	..	..	..
Jun	..	..	..	2 913	3 066	..	..	..	..
Jul	..	..	..	2 912	3 065	..	..	..	..
Aug	..	..	..	2 908	3 062	..	..	..	..
Sep	..	..	..	2 907	3 063	..	..	..	..
Oct	..	..	..	2 904	3 060	..	..	..	..
Nov	..	..	..	2 896	3 052	..	..	..	..
Dec	..	..	..	2 887	3 045	..	..	..	..
2007 Jan	..	..	..	2 876	3 032	..	..	..	..
Feb	..	..	..	2 876	3 032	..	..	..	..

3.3

Employee jobs: all industries[1,2]
Great Britain

continued   **Not seasonally adjusted**

Thousands

	Agriculture, hunting, forestry and fishing	Mining and quarrying, electricity, gas and water supply	Food products, beverages and tobacco	Manufacture of clothing, textiles and leather production	Wood and wood products	Paper, pulp, printing, publishing and recording media	Chemicals, chemical products and man-made fibres	Rubber and plastic products	Non-metallic mineral products, metal and metal products, nec	Machinery and equipment, nec	Electrical and optical equipment	Transport equipment	Coke, nuclear fuel and other manufacturing, nec
SIC 1992 Divisions or Classes	A,B 01-05	C,E 10-12, 40-41	DA 15-16	DB/DC 17-19	DD 20	DE 21-22	DG 24	DH 25	DI/DJ 26-28	DK 29	DL 30-33	DM 34-35	DF, DN 23, 36-37
	LMAL	LMAM	LMAN	LMAO	LMAP	LMAQ	LMAR	LMAS	LMAT	LMAU	LMAV	LMAW	LMAX
2005	226	149	410	129	77	394	195	196	496	273	324	320	199
2006	215	153	402	120	76	380	188	184	484	266	309	314	191
2005 Q3	219	151	412	126	76	390	192	190	494	271	321	316	195
Q4	215	149	409	122	75	387	189	187	484	268	317	315	191
2006 Q1	210	149	401	121	75	382	189	186	482	267	312	314	191
Q2	215	153	402	120	76	380	188	184	484	266	309	314	191
Q3	230	156	404	119	78	376	187	182	482	268	306	312	193
Q4	243	157	402	117	77	373	186	180	477	268	304	309	194
2006 Mar	..	149	401	121	75	382	189	186	482	267	312	314	191
Apr	..	150	401	120	74	381	188	186	481	266	311	314	191
May	..	151	400	120	75	380	188	185	481	267	309	314	191
Jun	..	153	402	120	76	380	188	184	484	266	309	314	191
Jul	..	153	403	120	76	379	188	184	482	267	308	312	193
Aug	..	154	404	119	78	377	187	183	481	268	308	311	193
Sep	..	156	404	119	78	376	187	182	482	268	306	312	193
Oct	..	156	404	119	77	375	187	182	482	268	305	311	193
Nov	..	156	404	118	77	374	187	181	478	269	305	310	193
Dec	..	157	402	117	77	373	186	180	477	268	304	309	194
2007 Jan	..	156	398	117	77	371	186	180	472	268	305	308	193
Feb	..	156	397	117	77	370	186	181	473	266	305	310	193

	Construction	Wholesale and retail trade and repairs	Hotels and restaurants	Transport and storage	Post and telecommunications	Financial intermediation	Real estate	Renting, research, computer and other business activities	Public administration and defence, compulsory social security	Education	Health and Social work activities	Other community social and personal activities
SIC 1992 Divisions or Classes	F 45	G 50-52	H 55	I 60-63	64	J 65-67	K 70	71-74	L 75	M 80	N 85	O 90-93
	LMAY	LMAZ	LMBA	LMBB	LMBC	LMBD	LMBE	LMBF	LMBG	LMBH	LOJV	LMBK
2005	1 168	4 478	1 814	1 076	491	1 049	443	3 828	1 460	2 286	3 188	1 385
2006	1 249	4 477	1 796	1 088	484	1 050	484	3 954	1 459	2 340	3 253	1 420
2005 Q3	1 213	4 473	1 799	1 087	488	1 047	456	3 901	1 455	2 284	3 201	1 380
Q4	1 216	4 605	1 781	1 081	498	1 047	469	3 955	1 461	2 335	3 231	1 376
2006 Q1	1 219	4 468	1 766	1 079	487	1 049	474	3 915	1 459	2 342	3 245	1 380
Q2	1 249	4 477	1 796	1 088	484	1 050	484	3 954	1 459	2 340	3 253	1 420
Q3	1 277	4 473	1 778	1 086	483	1 051	486	3 998	1 460	2 315	3 257	1 411
Q4	1 279	4 629	1 773	1 085	496	1 053	493	4 021	1 461	2 353	3 252	1 404

1 The data in this table have not been adjusted to reflect the 2001 Census population data.
2 Estimates for employee jobs and workforce jobs for Great Britain use the Annual Business Inquiry as a benchmark on which the quarterly movements are based.

Source: Office for National Statistics

3.4 Civil Service employment by department[1]

Full-time equivalents, Great Britain, not seasonally adjusted

		2006 Q2	2006 Q3	2006 Q4
Attorney General's Departments	GB3F	9 430	9 510	9 660
Cabinet Office	BBGD	1 620	1 610	1 660
Other Cabinet Office Agencies[2]	GB3G	780	780	780
HM Treasury	GB3H	1 160	1 130	1 110
Chancellor's other departments	GB3I	5 390	5 250	5 170
Charity Commission	GB3J	520	520	500
Communities and Local Government[2]	YEGA	5 610	5 560	5 520
Constitutional Affairs	GB3K	34 100	33 720	33 620
Culture, Media and Sport	DMTC	620	640	630
Defence	BCDW	87 260	85 690	84 670
Education and Skills	LNFW	4 170	4 060	3 940
Environment, Food and Rural Affairs	LNFX	13 100	12 730	11 580
Export Credits Guarantee Department	GB3L	260	250	270
Foreign and Commonwealth	BCDK	6 160	6 070	6 060
Health[3]	BAKR	6 100	6 020	5 870
HM Revenue and Customs	GB3M	97 360	95 780	94 880
Home Office[2]	BCDL	72 990	73 560	73 500
International Development	DMUA	1 780	1 740	1 750
Northern Ireland Office	BBGG	140	140	140
Office for Standards in Education	GB3N	2 280	2 300	2 470
Security and Intelligence Services	GB3O	4 890	4 890	4 960
Trade and Industry[2]	BCDQ	10 110	10 080	10 110
Transport	BCDR	19 120	18 950	18 770
Work and Pensions	LNGA	117 180	116 660	115 530
Central Governments Departments Total	GB3P	502 100	497 620	493 140
Scottish Executive	GB3Q	16 100	15 900	15 820
Welsh Assembly	GB3R	5 960	6 460	6 680
TOTAL	BCDX	524 160	519 980	515 640

1 Numbers are rounded to the nearest ten. Data not available are represented by "-".
2 The Office of the Third Sector (OTS) was established in May 2006. Employee numbers for OTS will not be available until Q4. For this publication, the employees are therefore still included with their former departments.
3 The Wine Standards Board (former NDPB) merged with the Food Standards Agency on 1 July 2006.

Source: Office for National Statistics

3.5 Intake and outflow of UK Regular Armed Forces Personnel

	Intake[1]						Outflow[2]					
	Financial Year					12 months to 1 October 2006	Financial Year					12 months to 1 October 2006
	2001-02	2002-03	2003-04	2004-05	2005-06		2001-02	2002-03	2003-04	2004-05	2005-06	
All Services[3]												
Total	23.7	26.3	23.5	17.6	18.1	19.5	24.7	24.1	23.4	23.4	23.3	24.0
Male	21.0	23.1	20.8	15.7	16.4	17.6	22.4	21.8	21.2	21.3	21.3	22.0
Female	2.7	3.3	2.7	1.9	1.7	2.0	2.4	2.3	2.2	2.1	2.0	2.0
Naval Service												
Total	5.0	5.2	4.1	3.7	3.9	3.9	5.8	5.3	4.8	4.6	4.5	4.4
Male	4.3	4.4	3.5	3.2	3.5	3.5	5.1	4.7	4.2	4.1	4.0	3.9
Female	0.7	0.8	0.6	0.5	0.5	0.5	0.7	0.6	0.5	0.5	0.5	0.5
Army												
Total	14.9	16.7	15.3	11.7	12.7	13.8	14.4	14.6	14.6	15.1	14.2	14.5
Male	13.7	15.1	14.0	10.8	11.7	12.7	13.3	13.4	13.5	14.0	13.2	13.5
Female	1.2	1.6	1.3	0.9	1.0	1.1	1.1	1.1	1.1	1.1	1.0	0.9
RAF[3]												
Total	3.8	4.4	4.2	2.2	1.5	1.7	4.5	4.2	4.0	3.7	4.6	5.2
Male	3.1	3.6	3.3	1.6	1.2	1.4	4.0	3.7	3.5	3.2	4.1	4.6
Female	0.7	0.9	0.9	0.5	0.3	0.4	0.6	0.6	0.6	0.5	0.5	0.6

1 Intake from civilian life, includes re-enlistments and rejoined reservists.
2 Outflow includes recalled reservists on release and outflow to the Home Service battalions of the Royal Irish Regiment.
3 Denotes provisional. Due to the introduction of a new Personnel Administration System for RAF, all data from 1st May 2006 and onwards are provisional and subject to review.

Figures are for UK Regular Forces (including both Trained and Untrained personnel), and therefore exclude Gurkhas, Full Time Reserve Service personnel, the Home Service battalions of the Royal Irish Regiment, mobilised reservists and Naval Activated Reservists.

Source: Defence Analytical Services Agency: 0207 218 4439

3.6 UK armed forces full-time strengths[1]

	1 Apr 2002	1 Apr 2003	1 Apr 2004	1 Apr 2005	1 Apr 2006	1 Oct 2006
All Services[2]						
Trained						
Total	187 110	188 520	190 190	188 050	183 180	179 420
UK regulars	181 680	182 780	184 590	182 840	178 300	174 590
Full Time Reserve Service	1 980	2 360	2 220	1 690	1 540	1 560
Gurkhas	3 450	3 380	3 390	3 520	3 330	3 280
Untrained						
Total	23 350	24 520	22 770	18 430	17 880	18 710
UK regulars	23 000	24 160	22 430	18 260	17 550	18 400
Gurkhas	350	380	330	170	330	310
Naval Service						
Trained						
Total	37 490	37 610	37 510	36 400	35 620	35 260
UK regulars	36 770	36 610	36 420	35 500	34 890	34 590
Full Time Reserve Service	720	1 010	1 090	900	720	670
Untrained						
Total	4 850	4 940	4 460	4 440	4 500	4 360
UK regulars	4 850	4 940	4 460	4 440	4 500	4 360
Army						
Trained						
Total	100 410	102 000	103 560	102 440	100 620	99 570
UK regulars	96 020	97 640	99 420	98 490	96 790	95 760
Full Time Reserve Service	940	990	750	430	490	540
Gurkhas	3 450	3 380	3 390	3 520	3 330	3 280
Untrained						
Total	14 380	14 880	13 650	10 970	11 260	12 060
UK regulars	14 030	14 490	13 320	10 800	10 940	11 750
Gurkhas	350	380	330	170	330	310
RAF[2]						
Trained						
Total	49 200	48 900	49 120	49 210	46 940	44 590
UK regulars	48 880	48 540	48 740	48 850	46 620	44 240
Full Time Reserve Service	320	360	380	360	330	350
Untrained						
Total	4 120	4 700	4 650	3 020	2 110	2 300
UK regulars	4 120	4 700	4 650	3 020	2 110	2 300

1 The full-time strength includes UK Regular Forces, Gurkhas and FTRS (Full Time Reserve Service) personnel.

2 Denotes provisional. Due to the introduction of a new Personnel Administration System for RAF, all data from 1st May 2006 and onwards are provisional and subject to review.

Due to the rounding methods used, totals may not always equal the sum of the parts. When rounding to the nearest 10, numbers ending in 5 have been rounded to the nearest multiple of 20 to prevent systematic bias.

Source: Defence Analytical Services Agency: 0207 218 4439

3.7 Number of workers employed in agriculture[1]

Thousands

	Regular workers					Seasonal or casual workers			All workers		
	Whole-time		Part-time								
	Male	Female	Male	Female	Total	Male	Female	Total	Male	Female	Total
	BAMY	BAMZ	BANA	BANB	BANC	BAND	BANE	BANF	BANG	BANH	BANI
1992 Jun	99.9	14.8	29.1	26.1	169.9	54.4	31.9	86.2	183.3	72.8	256.2
1993 Jun	96.5	13.7	29.8	25.3	165.3	55.0	30.4	85.4	181.3	69.4	250.7
1994 Jun	93.6	13.2	30.0	24.2	161.0	53.9	28.4	82.2	177.5	65.7	243.2
1995 Jun	90.4	13.0	30.0	24.1	157.4	56.5	27.2	83.7	176.8	64.3	241.2
1996 Jun	89.2	12.6	31.2	23.4	156.4	55.6	25.8	81.5	176.0	61.9	237.9
1997 Jun	87.5	12.6	31.2	23.1	154.4	55.3	25.5	80.9	174.0	61.2	235.2
1998 Jun[2]	88.0	13.1	29.7	24.7	155.6	55.6	23.8	79.5	172.8	62.2	235.0
1999 Jun	82.7	11.9	27.5	22.6	144.7	51.8	21.2	73.0	162.0	55.6	217.7
2000 Jun	73.4	10.3	24.6	20.6	128.9	45.9	18.5	64.4	143.9	49.4	193.3
2001 Jun[3]	69.0	10.9	22.0	18.9	120.8	44.6	18.6	63.2	135.6	48.5	184.0
	70.3	11.2	22.5	19.4	123.5	45.4	18.8	64.1	138.2	49.4	187.6
2002 Jun	64.7	11.5	21.7	18.4	116.3	46.2	18.0	64.2	132.6	47.9	180.6
2003 Jun	60.4	10.0	21.0	17.0	108.4	44.8	17.8	62.6	126.2	44.8	170.9
2004 Jun	58.1	9.8	23.5	17.4	108.8	49.6	18.6	68.3	131.2	45.8	177.0
2005 Jun	57.2	10.3	24.5	17.2	109.2	46.4	18.7	65.1	128.1	46.2	174.3
2006 Jun	53.6	10.4	24.3	17.1	105.4	44.4	19.6	64.0	122.3	47.1	169.4

1 Figures exclude farmers, partners, directors and their spouses, salaried managers, school children and most trainees. Includes estimates for minor holdings.

2 In 1998, fundamental changes were introduced to the labour questions on the June Agricultural and Horticultural Census in England, Wales and Scotland. It appears that this change in questions may have led to the recording of additional Labour who were not previously included in the returns. The change in questions has also led to a redistribution of labour between the various categories. We therefore advise caution when comparing the results from 1998 onwards with previous years.

3 Due to an English register improvement only the top figure for 2001 is directly comparable with June 2000, while the bottom figure for 2001 is only comparable with data from June 2002.

Source: Department for Environment, Food and Rural Affairs: 01904 455095

3.8 Unemployment in United Kingdom
Analysis by duration[1]

Thousands, seasonally adjusted[1]

	Males				Females			
	Up to 26 weeks	Over 26 and up to 52 weeks	Over 52 weeks	Total	Up to 26 weeks	Over 26 and up to 52 weeks	Over 52 weeks	Total
	MGYK	MGYM	MGYO	MGSD	MGYL	MGYN	MGYP	MGSE
1995 Q1	571	247	798	1 617	446	145	286	877
Q2	551	254	776	1 581	449	143	269	861
Q3	580	229	766	1 575	462	149	257	869
Q4	559	245	708	1 512	456	154	230	840
1996 Q1	581	265	693	1 539	437	132	221	790
Q2	591	246	680	1 517	458	143	220	820
Q3	579	227	664	1 471	458	133	219	809
Q4	543	205	653	1 400	471	133	223	827
1997 Q1	512	189	597	1 297	443	126	216	785
Q2	550	178	538	1 265	459	121	203	783
Q3	533	173	491	1 197	450	116	185	750
Q4	523	175	443	1 141	439	109	171	719
1998 Q1	512	171	418	1 101	448	98	163	709
Q2	518	160	396	1 074	462	93	160	715
Q3	550	164	377	1 092	446	102	144	692
Q4	556	166	356	1 079	445	92	147	684
1999 Q1	561	165	353	1 080	450	99	147	695
Q2	536	165	359	1 059	450	102	131	684
Q3	513	160	353	1 026	438	100	138	676
Q4	504	144	355	1 002	442	108	132	682
2000 Q1	515	142	326	984	458	108	126	691
Q2	500	140	317	957	420	100	122	642
Q3	476	137	297	910	429	92	114	635
Q4	486	136	289	912	415	87	107	609
2001 Q1	475	128	283	885	400	85	101	586
Q2	481	131	269	882	396	87	107	591
Q3	504	132	261	897	401	82	104	586
Q4	529	132	253	914	432	76	101	609
2002 Q1	533	147	239	919	419	77	97	593
Q2	536	147	227	910	441	71	94	606
Q3	571	141	234	945	439	78	98	615
Q4	526	148	218	891	443	85	95	623
2003 Q1	557	130	239	926	425	83	89	597
Q2	537	131	218	886	410	74	94	578
Q3	531	145	223	899	434	75	95	604
Q4	502	146	227	876	414	74	89	577
2004 Q1	489	141	212	841	412	82	97	591
Q2	503	141	197	841	419	86	86	592
Q3	492	133	195	821	420	75	84	579
Q4	494	143	192	829	418	77	87	583
2005 Q1	490	137	205	832	415	75	89	579
Q2	487	137	209	833	424	77	98	599
Q3	500	146	212	859	409	95	84	588
Q4	535	143	238	916	439	105	94	638
2006 Q1	531	166	235	932	454	112	101	667
Q2	546	177	252	975	477	126	105	708
Q3	545	176	273	994	479	117	121	716
Q4	530	168	266	964	481	112	130	723

1 Seasonally adjusted estimates are subject to periodic revision.

Source: Labour Force Survey, Office for National Statistics: 020 7533 6094

3.9 Claimant count in United Kingdom
Analysis of claimant by duration - computerised claims only

Thousands, seasonally adjusted

	Males				Females			
	Up to 26 weeks	Over 26 and up to 52 weeks	Over 52 weeks	Total[1]	Up to 26 weeks	Over 26 and up to 52 weeks	Over 52 weeks	Total[1]
	AGXK	ELNP	ELON	AGNG	JLGK	JLGJ	JLGL	JLGI
2001	449.4	125.4	158.8	733.6	160.4	35.1	32.5	227.9
2002	457.4	124.2	126.7	708.3	163.6	35.5	27.6	226.8
2003	451.2	127.1	114.7	693.0	166.3	37.2	26.5	230.1
2004	408.8[†]	113.7	108.2[†]	630.7[†]	153.2[†]	34.9	26.7	214.7
2005	423.4	113.3	98.3	635.0	159.2	35.6	25.2[†]	220.0
2006	438.5	136.4[†]	119.0	694.0	171.5	43.6	30.8	245.9[†]
2003 Feb	459.0	125.8	116.4	701.2	167.9	35.5	26.2	229.6
Mar	457.1	126.5	115.7	699.3	168.2	36.1	26.2	230.5
Apr	456.0	124.8	113.9	694.7	169.9	35.4	25.7	231.0
May	462.0	127.1	114.6	703.7	169.8	36.6	26.4	232.8
Jun	461.4	128.2	114.2	703.8	169.1	37.4	26.3	232.8
Jul	455.7	128.6	113.9	698.2	167.7	38.1	26.4	232.2
Aug	449.7	128.9	114.3	692.9	166.0	38.8	26.7	231.5
Sep	446.8	128.5	114.0	689.3	165.2	38.7	26.7	230.6
Oct	440.9	129.1	114.1	684.1	163.5	38.9	26.9	229.3
Nov	436.9	126.9	113.6	677.4	161.6	38.2	26.9	226.7
Dec	432.2	126.1	113.7	672.0	160.4	37.7	27.2	225.3
2004 Jan	428.2[†]	125.0[†]	113.2[†]	666.4[†]	158.8[†]	37.6[†]	27.3	223.7[†]
Feb	425.7	122.5	112.9	661.1	158.1	36.8	27.2	222.1
Mar	418.8	121.4	112.1	652.3	156.4	36.6	27.2[†]	220.2
Apr	416.5	118.5	111.4	646.4	154.9	36.1	27.4	218.4
May	406.9	116.8	110.7	634.4	153.0	35.9	27.3	216.2
Jun	402.4	113.7	109.7	625.8	151.6	35.0	27.0	213.6
Jul	400.7	110.5	107.9	619.1	149.0	34.2	26.8	210.0
Aug	400.2	109.8	106.7	616.7	150.5	33.8	26.5	210.8
Sep	400.6	108.5	105.8	614.9	150.7	33.6	26.4	210.7
Oct	403.9	105.5	104.1	613.5	151.1	32.9	25.9	209.9
Nov	401.7	106.4	102.8	610.9	151.5	33.1	25.8	210.4
Dec	400.2	105.4	101.4	607.0	152.2	33.1	25.4	210.7
2005 Jan	400.3	104.2	99.4	603.9	152.7	32.9	25.5	211.1
Feb	403.2	103.7	98.8	605.7	152.6	33.0	25.2	210.8
Mar	409.9	104.4	98.0	612.3	154.1	33.1	25.0	212.2
Apr	413.9	106.2	97.0	617.1	156.8	33.8	24.6	215.2
May	426.4	106.8	96.2	629.4	158.6	33.9	24.5	217.0
Jun	430.4	108.7	96.4	635.5	160.0	34.3	24.6	218.9
Jul	430.3	112.1	96.5	638.9	160.5	35.2	24.7	220.4
Aug	430.1	114.8	96.2	641.1	160.3	35.9	24.6	220.8
Sep	429.6	119.5	97.4	646.5	160.5	37.4	25.1	223.0
Oct	432.8	122.8	99.3	654.9	162.8	38.1	25.5	226.4
Nov	435.9	127.4	101.2	664.5	164.8	39.5	26.3	230.6
Dec	438.0	128.7	103.0	669.7	166.7	40.2	26.7	233.6
2006 Jan	435.3	129.8	105.2	670.3	166.6	41.1	27.3	235.0
Feb	441.1	133.0	108.1	682.2	168.8	41.8	28.2	238.8
Mar	446.3	134.3	110.9	691.5	171.2	41.9	28.6	241.7
Apr	446.1	138.1	114.0	698.2	170.5	43.5	29.6	243.6
May	443.6	140.0	117.5	701.1	172.0	43.9	30.2	246.1
Jun	442.2	141.4	119.7	703.3	171.6	44.7	30.9	247.2
Jul	438.2	141.8	122.3	702.3	171.2	45.5	31.6	248.3
Aug	435.4	139.9	124.2	699.5	172.1	45.2	32.0	249.3
Sep	436.0	138.8	125.9	700.7	173.4	44.8	32.7	250.9
Oct	433.8	138.1	126.9	698.8	174.2	44.6	32.9	251.7
Nov	432.8	132.6	127.1	692.5	173.7	43.5	33.0	250.2
Dec	431.2	129.5	126.3	687.0	172.2	42.9	32.8	247.9
2007 Jan	421.8	126.1	125.1	673.0	170.8	42.4	32.8	246.0
Feb	421.8	124.6	125.1	671.5	170.3	41.8	32.8	244.9
Mar	417.0	122.5	123.9	663.4	169.7	41.3	32.6	243.6

1 Total computerised claims only.

Sources: Jobcentre Plus Administrative;
Labour Market Statistics;
Helpline: 020 7533 6094

3.10 Claimant count

Thousands

| | United Kingdom | | | | | | Great Britain | |
| | Not seasonally adjusted | | Seasonally adjusted[1] | | | | Seasonally adjusted[1] | |
	Total	Percentage rate[2]	Males	Females	Total	Percentage rate[2]	Total	Percentage rate[2]
	BCJA	BCJB	DPAE	DPAF	BCJD	BCJE	DPAG	DPAJ
2001	983.0	3.2	739.6	230.3	969.9	3.2	930.5	3.1
2002	958.8	3.1	717.1	229.6	946.6	3.1	910.2	3.0
2003	945.9	3.0	700.3	232.8	933.0	3.0	898.5	3.0
2004	866.1	2.8	636.2†	217.1	853.3†	2.7	822.5†	2.7
2005	874.4	2.8	639.7	222.0	861.7	2.7	833.1	2.7
2006	956.7	3.1	697.3	247.4†	944.7	3.0	916.9	3.0
2004 Feb	957.0	3.0	667.2†	224.9†	892.1†	2.8	859.3†	2.8
Mar	932.0	3.0	658.2	222.8	881.0	2.8	848.8	2.8
Apr	905.2	2.9	651.2	220.7	871.9	2.8	840.1	2.8
May	869.7	2.8	639.8	218.3	858.1	2.7	826.9	2.7
Jun	840.5	2.7	631.0	215.9	846.9	2.7	816.3	2.7
Jul	841.5	2.7	624.3	212.1	836.4	2.7	806.5	2.6
Aug	847.6	2.7	621.7	212.8	834.5	2.7	804.6	2.6
Sep	827.8	2.6	620.1	212.8	832.9	2.7	803.1	2.6
Oct	806.8	2.6	619.2	212.3	831.5	2.6†	801.9	2.6
Nov	803.0	2.6	616.6	212.9	829.5	2.6	800.0	2.6
Dec	810.2	2.6	612.7	213.4	826.1	2.6	797.1	2.6
2005 Jan	872.1	2.8	609.8	213.5	823.3	2.6	794.2	2.6
Feb	885.0	2.8	611.1	212.9	824.0	2.6	795.0	2.6
Mar	882.3	2.8	617.6	214.4	832.0	2.6	803.1	2.6
Apr	871.8	2.8	622.1	217.6	839.7	2.7	810.9	2.6
May	867.6	2.7	634.7	219.3	854.0	2.7	825.3	2.7
Jun	858.2	2.7	640.4	221.0	861.4	2.7	832.7	2.7
Jul	871.0	2.8	643.3	222.4	865.7	2.7	837.3	2.7
Aug	880.7	2.8	645.5	222.8	868.3	2.7	840.1	2.7
Sep	871.5	2.8	650.9	224.9	875.8	2.8	847.7	2.8
Oct	864.8	2.7	659.1	228.3	887.4	2.8	859.3	2.8
Nov	875.3	2.8	668.3	232.2	900.5	2.8	871.9	2.8
Dec	892.7	2.8	673.3	235.1	908.4	2.9	880.1	2.9
2006 Jan	955.3	3.0	674.2	236.7	910.9	2.9	882.6	2.9†
Feb	984.7	3.1	686.0	240.4	926.4	2.9	898.0	2.9
Mar	989.1	3.1	695.4	243.4	938.8	3.0	910.4	3.0
Apr	981.2	3.1	701.9	245.2	947.1	3.0	918.8	3.0
May	965.7	3.1	704.3	247.6	951.9	3.0	923.6	3.0
Jun	952.9	3.0	706.7	248.5	955.2	3.0	927.3	3.0
Jul	960.8	3.0	705.4	249.7	955.1	3.0	927.4	3.0
Aug	958.9	3.0	702.7	250.6	953.3	3.0	925.8	3.0
Sep	952.9	3.0	704.2	252.5	956.7	3.0	929.1	3.0
Oct	933.7	3.0	701.8	253.3	955.1	3.0	927.4	3.0
Nov	922.1	2.9	695.5	251.7	947.2	3.0	920.0	3.0
Dec	923.5	2.9	689.8	249.3	939.1	3.0	912.3	3.0
2007 Jan	965.1	3.1	675.8	247.3	923.1	2.9	897.0	2.9
Feb	974.9	3.1	674.0	246.0	920.0	2.9	894.2	2.9
Mar	956.0	3.0	666.1	244.7	910.8	2.9	885.1	2.9

1 The seasonally adjusted series relate only to claimants aged 18 or over in order to maintain the consistent series, available back to 1971 (1974 for the regions - see p.608 of the December 1990 *Employment Gazette* and pS16 of the April 1994 issue for the list of discontinuities taken into account). It also takes into account the effect of the change in benefit eligibility rules introduced with Jobseeker's Allowance (see p.219-24, Labour Market Trends, May 2000). The latest national and regional seasonally adjusted claimant count figures are provisional and are subject to revision mainly in the following month.

2 Percentage rates have been calculated by expressing the number of claimants as a percentage of the estimated total workforce (the sum of claimants, employees jobs, self-employed, HM Forces and participants on work related government training programmes) at mid-2005 estimates for 2005 and 2006 figures and at the corresponding mid-year estimates for earlier years.

Sources: Jobcentre Plus Administrative;
Labour Market Statistics;
Helpline: 020 7533 6094

3.11 Unemployed
Analysis by Government Office Regions

Thousands, seasonally adjusted

	North East	North West	Yorkshire and the Humber	East Midlands	West Midlands	East	London	South East	South West	England	Wales	Scotland	Great Britain	Northern Ireland	United Kingdom[1]
	YCMP	YCMQ	YCMR	YCMS	YCMT	YCMU	YCMV	YCMW	YCMX	YCMY	YCMZ	YCNA	YCNB	ZSFA	MGSC
2000 Q2	105	171	148	101	156	100	271	137	105	1 295	80	178	1 552	49	1 599
Q3	105	172	143	100	145	101	254	130	101	1 250	88	167	1 505	41	1 545
Q4	90	170	148	97	152	101	250	140	95	1 243	76	157	1 476	45	1 521
2001 Q1	88	167	129	97	143	97	242	140	96	1 200	79	147	1 426	46	1 472
Q2	86	171	130	105	140	100	234	133	88	1 188	80	159	1 427	46	1 472
Q3	82	163	127	97	138	110	249	143	90	1 198	72	167	1 437	46	1 483
Q4	84	172	122	96	144	109	278	143	89	1 236	76	168	1 481	44	1 523
2002 Q1	86	172	122	99	145	103	262	151	86	1 227	74	166	1 467	46	1 511
Q2	75	179	128	97	148	102	258	162	92	1 241	75	159	1 475	43	1 515
Q3	72	179	135	100	155	108	266	169	100	1 284	70	161	1 515	47	1 561
Q4	84	161	121	102	148	113	250	168	101	1 247	69	156	1 472	43	1 514
2003 Q1	77	161	129	85	158	129	265	163	96	1 263	67	151	1 481	42	1 523
Q2	70	163	124	91	147	108	274	166	85	1 229	63	134	1 426	41	1 464
Q3	76	164	120	99	153	112	276	163	82	1 245	66	150	1 461	43	1 504
Q4	74	154	121	96	147	98	263	162	76	1 191	67	148	1 406	48	1 453
2004 Q1	67	148	119	101	144	98	266	161	75	1 179	65	149	1 393	40	1 432
Q2	64	146	112	90	144	108	269	154	93	1 181	59	154	1 394	39	1 433
Q3	70	148	113	88	130	102	274	154	83	1 161	67	136	1 364	38	1 400
Q4	76	154	114	91	125	107	272	148	83	1 171	58	148	1 377	36	1 411
2005 Q1	69	158	108	93	124	109	257	156	92	1 167	64	144	1 374	37	1 411
Q2	83	147	118	92	123	110	275	162	82	1 192	63	140	1 395	39	1 433
Q3	80	150	113	98	123	119	260	171	95	1 209	65	142	1 416	34	1 447
Q4	79	162	137	103	139	130	288	180	101	1 318	68	136	1 521	35	1 554
2006 Q1	82	165	136	112	139	138	304	192	92	1 360	67	139	1 566	35	1 599
Q2	75	178	145	121	154	144	315	202	96	1 430	81	141	1 652	34	1 683
Q3	85	190	152	119	164	143	321	195	100	1 469	77	131	1 677	38	1 711
Q4	81	178	152	130	175	128	315	188	98	1 444	74	139	1 656	34	1 687

Unemployment rate[2]

	YCNC	YCND	YCNE	YCNF	YCNG	YCNH	YCNI	YCNJ	YCNK	YCNL	YCNM	YCNN	YCNO	ZSFB	MGSX
2006 Q4	6.5	5.3	6.0	5.8	6.5	4.5	7.9	4.3	3.8	5.6	5.2	5.2	5.5	4.2	5.5

1 Due to slight methodological differences between the way the national and regional LFS estimates have been interim adjusted for the 2001 Census, there may be small differences between the UK totals and the sum of the regional components.

2 Unemployed as a percentage of total economically active (the sum of unemployed and those in employment).

Source: Labour Force Survey, Office for National Statistics: 020 7533 6094

Labour market

3.12 Claimant count[1]
Analysis by Government Office Regions

Thousands, seasonally adjusted

	North East	North West	Yorkshire and the Humber	East Midlands	West Midlands	East	London	South East	South West	Wales	Scotland	Northern Ireland
	DPDG	IBWA	DPAX	DPAY	DPBC	DPDJ	DPDK	DPDL	DPBB	DPBE	DPBF	DPBG
1999	79.9	153.8	123.0	76.2	119.7	76.5	203.1	95.3	75.3	64.1	130.4	50.7
2000	72.2	136.9	107.0	69.4	108.0	64.1	174.5	78.9	61.8	57.3	116.3	42.1
2001	62.7	123.5	96.0	63.6	99.0	55.0	154.9	66.6	52.7	51.2	105.2	39.5
2002	57.9	118.1	88.8	58.7	93.7	56.6	166.0	71.2	50.1	47.1	102.0	36.4
2003	52.8	111.7	83.7	58.9	94.7	58.1	170.7	75.6	48.3	44.6	99.5	34.6
2004	46.3	99.2	73.4	52.5	88.3	55.4	162.8	70.7	41.9	40.2	92.0	30.8
2005	45.9[†]	101.3	76.0	54.1	93.9	58.1	162.9[†]	71.6	42.2	41.2	85.9	28.6
2006	50.2	115.5	87.3[†]	62.0	108.3	65.5[†]	166.8	81.7[†]	48.0	44.2	87.3[†]	27.8
2003 Oct	51.1	108.7	81.6	58.8	94.2	57.3	170.2	76.0	47.4	43.1	98.9	34.7
Nov	50.7	107.0	80.0	57.8	93.5	57.3	169.3	75.8	46.5	42.7	98.3	34.1
Dec	50.1	106.0	78.7	57.2	93.0	56.9	168.9	75.3	45.9	42.2	97.8	34.0
2004 Jan	49.8[†]	104.6[†]	78.3[†]	56.2[†]	93.0[†]	56.7[†]	167.8	75.0[†]	45.3[†]	42.0[†]	97.0[†]	33.5
Feb	48.5	104.1	77.6	55.2	93.0	56.6	166.6	74.3	44.7	41.9	96.8	32.8
Mar	47.6	102.9	76.4	54.6	91.3	56.3	165.4[†]	73.3	43.9	41.5	95.6	32.2
Apr	47.5	101.3	75.6	53.7	89.7	56.0	165.5	72.3	42.7	41.4	94.4	31.8
May	46.6	99.7	73.9	52.4	88.2	55.4	165.2	71.1	41.6	40.4	92.4	31.2
Jun	45.6	98.3	72.7	51.8	87.7	54.7	163.2	70.2	41.0	39.8	91.3	30.6
Jul	45.4	96.7	71.6	51.1	86.7	54.6	162.0	68.5	40.4	39.5	90.0	29.9[†]
Aug	44.9	97.0	71.9	50.8	86.0	54.7	161.0	68.6	40.3	39.4	90.0	29.9
Sep	44.8	96.9	71.4	50.8	85.8	54.8	160.1	68.6	40.4	39.3	90.2	29.8
Oct	45.1	96.5	71.1	50.9	86.0	55.0	158.8	69.2	40.6	39.2	89.5	29.6
Nov	44.8	96.4	70.5	51.4	85.8	54.9	158.8	68.8	40.8	39.0	88.8	29.5
Dec	44.7	96.0	69.8	50.9	85.9	55.2	158.6	68.2	40.7	39.1	88.0	29.0
2005 Jan	43.9	94.5	70.1	50.8	85.6	55.3	158.6	68.3	40.8	38.9	87.4	29.1
Feb	44.3	95.0	70.6	50.4	85.3	55.2	159.4	67.9	41.0	39.0	86.9	29.0
Mar	44.9	96.3	72.0	51.8	85.3	56.1	161.5	68.8	41.2	39.2	86.0	28.9
Apr	44.9	97.9	73.2	51.8	87.6	56.3	162.2	70.1	41.3	39.5	86.1	28.8
May	45.4	99.6	74.4	52.8	94.7	57.1	162.2	70.4	41.8	40.5	86.4	28.7
Jun	45.9	100.8	75.6	53.9	95.4	58.0	162.4	71.6	42.0	41.3	85.8	28.7
Jul	46.2	102.0	76.2	54.6	96.6	58.9	162.2	71.6	42.6	41.7	84.7	28.4
Aug	46.6	102.9	76.6	54.6	96.3	58.7	163.7	71.7	42.2	41.7	85.1	28.2
Sep	46.9	104.1	78.1	55.3	97.6	59.1	164.2	72.6	42.3	41.9	85.6	28.1
Oct	47.3	105.9	79.7	56.5	99.3	60.1	165.7	73.6	43.0	42.9	85.3	28.1
Nov	47.4	107.6	81.9	58.0	101.1	60.9	166.1	75.4	43.9	44.0	85.6	28.6
Dec	47.4	108.4	83.5	58.7	102.3	61.6	167.2	77.4	43.8	44.1	85.7	28.3
2006 Jan	47.2	109.1	84.0	58.7	102.6	62.3	168.0	78.0	44.0	43.8	84.9	28.3
Feb	48.7	111.9	85.3	59.9	105.0	63.1	168.1	79.9	45.3	44.3	86.5	28.4
Mar	49.3	113.7	86.5	60.9	107.1	64.3	167.8	81.7	46.3	44.9	87.9	28.4
Apr	49.7	115.0	87.1	61.9	108.7	65.5	167.8	81.7	47.9	45.2	88.3	28.3
May	50.2	115.8	87.9	62.3	108.8	65.5	167.9	82.8	48.6	45.0	88.8	28.3
Jun	50.9	116.8	88.2	62.6	108.9	65.8	168.2	83.2	49.1	44.8	88.8	27.9
Jul	50.5	116.8	88.4	62.7	109.3	65.8	168.3	83.7	49.2	44.2	88.5	27.7
Aug	50.7	116.9	88.3	63.2	109.5	65.6	166.5	83.5	49.4	44.2	88.0	27.5
Sep	51.2	117.9	88.7	63.4	110.1	66.7	167.0	83.2	49.5	44.0	87.4	27.6
Oct	51.2	118.1	88.7	63.2	109.8	67.4	165.9	82.7	49.2	44.0	87.2	27.7
Nov	51.4	117.4	87.9	62.7	109.9	67.4	164.3	80.9	48.8	43.3	86.0	27.2
Dec	51.8	117.1	87.0	62.2	110.0	66.8	161.9	79.4	48.5	42.8	84.8	26.8
2007 Jan	51.0	115.3	85.8	61.7	109.5	66.2	158.9	77.8	47.2	42.2	81.4	26.1
Feb	51.4	115.3	85.3	61.6	109.0	65.7	157.4	76.8	47.3	42.5	81.9	25.8
Mar	51.3	114.3	84.3	61.2	108.1	64.7	156.3	75.4	46.7	42.1	80.7	25.7

Claimant count rate[2]

	North East	North West	Yorkshire and the Humber	East Midlands	West Midlands	East	London	South East	South West	Wales	Scotland	Northern Ireland
	DPDM	IBWC	DPBI	DPBJ	DPBN	DPDP	DPDQ	DPDR	DPBM	DPBP	DPBQ	DPBR
2007 Mar	4.4	3.3	3.2	2.9	3.9	2.4	3.3	1.7	1.8	3.0	3.0	3.0

1 The seasonally adjusted series relate only to claimants aged 18 or over in order to maintain the consistent series, available back to 1971 (1974 for the regions - see p.608 of the December 1990 *Employment Gazette* and pS16 of the April 1994 issue for the list of discontinuities taken into account). It also takes into account the effect of the change in benefit eligibility rules introduced with Jobseeker's Allowance (see p.219-24, Labour Market Trends, May 2000). The latest national and regional seasonally adjusted claimant count figures are provisional and are subject to revision mainly in the following month.

2 Percentage rates have been calculated by expressing the number of claimants as a percentage of the estimated total workforce (the sum of claimants, employees jobs, self-employed, HM Forces and participants on work related government training programmes) at mid-2005 estimates for 2005 and 2006 figures and at the corresponding mid-year estimates for earlier years.

Sources: Jobcentre Plus Administrative;
Labour Market Statistics;
Helpline: 020 7533 6094

3.13 Vacancies by industry
Standard Industrial Classification (1992)

United Kingdom (thousands), seasonally adjusted

	All vacancies[1]	Energy and water[2]	Manufacturing	Construction	Distribution, hotels & restaurants	Transport & communications	Finance & business services	Education, health & public admin[3]	Other services[2]	Total services
Levels (thousands)										
	AP2Y	AP32	AP33	AP34	AP35	AP36	AP37	AP38	AP39	AP3A
2006 Mar	589.7	3.7	48.4	19.6	161.1	39.6	149.2	134.8	33.2	517.9
Apr	587.7	3.7	48.9	19.1	163.3	38.3	147.4	132.9	34.2	516.1
May	584.7	4.1	49.1	18.5	163.3	37.5	148.9	129.8	33.5	513.0
Jun	589.1	4.2	49.0	18.5	165.4	38.7	153.2	129.5	30.7	517.5
Jul	593.6	4.2	47.8	18.6	163.8	39.6	156.1	131.8	31.6	522.9
Aug	601.9	3.9	48.4	20.6	166.0	41.5	159.2	134.4	28.0	529.1
Sep	598.9	3.9	48.4	20.5	166.4	39.8	159.1	132.8	28.0	526.1
Oct	600.6	3.9	47.9	20.8	167.8	39.7	160.6	131.0	28.9	528.0
Nov	599.1	3.8	48.0	19.4	166.6	40.8	160.8	132.6	27.1	527.9
Dec	602.0	3.7	48.8	19.8	169.3	40.7	163.5	132.7	23.5	529.7
2007 Jan	607.8	3.5	50.5	19.5	171.6	42.4	165.7	134.9	19.7	534.3
Feb	619.7	3.9	52.5	19.6	176.6	41.8	166.1	137.2	22.0	543.7
Mar	635.5	4.3	54.5	20.4	180.8	42.3	166.8	140.0	26.4	556.3
Ratio per 100 employee jobs										
	AP2Z	AP3B	AP3C	AP3D	AP3E	AP3F	AP3G	AP3H	AP3I	AP3J
2006 Mar	2.3	2.1	1.5	1.5	2.5	2.5	2.9	2.0	2.4	2.4
Apr	2.3	2.1	1.5	1.5	2.5	2.4	2.8	2.0	2.5	2.4
May	2.2	2.3	1.5	1.4	2.5	2.4	2.9	1.9	2.4	2.4
Jun	2.3	2.4	1.5	1.4	2.6	2.5	3.0	1.9	2.2	2.4
Jul	2.3	2.4	1.5	1.5	2.6	2.5	3.0	1.9	2.3	2.5
Aug	2.3	2.2	1.5	1.6	2.6	2.7	3.1	2.0	2.0	2.5
Sep	2.3	2.2	1.5	1.6	2.6	2.5	3.1	2.0	2.0	2.5
Oct	2.3	2.2	1.5	1.6	2.6	2.5	3.1	1.9	2.1	2.5
Nov	2.3	2.1	1.5	1.5	2.6	2.6	3.1	2.0	2.0	2.5
Dec	2.3	2.1	1.5	1.5	2.6	2.6	3.2	2.0	1.7	2.5
2007 Jan	2.3	2.0	1.5	1.5	2.7	2.7	3.2	2.0	1.4	2.5
Feb	2.4	2.2	1.6	1.5	2.8	2.7	3.2	2.0	1.6	2.6
Mar	2.4	2.4	1.7	1.6	2.8	2.7	3.2	2.1	1.9	2.6

1 Exludes Agriculture, Forestry and Fishing.
2 Not seasonally adjusted. 'Energy and water' and 'Other services' do not display seasonality. Therefore the unadjusted series is the best estimate of a 'seasonally adjusted' series.
3 Includes both public and private sectors.

Sources: ONS Vacancy Survey;
Labour Market Statistics Helpline: 020 7533 6094

3.14 Labour disputes[1]

Thousands

	Workers beginning involvement in period in any dispute	Total working days lost[2]						
		All industries and services	Manufacturing	Transport, storage and communication	Public administration and defence	Education	Health and social work	All other industries and services
SIC 1992		*All classes*	*15-37*	*60-64*	*75*	*80*	*85*	*All other classes*
	BBFV	BBFW	BBFX	BBFY	BBFZ	BBGA	BBGB	BBGC
2003	123	499	63	126	138	131	15	25
2004	272	905	31	44	437	379	4	10
2005	92	157	16	33	23	43	–	43
2006	711	755	18	41	627	31	5	33
2005 Apr	3	6	–	3	–	1	–	1
May	26	32	2	2	5	17	–	6
Jun	2	5	2	1	–	–	–	3
Jul	5	15	4	10	–	–	–	–
Aug	5	17	1	3	3	–	–	10
Sep	4	29	6	8	1	–	–	14
Oct	4	7	–	3	2	1	–	–
Nov	19	19	–	–	3	15	–	1
Dec	13	15	–	2	5	–	–	8
2006 Jan	45	77	–	5	69	–	–	3
Feb	2	14	–	10	1	1	–	2
Mar	577	482	–	2	461	17	–	1
Apr	2	3	–	–	–	1	–	–
May	50	83	2	2	70	4	–	6
Jun	2	6	2	3	–	–	–	–
Jul	8	14	4	2	4	1	2	1
Aug	2	6	1	1	1	–	1	3
Sep	5	23	–	1	16	2	2	1
Oct	7	13	3	1	2	2	–	5
Nov	5	23	5	6	–	2	–	11
Dec	7	11	–	8	2	–	–	–
2007 Jan	135	120	–	1	115	2	1	2
Feb	3	4	–	–	3	–	–	–

1 Excludes stoppages involving fewer than 10 workers or lasting less than one day except any in which the total number of working days lost are 100 or more. There may be some under-recording of small or short stoppages; this would have much more effect on the total stoppages than on working days lost.

2 The working days lost figures relate to the total working days lost within each of the periods shown as a result of stoppages *in progress* in that period, whether the stoppages began in that period or earlier.

Source: Office for National Statistics: 01633 819205

4 Social services

4.1 National Insurance and Child Benefit
Great Britain

Thousands

| | National Insurance | | | | Child Benefit[1,6] | |
| | Persons in receipt of Jobseeker's Allowance (contributions based)[2] | New claims Incapacity Benefit (Weekly averages)[5] | At end of period | | Families receiving benefit | Children in families receiving benefits |
			State Pension[3]	Widows/ Bereavement Benefit[4]		
	BDAD	BDAA	BDAE	BMCR	BDAG	BDAH
2005 May	145	12.5	10 526	183	7 073	12 573
Jun	..	13.7	..	..	..	..
Jul	..	12.2	..	..	..	..
Aug	145	12.6	10 547	178	7 135	12 698
Sep	..	13.3	..	..	..	..
Oct	..	12.5	..	..	..	..
Nov	141	13.7	10 557	172	6 986	12 323
Dec	..	10.7	..	..	..	..
2006 Jan	..	12.2	..	..	..	..
Feb	158	13.9	10 564	169	7 047	12 444
Mar	..	13.5	..	..	..	..
Apr	..	10.0	..	..	..	..
May	143	11.8	10 587	165	7 125	12 604
Jun	..	13.3	..	..	..	..
Jul	..	12.3	..	..	..	..
Aug	137	13.6	10 626	161	7 198	12 750
Sep	..	13.7	..	..	..	..
Oct	..	14.1	..	..	..	..
Nov	..	15.3	..	..	..	..
Dec	..	11.4	..	..	..	..

1 Child Benefit figures are taken from the Child Benefit Computer System 5% scan in the months shown. Figures exclude overseas cases.
2 Jobseeker's Allowance figures have been derived by applying 100% WPLS proportions to 5% data. This figure is based on Contribution Based only Jobseekers Allowance.
3 Excluding pensioners in receipt of non-contributory State Pension awarded under National Insurance Acts 1970 and 1971. Also excludes overseas and Channel Islands.

4 Includes all Widow's Benefit and Bereavement Benefit except Widow's Payment and Bereavement Payment. Excludes overseas and Channel Island cases.
5 The figures for Incapacity Benefit are calculated from 100% counts but are provisional and therefore subject to amendment.
6 Child Benefit is the responsibility of HM Revenue and Customs.

Source: Department for Work and Pensions: 0191 225 9900

4.2 Child and Working Tax Credit[1]
United Kingdom

Thousands

| | Families in work receiving credit: | | | No of children in these families |
	All families	Two-adult families	One-adult families	
	WMPT	WMPU	WMPV	WMPW
2004 Apr	4 541	3 363	1 179	7 668
2004 Jul[2]	4 610	3 390	1 220	7 760
2004 Dec	4 518	3 310	1 209	7 455
2005 Apr	4 638	3 378	1 260	7 624
2005 Dec	4 538	3 261	1 277	7 324
2006 Apr	4 601	3 307	1 294	7 446
2006 Dec	4 526	3 237	1 289	7 292

1 For further information refer to Section 4 of the *Annual Supplement* in the January edition of *Monthly Digest*.

2 July figures rounded to nearest 10 thousand.

Source: Board of Inland Revenue: 020 7438 6275

Social services

4.3 Income Support/Pension Credit/Jobseeker's Allowance (income based)
Great Britain

In a week in the month shown, thousands

	Income support[1]					Pension Credit[6]	Jobseeker's Allowance (income based)[7]		
	Aged 60 and over[2,6]	Incapacity benefits[3]	Lone parents[4]	Others[5]	All cases		With contribution based benefit	Without contribution based benefit	All cases
	BALZ	BAMD	BAME	BAMF	BAMG	A4EK	DMUB	DMUC	DMUD
2003 May	1 778	1 215	853	168	4 014	..	19	640	659
Aug	1 800	1 221	851	168	4 041	..	17	618	635
Nov	..	1 221	832	167	2 220	2 085	15	584	599
2004 Feb	..	1 221	830	166	2 217	2 282	16	625	641
May	..	1 205	823	164	2 193	2 491	14	576	590
Aug	..	1 207	818	166	2 191	2 593	12	576	588
Nov	..	1 206	797	165	2 167	2 630	13	553	566
2005 Feb	..	1 200	793	160	2 153	2 655	15	600	615
May	..	1 194	789	157	2 140	2 683	14	596	610
Aug	..	1 190	789	159	2 138	2 697	15	620	635
Nov	..	1 189	779	160	2 127	2 708	14	633	647
2006 Feb	..	1 188	777	158	2 123	2 709	15	702	717
May	..	1 183	775	157	2 115	2 717	14	690	704
Aug	..	1 189	783	157	2 129	2 728	13	695	708

1 IS claimants have been assigned to a statistical group according to a hierarchy. The order is as shown in the table, i.e. "Aged 60 and over", "Incapacity Benefits" etc. For example, lone parents with both Incapacity Benefits and Income Support will fall into the "Incapacity Benefits" category.
2 "Aged 60 and over" are benefit units where the claimant and/or partner is aged 60 or over.
3 "Incapacity Benefits" refer to claimants aged under 60 claiming Incapacity Benefit (IB) or Severe Disablement Allowance (SDA), including IB credits only cases.
4 "Lone Parents" are single recipients of Income Support aged under 60 with a child under 16 who are not in receipt of IB/SDA.
5 "Others" are recipients of Income Support not in one of the other categories.
6 Since 6th October 2003, Income Support for claimants aged 60 or over have been paid via the new Pension Credit. Pension Credit eligibility is also more generous than prior to 6th October 2003, increasing the numbers of pensioners in receipt.
7 JSA figures have been derived by applying 100% WPLS proportions to 5% totals.

Source: Department for Work and Pensions

4.4 Family health services

Thousands

	England and Wales						Scotland			
	Pharmaceutical services	Dental services			Ophthalmic services[1]		Pharmaceutical services	Dental services	Ophthalmic services	
	Number of prescriptions items dispensed by chemists etc[2]	Completed courses of treatment and cases of occasional treatment[3]	Personal dental services	Total courses of treatment[5]	Sight tests	Pairs of spectacles paid for by HAs under the Voucher Scheme	Number of prescription items dispensed[4]	Completed courses of adult treatment and cases of occasional treatment[3]	Sight tests paid for	Pairs of spectacles paid for by SHBs under the Voucher Scheme
	CKQJ	BDDB	F93Q	G92F	BDDC	BDDD	BDDE	BDDF	BDDG	BDDH
2004	740 389	26 604	1 616	28 220	..	..	74 335	2 942	943	462
2005	776 925	19 914	7 631	27 545	..	..	76 427	2 904	942	454
2006	..	..	..	29 579	..	..	..	2 920	..	..
2003 Q3	174 725	7 021	108	7 129	5 160	1 850	17 843	713	229	111
Q4	188 324	7 252	125	7 377	..	..	18 560	725	221	109
2004 Q1	177 162	6 795	175	6 970	5 331	1 921	17 936	731	243	117
Q2	181 577	6 885	249	7 134	..	..	18 545	745	237	118
Q3	184 288	6 411	461	6 872	5 466	1 979	18 599	728	236	116
Q4	197 362	6 513	731	7 244	..	..	19 255	738	227	111
2005 Q1	183 181	5 598	1 224	6 822	5 339	1 896	18 271	719	235	113
Q2	193 562	5 334	1 794	7 128	..	..	19 374	749	244	119
Q3	193 063	4 597	2 140	6 737	5 530	1 988	19 097	712	237	113
Q4	207 119	4 385	2 473	6 858	..	..	19 685	724	226	109
2006 Q1	196 783	4 103	2 532	6 635	5 497	1 942	..	727	252	117
Q2	200 015	..	..	4 819[6]	..	..	..	743	371	114
Q3	..	..	..	8 867[6]	5 659	2 051	..	710	375	104
Q4	..	..	..	9 258[6]	..	..	..	740	..	..

1 Data on Ophthalmic Services are collected six-monthly and presented against the second quarter covered.
2 The data covers all prescriptions dispensed by community pharmacists and appliance contractors, dispensing doctors, and prescriptions submitted by prescribing doctors for items personally administered.
3 Number scheduled for payment in the General Dental Service.
4 Includes prescriptions dispensed by Community Pharmacies, appliance suppliers, dispensing doctors and stock orders.
5 Some early information relates only to the General Dental Service.
6 A new NHS dental contract was introduced on 1 April 2006. Information based on the new contract are not comparable with information under the old contractual arrangements. Data cannot be separated between GDS and PDS contracts from 1 April 2006 and data only for England have been provided under the new contract. Information for 2006 Q2 is based on incomplete data as this is the period immediately following the introduction of the new contract. The data reported in later quarters are more complete as activity levels and the reporting cycle have matured.

Sources: The Health and Social Care Information Centre; NHS Scotland and the National Assembly for Wales

5 Law enforcement

5.1 Recorded crime statistics
England and Wales

Thousands

	Violence against the person	Sexual offences	Burglary	Robbery	Theft and handling stolen goods	Fraud and forgery	Drug offences	Criminal damage	Other	Total
1998/99	502.8	36.2	953.2	66.8	2 191.4	279.5	135.9	879.6	63.6	5 109.0
1999/2000	581.0	37.8	906.5	84.3	2 223.6	334.8	121.9	945.7	65.7	5 301.3
2000/2001	600.9	37.3	836.0	95.2	2 145.4	319.3	113.5	960.1	63.2	5 170.9
2001/2002[1]	650.3	41.4	878.5	121.4	2 267.0	314.9	121.4	1 064.5	65.7	5 525.1
2002/03[2,5]	845.1	49.2	890.1	110.3	2 411.6	331.1	143.3	1 120.6	73.7	5 975.0
2003/04[3,5]	967.2	52.7	820.0	103.7	2 312.9	319.6	143.5	1 218.5	75.5	6 013.6
2004/05[4,5]	1 048.2	62.1	681.1	90.7	2 069.4	280.5	145.5	1 198.2	64.9	5 640.6
2005/06[5]	1 059.9	62.1	645.1	98.2	2 019.3	233.0	178.5	1 184.7	75.7	5 556.5
	BEAB	BEAC	BEAD	BEAE	BEAF	BEAG	LQMO	BEAH	BEAI	BEAA
2003 Q2	236.3	12.8	221.6	27.6	605.8	84.6	34.2	303.7	19.1	1 545.7
Q3	253.0	14.1	208.7	26.2	591.7	81.2	36.2	281.2	19.7	1 512.0
Q4	236.9	12.6	196.4	24.6	560.7	76.2	37.4	307.7	18.1	1 470.6
2004 Q1	241.0	13.2	193.3	25.4	554.7	77.7	35.7	325.9	18.5	1 485.4
Q2	266.3	15.1	177.3	23.4	541.7	74.0	33.6	311.7	17.5	1 460.6
Q3	269.2	17.4	169.9	21.6	530.0	71.5	35.5	280.6	16.7	1 412.4
Q4	262.0	14.9	167.2	23.1	512.3	70.0	38.7	302.0	15.2	1 405.4
2005 Q1	250.7	14.7	166.6	22.5	485.4	65.0	37.7	308.8	15.6	1 367.0
Q2	277.6	16.7	162.0	24.2	516.1	63.1	41.5	302.1	19.2	1 422.5
Q3	278.2	16.6	160.7	24.0	514.5	60.9	42.0	277.7	19.8	1 394.5
Q4	262.4	15.0	164.1	24.6	503.4	55.7	46.7	305.2	18.8	1 395.9
2006 Q1	241.5	13.7	158.3	25.4	485.0	53.0	48.2	299.4	17.8	1 342.3
Q2	278.2†	15.7†	154.3†	25.3	496.4†	53.5†	48.0	301.6†	20.8	1 393.8†
Q3	276.8	15.9	152.5	24.2	490.7	52.0	45.8	281.6	19.3†	1 358.8
Q4	257.7	13.3	158.0	26.6	490.0	47.2	48.2	309.9	17.9	1 368.8

1 Some forces adopted the principles of the National Crime Recording Standard in advance of its national implementation on 1 April 2002. For 2001/02 as a whole it has been calculated that this in itself has inflated the total number of crimes recorded by 5%, although the impact differs for each offence group.
2 The National Crime Recording Standard (NCRS) was introduced across all police forces from April 2002, and this has increased the recorded crime figures significantly. For 2002/03 it has been estimated that the implementation of the Standard has inflated the total number of recorded crimes by 10%, although the impact differs for each offence group. Violence against the person was particularly affected. Due to the introduction of the NCRS in April 2002, figures before and after this date are not directly comparable.

3 Much of the increase in violence against the person in 2003/04 is likely to be due to the continuing impact of changes in recording.
4 The Sexual Offences Act 2003, introduced in May 2004, re-defined many sexual offences. This change in legislation could, in itself, account for much of the increase in recorded sexual offences and means figures for 2004/05 are not comparable with earlier years.
5 Figures for the British Transport Police have been added to these statistics as from April 2002 onwards.

Source: Home Office: 020 7035 0307

5.2 Crimes and offences recorded by the police[1,2]
Scotland

Thousands

	Non-sexual crimes of violence	Crimes of indecency	Crimes of dishonesty	Fire raising, vandalism etc	Other crimes	Motor vehicle offences	Miscellaneous offences	Total crimes and offences (annual)
	BEBC	BEBD	BEBE	BEBF	BEBG	BEBI	BEBH	BEBB
2001	15.1	6.0	239.8	94.9	65.2	362.1	162.5	945.8
2002	16.5	6.5	235.7	95.6	72.9	341.3	167.5	935.9
2003	15.2	6.6	210.8	100.1	74.3	409.4	176.7	993.1
2004	15.2	7.4	214.4	124.8	78.6	428.2	209.4	1 078.0
2005	13.6	6.7	191.8	128.3	79.4	381.4	216.9	1 018.2
2003 Q1	3.9	1.6	51.9	25.9	17.1	90.3	41.5	232.1
Q2	3.9	1.7	54.3	26.1	18.3	107.2	45.6	257.0
Q3	3.8	1.6	54.6	23.4	19.7	101.3	47.1	251.6
Q4	3.6	1.7	50.0	24.7	19.2	110.6	42.5	252.4
2004 Q1	3.8	1.8	52.1	29.6	20.3	107.5	45.8	260.8
Q2	4.2	2.0	55.4	32.9	20.2	107.9	57.5	280.1
Q3	3.8	1.8	56.0	32.0	19.6	110.0	56.2	279.4
Q4	3.4	1.8	50.9	30.3	18.5	102.8	49.9	257.7
2005 Q1	3.3	1.7	48.1	33.3	18.9	98.0	50.7	254.0
Q2	3.4	1.6	48.5	32.5	20.3	97.7	56.8	260.8
Q3	3.6	1.7	48.0	29.7	19.2	89.4	53.8	245.4
Q4	3.3	1.7	47.2	32.8	21.0	96.3	55.6	258.0
2006 Q1	3.5	1.6	44.1	32.9	21.4	90.9	53.3	247.4
Q2	3.7	1.8	46.2	33.4	21.9	93.7	59.0	259.8
Q3	3.6	1.9	47.3	31.6	21.0	92.2	62.7	260.2

1 Components may not add to totals due to separate rounding.
2 The introduction of the Scottish Crime recording Standard on 1 April 2004 has increased the number of minor crimes recorded, such as minor crimes of vandalism and petty thefts.

Sources: The Scottish Executive Justice Analytical Services Division;
Tel: 0131 244 2635

6 Agriculture, food, drinks and tobacco

6.1 Land use and crop areas[1]
Area at the June Survey

Thousand hectares

		2000	2001	2002	2003	2004	2005	2006
Total agricultural area	BFAH	18 311	18 594	18 537	18 464	18 432	18 502	18 713
Crops	BFAA	4 665	4 493	4 604	4 475	4 589	4 437	4 340
Bare fallow	BFAB	37	43	33	29	29	140	150
All grasses	BFAC	6 589	6 789	6 761	6 884	6 866	6 904	7 104
Sole right rough grazing	BFAD	4 445	4 435	4 488	4 329	4 326	4 354	4 491
Set aside	DMNF	567	800	612	689	559	559	513
All other land on agricultural holdings, including woodland	BFAE	780	801	806	820	825	872	874
Total land on agricultural holdings	BFAF	17 083	17 361	17 303	17 227	17 195	17 266	17 472
Common rough grazing (estimated)	BFAG	1 228	1 232	1 234	1 236	1 237	1 236	1 241
Crops	BFAA	4 665	4 493	4 604	4 475	4 589	4 437	4 340
Cereals	BFAJ	3 348	3 014	3 245	3 057	3 130	2 919	2 861
Wheat	BFAK	2 086	1 635	1 996	1 837	1 990	1 867	1 833
Barley (winter and spring)	BFAL	1 128	1 245	1 101	1 076	1 007	938	881
Oats	BFAM	109	112	126	121	108	90	121
Mixed corn[2]	BFAN	2	3	4	4	..	..	..
Rye	BFAO	7	5	5	4	6	..	..
Triticale[2]	DMNH	16	14	14	15	15	13	13
Mixed corn and Triticale	C6GX	..	..	..	..	15	13	13
Mixed corn, Triticale and Rye	EFO7	..	..	..	..	21	13	13
Other arable crops (excluding potatoes)	DMNI	979	1 141	1 024	1 098	1 136	1 211	1 172
Oilseed rape[3]	BFAP	332	404	357	460	498	519	500
Sugar beet, not for stock feeding	BFAQ	173	177	169	162	154	148	130
Hops	DMNJ	2	2	2	2	2	1	1
Peas for harvesting dry and field beans	DMNK	208	275	249	235	242	239	231
Linseed	DMNL	71	31	12	32	30	45	33
Other crops	DMNM	192	214	204	201	203	252	278
Potatoes	BFAR	166	165	158	145	148	137	140
Horticultural	BFAV	172	173	176	176	175	170	166
Vegetables grown in the open	DMNN	119	120	124	125	125	121	119
Orchard fruits	BFBG	28	28	26	25	24	23	23
Soft fruit	DMNO	10	9	9	9	9	9	10
Orchard fruits and Soft fruit	EFO8	..	..	..	..	..	32	33
Ornamentals	DMNP	14	14	15	14	15	14	12
Glasshouse crops	DMNQ	2	2	2	2	2	2	2

1 Figures include estimates for minor holdings. For further information refer to Section 6 of the *Annual Supplement* in the January edition of *Monthly Digest*.

2 From 2004 onwards data for Mixed corn and Triticale amalgamated.
3 Area grown not on set-aside land.

Source: Department for Environment, Food and Rural Affairs: 01904 455095

6.2 Crops: yields and production[1]

		Yields per hectare (tonnes)						Production (thousand tonnes)				
		2002	2003	2004	2005	2006		2002	2003	2004	2005	2006
Agricultural crops												
Wheat	BFBJ	8.00	7.78	7.77	7.96	8.00	BADO	15 973	14 282	15 468	14 863	14 735
Barley (winter and spring)	BFBK	5.57	5.91	5.76	5.86	5.90	BADP	6 128	6 360	5 799	5 495	5 239
Oats	BFBO	6.00	6.16	5.83	5.84	6.00	BADQ	753	749	626	532	728
Sugar beet	BFBL	56.54	56.55	57.50	..	..	BADR	9 559	9 168	8 850	..	..
Potatoes	BFBM	43.96	40.74	42.47	..	..	BADS	6 966	5 918	6 316	..	..

		2000 /01	2001 /02	2002 /03	2003 /04	2004 /05		2000 /01	2001 /02	2002 /03	2003 /04	2004 /05
Horticultural crops[2]												
Field vegetables												
Brussels sprouts	BFBR	12.5	13.4	13.3	11.5	12.4	BADT	67.3	54.8	42.7	55.8	42.5
Cabbage, inc. savoy and spring greens	BFBS	86.8	88.5	88.6	80.3	94.7	BADU	273.2	295.4	255.2	245.6	290.9
Cauliflowers	BFBT	13.6	11.5	12.4	11.2	12.0	BADV	156.1	107.4	115.8	126.3	165.3
Carrots	BFBU	58.4	63.3	60.6	52.2	70.1	BADW	725.8	760.0	731.2	614.3	659.8
Turnips and swedes	BFBV	35.1	35.3	38.3	13.8	16.8	BADX	132.1	141.8	104.7	96.5	103.8
Beetroot	BFBW	35.5	36.4	33.5	34.9	41.8	BADY	67.1	68.6	56.3	58.8	53.9
Onions dry bulb	BFBX	41.9	35.5	41.8	40.7	40.8	BADZ	392.7	374.9	283.4	373.6	340.9
Peas green for market (in pod weight)	BFBY	7.4	6.7	6.8	6.5	7.9	BAEA	6.7	6.2	7.2	5.9	5.9
Peas green for processing (shelled weight)	BFBZ	4.7	4.4	4.5	4.0	3.7	BAEB	184.5	161.0	169.3	167.6	130.3
Lettuce	BFCA	21.5	23.3	23.2	22.4	18.1	BAEC	135.8	123.9	109.9	125.6	140.9
Protected crops												
Tomatoes	BFCB	422.6	412.6	425.5	437.2	416.0	BAED	113.0	109.1	100.9	75.6	78.5
Cucumbers	BFCC	447.5	431.4	435.8	557.8	472.0	BAEE	79.8	71.5	73.6	77.0	61.4
Lettuce	BFCP	35.4	43.8	33.9	39.3	37.3	BAEF	18.7	20.9	16.0	16.6	10.8
Fruit												
Dessert apples	BAEG	13.1	16.1	11.9	13.4	18.0	BFCD	101.3	104.4	84.0	69.0	96.3
Cooking apples	BAEH	18.5	23.7	17.1	18.8	27.5	BFCE	107.5	107.4	95.3	74.9	78.2
Soft fruit	BAEI	..	..	..	..	..	BFCF	65.4	64.6	66.7	79.6	85.9
Pears	BAEJ	14.4	15.3	17.1	17.0	13.6	BFBQ	26.6	38.5	34.2	29.6	22.7

1 For further information refer to Section 6 of the *Annual Supplement* in the January edition of *Monthly Digest*.

2 Yield data are marketed yield and production data are home production marketed.

Source: Department for Environment, Food and Rural Affairs

6.3 Livestock[1]

Thousands

		2000 Dec	2001 Jun	2001 Dec	2002 Jun	2002 Dec	2003 Jun	2003 Dec	2004 Jun	2004 Dec	2005 Jun	2005 Dec	2006 Jun
Total cattle and calves	BFCG	10 878	10 602	10 159	10 345	10 381	10 508	10 519	10 588	10 425	10 392	10 160	10 270
Dairy cows	BFCH	2 339	2 251	2 203	2 227	2 229	2 191	2 207	2 129	2 152	2 063	2 074	2 066
Beef cows	BFCI	1 783	1 708	1 673	1 657	1 694	1 698	1 702	1 736	1 733	1 762	1 657	1 733
Heifers in calf	BFCJ	684	701	691	728	684	679	678	690	680	638	676	645
Total sheep and lambs	BFCM	27 591	36 716	24 434	35 834	24 898	35 812	24 572	35 817	24 688	35 416	23 933	34 722
Ewes and shearlings	CKUQ	18 513	17 921	16 082	17 630	16 469	17 580	16 337	17 630	16 308	16 935	15 633	16 637
Lambs under one year old	BFCP	7 769	17 769	7 219	17 310	7 233	17 322	7 078	17 238	7 067	17 488	7 146	17 058
Total pigs	BFCQ	5 948	5 845	5 845	5 588	5 330	5 046	4 842	5 159	4 787	4 862	4 724	4 933
Sows in pig and other sows for breeding	CKUU	497	527	482	483	446	442	444	449	413	404	376	401
Gilts in pig	CKUR	81	71	65	74	74	73	70	66	63	67	65	67
Total fowls	CKUS	..	..	..	..	..	..	..	..	..	..	..	..
Total table chicken	CKUT	..	112 531	..	105 137	..	116 738	..	119 888	..	111 475	..	110 672
Birds in laying flock	CKUV	..	29 895	..	28 778	..	29 274	..	29 655	..	29 544	..	28 632
Growing pullets up to point of lay	CKUW	..	9 367	..	9 784	..	8 286	..	8 156	..	10 928	..	9 625

1 Figures include estimates for minor holdings. For further details refer to section 6 of the *Annual Supplement* in the January edition of *Monthly Digest*.

Source: Department for Environment, Food and Rural Affairs

6.4 Animals slaughtered and meat produced
Monthly averages or totals for four or five week periods

	Animals slaughtered (thousands)							Meat produced (thousand tonnes)						
	Steers, heifers and young bulls	Cows and adult bulls	Calves	Ewes and rams	Other sheep and lambs	Sows and boars	Other pigs	Poultry[2]	Beef and veal	Mutton and lamb	Pork	Poultry[2]	Offal[3]	Total
	BFHA	BFHB	BFHC	BFHD	BFHE	BFHF	BAKP	JYXD	BFHK	BFHL	BFHM	JYXE	BFHN	BFHJ
2001[1]	173	–	8	144	936	15	871	72 175	54.3	21.6	49.7	130.5	20.5	276.6
2002[1]	182	–	8	160	1 098	20	761	71 828	58.3	25.3	48.3	129.7	21.2	283.8
2003[1]	182	–	7	160	1 098	20	761	73 460	58.3	25.3	48.3	130.8	21.2	283.8
2004[1,4]	191	–	9	165	1 126	20	763	73 477	61.2	26.6	49.9	130.3	21.5	289.5
2005	190	1	9	183	1 174	17	748	75 218	63.5	27.6	48.9	131.8	21.7	293.4
2004 Dec[4]	230	–	12	209	1 446	22	890	66 120	73.6	33.3	59.5	117.5	22.8	306.7
2005 Jan	187	–	10	212	1 247	21	867	91 184	61.4	30.6	58.7	163.3	24.8	338.7
Feb	182	–	9	166	941	18	696	71 905	60.1	23.1	46.1	124.7	20.2	274.1
Mar	170	–	8	163	977	18	648	67 891	56.5	24.1	42.6	116.0	19.1	258.2
Apr	221	–	6	196	1 061	21	836	83 732	73.5	27.1	55.1	143.3	23.7	322.7
May	178	–	5	156	796	16	667	68 230	59.1	20.2	43.8	121.8	19.6	264.5
Jun	174	–	7	154	979	16	691	68 815	58.1	23.1	45.3	122.5	20.0	268.9
Jul	202	–	11	196	1 324	20	837	87 521	67.5	30.6	53.7	153.7	24.7	330.3
Aug	173	–	12	175	1 216	16	686	69 150	57.5	27.8	45.4	119.6	20.4	270.6
Sep	195	–	14	190	1 303	14	707	68 578	65.0	29.6	46.9	116.6	21.0	279.2
Oct	227	–	14	234	1 610	16	881	86 954	74.9	36.1	55.9	151.6	26.1	344.7
Nov	198	9	9	182	1 374	15	744	71 484	68.0	31.0	48.2	126.6	22.3	296.2
Dec	174	10	7	170	1 264	12	711	67 173	60.3	28.1	44.7	122.3	20.9	276.3
2006 Jan	217	18	7	221	1 341	17	818	80 586	77.7	31.7	53.8	145.0	25.0	333.3
Feb	175	19	6	173	1 052	14	685	68 195	63.8	25.1	45.7	116.1	20.3	271.1
Mar	176	21	5	172	1 039	15	681	68 295	65.0	25.4	45.5	114.6	20.4	270.9
Apr	202	24	3	199	1 090	17	783	85 971	74.3	27.1	50.3	144.7	24.1	320.5
May	179	25	2	159	831	14	665	69 034	67.5	20.3	43.4	119.8	20.3	271.3
Jun	170	26	3	163	965	14	666	67 676	64.7	22.6	42.9	120.9	20.4	271.5
Jul	202	38	5	212	1 309	20	832	83 915	78.8	30.0	53.4	149.0	25.3	336.5
Aug	152	31	4	184	1 216	15	686	67 886	59.4	27.5	44.8	118.8	20.4	270.8
Sep	177	37	4	192	1 302	17	726	68 308	69.0	29.3	48.7	117.2	21.5	285.7
Oct	217	53	4	221	1 587	21	915	84 799	86.5	35.7	58.4	153.3	27.2	361.0
Nov	183	47	3	179	1 221	17	749	69 364	74.2	28.0	48.6	124.4	22.4	297.6

1 Annual averages.
2 Includes chickens, turkeys, ducks and geese.
3 Includes poultry offal.
4 2004 is a 53 week statistical year; December is a 5 week statistical month rather than the usual 4 week statistical month.

Source: Department for Environment, Food and Rural Affairs: 01904 455097

6.5 Cereals and cereal products
Monthly averages or totals for four or five week periods. Stocks refer to the end of the period

Thousand tonnes

| | Wheat and flour | | | | | | Oats | | | | Barley | | | |
	Sales of home-grown wheat for food	Wheat milled Home-produced	Imported	Stocks[1] (including flour as wheat)	Flour produced	Flour disposals	Sales of home-grown oats for milling	Oats milled	Products of oat-milling	Stocks	Sales of home-grown barley for food[2]	Disposals for food and brewing	Stocks	Breakfast cereals:[3] production
	BFDA	BFDB	BFDC	BFDD	BFDE	BFDF	BFDG	BFDH	BFDI	BFDJ	BFDK	BFDL	BFDM	BFDN
2002	398	388	81	840	369	368	26	26	16	52	251	240	1 300	29
2003	403	395	71	739	365	364	27	27	16	44	260	256	1 096	27
2004	405	399	68	687	370	370	26	27	16	44	208	211	976	29
2005	386	381	89	646	368	369	28	28	17	33	231	218	880	32
2006	397	392	70	673	366	366	27	27	16	41	212	214	949	30
2004 Q1	427	412	65	818	379	382	28	26	15	54	173	220	1 146	27
Q2	396	393	61	685	364	363	26	26	16	45	102	193	767	29
Q3	387	404	62	557	369	369	22	26	16	34	354	238	836	30
Q4	408	387	82	688	369	367	30	29	17	41	201	195	1 154	29
2005 Q1	387	376	82	735	359	361	28	28	17	40	232	265	1 000	31
Q2	387	380	90	638	370	370	30	29	18	29	110	183	724	34
Q3	386	385	93	567	376	375	27	27	16	29	350	206	916	31
Q4	412	396	76	653	372	371	31	29	17	42	197	209	1 191	30
2006 Q1	398	392	69	652	364	365	30	29	17	40	158	198	979	32
Q2	402	394	70	554	366	364	31	32	18	28	95	175	700	32
Q3	398	387	73	679	363	364	29	28	17	44	178	215	1 131	30
Q4	402	394	68	614	366	365	30	30	18	36	135	186	893	31
2006 Jan	370	363	67	689	339	344	27	26	15	42	169	212	1 062	33
Feb	376	363	62	664	334	332	32	30	17	40	150	194	977	29
Mar	449	450	77	604	418	418	32	31	18	37	154	189	899	33
Apr	381	370	66	575	345	344	25	30	17	29	103	175	804	31
May	384	376	62	562	346	344	32	31	18	27	99	173	706	30
Jun	442	437	81	523	407	405	37	35	20	26	84	178	590	35
Jul	361	372	73	519	349	351	22	28	16	27	148	155	644	32
Aug	355	368	73	542	348	347	31	31	18	32	384	189	872	31
Sep	447	441	83	550	415	414	41	37	21	44	438	218	1 172	36
Oct	412	397	71	663	367	371	31	32	18	45	209	213	1 154	32
Nov	386	378	72	384	357	359	34	35	21	20	223	229	889	28
Dec	439	429	82	402	405	405	33	36	20	17	223	252	855	26

1 Stocks held by wheat millers, feed compounders, cereal breakfast food manufacturers, brewers, maltsters and distillers, merchants and dealers.
2 Sales of UK grown barley to brewers, maltsters and distillers.
3 Other than oatmeal and oatmeal flakes.

Source: Department for Environment, Food and Rural Affairs: 01904 455076

6.6 Production of compound feedingstuffs
Monthly averages

Thousand tonnes

	Cattle feed	Calf feed	Pig feed	Poultry feed	Other compounds	Total
	BFFB	BFFC	BFFD	BFFE	BFFF	BFFA
1997	284.9	16.5	200.5	234.0	92.7	834.9
1998	277.1	14.3	208.0	226.1	95.3	826.9
1999	305.2	13.0	185.9	219.3	108.6	837.6
2000	286.0	13.0	160.9	214.5	97.3	776.4
2001	304.2	12.3	150.0	226.9	94.7	793.2
2002	288.3	11.8	137.1	243.2	89.0	774.5
2003	306.3	12.9	116.9	230.7	95.2	766.9
2004	299.4	12.9	121.9	229.0	99.3	767.5
2005	280.3	12.1	119.4	219.2	95.5	731.6
2006	280.9	11.9	119.4	217.8	95.4	730.4
2004 Q3	264.3	11.4	123.4	236.3	62.0	702.2
Q4	330.2	15.5	127.2	224.7	89.1	791.9
2005 Q1	311.1	14.7	116.3	211.1	150.8	808.7
Q2	243.3	10.7	116.4	219.7	80.5	675.7
Q3	254.0	10.3	119.0	231.1	60.7	680.2
Q4	312.7	12.9	125.9	214.9	90.2	761.7
2006 Q1	332.0	13.1	116.8	193.9	164.1	824.5
Q2	273.3	10.6	121.8	207.7	95.2	713.4
Q3	291.5	11.0	123.7	219.1	78.4	729.1
Q4	271.5	10.3	123.4	222.1	71.2	703.6

Source: Department for Environment, Food and Rural Affairs: 01904 455076

6.7 Potatoes and sugar[1]
Monthly averages, calendar months or totals for four or five week periods

Thousand tonnes

| | Potatoes | | | | Sugar (as refined) | | | | |
| | Movement into human consumption in the United Kingdom | | | | | Disposals | | | |
	From home crop	Imports[2,3]	Exports[3]	Stocks[4]	Production from home- grown sugar beet	Total New Supply[5]	For food in the United Kingdom	Stocks	Glucose: production
	BFGA	BFGB	BFGC	BFGD	BFGF	BFGG	BFGH	BFGI	BFGK
2002	417	150	30	3 386	1 430.0	2 197.0	..	..	60.6
2003	400	142	31	2 915	1 368.0	1 800.0	..	..	61.2
2004	391	148	26	2 820	1 390.0	1 874.0	..	..	61.4
2005	361	124	27	2 509	1 300.0	1 859.0	..	..	57.9
2006	355	..	..	..	..	..	..	..	46.7
2005 Nov	440	69	32	..	293.8	177.6	176.9	523.4	51.6
Dec	385	171	40	2 509	265.8	153.0	152.3	709.4	35.6
2006 Jan	368	..	..	..	134.4	137.9	131.8	779.2	45.8
Feb	343	..	..	..	0.1	144.1	143.4	731.9	44.5
Mar	377	..	..	..	2.9	151.6	151.3	627.5	50.7
Apr	301	..	..	..	3.3	165.0	164.4	525.6	47.4
May	305	..	..	..	3.1	151.9	151.3	428.9	49.7
Jun	281	..	..	..	..	..	..	..	44.8
Jul	277	..	..	..	..	..	..	..	47.6
Aug	390	..	..	..	..	..	..	..	47.8
Sep	444	..	..	..	..	..	..	..	45.7
Oct	521	..	..	..	..	..	..	..	47.7
Nov	420	..	..	..	..	..	..	..	47.0
Dec	368	..	..	..	..	..	..	..	41.2

*Note: The annual figures for sugar are calendar year totals, rather than 12 month averages.

1 For further information refer to Section 6 of the *Annual Supplement* in the January edition of *Monthly Digest*.

2 Includes Channel Isles exports to Great Britain.

3 Trade data provided by British Potato Council and Dept. of Agriculture and Rural Development in Northern Ireland. Figures currently unavailable for 2006.

4 Estimate of end - December stocks based on Potato Marketing returns.

5 Total New supply (including imports) for use by UK food and other industries (including sugar used in the chemical industry). For further information: http://statistics.defra.gov.uk/esg/publications/auk/2005/5-7.xls

Sources: Department for Environment, Food and Rural Affairs; 01904 455067 (glucose); 020 7238 3279 (sugar); 01904 455068 (potatoes)

6.8 Production of bacon, ham and canned meat and meat stocks in cold storage[1]
Monthly averages or totals for four or five week periods   Monthly averages or end of period stocks

Thousand tonnes

| | Bacon and ham | Meat stocks in cold storage[2,3] | | | | |
	Production	Beef and veal	Mutton and lamb	Pork	Offal	Total
	BAKQ	BFIF	BFIG	BFIH	BFII	BFIE
2001	16.9	..	..	..	..	..
2002	16.4	..	..	..	..	..
2003	16.9	..	..	..	..	..
2004	17.6	..	..	..	..	..
2005	17.8	..	..	..	..	..
2005 May	..	..	..	..	..	..
Jun	18.0	28.8	7.6	8.5	1.8	46.7
Jul	..	..	..	..	..	..
Aug	..	..	..	..	..	..
Sep	17.1	26.7	8.2	9.0	2.5	46.5
Oct	..	..	..	..	..	..
Nov	..	..	..	..	..	..
Dec	19.0	25.2	7.7	9.4	2.1	44.3
2006 Jan	..	..	..	..	..	..
Feb	..	..	..	..	..	..
Mar	16.0	26.6	6.6	10.8	1.4	45.4
Apr	..	..	..	..	..	..
May	..	..	..	..	..	..
Jun	17.0	..	..	..	..	..
Jul	..	..	..	..	..	..
Aug	..	..	..	..	..	..
Sep	16.6	..	..	..	..	..

1 Owing to change in methodology, the data are now collected on a quarterly basis, and consequently, cannot be provided for the intermediate months.

2 Stocks held in cold stores for private concerns or in undischarged cargos are not included.

3 The stocks held in Public Coldstores in the United Kingdom survey was discontinued in March 2006. As a result, stocks data is no longer published.

Source: Department for Environment, Food and Rural Affairs: 01904 455096

6.9 Fish, oils and fats
Monthly averages, calendar months or totals for four or five week periods; stocks: end of period

Thousand tonnes

	Fresh and frozen fish: UK landings	Oilseeds and nuts			Vegetable oil		Marine oil		Margar-ine: produc-tion	Solid cooking fat	Other table spreads
		Crushed	Crude oil produced	Stocks[5]: crude oil equiv-alent	Crude oil equivalent		Crude oil equivalent				
					Disposals[1]	Stocks[2,5]	Usage[3]	Stocks[4,5]			
	BFJA	BFJE	BFJF	BFJG	BFJJ	BFJK	BFJL	BFJM	BFJN	BFJO	BFJP
2001[6]	..	2 251.6	785.9	17.3	2 068.0	95.9	1.9	–	124.3	120.7	284.9
2002[6]	..	2 332.3	804.9	10.4	2 065.9	88.9	2.1	–	114.4	114.4	300.8
2003[6]	..	2 210.3	768.9	13.2	2 213.7	86.5	2.1	–	135.9	130.9	305.9
2004	..	2 128.2	747.5	23.1	2 058.2	170.8	1.7	..	114.5	130.5	316.5
2005	..	..	..	..	2 043.6	166.9	1.2	..	115.9	117.0	292.7
2005 Dec	11.1	–	–	–	–	–	–	–	–	–	–
2006 Jan	50.2	..	..	..	..	..	..	..	..	..	..
Feb	22.5	..	..	..	..	..	..	..	..	..	..
Mar	17.3	..	..	..	..	..	..	..	..	..	..
Apr	20.8	..	..	..	..	..	..	..	..	..	..
May	10.3	..	..	..	..	..	..	..	..	..	..
Jun	11.3	..	..	..	..	..	..	..	..	..	..
Jul	31.6	..	..	..	..	..	..	..	..	..	..
Aug	39.6	..	..	..	..	..	..	..	..	..	..
Sep	15.7	..	..	..	..	..	..	..	..	..	..
Oct	30.9	..	..	..	..	..	..	..	..	..	..
Nov	9.6	..	..	..	..	..	..	..	..	..	..
Dec	8.3	..	..	..	..	..	..	..	..	..	..
2007 Jan	64.7	..	..	..	..	..	..	..	..	..	..
Feb	72.1	..	..	..	..	..	..	..	..	..	..

1 This series contains revisions following the incorporation of revised trade figures.
2 Comprising stocks of crude and refined oils held by seed crushers, oil refiners and manufacturers of margarine, solid cooking fat and other table spreads.
3 For the manufacture of margarine, solid cooking fat and other table spreads only.
4 Including quantities held by hardeners and refiners of oil and manufacturers of margarine.
5 Stocks are as at the end of December.
6 Figures for 2001 - 2003 are shown in actual annual totals.

Sources: Department for Environment, Food and Rural Affairs;
020 7238 5913 (fish landings);
01904 455061 (oils and fats)

6.10 Milk, milk products and eggs[1]
Monthly averages or calendar months; stocks: end of period

	Million litres				Thousand tonnes										Supply of hen eggs for human consump-tion (million dozen)[1,2]
					Condensed and evaporated milk		Milk powder				Butter		Cheese		
							Full-cream		Skimmed						
	Liquid milk[3,6]	Milk for manufac-ture[4,6]	Other dis-posals[5,6]	Total milk dis-posals	Pro-duction	Stocks	Pro-duction	Stocks	Pro-duction	Stocks	Pro-duction	Stocks	Pro-duction	Stocks	
	BFKB	BFKC	JYXF	BFKA	BFKH	BFKI	BFKJ	BFKK	BFKL	BFKM	BFKD	BFKE	BFKF	BFKG	BFKN
2001	563	563	43	1 168	13.4	9.7	7.3	6.2	5.9	12.4	10.5	18.4	32.3	15.0	70.20
2002	569	574	42	1 184	14.5	9.0	8.7	5.2	7.2	28.4	11.3	19.4	30.3	12.4	70.17
2003	563	595	44	1 202	13.2	7.2	8.5	3.4	9.6	50.8	10.9	17.5	28.7	7.1	71.74
2004	558	560	45	1 164	13.4	7.7	6.7	2.0	7.3	20.7	10.1	9.2	29.3	11.1	75.54
2005	555	541	59	1 155	11.9	4.8	4.5	1.9	5.8	10.1	10.8	2.9	32.0	3.3	73.94
2005 Jul	549	561	73	1 183	10.1	4.3	5.8	2.7	4.9	11.5	9.8	5.1	34.2	8.0	73.36
Aug	541	558	57	1 156	10.6	3.6	4.4	3.0	5.1	10.9	10.9	5.1	35.0	8.0	73.36
Sep	544	490	50	1 084	10.6	3.1	2.3	1.9	4.6	10.8	10.7	3.7	31.6	7.2	73.36
Oct	579	453	61	1 094	11.2	3.0	2.2	1.8	3.4	10.2	11.3	3.7	29.2	7.2	76.21
Nov	556	438	52	1 047	11.9	2.6	1.9	1.3	2.6	10.3	9.7	3.7	28.2	7.2	76.21
Dec	580	472	64	1 117	13.0	4.8	4.3	1.9	4.7	10.1	9.6	2.9	28.7	3.3	76.21
2006 Jan	570	513	70	1 153	..	3.2	..	1.5	..	9.2	10.9	2.9	32.7	3.3	75.30
Feb	528	481	53	1 062	..	3.4	..	2.3	..	3.7	9.2	2.8	30.0	3.3	75.30
Mar	589	567	40	1 195	..	1.4	..	2.2	..	2.5	10.9	3.4	34.9	2.6	75.30
Apr	555	579	75	1 208	..	2.4	..	3.0	..	3.1	9.6	4.6	35.3	2.6	72.39
May	585	650	62	1 297	..	1.0	..	2.6	..	4.3	10.4	6.6	37.9	2.6	72.39
Jun	556	582	59	1 198	..	0.9	..	2.8	..	6.0	9.7	6.9	34.8	2.6	72.39
Jul	561	548	65	1 174	..	1.3	..	5.2	..	5.3	9.1	6.9	34.6	2.6	73.44
Aug	556	511	55	1 123	..	1.2	..	4.6	..	4.4	9.5	6.8	33.5	2.6	73.44
Sep	544	472	61	1 077	..	1.4	..	2.4	..	2.2	8.8	6.7	32.4	2.6	73.44
Oct	565	456	67	1 089	..	1.4	..	0.9	..	2.4	9.2	6.7	30.8	2.6	76.29

1 Includes first and second quality eggs broken out.
2 This series has been revised as a result in survey methodology - see Explanatory Notes in the January edition of Monthly Digest.
3 Includes wholesale and direct sellers utilisation of milk for liquid milk.
4 Includes wholesale and direct sellers utilisation of milk for the manufacture of milk products.
5 Includes dairy wastage, stock changes and exports of raw milk.
6 Suckled milk, milk used on farm for farmhouse consumption, milk fed to livestock and farm waste are excluded. Utilisation of imported raw milk is included.

Source: Department for Environment, Food and Rural Affairs: 01904 455095

6.11 Beverages and confectionery
Monthly averages, calendar months or totals for four or five week periods; stocks: end of period

	Chocolate and sugar confectionery		Tea		Raw coffee	
	Production	Disposals	Disposals[1]	Stocks	Disposals	Stocks
	BFLG	BFLH	BFLJ	BFLK	BFLL	BFLM
2000	70.91	88.78	12.0	27.6	9.1	7.9
2001	69.60	88.82	11.0	31.2	8.7	12.5
2002	66.47	87.88	11.3	29.3	9.6	8.5
2003	65.02	88.79	10.0	24.3	9.1	8.9
2004	61.66	87.69	13.0	18.9	10.7	11.1
2005	57.08	84.87	10.0	19.0	9.5	9.9
2006	52.38	83.03	9.4	20.7	9.6	6.2
2005 Jul	47.13	71.51	..	..	..	..
Aug	50.54	81.59	11.50	19.0	6.10	3.30
Sep	67.76	105.37	..	..	..	..
Oct	72.47	107.66	..	..	..	..
Nov	64.37	99.10	6.60	19.0	10.40	3.20
Dec	45.51	75.45	..	..	..	..
2006 Jan	41.12	65.62	..	..	..	..
Feb	50.35	76.60	7.00	19.1	10.70	3.60
Mar	65.23	92.91	..	..	..	..
Apr	55.03	78.41	..	..	..	..
May	45.78	74.44	6.50	20.7	10.10	3.40
Jun	37.64	67.40	..	..	..	..
Jul	40.56	66.48	..	..	..	..
Aug	51.56	83.92	10.70	22.6	9.10	4.30
Sep	57.18	96.01	..	..	..	..
Oct	64.65	115.77	..	..	..	..
Nov	61.91	95.87	13.30	20.7	8.40	5.20
Dec	57.59	83.65	..	..	..	..

1 Excluding exports.

Source: Department for Environment, Food and Rural Affairs: 020 7270 8560

6.12 Tobacco products released for home consumption
Monthly averages or calendar months

	Million			Thousand kilogrammes			
	Cigarettes			Other tobacco products			Total tobacco products other than cigarettes
	Home-produced	Imported	Total	Cigars	Hand-rolling	Other[1]	
	LUQN	LUQO	LUQP	LUQQ	LUQR	LUQS	LUQT
2001	47 689	6 828	54 517	1 019	2 825	750	4 595
2002	49 574	6 514	56 088	969	2 864	688	4 522
2003	49 096	4 856	53 952	902	2 893	589	4 384
2004	48 166	4 454	52 620	826	3 052	549	4 428
2005	45 922	4 322	50 244	758	3 189	499	4 445
2006 Jan	4 590	379	4 969	67	285	44	396
Feb	2 809	307	3 116	42	228	29	299
Mar	3 237	339	3 575	56	260	34	350
Apr	8 980	1 076	10 056	133	692	77	901
May	296	10	306	5	46	10	60
Jun	4 847	357	5 204	40	200	34	274
Jul	1 681	173	1 854	57	280	35	372
Aug	3 115	349	3 464	47	255	31	333
Sep	3 929	412	4 341	66	305	38	410
Oct	3 916	360	4 276	55	318	33	406
Nov	3 883	383	4 266	55	269	38	362
Dec	2 950	356	3 306	66	272	37	374

1 Excluding snuff.

Source: HM Revenue and Customs: 020 7147 0593

6.13 Alcoholic drink

			Thousand hectolitres							Thousand hectolitres of alcohol				
			Released for home consumption							Released for home consumption			Production of potable spirits[1]	
			Wine of fresh grapes				Made wine			Spirits				
			Still											
	Beer pro-duction[7]	Beer[7]	Not exceeding 15%[2]	Over 15%	Sparkling	Total	Coolers[3]	Other	Cider and perry	Home-produced whisky	Spirit-based coolers[4]	Other[5]	Home-produced whisky	Other
	BFNK	BAYL	BFNO	BFNP	BFNS	BFNT	BAYM	BAYN	BFNW	BFNX	YZUJ	BFNY	BAYO	BAYP
2002	56 672	59 384	10 318.7	325.3	577.9	11 221.9	1 606.2	339.2	5 939.2	320.7	105.2	688.9	3 905.7	602.5
2003	58 014	60 301	10 646.9	296.4	640.1	11 583.5	423.2	351.4	5 876.1	318.3	124.4	744.3	3 936.6	616.0
2004	57 459	59 195	11 768.2	297.8	675.6	12 741.5	508.0	333.9	6 138.8	319.3	114.3	792.4	3 529.4	551.5
2005	56 255	57 572	12 117.1	305.7	720.6	13 143.4	597.5	333.9	6 376.9	300.7	84.2	821.7	3 758.6	606.0
2006	53 763	55 748	11 657.9	301.5	715.0	12 674.5	527.8	316.7	7 522.6	282.6	64.8	766.9	3 985.7	499.5
2003 Jul	5 449	5 633	908.5	15.2	45.9	969.5	41.1	27.6	534.8	22.5	11.6	57.0	..	..
Aug	5 170	5 354	887.4	16.1	52.4	955.9	41.6	24.1	583.6	23.2	12.5	61.0	..	..
Sep	4 712	5 124	795.0	16.3	37.4	848.7	25.1	27.6	491.8	22.0	9.6	51.9	884.2	146.8
Oct	5 225	5 299	1 027.4	36.4	60.7	1 124.5	36.1	36.9	485.4	33.5	12.8	76.4	..	..
Nov	4 848	5 509	1 273.1	66.7	124.1	1 463.9	52.0	49.0	486.8	50.8	13.5	106.1	..	..
Dec	5 324	5 575	859.5	46.4	80.1	986.0	43.5	28.6	597.6	34.7	11.2	79.6	994.2	156.2
2004 Jan[6]	3 153	3 322	832.8	20.6	53.9	907.3	36.1	24.2	339.2	16.9	9.2	54.3	..	..
Feb	3 815	3 955	764.0	12.8	31.9	808.7	25.1	21.5	427.8	19.5	6.0	46.4	..	..
Mar	5 168	5 446	933.0	15.7	40.8	989.5	33.7	33.9	485.9	24.0	8.6	60.4	896.6	131.9
Apr	4 677	4 612	896.2	15.5	34.7	946.4	19.4	19.1	519.8	21.6	7.9	53.2	..	..
May	5 196	5 264	967.9	16.1	39.3	1 023.3	31.3	24.4	553.0	25.2	11.8	62.9	..	..
Jun	5 391	5 513	968.5	16.9	49.1	1 034.6	35.6	25.1	551.3	23.3	9.9	63.9	976.1	129.8
Jul	4 700	4 782	1 023.1	18.2	54.6	1 095.8	35.5	36.7	541.9	23.3	10.4	57.9	..	..
Aug	5 416	5 171	982.7	15.6	46.1	1 044.4	44.7	26.1	585.4	23.3	8.4	60.2	..	..
Sep	4 696	5 106	985.5	20.3	44.9	1 050.7	50.6	28.5	460.4	22.1	8.8	64.4	844.0	120.4
Oct	4 517	4 836	1 132.8	32.8	64.5	1 230.1	50.8	28.9	525.6	34.1	8.9	76.3	..	..
Nov	5 336	5 042	1 233.5	61.2	107.6	1 402.3	62.4	42.0	579.1	48.3	12.9	101.4	..	..
Dec	5 394	6 146	1 047.9	52.3	108.3	1 208.5	82.7	31.1	569.4	37.6	11.4	91.0	812.6	169.4
2005 Jan[6]	3 072	3 094	791.4	17.0	56.8	865.2	38.1	20.7	332.7	15.6	4.6	51.9	..	..
Feb	3 918	3 924	770.1	14.2	37.8	822.1	30.4	16.4	374.7	16.8	4.1	44.8	..	..
Mar	5 119	5 355	1 116.7	17.8	43.4	1 177.9	53.1	32.2	532.8	22.8	7.5	64.3	854.2	134.1
Apr	4 336	4 341	968.4	14.9	39.0	1 022.2	49.3	15.9	522.4	22.4	6.5	61.1	..	..
May	5 072	5 190	911.0	14.7	38.4	964.2	38.4	28.2	507.3	21.7	7.2	61.1	..	..
Jun	5 121	5 368	1 040.5	17.4	49.7	1 107.7	52.5	25.9	609.9	23.6	8.3	68.5	1 057.3	168.0
Jul	5 012	5 054	1 077.2	14.8	55.4	1 147.4	53.6	25.8	578.1	22.6	8.0	60.1	..	..
Aug	4 987	5 271	964.7	15.3	43.1	1 023.0	45.9	22.3	608.5	18.3	7.6	57.0	..	..
Sep	4 612	4 603	970.3	19.2	57.6	1 047.1	47.5	30.0	577.2	24.0	5.0	62.3	863.4	133.8
Oct	4 742	4 828	1 064.5	39.3	71.2	1 175.0	51.1	32.9	518.2	32.1	7.2	74.8	..	..
Nov	5 284	5 367	1 316.5	60.6	114.3	1 491.4	64.1	51.2	623.8	41.9	9.1	104.1	..	..
Dec	4 980	5 177	1 125.8	60.6	113.9	1 300.3	73.5	32.4	591.5	38.9	9.1	111.7	983.8	170.2
2006 Jan[6]	3 564	3 157	693.6	11.5	46.9	751.9	24.8	19.7	359.4	13.0	3.3	32.2	..	..
Feb	3 105	3 748	843.4	14.0	41.2	898.6	31.6	16.6	437.8	16.0	3.7	42.9	..	..
Mar	5 218	5 492	1 095.5	18.9	41.4	1 155.8	38.1	31.9	527.8	21.6	5.0	59.4	1 019.7	140.3
Apr	4 029	4 005	955.0	16.9	40.5	1 012.5	42.8	19.2	560.1	21.8	5.6	59.8	..	..
May	4 784	5 394	891.6	15.9	46.5	954.0	35.2	22.2	647.9	20.1	5.1	55.0	..	..
Jun	5 295	5 362	961.7	17.8	54.9	1 034.4	49.8	25.6	695.7	24.2	8.2	75.0	1 222.8	118.1
Jul	4 851	4 557	980.1	13.8	57.4	1 051.4	50.1	24.2	753.5	16.8	4.5	50.5	..	..
Aug	4 570	4 900	999.3	17.0	49.7	1 066.0	49.6	25.2	849.8	21.0	7.0	64.4	..	..
Sep	4 204	4 331	969.1	21.6	53.8	1 044.5	39.8	27.7	690.1	20.9	4.5	61.9	909.4	110.4
Oct	4 667	4 740	974.9	34.8	65.7	1 075.5	47.6	38.1	682.5	31.6	5.7	72.8	..	..
Nov	4 053	4 435	1 242.6	67.5	106.9	1 417.0	53.7	42.9	695.3	38.2	4.9	100.5	..	..
Dec	5 423	5 627	1 051.1	51.8	110.1	1 213.0	64.7	23.5	622.8	37.4	7.3	92.5	833.8	130.7
2007 Jan	3 241	3 220	942.2	20.1	65.0	1 027.4	41.9	22.7	520.1	19.1	4.5	61.5	..	..

1 Data are available only quarterly.
2 Percentage alcohol by volume.
3 Made wine with alcoholic strength 1.2% to 5.5%, includes alcoholic lemonade of appropriate strength.
4 From 28 April 2002 duty on spirit-based ready-to-drink (RTDs) products is charged at the same rate as spirits per litre of alcohol. Until September 2002, RTDs were recorded under the imported and spirits. Customs and Excise have now been able to estimate the amount of RTDs under the spirits and remove them from the spirits clearances. Spirit-based RTDs were previously dutied at the made wine rate.

5 Includes imported spirits.
6 Due to the effect of the holiday period, these figures are subject to greater un-certainty than usual.
7 HMRC revised the beer production and clearances data back to April 2005 with the latest available information.

Source: HM Revenue and Customs: 020 7147 0593

7 Production, output and costs

7.1 Output of the production industries

Average 2003 = 100

	Total production industries	Mining and quarrying	Total manufact- uring industries	Food, drink and tobacco	Textiles, leather and clothing	Coke ref petrol and nuclear fuels	Chemicals and man-made fibres	Basic metals and metal products	Engineering and allied industries	Other manufact- uring	Electricity, gas and water
SIC 2003 Sub-section	Sect C+D+E	Sect C	Sect D	DA	DB_DC	DF	DG	DJ	DK_DM	DD_DN	Sect E
Weights	*1000*	*118*	*792*	*118*	*26*	*13*	*87*	*81*	*237*	*229*	*90*
	CKYW	CKYX	CKYY	CKZA	AGVO	CKZF	CKZG	CKZJ	AGXS	AGXQ	CKYZ
2001	102.3	105.0	102.5	98.0	110.1	106.9	99.3	101.4	107.1	100.4	98.0
2002	100.3	105.4	99.8	100.0	101.8	108.3	99.1	102.4	98.5	99.8	98.4
2003	100.0	100.0	100.0	100.0	100.0	100.0	100.0	100.0	100.0	100.0	100.0
2004	100.8	92.1	102.0	101.6	90.1	105.8	103.4	103.1	104.3	100.1	101.1
2005	98.9	83.4	101.0	102.3	88.1	109.9	104.3	103.2	103.3	96.8	100.9
2006	99.0	76.8	102.5	102.1	85.2	105.2	107.9	104.6	107.4	96.5	98.1

Seasonally adjusted

2002 Q3	100.2	101.0	100.3	100.7	101.0	103.5	100.0	102.6	99.3	100.2	99.2
Q4	100.2	105.7	99.4	99.3	96.5	108.4	98.0	102.3	98.8	99.5	99.7
2003 Q1	99.9	105.0	99.3	100.1	99.4	104.4	98.3	100.0	98.9	99.3	98.1
Q2	99.4	99.8	99.4	99.4	99.5	100.7	99.4	99.5	99.4	99.1	98.9
Q3	100.0	98.9	100.0	100.2	101.6	97.9	99.8	99.7	99.6	100.5	100.6
Q4	100.8	96.3	101.3	100.4	99.5	97.0	102.5	100.7	102.1	101.1	102.3
2004 Q1	100.9	94.3	101.7	100.4	93.1	108.5	104.7	101.0	102.7	101.1	102.2
Q2	101.3	94.8	102.4	102.6	90.2	105.2	103.8	103.6	104.4	100.4	100.7
Q3	100.3	90.9	101.6	101.3	89.3	103.4	102.1	104.1	104.6	98.9	101.0
Q4	100.6	88.6	102.4	102.0	88.0	106.1	102.9	103.7	105.6	99.9	100.6
2005 Q1	99.6	86.2	101.5	102.2	86.3	122.6	103.6	103.5	102.8	98.9	100.1
Q2	99.3	86.9	100.9	103.0	89.4	110.3	103.1	103.4	103.2	96.6	101.8
Q3	98.6	80.0	101.1	102.2	88.4	106.4	104.5	102.8	104.5	96.1	101.2
Q4	98.0	80.4	100.4	101.9	88.4	100.4	105.8	102.9	102.8	95.5	100.6
2006 Q1	98.9	80.4	101.4	101.8	85.9	104.8	105.5	103.8	105.5	96.2	100.6
Q2	99.0	77.5	102.3	101.9	85.0	106.1	107.6	104.6	107.2	96.4	97.9
Q3	99.2	74.8	103.0	101.8	85.0	104.8	110.0	105.2	108.2	96.8	97.7
Q4	99.0	74.3	103.1	102.7	84.8	105.2	108.6	105.0	108.7	96.6	96.1
2007 Q1	99.1	75.3	102.8	102.3	83.8	111.9	108.4	104.3	108.7	96.0	97.3
2005 Apr	99.4	86.8	100.9	101.4	88.6	117.3	102.6	104.4	103.1	97.1	102.0
May	99.3	87.8	100.7	103.3	88.8	108.3	102.1	104.1	103.1	96.2	101.3
Jun	99.4	86.2	101.0	104.2	90.7	105.4	104.6	101.7	103.3	96.3	102.2
Jul	99.2	82.8	101.4	103.5	89.2	106.7	104.2	103.2	104.5	96.6	101.5
Aug	98.1	75.5	101.1	101.8	87.8	105.6	105.5	102.6	104.8	95.9	101.3
Sep	98.4	81.6	100.6	101.3	88.1	106.9	103.9	102.7	104.1	95.8	100.7
Oct	97.5	80.6	99.9	101.4	87.2	102.2	105.0	102.5	102.6	94.9	98.2
Nov	98.1	79.3	100.4	102.1	87.8	98.8	104.8	103.0	102.9	95.9	102.4
Dec	98.6	81.3	100.8	102.4	90.1	100.2	107.5	103.1	103.0	95.8	101.3
2006 Jan	98.7	82.1	101.1	101.8	86.8	105.7	105.5	103.6	104.3	96.1	100.0
Feb	98.6	80.2	101.2	101.7	85.6	106.4	105.5	103.2	105.3	95.8	99.6
Mar	99.3	79.0	102.0	101.8	85.3	102.3	105.5	104.5	106.9	96.7	102.4
Apr	98.7	78.8	101.8	101.8	84.4	103.9	106.4	104.2	106.8	95.8	98.2
May	99.2	78.1	102.5	101.4	84.9	107.4	108.7	103.7	107.1	97.1	97.4
Jun	99.1	75.7	102.7	102.4	85.9	107.0	107.7	105.8	107.6	96.4	98.0
Jul	99.1	75.2	102.7	101.7	84.5	104.2	109.3	105.2	107.9	96.6	98.0
Aug	99.1	73.1	103.1	101.6	85.2	105.7	109.8	105.6	108.0	97.4	97.6
Sep	99.5	76.1	103.2	102.2	85.1	104.4	111.0	104.7	108.8	96.4	97.4
Oct	98.9	75.3	102.9	102.8	84.0	100.6	108.3	105.0	108.5	96.6	94.2
Nov	99.2	75.1	103.1	102.1	85.0	106.2	108.3	105.4	108.8	96.7	96.9
Dec	99.1	72.5	103.2	103.4	85.3	108.9	109.1	104.5	108.7	96.6	97.1
2007 Jan	99.2[†]	74.3[†]	103.1[†]	102.5[†]	84.4[†]	111.8[†]	109.1[†]	103.9[†]	109.2[†]	96.1[†]	97.5[†]
Feb	98.9	76.4[†]	102.3	101.9	83.1	111.3	108.4	104.4	107.9	95.5	97.6
Mar	99.1	75.3	102.9	102.3	84.0	112.7	107.7	104.8	108.9	96.2	97.0

7.1 Output of the production industries
continued

Average 2003 = 100

Summary - Not seasonally adjusted

	Total production industries	Mining and quarrying	Total manufact-uring industries	Food, drink and tobacco	Textiles, leather and clothing	Coke ref petrol and nuclear fuels	Chemicals and man-made fibres	Basic metal and metal products	Engineering and allied industries	Other manufact-uring	Electricity, gas and water
SIC 2003 Sub-section	Sect C+D+E	Sect C	Sect D	DA	DB_DC	DF	DG	DJ	DK_DM	DD_DN	Sect E
Weights	1000	118	792	118	26	13	87	81	237	229	90
	AGVZ	AGVT	AGVV	AGUV	AGWR	AGUX	AGUZ	AGVF	AGXT	AGXR	AGVX
2001	102.3	105.0	102.5	98.0	110.1	106.9	99.3	101.4	107.1	100.4	98.0
2002	100.3	105.4	99.8	100.0	101.8	108.3	99.1	102.4	98.5	99.8	98.4
2003	100.0	100.0	100.0	100.0	100.0	100.0	100.0	100.0	100.0	100.0	100.0
2004	100.8	92.1	102.0	101.6	90.1	105.8	103.4	103.1	104.3	100.1	101.1
2005	98.9	84.2	100.9	102.0	88.0	109.6	104.5	103.1	103.3	96.6	101.1
2006	99.1	77.5	102.4	101.7	85.1	104.9	108.2	104.5	107.4	96.4	98.2
Not seasonally adjusted [3]											
2002 Q3	97.3	94.2	99.4	100.2	100.9	105.1	100.3	102.1	96.0	100.8	84.5
Q4	103.2	111.7	101.7	107.7	98.3	109.1	97.0	101.0	101.6	101.2	107.1
2003 Q1	100.8	109.6	98.2	94.1	98.6	104.1	98.9	101.7	98.9	97.8	113.3
Q2	98.0	97.2	99.0	97.5	98.7	98.3	100.0	100.2	99.2	98.9	91.1
Q3	97.6	91.7	99.8	100.3	101.4	98.9	100.5	100.0	97.4	101.7	85.6
Q4	103.5	101.5	103.0	108.1	101.3	98.7	100.5	98.1	104.5	101.7	110.0
2004 Q1	102.8	98.7	101.7	96.1	92.1	108.3	106.8	103.4	103.8	100.4	118.2
Q2	99.7	93.2	101.5	99.7	91.3	102.8	103.7	103.6	103.3	99.9	92.6
Q3	97.6	84.0	101.0	101.3	89.0	104.8	101.9	104.1	102.0	99.7	85.3
Q4	103.0	92.7	103.9	109.2	88.2	107.3	101.2	101.3	108.2	100.2	108.4
2005 Q1	100.2	91.0	99.7	96.8	83.8	122.5	103.5	104.7	101.4	96.8	116.0
Q2	98.8	86.9	101.1	100.0	89.6	107.8	105.0	104.2	104.1	96.9	93.7
Q3	96.6	74.4	101.1	102.4	89.4	107.7	106.3	102.7	102.3	97.4	86.4
Q4	100.2	84.3	101.6	108.6	89.1	100.2	103.4	100.6	105.3	95.3	108.3
2006 Q1	100.8	85.0	101.3	96.7	84.5	103.6	107.6	106.8	106.6	95.7	116.4
Q2	98.0	77.8	102.0	100.0	84.5	104.6	108.7	104.9	106.9	96.0	89.9
Q3	96.2	69.4	101.7	101.0	85.1	106.4	109.9	104.2	104.2	97.0	83.5
Q4	101.2	77.7	104.5	109.1	86.4	104.9	106.4	102.2	111.7	96.7	103.0
2007 Q1	100.4	79.4	102.1	96.5	82.8	112.0	110.5	107.1	108.1	95.3	112.9
2005 Apr	97.7	90.8	98.3	97.2	85.6	102.9	102.7	102.7	99.6	95.5	101.8
May	97.7	87.9	99.8	99.3	89.7	103.5	103.8	104.4	101.8	95.6	92.3
Jun	100.8	81.8	105.2	103.6	93.5	117.1	108.6	105.5	110.9	99.5	87.1
Jul	94.4	78.9	97.7	99.0	86.7	112.1	101.8	100.9	98.3	94.1	85.4
Aug	93.1	67.8	97.7	101.6	87.9	104.5	106.2	100.9	95.1	94.9	85.8
Sep	102.3	76.6	107.8	106.5	93.7	106.6	111.0	106.5	113.5	103.3	87.9
Oct	99.4	83.6	102.2	107.7	90.9	95.6	105.4	104.7	101.5	99.7	95.4
Nov	104.0	82.4	106.3	107.6	96.0	100.3	107.2	107.8	109.6	102.9	111.8
Dec	97.1	86.9	96.3	110.5	80.3	104.8	97.6	89.5	104.8	83.2	117.7
2006 Jan	95.6	88.5	93.9	89.8	78.7	101.2	104.6	101.1	96.0	88.6	120.0
Feb	96.4	79.5	96.8	91.7	81.1	107.2	101.7	102.9	100.8	92.5	114.7
Mar	110.2	87.2	113.2	108.4	93.8	102.5	116.7	116.3	122.9	106.0	114.6
Apr	93.5	82.2	94.8	94.9	78.1	95.4	100.2	99.8	97.3	90.1	97.6
May	99.6	79.0	103.8	102.0	87.8	102.9	113.4	106.3	107.1	98.7	88.8
Jun	101.0	72.3	107.2	103.2	87.5	115.6	112.5	108.5	116.3	99.3	83.2
Jul	94.1	71.4	98.7	98.1	81.6	108.5	106.1	102.5	101.8	93.0	83.0
Aug	94.3	65.2	99.9	102.3	85.1	107.0	109.8	104.3	98.8	95.8	82.5
Sep	100.4	71.5	106.4	102.5	88.6	103.7	113.8	105.8	112.1	102.2	85.1
Oct	102.4	78.3	107.3	109.5	90.5	98.8	112.5	110.0	109.2	103.5	90.9
Nov	105.6	78.2	109.7	109.0	94.2	99.7	110.1	109.7	117.6	104.1	105.6
Dec	95.6	76.5	96.5	108.6	74.5	116.1	96.5	86.9	108.3	82.6	112.6
2007 Jan	97.2[†]	79.0[†]	97.7[†]	92.9[†]	79.7[†]	107.6[†]	111.2[†]	103.2[†]	101.0[†]	91.1	116.7[†]
Feb	95.9	75.6	96.9	90.5	78.6	105.9	105.0	103.7	101.9	91.2[†]	113.1
Mar	108.1	83.5	111.6	106.1	90.1	122.3	115.4	114.5	121.4	103.7	108.9

7.1
continued **Output of the production industries**

	Detailed analysis							
	Mining and quarrying				Textiles, leather and clothing		Coke ref petrol and nuclear fuels	Chemicals and man-made fibres
	Oil and gas	Coal	Other mining and quarrying	Food, drink and tobacco	Textiles and textile products	Leather and leather products		
SIC 2003 Sub-section	C_1	C_11	CB	DA	DB	DC	DF	DG
Weights	107	3	8	118	24	3	13	87
	CKZO	CKZP	CKZQ	CKZA	CKZB	CKZC	CKZF	CKZG
2001	107.3	112.6	80.4	98.0	107.2	140.0	106.9	99.3
2002	105.9	105.9	98.7	100.0	99.7	122.5	108.3	99.1
2003	100.0	100.0	100.0	100.0	100.0	100.0	100.0	100.0
2004	91.6	85.8	101.4	101.6	91.8	74.6	105.8	103.4
2005	81.7	66.9	110.1	102.3	90.2	68.9	109.9	104.3
2006	74.5	63.7	109.9	102.1	86.8	69.8	105.2	107.9
Seasonally adjusted [1]								
2002 Q3	101.1	101.3	97.9	100.7	99.0	120.5	103.5	100.0
Q4	106.4	98.9	98.0	99.3	94.9	112.1	108.4	98.0
2003 Q1	105.1	106.6	101.7	100.1	97.8	115.3	104.4	98.3
Q2	99.5	104.8	101.6	99.4	99.2	102.5	100.7	99.4
Q3	99.1	89.9	100.2	100.2	102.6	91.5	97.9	99.8
Q4	96.3	98.7	96.5	100.4	100.4	90.7	97.0	102.5
2004 Q1	94.4	85.4	95.8	100.4	94.8	76.8	108.5	104.7
Q2	94.5	84.5	101.1	102.6	91.3	79.8	105.2	103.8
Q3	90.2	89.4	100.7	101.3	91.0	72.9	103.4	102.1
Q4	87.2	83.7	108.0	102.0	90.1	68.8	106.1	102.9
2005 Q1	84.8	65.2	110.2	102.2	88.2	69.1	122.6	103.6
Q2	85.7	63.0	110.2	103.0	91.3	70.9	110.3	103.1
Q3	78.0	69.5	108.3	102.2	90.5	69.2	106.4	104.5
Q4	78.2	69.7	111.6	101.9	90.7	66.5	100.4	105.8
2006 Q1	78.5	76.0	107.1	101.8	87.4	71.3	104.8	105.5
Q2	74.9	70.5	112.8	101.9	87.1	66.0	106.1	107.6
Q3	72.5	53.5	110.1	101.8	86.4	71.4	104.8	110.0
Q4	72.0	54.9	109.7	102.7	86.3	70.5	105.2	108.6
2007 Q1	72.8	51.2	114.9	102.3	85.1	71.8	111.9	108.4
2005 Apr	85.5	62.9	110.8	101.4	90.3	72.3	117.3	102.6
May	86.7	62.6	110.0	103.3	90.8	70.5	108.3	102.1
Jun	84.8	63.5	109.9	104.2	92.9	70.0	105.4	104.6
Jul	81.5	56.9	108.1	103.5	91.2	70.7	106.7	104.2
Aug	73.1	70.0	108.4	101.8	89.9	68.3	105.6	105.5
Sep	79.5	81.5	108.5	101.3	90.2	68.5	106.9	103.9
Oct	78.6	70.5	109.8	101.4	89.8	63.5	102.2	105.0
Nov	76.9	67.9	113.1	102.1	90.1	66.2	98.8	104.8
Dec	79.2	70.9	111.9	102.4	92.3	69.6	100.2	107.5
2006 Jan	80.1	83.7	107.3	101.8	88.5	70.8	105.7	105.5
Feb	78.3	75.0	106.1	101.7	87.2	71.4	106.4	105.5
Mar	77.0	69.2	108.0	101.8	86.7	71.8	102.3	105.5
Apr	76.5	72.9	110.6	101.8	86.5	64.6	103.9	106.4
May	75.4	72.3	113.8	101.4	86.8	66.5	107.4	108.7
Jun	72.9	66.4	113.9	102.4	88.0	66.8	107.0	107.7
Jul	72.8	56.4	111.0	101.7	86.5	65.7	104.2	109.3
Aug	70.8	48.4	110.5	101.6	86.5	73.5	105.7	109.8
Sep	74.0	55.7	108.7	102.2	86.2	75.1	104.4	111.0
Oct	73.2	56.5	108.1	102.8	85.5	70.6	100.6	108.3
Nov	72.9	56.8	109.0	102.1	86.5	70.9	106.2	108.3
Dec	69.9	51.5	112.1	103.4	87.0	69.9	108.9	109.1
2007 Jan	71.8	54.7†	112.5†	102.5†	85.6†	73.5†	111.8†	109.1†
Feb	73.9†	50.5	115.5	101.9	84.4	71.2	111.3	108.4
Mar	72.7	48.3	116.6	102.3	85.4	70.6	112.7	107.7

7.1 Output of the production industries

Average 2003 = 100

| | Detailed analysis (continued) | | | | | | | | | |
| | Engineering and allied industries | | | | Other manufacturing | | | | | |
	Basic metal and metal products	Machinery and equipment	Electrical and optical equipment	Transport equipment	Wood and wood products	Pulp, paper, printing and publishing	Rubber and plastic products	Non-metallic mineral products	Other manufacturing NES	Electricity, gas and water
SIC 2003 Sub-section	DJ	DK	DL	DM	DD	DE	DH	DI	DN	Sect E
Weights	*81*	*66*	*85*	*86*	*15*	*108*	*41*	*30*	*35*	*90*
	CKZJ	CKZK	CKZL	CKZM	CKZD	CKZE	CKZH	CKZI	CKZN	CKYZ
2001	101.4	104.2	118.7	97.9	96.6	101.3	103.2	96.0	99.9	98.0
2002	102.4	98.3	102.6	94.8	99.2	101.4	99.2	94.5	100.5	98.4
2003	100.0	100.0	100.0	100.0	100.0	100.0	100.0	100.0	100.0	100.0
2004	103.1	105.8	101.8	105.8	101.8	99.1	98.5	105.8	99.3	101.1
2005	103.2	109.0	96.9	105.3	97.4	94.0	94.9	105.5	99.8	100.9
2006	104.6	114.0	98.2	111.4	94.9	91.7	98.0	107.5	100.7	98.1
Seasonally adjusted [1]										
2002 Q3	102.6	99.1	102.4	96.5	100.7	101.8	99.9	95.2	99.6	99.2
Q4	102.3	96.1	102.9	96.8	101.1	101.1	97.9	94.6	99.9	99.7
2003 Q1	100.0	96.6	100.5	99.0	97.6	100.0	97.8	98.3	100.2	98.1
Q2	99.5	100.1	99.5	98.8	97.1	99.6	98.2	98.4	99.8	98.9
Q3	99.7	100.8	99.8	98.6	101.2	99.9	101.5	101.0	100.7	100.6
Q4	100.7	102.5	100.2	103.5	104.1	100.5	102.5	102.3	99.2	102.3
2004 Q1	101.0	100.4	100.0	107.1	100.1	100.8	101.1	104.5	99.2	102.2
Q2	103.6	107.8	102.6	103.7	104.3	99.1	99.0	106.3	99.2	100.7
Q3	104.1	107.2	102.5	104.7	101.8	98.0	96.3	105.8	97.8	101.0
Q4	103.7	107.7	101.9	107.7	101.2	98.5	97.6	106.6	101.0	100.6
2005 Q1	103.5	109.2	97.0	103.7	100.6	96.2	96.5	108.9	100.9	100.1
Q2	103.4	108.3	96.9	105.5	95.8	94.1	94.6	104.3	100.2	101.8
Q3	102.8	108.6	98.1	107.5	98.0	93.5	94.5	103.3	99.1	101.2
Q4	102.9	109.7	95.7	104.5	95.2	92.2	94.1	105.4	99.2	100.6
2006 Q1	103.8	110.8	97.8	109.0	93.2	92.6	97.0	105.2	99.8	100.6
Q2	104.6	113.7	98.8	110.4	95.5	91.3	98.6	106.7	101.2	97.9
Q3	105.2	115.9	98.0	112.4	93.9	91.7	98.7	109.3	100.8	97.7
Q4	105.0	115.4	98.3	113.6	96.9	91.3	97.9	108.9	101.0	96.1
2007 Q1	104.3	117.9	98.1	111.9	96.2	90.8	96.0	107.8	101.5	97.3
2005 Apr	104.4	108.4	97.0	104.9	96.6	94.1	95.2	105.0	102.2	102.0
May	104.1	107.9	96.6	105.8	95.7	94.0	93.8	104.3	99.2	101.3
Jun	101.7	108.6	97.0	105.6	95.2	94.2	94.8	103.6	99.0	102.2
Jul	103.2	108.9	97.4	108.0	96.2	94.8	94.4	103.0	99.5	101.5
Aug	102.6	108.6	98.8	107.9	99.7	92.9	94.7	103.4	98.7	101.3
Sep	102.7	108.4	98.1	106.6	98.2	92.8	94.5	103.4	99.1	100.7
Oct	102.5	108.7	96.4	104.0	95.9	92.0	93.2	104.6	96.9	98.2
Nov	103.0	109.8	95.7	104.6	95.3	92.7	94.0	105.3	100.0	102.4
Dec	103.1	110.7	95.0	104.8	94.3	91.7	95.1	106.2	100.8	101.3
2006 Jan	103.6	110.5	96.7	106.9	92.4	92.5	96.3	107.1	99.4	100.0
Feb	103.2	110.1	97.8	109.0	92.5	92.2	96.6	104.4	99.8	99.6
Mar	104.5	111.7	98.8	111.2	94.6	93.2	98.0	104.2	100.2	102.4
Apr	104.2	113.0	97.9	110.7	93.8	91.8	97.6	105.2	98.9	98.2
May	103.7	113.6	99.4	109.9	95.4	91.8	99.7	107.2	102.4	97.4
Jun	105.8	114.7	99.2	110.5	97.3	90.4	98.4	107.7	102.4	98.0
Jul	105.2	115.3	98.1	111.9	93.2	91.6	98.4	108.4	100.9	98.0
Aug	105.6	114.8	98.8	111.9	94.8	92.0	99.3	110.3	101.7	97.6
Sep	104.7	117.5	97.1	113.5	93.7	91.4	98.3	109.3	99.6	97.4
Oct	105.0	115.6	97.6	113.8	95.8	91.5	98.4	108.6	100.2	94.2
Nov	105.4	115.1	99.2	113.4	97.6	91.2	97.7	108.8	101.8	96.9
Dec	104.5	115.7	98.2	113.6	97.4	91.1	97.5	109.3	101.0	97.1
2007 Jan	103.9†	118.3†	98.5†	112.7†	96.2†	90.8†	96.7†	107.9†	101.9†	97.5†
Feb	104.4	117.0	97.6	111.0	94.5	90.6	95.7	107.1	100.9	97.6
Mar	104.8	118.5	98.3	112.0	97.8	91.2	95.5	108.5	101.6	97.0

7.1 Output of the production industries
continued

	Market Sector analysis					
	Consumer durables	Consumer non-durables	Capital goods industries	Intermediate goods and energy		
				Total	Energy	Intermediate goods
SIC 2003 Weights[2]	36	272	213	478	212	266
	UFIU	UFJS	UFIL	JMOH	UFJB	UFJL
2001	101.2	99.4	106.8	102.3	103.4	101.4
2002	101.7	99.9	98.2	101.5	102.9	100.4
2003	100.0	100.0	100.0	100.0	100.0	100.0
2004	104.6	100.0	103.7	99.7	96.4	102.3
2005	102.5	99.4	103.6	96.2	91.4	100.0
2006	104.6	99.4	107.5	94.6	86.2	101.3
Seasonally adjusted [1]						
2002 Q3	100.4	100.5	98.7	100.8	100.4	101.1
Q4	101.6	98.7	98.4	101.7	103.7	100.1
2003 Q1	99.7	99.0	98.7	101.0	102.2	99.9
Q2	99.3	99.2	99.1	99.6	99.4	99.6
Q3	99.9	100.6	99.8	99.7	99.5	99.8
Q4	101.2	101.2	102.4	99.8	98.9	100.6
2004 Q1	102.6	100.4	102.2	100.4	98.5	102.0
Q2	104.9	100.4	103.4	100.6	97.6	103.0
Q3	106.3	99.1	104.0	98.9	95.6	101.5
Q4	104.7	99.8	105.1	98.7	94.0	102.5
2005 Q1	105.3	99.6	102.8	97.8	93.4	101.2
Q2	102.0	99.4	103.4	97.3	93.7	100.1
Q3	101.3	99.3	105.1	95.1	89.5	99.6
Q4	101.5	99.4	103.2	94.7	89.0	99.3
2006 Q1	103.0	99.4	105.5	95.3	89.4	100.0
Q2	105.5	99.2	107.0	94.8	86.5	101.4
Q3	104.0	99.6	108.3	94.6	84.9	102.3
Q4	106.0	99.6	109.2	93.7	84.0	101.4
2007 Q1	103.1	98.9	109.2	94.4	85.3	101.6
2005 Apr	104.5	98.5	103.0	97.9	94.2	100.8
May	101.0	99.3	103.3	97.3	93.9	100.0
Jun	100.6	100.6	103.9	96.6	93.2	99.3
Jul	100.8	100.4	105.2	95.8	91.2	99.5
Aug	101.2	99.0	105.4	94.2	87.0	99.9
Sep	101.9	98.6	104.7	95.2	90.2	99.2
Oct	101.2	98.5	103.0	94.2	88.2	99.0
Nov	101.0	99.4	103.5	94.7	88.9	99.3
Dec	102.4	100.3	103.2	95.3	89.7	99.7
2006 Jan	101.3	99.5	104.4	95.6	90.1	100.0
Feb	102.3	99.3	105.5	94.8	89.0	99.4
Mar	105.5	99.4	106.5	95.6	89.2	100.7
Apr	105.9	99.1	106.5	94.6	87.3	100.3
May	105.4	99.5	107.0	95.0	86.7	101.6
Jun	105.2	99.0	107.6	94.9	85.5	102.3
Jul	103.6	99.3	108.1	94.6	85.2	102.0
Aug	103.9	99.4	107.8	94.7	84.0	103.2
Sep	104.5	100.0	108.9	94.6	85.6	101.8
Oct	104.0	99.4	109.2	93.5	83.6	101.5
Nov	106.7	99.2	109.2	94.2	84.9	101.7
Dec	107.2	100.2	109.2	93.3	83.6	101.1
2007 Jan	102.9[†]	99.2[†]	109.8[†]	94.2	84.9[†]	101.6[†]
Feb	102.3	98.7	108.4	94.4[†]	85.9	101.2
Mar	104.1	98.7	109.3	94.5	85.1	101.9

Note: The figures contain, where appropriate, an adjustment for stock changes.

1 Unadjusted data may be obtained from the Office for National Statistics, IOP Branch, Government Buildings, Cardiff Road, Newport, NP10 8XG.

2 These sum to the total of 1 000 for the production industries.
3 Includes adjustments to standardise the length of months.

Source: Office for National Statistics: 01633 812319

7.2 Productivity jobs and output per filled job[1]

2003 = 100

	Whole economy[2]	Total production industries	Total mining quarrying electricity gas & water supply	Total manufac- turing indus- tries	Food, drink and tobacco	Manufacturing industries						
						Textiles, footwear, clothing and leather	Pulp, paper & paper products, printing and publishing	Chemicals and man-made fibres	Other non- metalic mineral products	Basic metals and fabri- cated metal products	Engi- neering and related industries	Other manufactur- ing
SIC 1992 Sub-section		Sect C+D+E	Sect C+E	Sect D	DA	DB_DC	DE	DG	DI	DJ	DK_DM	DD+DF+DH+DN
Productivity jobs												
	LNNM	LNOJ	LOIW	LNOK	LNOL	LOIS	LOIM	LOIN	LZYL	LZYP	LOIT	LOIZ
2001	98.4	110.3	107.5	110.5	106.2	132.0	101.6	103.1	110.5	109.3	117.0	105.6
2002	99.1	105.4	104.1	105.5	103.6	117.3	100.5	103.7	103.4	105.0	108.5	103.2
2003	100.0	100.0	100.0	100.0	100.0	100.0	100.0	100.0	100.0	100.0	100.0	100.0
2004	100.8	95.4	93.4	95.5	98.9	89.5	95.2	95.5	99.3	95.7	94.5	96.0
2005	101.7	91.3	93.8	91.2	96.6	81.0	91.2	90.5	93.6	89.9	91.5	90.4
2006	102.4	89.2	97.7	88.8	94.8	75.2	90.8	86.8	87.5	90.3	88.4	87.5
Seasonally adjusted												
2003 Q1	99.7	102.5	102.9	102.4	101.5	106.4	100.4	102.9	102.0	101.8	103.3	102.4
Q2	99.9	100.7	101.3	100.7	100.4	102.4	100.3	99.9	100.1	100.8	100.7	101.1
Q3	100.1	99.1	99.3	99.1	99.2	97.8	100.3	98.7	99.1	99.1	98.9	99.2
Q4	100.2	97.7	96.5	97.8	98.9	93.4	99.0	98.5	98.8	98.3	97.1	97.3
2004 Q1	100.6	96.6	94.1	96.7	99.7	92.8	96.8	96.8	99.1	96.7	95.6	97.4
Q2	100.7	96.0	92.8	96.1	99.5	90.4	96.3	96.3	99.6	96.2	94.8	96.8
Q3	100.7	94.9	93.4	95.0	98.5	87.8	94.3	95.2	99.4	95.4	93.8	95.7
Q4	101.1	94.2	93.4	94.2	98.0	87.1	93.4	93.5	99.2	94.4	93.7	94.0
2005 Q1	101.4	92.9	92.9	93.0	97.4	85.7	91.7	92.7	97.7	92.7	93.1	91.5
Q2	101.6	91.7	93.6	91.6	96.4	83.0	91.8	91.7	94.7	89.7	91.9	90.5
Q3	101.8	90.6	94.2	90.4	96.2	79.0	90.9	89.6	92.2	88.2	91.0	89.8
Q4	101.8	90.0	94.5	89.7	96.3	76.3	90.6	87.9	89.6	89.1	89.9	89.6
2006 Q1	102.0	89.7	94.4	89.4	95.5	75.8	90.9	87.1	88.6	90.5	89.2	88.4
Q2	102.3	89.4	96.6	89.0	94.5	75.1	91.1	86.7	88.0	90.6	88.8	87.6
Q3	102.5	89.2	99.4	88.7	94.4	74.9	90.8	86.3	87.3	90.7	88.3	87.0
Q4	102.7	88.7	100.3	88.0	94.6	75.1	90.3	86.9	86.0	89.3	87.4	86.8
Output per filled job												
	LNNN	LNNW	LOJA	LNNX	LNNY	LNOG	LNOA	LNOB	LZYM	LZYQ	LNOH	LOJD
2001	97.2	92.7	95.0	92.7	92.3	83.3	99.6	96.3	86.9	92.7	91.4	96.2
2002	98.2	95.1	98.4	94.6	96.6	86.6	100.8	95.5	91.3	97.5	90.8	97.7
2003	100.0	100.0	100.0	100.0	100.0	100.0	100.0	100.0	100.0	100.0	100.0	100.0
2004	102.5	105.6	102.6	106.8	102.7	100.4	104.1	108.3	106.5	107.7	110.4	104.4
2005	103.6	108.3	96.6	110.7	105.9	108.8	103.0	115.3	112.8	114.7	112.9	109.4
2006	105.7	110.9	87.7	115.4	107.7	112.9	101.1	124.4	122.9	115.9	121.3	113.7
Seasonally adjusted												
2003 Q1	99.0	97.5	99.2	96.9	98.6	93.1	99.6	95.4	96.3	98.3	95.7	97.1
Q2	99.4	98.6	98.1	98.7	98.9	96.9	99.4	99.5	98.3	98.7	98.6	97.8
Q3	100.3	100.8	100.3	100.9	101.0	103.6	99.6	101.1	101.9	100.6	100.6	101.4
Q4	101.3	103.2	102.3	103.5	101.5	106.3	101.4	104.0	103.6	102.4	105.1	103.7
2004 Q1	101.6	104.4	103.7	105.2	100.6	100.0	104.1	108.1	105.4	104.4	107.4	104.0
Q2	102.5	105.5	104.7	106.5	103.1	99.5	103.0	107.7	106.7	107.7	110.0	103.9
Q3	102.7	105.7	101.7	106.9	102.8	101.4	103.9	107.2	106.4	109.1	111.4	102.9
Q4	103.1	106.8	100.1	108.6	104.1	100.8	105.4	110.0	107.3	109.8	112.6	106.8
2005 Q1	103.1	107.2	99.0	109.1	104.9	100.5	104.9	111.8	111.4	111.6	110.3	111.4
Q2	103.3	108.3	99.5	110.1	106.8	107.4	102.5	112.4	110.0	115.2	112.1	109.0
Q3	103.6	108.8	94.2	111.8	106.2	111.6	102.8	116.7	112.0	116.6	114.7	109.2
Q4	104.3	108.9	93.9	111.8	105.9	115.6	101.8	120.2	117.6	115.4	114.2	108.0
2006 Q1	105.0	110.2	94.0	113.4	106.5	113.0	101.9	121.0	118.7	114.7	118.2	111.4
Q2	105.5	110.7	89.0	114.9	107.8	112.9	100.3	124.1	121.2	115.3	120.6	114.2
Q3	105.9	111.2	84.7	116.1	107.8	113.2	100.9	127.4	125.2	115.9	122.4	114.4
Q4	106.4	111.6	83.1	117.0	108.6	112.7	101.1	124.9	126.5	117.6	124.2	114.8

Note: The full productivity and unit wage costs data sets with associated articles can be found on the National Statistics website at: www.statistics.gov.uk/productivity.

1 Output per filled job is the ratio of the output index numbers published in Table 7.1 and productivity jobs. A monthly series for total manufacturing industries is presented in Table 7.3.

2 Whole economy output per job is based on Gross Value Added at Basic Prices.

Source: Office for National Statistics

7.3 Key Productivity Measures

2003=100

	Whole economy				Manufacturing industry	
	Implied GDP deflator[1]	Labour costs per unit of output	Wages and salaries per unit of output	Output per worker[2]	Wages and salaries per unit of output	Output per filled job
	YBGB	LNNL	LNNK	A4YM	LNNQ	LNNX
1999	90.9	88.9	90.6	93.6	100.9	85.3
2000	92.1	91.5	92.9	96.1	99.5	89.8
2001	94.1	94.8	96.5	97.3	100.6	92.7
2002	97.0	97.0	98.2	98.3	102.1	94.6
2003	100.0	100.0	100.0	100.0	100.0	100.0
2004	102.6	102.1	101.3	102.2	97.1	106.8
2005	104.9	105.6	103.9	103.3	97.1	110.7
2006	107.4	107.9	106.0	105.3	97.9	115.4
2000 Q4	92.5	93.0	94.5	96.8	99.1	92.0
2001 Q1	93.4	94.4	96.3	97.3	99.3	92.9
Q2	94.0	94.6	96.4	97.1	101.2	91.9
Q3	93.9	95.0	96.6	97.5	100.3	93.4
Q4	95.0	95.4	96.8	97.5	101.5	92.7
2002 Q1	96.1	96.1	97.5	98.0	101.7	93.4
Q2	96.9	97.0	98.4	97.9	102.9	93.5
Q3	97.3	97.2	98.4	98.6	101.4	95.7
Q4	97.6	97.8	98.5	98.6	102.4	95.7
2003 Q1	98.8	98.4	99.1	99.2	101.8	96.9
Q2	99.8	99.7	100.0	99.2	100.6	98.7
Q3	100.5	100.9	100.6	100.3	99.6	100.9
Q4	100.9	101.0	100.2	101.3	98.0	103.5
2004 Q1	101.1	101.2	100.3	101.4	97.3	105.2
Q2	102.4	101.6	101.0	102.3	97.2	106.5
Q3	103.0	102.0	101.4	102.5	97.2	106.9
Q4	103.9	103.5	102.5	102.7	96.6	108.6
2005 Q1	104.1	104.2	103.2	102.8	97.0	109.1
Q2	104.6	105.1	103.6	103.1	96.6	110.1
Q3	104.8	106.2	104.2	103.2	96.7	111.8
Q4	106.1	106.9	104.7	104.1	97.9	111.8
2006 Q1	106.1	107.7	105.3	104.5	98.1†	113.4
Q2	106.7	107.2	105.6	105.1	98.0	114.9
Q3	108.0	108.1	106.3	105.6	97.9	116.1
Q4	108.8	108.4	106.7	106.1	97.8	117.0
2004 Jul	..	..	..	..	98.1	105.9
Aug	..	..	..	..	97.3	106.6
Sep	..	..	..	..	96.1	108.2
Oct	..	..	..	..	97.1	107.6
Nov	..	..	..	..	96.2	109.0
Dec	..	..	..	..	96.5	109.1
2005 Jan	..	..	..	..	96.5	109.1
Feb	..	..	..	..	96.2	110.0
Mar	..	..	..	..	98.4	108.3
Apr	..	..	..	..	97.0	109.6
May	..	..	..	..	96.5	109.9
Jun	..	..	..	..	96.4	110.7
Jul	..	..	..	..	96.2	111.7
Aug	..	..	..	..	96.7	111.8
Sep	..	..	..	..	97.2	111.7
Oct	..	..	..	..	98.0	111.2
Nov	..	..	..	..	97.7	111.8
Dec	..	..	..	..	97.9	112.4
2006 Jan	..	..	..	..	98.1	112.9
Feb	..	..	..	..	98.5†	113.1
Mar	..	..	..	..	97.7	114.2
Apr	..	..	..	..	98.7	114.1
May	..	..	..	..	97.4	115.1
Jun	..	..	..	..	97.8	115.6
Jul	..	..	..	..	97.5	115.6
Aug	..	..	..	..	98.0	116.2
Sep	..	..	..	..	98.2	116.5
Oct	..	..	..	..	98.3	116.5
Nov	..	..	..	..	97.7	117.1
Dec	..	..	..	..	97.4	117.4
2007 Jan	..	..	..	..	97.4	117.6†
Feb	..	..	..	..	97.8	117.2

Note: The full productivity and unit wage costs data sets with associated articles can be found on the National Statistics website at: www.statistics.gov.uk/productivity.

1 Based on the sum of expenditure components of GDP at current and constant market prices.
2 Whole Economy output per worker is the ratio of Gross Value Added (GVA) at Basic Prices and Labour Force Survey (LFS) total employment.

Source: Office for National Statistics

53

8 Energy

8.1 Inland energy consumption: primary fuel input basis

Million tonnes of oil equivalent

| | Unadjusted | | | | | | | Seasonally adjusted and temperature corrected (annual rate | | | | | | |
| | | | | Primary electricity | | | | | | | Primary electricity | | | |
	Coal[1]	Petro-leum[2]	Natural gas[3]	Nuclear	Natural flow hydro[4]	Net imports	Total	Coal	Petro-leum	Natural gas	Nuclear[5]	Natural flow hydro[5]	Net imports[5]	Total
	BHBB	BHBC	BHBD	BHBE	BHBF	BHBM	BHBA	BHBH	BHBI	BHBJ	BHBK	BHBL	BHBN	BHBG
2001	42.5	75.9	96.6	20.8	0.4	0.9	237.0	42.9	76.4	96.7	20.8	0.4	0.9	238.1
2002	39.3	73.5	95.4	20.1	0.5	0.7	229.5	40.1	74.9	98.7	20.0	0.5	0.7	235.0
2003	42.4	73.0	95.8	20.0	0.4	0.2	231.9	43.5	74.0	97.7	20.0	0.4	0.2	235.7
2004	41.2	75.3	97.7	18.2	0.6	0.6	233.6	41.8	76.5	100.0	18.1	0.6	0.6	237.7
2005	42.4	77.0	95.1	18.4	0.7	0.7	234.3	42.7	78.0	95.5	18.4	0.7	0.7	236.0
2002 Sep	2.9	6.3	5.9	1.7	–	–	16.9	35.6	76.6	92.8	20.0	0.4	0.4	225.8
Oct	3.5	5.6	8.3	1.3	–	0.1	18.8	42.4	69.6	99.0	17.4	0.3	0.6	229.4
Nov	4.0	5.9	9.0	1.4	–	0.1	20.5	46.3	72.8	102.5	17.5	0.5	1.2	240.7
Dec	4.7	5.8	10.7	2.1	–	0.1	23.4	42.0	70.5	107.9	21.9	0.3	1.4	244.0
2003 Jan	3.7	6.3	11.6	1.8	–	0.1	23.5	40.2	74.3	110.3	20.4	0.4	0.6	246.1
Feb	4.0	6.0	10.4	1.8	–	–	22.2	45.4	74.1	107.8	21.5	0.3	0.1	248.9
Mar	4.2	6.0	9.5	2.0	–	–	21.8	43.6	69.5	106.6	21.1	0.3	0.1	241.2
Apr	3.4	6.2	7.5	1.6	–	–	18.5	45.0	82.2	94.3	20.2	0.3	0.1	242.1
May	3.0	6.0	6.7	1.6	–	–	17.1	40.3	74.4	97.2	20.2	0.7	0.3	233.1
Jun	3.3	6.3	5.2	1.9	–	–	16.8	50.1	78.9	86.3	21.5	0.5	–0.1	237.2
Jul	2.8	6.1	5.2	1.3	–	–	15.4	44.0	74.4	82.7	18.1	0.5	–	219.7
Aug	2.6	6.1	5.0	1.4	–	–	15.1	42.7	69.7	82.8	17.7	0.5	0.3	213.7
Sep	3.2	6.4	5.9	2.0	–	–	17.4	39.4	77.1	91.3	23.5	0.4	–0.6	231.1
Oct	3.9	6.2	8.5	1.4	–	–	20.1	46.7	75.9	98.2	18.5	0.3	–	239.7
Nov	3.4	5.8	9.3	1.5	–	–	20.0	39.2	70.5	104.4	17.6	0.3	0.3	232.4
Dec	4.7	6.4	10.9	1.9	0.1	0.1	24.1	41.5	77.2	110.6	19.7	0.4	1.0	250.5
2004 Jan	3.8	6.2	11.3	1.6	0.1	0.1	23.1	41.3	73.3	110.6	18.5	0.6	0.7	245.1
Feb	3.8	5.8	10.5	1.6	0.1	–	21.8	44.5	73.4	114.1	19.7	0.5	0.6	252.5
Mar	4.5	6.0	10.5	2.1	–	–	23.1	44.4	68.3	110.7	22.4	0.4	–	246.2
Apr	3.2	6.2	8.2	1.5	–	–	19.2	42.7	81.0	102.1	18.2	0.5	0.5	245.0
May	2.7	7.0	6.8	1.3	–	–	17.8	37.4	86.3	100.0	16.7	0.6	0.4	241.5
Jun	2.9	5.7	5.6	1.5	–	0.1	15.8	41.6	70.8	89.4	16.8	0.6	0.8	219.9
Jul	2.6	7.3	5.7	1.5	–	0.1	17.2	38.8	88.9	86.3	19.7	0.6	0.8	235.1
Aug	2.6	5.9	5.3	1.4	–	0.1	15.3	42.7	67.3	84.6	17.3	0.8	0.7	213.4
Sep	3.4	6.2	5.6	1.4	0.1	–	16.7	41.7	75.3	89.3	16.8	0.9	0.6	224.5
Oct	3.7	7.2	8.2	1.4	0.1	0.1	20.6	44.9	89.3	100.4	18.0	0.8	1.2	254.5
Nov	3.8	6.0	9.5	1.4	0.1	0.1	20.8	43.7	72.5	106.0	16.8	0.5	0.7	240.3
Dec	4.5	7.0	10.6	1.6	0.1	0.1	23.9	40.0	84.6	108.7	17.0	0.5	0.7	251.5
2005 Jan	4.1	6.7	11.0	1.9	0.1	0.1	23.8	45.3	81.8	111.0	21.5	0.6	0.6	260.8
Feb	4.2	5.9	10.3	1.6	–	–	22.0	48.7	66.4	108.3	19.0	0.5	0.3	243.0
Mar	4.4	6.3	9.8	1.6	0.1	–	22.3	45.0	82.0	106.9	17.4	0.6	0.6	252.5
Apr	3.3	6.7	8.4	1.4	–	–	19.9	42.7	83.1	98.9	17.6	0.6	0.6	243.5
May	2.8	6.2	7.1	1.5	–	0.1	17.8	37.9	76.7	96.0	19.1	0.8	1.0	231.5
Jun	2.9	6.5	5.5	1.6	–	0.1	16.5	42.1	80.0	84.6	17.7	0.8	0.6	225.9
Jul	2.6	6.2	5.4	1.6	–	–	15.8	39.1	70.7	80.3	21.2	0.7	0.6	212.6
Aug	2.6	6.3	5.1	1.7	–	0.1	15.7	40.2	75.3	78.2	21.2	0.7	1.0	216.7
Sep	2.9	6.7	5.8	1.3	–	–	16.8	36.2	84.9	89.7	15.9	0.8	0.4	227.8
Oct	3.3	6.1	7.1	1.3	0.1	0.1	17.9	41.0	76.4	96.0	16.6	0.8	0.9	231.8
Nov	4.4	6.9	9.4	1.4	0.1	0.1	22.3	51.9	82.2	98.1	17.3	0.7	1.0	251.2
Dec	5.1	6.5	10.3	1.6	0.1	0.1	23.6	44.0	77.1	98.3	16.8	0.5	1.0	237.7
2006 Jan	5.0	6.2	10.8	1.7	0.1	0.1	23.8	53.5	72.4	98.3	19.8	0.7	0.8	245.5
Feb	4.6	6.1	10.0	1.5	0.1	–	22.3	52.3	74.8	96.6	18.5	0.5	0.2	243.0
Mar	5.0	7.3	10.3	1.8	0.1	0.1	24.5	49.6	80.9	96.7	18.7	0.6	0.9	247.4
Apr	3.3	6.1	7.9	1.5	0.1	0.1	19.1	43.4	78.8	90.8	19.4	0.7	1.2	234.4
May	3.4	6.9	6.3	1.5	0.1	0.1	18.2	46.8	84.7	89.4	19.5	0.9	1.2	242.5
Jun	3.2	5.9	5.1	1.4	–	–	15.6	47.2	73.2	80.8	15.7	0.8	0.5	218.3
Jul	3.3	6.4	4.7	1.4	–	–	15.8	53.0	79.3	73.8	19.3	0.9	0.5	226.9
Aug	3.0	6.5	4.9	1.5	–	0.1	16.1	47.7	74.0	76.5	19.1	0.9	0.8	219.0
Sep	3.2	6.1	5.3	1.3	0.1	0.1	16.0	40.1	76.9	87.0	15.1	0.9	0.7	220.8
Oct	3.3	6.0	7.0	1.0	0.1	0.1	17.5	42.0	78.1	93.6	13.1	0.9	0.8	228.4
Nov	4.4	6.9	8.8	1.1	0.1	0.1	21.4	50.7	84.3	97.6	12.8	0.8	0.9[†]	247.2[†]
Dec	4.7	7.2	9.9	1.2	0.1	0.1	23.2	42.4	88.7	102.3	12.7	0.7	0.8[†]	247.6[†]
2007 Jan	4.6[†]	6.8[†]	10.2	1.2	0.1	0.1	23.0[†]	51.3[†]	84.0[†]	101.5	14.0	0.9	0.7	252.4
Feb	3.7	5.9	9.7	1.1	0.1	–	20.5	43.5	74.1	104.0	13.3	0.7	0.4	236.0

1 Include solid renewable sources (wood, straw and waste), geothermal and active solar heat,net foreign trade and stock changes in other solid fuels.

2 Excludes non-energy use. A statistical month adjustment has been removed.

3 Includes gas used during production, colliery methane, landfill gas and sewage gas. Excludes gas flared or re-injected and non-energy use of gas. A statistical adjustment has been removed.

4 Includes generation at wind stations. Excludes generation from pumped storage stations.

5 Not seasonally adjusted or temperature corrected.

Source: Department of Trade and Industry: 020 7215 2698

8.2 Supply and use of fuels[1]

Thousand tonnes of oil equivalent

		2005	2006	2005 Q1	2005 Q2	2005 Q3	2005 Q4	2006 Q1	2006 Q2	2006 Q3	2006 Q4
Supply											
Indigenous production	BHCE	215 447	196 637	59 891	55 269	45 865	54 421	57 011	49 090	42 355	48 181
Imports	DMNT	134 702	148 795	32 714	33 211	33 835	34 941	37 774	34 836	35 457	40 728
Exports	BHCH	−100 519	−96 290	−25 609	−27 464	−22 967	−24 479	−23 589	−25 057	−24 043	−23 602
Marine bunkers	DMNU	−2 180	−1 998	−495	−566	−600	−519	−450	−583	−487	−478
Stock change[2]	BHCI	−637	−2 273	4 721	−3 425	−4 771	2 838	3 205	−2 363	−2 665	−450
Primary supply	LURA	246 813	244 871	71 223	57 027	51 361	67 202	73 952	55 922	50 618	64 379
Statistical difference[3]	BHCO	−71	−524	145	268	−546	63	110	29	−368	−295
Primary demand	LURB	246 884	245 396	71 078	56 759	51 908	67 139	73 842	55 893	50 986	64 674
Transfers[4]	LURC	−114	752	135	−22	−33	−194	116	81	202	352
Transformation	LURD	−54 371	−55 523	−14 868	−12 781	−12 345	−14 377	−15 365	−12 485	−12 648	−15 025
Electricity generation	LURE	−51 107	−51 592	−14 150	−11 779	−11 564	−13 614	−14 557	−11 761	−11 629	−13 645
Heat generation[5]	SKYM	−867	−851	−261	−195	−169	−241	−269	−183	−158	−241
Petroleum refineries	YAPL	84	−322	135	−179	−7	134	171	138	−175	−456
Coke manufacture	YAPM	−38	−38	4	10	−24	−28	−12	−3	−25	1
Blast furnaces	YAPN	−2 455	−2 720	−598	−643	−586	−629	−698	−680	−660	−682
Patent fuel manufacture	YAPO	11	−	1	5	4	1	−1	3	−	−1
Energy industry use	YAPP	16 523	15 600	4 344	4 135	3 841	4 204	4 426	3 823	3 595	3 757
Losses	YAPQ	3 765	3 890	1 122	844	799	999	1 210	829	862	989
Final consumption	YAPR	172 111	171 136	50 878	38 976	34 891	47 366	52 956	38 837	34 087	45 256
Iron and steel	YAPS	1 762	1 781	450	457	413	443	476	460	416	429
Other industries	YAPT	31 333	31 470	9 427	7 266	6 410	8 229	10 121	7 131	6 271	7 947
Transport	YAPU	59 225	59 882	14 008	14 889	15 326	15 002	14 361	15 030	15 603	14 888
Domestic	YAPV	46 979	46 032	17 662	8 847	5 539	14 931	18 401	8 782	5 241	13 608
Public administration	YAPW	7 162	7 004	2 355	1 554	1 225	2 028	2 316	1 540	1 173	1 975
Commercial	YAPX	9 866	10 209	2 883	2 261	2 068	2 653	3 039	2 175	2 146	2 848
Agriculture	YAPY	990	954	268	221	224	277	219	236	204	295
Miscellaneous	YAPZ	2 211	2 030	726	517	347	620	771	410	283	565
Non energy use	BHCN	12 583	11 774	3 099	2 963	3 339	3 183	3 250	3 075	2 749	2 701

8.2 Supply and use of fuels[1]
continued

Thousand tonnes of oil equivalent

		2005	2006	2005 Q1	2005 Q2	2005 Q3	2005 Q4	2006 Q1	2006 Q2	2006 Q3	2006 Q4
Final consumption by user											
Iron and steel industry											
Coal and other manufactured fuels[6]	YAQA	593	..	130	149	149	165	151	155	142	162
Petroleum products	BHTF	15	..	6	2	2	5	9	–	–	3
Natural gas[7]	YAQB	723	..	206	198	153	166	207	195	165	159
Electricity	BHTE	–	..	109	107	108	108	109	109	108	106
Total[8]	YAPS	1 762	1 781	450	457	413	443	476	460	416	429
Other industries											
Coal and other manufactured fuels[6]	YAQC	1 427	..	340	330	364	393	440	396	463	505
Petroleum products	BHTM	7 051	..	2 076	1 618	1 503	1 853	2 376	1 600	1 565	2 044
Natural gas[7]	YAQD	12 067	..	4 207	2 612	1 992	3 255	4 594	2 461	1 687[†]	2 720
Renewables and waste[9]	YAQE	151	..	49	35	28	38	49	35	29	39
Electricity	BHTL	9 785	..	2 542	2 458	2 309	2 476	2 449	2 426	2 314	2 426
Total[8]	YAPT	31 333	31 470	9 427	7 266	6 410	8 229	10 121	7 131	6 271	7 947
Transport											
Petroleum products	BHTQ	58 485	..	13 824	14 705	15 140	14 815	14 177	14 840	15 424	14 699
Electricity	BHTP	740	..	184	184	186	187	185	189	179	188
Total[8]	YAPU	59 225	59 882	14 008	14 889	15 326	15 002	14 361	15 030	15 603	14 888
Domestic											
Coal and other manufactured fuels[6]	YAQF	698	..	207	158	160	172	213	177	168	184
Petroleum products	BHTW	3 093	..	1 081	560	469	983	1 090	719	484	901
Natural gas[7]	YAQG	32 836	..	13 350	5 847	2 825	10 813	13 881	5 629	2 515	9 617
Renewables and waste[9]	YAQH	256	..	96	49	27	84	96	49	27	84
Electricity	BHTV	10 044	..	2 906	2 224	2 053	2 861	3 100	2 199	2 043	2 805
Total[8]	YAPV	46 979	46 032	17 662	8 847	5 539	14 931	18 401	8 782	5 241	13 608
Other final users[10]											
Coal and other manufactured fuels[6]	YAQI	23	..	6	5	5	7	7	11	16	7
Petroleum products	BHNC	1 754	..	460	474	496	325	394	353	409	374
Natural gas[7]	YAQJ	9 170	..	3 225	1 919	1 305	2 722	3 344	1 847	1 313	2 807
Renewables and waste[9]	YAQK	193	..	68	38	21	66	68	38	21	66
Electricity	BHNB	8 683	..	2 312	2 049	2 000	2 322	2 372	2 041	2 009	2 294
Total[8]	BHND	20 229	..	6 232	4 554	3 865	5 578	6 346	4 361	3 806	5 684
Total final users	BHNE	159 527	..	47 779	36 013	31 552	44 183	49 706	35 763	31 338	42 556

1 Layout comparable with annual balances published in Table 1.1 of DUKES 2005.
2 Stock fall (+), stock rise (-).
3 Primary supply minus primary demand.
4 Annual transfers should ideally be zero. For manufactured fuels differences occur in the rescreening of coke to breeze. For oil and petroleum products differences arise due to small variations in the calorific values used.
5 Generation of heat for sale under the provision of a contract.

6 Includes all manufactured solid fuels, benzole, tars, coke oven gas and blast furnace gas.
7 Includes colliery methane.
8 Includes heat sold.
9 Includes geothermal and solar heat. Latest quarter is estimated from the previous year and adjusted according to average annual rate of change over the last three years.
10 Includes public administration, commercial, agriculture and miscellaneous use.

Source: Department of Trade and Industry: 020 7215 2698

8.3 Coal supply

Thousand tonnes

	Production			Net imports	Imports[2]	Exports
	Deep-mined	Opencast	Total[1]			
	BHDC	BHDD	BHDB	BHDE	BHDF	BHDG
2002	16 391	13 148	29 989	28 149	28 686	537
2003	15 633	12 126	28 279	31 349	31 891	543
2004	12 542	11 993	25 096	35 531	36 153	622
2005	9 563	10 445	20 498	43 433	43 968	536
2006	9 439	8 635	18 588	49 776	50 256	480
2005 Sep	1 130	1 013	2 193	3 722	3 764	41
Oct	961	813	1 822	4 002	4 039	37
Nov	967	736	1 737	4 486	4 533	47
Dec	1 271	862	2 183	3 316	3 346	29
2006 Jan	1 029	526	1 588	4 055	4 090	35
Feb	995	833	1 871	4 019	4 056	37
Mar	1 048	1 012	2 108	4 325	4 361	37
Apr	761	679	1 477	3 894	3 948	54
May	840	757	1 640	3 928	3 951	23
Jun	940	860	1 848	3 974	4 017	42
Jul	615	497	1 154	4 469	4 509	40
Aug	326	566	929	4 087	4 105	18
Sep	692	813	1 554	3 889	3 916	27
Oct	735	717	1 501	4 134	4 219	85
Nov	754	704	1 511	4 647	4 691	44
Dec	703	672	1 406	4 356	4 393	37
2007 Jan	600	491	1 123	5 170†	5 267†	98
Feb	561	723	1 326	3 753	3 790	37

1 Includes an estimate for slurry.
2 Figures are as recorded in the Overseas Trade Statistics of the United Kingdom (OTS) except that import and export figures for recent months are estimated on the basis of information available for the extra-EC trade until monthly statistics for Intra-EC trade become available from HM Revenue and Customs.

Source: Department of Trade and Industry: 020 7215 2698

8.4 Inland use and stocks of coal
Stocks: end of period

Thousand tonnes

	Inland use									
		Fuel producers (consumption)				Final users[1]				
			Secondary							
	Primary: collieries	Electricity generators[2]	Heat generation[3]	Coke ovens	Other conversion industries[4]	Industry[5]	Domestic[5,6]	Other[5,7]	Total inland consumption	Stocks[8]
	BHEB	BHEC	SKYY	BHED	BHEE	BHEF	BHEG	BHEI	BHEA	BHEJ
2002	9	47 741	717	6 533	436	1 809	1 285	22	58 552	2 482
2003	6	52 463	622	6 612	396	1 856	1 042	24	63 021	1 624
2004	8	50 444	478	6 382	327	1 846	941	22	60 447	1 192
2005	6	52 084	453	6 603	266	1 791	614	34	61 850	1 101
2006	4	57 685	483†	7 049	276	1 994	676	57	68 225	830
2005 Sep	–	3 156	39	677	27	193	55	3	4 150	942
Oct	–	3 925	35	534	19	177	39	3	4 733	973
Nov	–	5 681	35	534	17	135	44	5	6 451	1 065
Dec	1	6 672	44	664	30	187	67	3	7 668	1 101
2006 Jan	–	6 609	42	538	27	155	58	4	7 432	1 060
Feb	1	6 020	42	513	23	180	61	4	6 843	1 080
Mar	–	6 499	50	674	28	174	67	3	7 495	1 040
Apr	–	4 075	35	550	23	137	39	6	4 865	1 046
May	–	4 123	35	537	24	144	60	4	4 928	992
Jun	–	3 537	43	675	26	142	57	5	4 487	1 000
Jul	–	3 899	31	568	20	162	46	10	4 737	879
Aug	–	3 469	31	542	22	179	55	11	4 309	813
Sep	–	3 562	39	676	31	167	53	2	4 530	969
Oct	1	4 083	42	553	16	173	53	1	4 921	1 091
Nov	–	5 829	42	540	20	187	57	6	6 681	920
Dec	1	5 980	52	682	17	194	69	2	6 997	830
2007 Jan	–	5 893	32	679	21	115	46†	2	6 789†	880†
Feb	1	4 504	32	547	20	185	51	4	5 345	908

1 Coal-fired power stations belonging to major electricity generating companies.
2 Low temperature carbonisation and patent fuel plants.
3 Includes estimated proportion of total imports.

4 Including miners' coal.
5 Disposals by colleries and open cast sites.
6 Includes public administration and commerce.
7 From 1999 includes heat generation.

Source: Department of Trade and Industry: 020 7215 2698

8.5 Natural gas production and supply

Gigawatt hours

	Upstream gas industry						Downstream gas industry					Percentage of net gas available for consumption in the UK	
			Less		Plus			Less					
	Gross gas production[1]	Producers own use[2]	Exports[3]	Stock change and other net losses	Imports	Gas available at terminals[4]	Gas input into transmission system[5]	Operators own use	Stock changes	Metering differences	Gas output from transmission system[6]	Indigenous	Imported
	BAWX	DMUE	BAWY	DMUF	BAWZ	BAXA	DMUG	DMUH	DMUI	DMUJ	BAXD	BAXB	BAXC
2002	1 204 713	79 364	150 731	–	60 493	1 036 738	1 035 236	7 017	7 356	1 821	1 019 042	94.0	5.8
2003	1 196 117	76 839	177 039	–	86 298	1 028 538	1 029 922	7 828	–3 492	–1 280	1 026 866	91.6	8.4
2004	1 115 744	76 899	114 111	–	133 035	1 057 769	1 059 307	6 560	6 235	137	1 046 375	87.4	12.6
2005	1 017 813	73 652	96 181	–	173 328	1 021 308	1 023 472	6 555	–1 321	2 880	1 015 358	83.0	17.0
2006	929 783	69 245	120 591	–	244 031	983 978	983 831	5 831	6 435	4 544	967 021	75.2	24.8
2006 Mar	96 770	6 576	5 868	–	25 342	109 668	109 637	643	–2 955	350	111 599	76.9	23.1
Apr	85 780	6 184	9 847	–	16 296	86 045	86 024	476	1 217	270	84 061	81.1	18.9
May	76 390	5 719	15 087	–	12 242	67 826	67 820	389	1 431	379	65 621	82.0	18.0
Jun	65 648	5 257	10 660	–	6 584	56 315	56 310	247	3 508	436	52 119	88.3	11.7
Jul	58 952	5 242	13 588	–	13 649	53 771	53 742	479	5 740	475	47 048	74.6	25.4
Aug	59 561	4 759	11 466	–	13 822	57 158	57 119	353	5 759	365	50 642	75.8	24.2
Sep	68 156	5 274	16 623	–	12 353	58 612	58 581	481	3 107	502	54 491	78.9	21.1
Oct	74 762†	5 582	13 726	–	21 876	77 330	77 359	379	2 243	354	74 383	71.7	28.3
Nov	77 660	5 934†	7 146	–	30 551	95 131	95 103	481	–75	342	94 355	67.9	32.1
Dec	77 617	6 114	6 342	–	40 730	105 891	105 860	543	–2 749	368	107 698	61.5	38.5
2007 Jan	80 441	5 698	6 959	–	39 245†	107 029	107 056	529	–5 010	462	111 075	63.3	36.7
Feb	72 687	5 265	6 347	..	38 273	99 348	99 284	597	–7 534	392	105 829	61.5	38.5

1 Includes waste and own use but excludes gas flared.
2 Gas used for drilling, production and pumping operations.
3 Includes exports direct from the UKCS as well as others carried out by the downstream gas industry from the national transmission system.
4 Gas available at terminals for consumption in the UK as recorded by the terminal operators.
5 Gas input into inland transmission systems. It includes public gas supply, direct supply by North Sea producers, third party supplies, and stock changes. Figures differ from gas available for consumption in the UK mainly because of additional stock changes at local distribution zones. The figures also differ from total consumption (expressed in oil equivalent in Table 8.1) because they exclude producers' and operators' own use and losses.
6 Including public gas supply, direct supplies by North Sea producers, third party supplies and stock changes.

Source: Department of Trade and Industry: 020 7215 2698

8.6 Fuel used by and electricity production and availability from the electricity supply industry[1]

	Million tonnes of oil equivalent					Terawatt hours							
	Fuel used							Electricity supplied by type of plant					Total electricity available[7]
	Coal[2]	Gas[2]	Nuclear electricity	Hydro-electricity	Total[3]	Electricity generated	Own use[4]	Conventional Thermal[5]	Combined Cycle Gas Turbine	Nuclear	Other[6]	Total	
	FTAJ	WSFA	FTAL	FTAM	FTAN	BHJF	BHJJ	FTAB	BAYK	FTAC	FTAD	BHJK	BHJL
2002	28.62	25.04	20.10	0.34	75.07	354.00	19.21	128.80	121.89	81.09	3.81	334.78	350.75
2003	31.57	24.48	20.04	0.22	77.34	362.60	20.29	140.20	118.55	81.91	2.71	342.31	356.39
2004	30.37	26.18	18.16	0.34	76.18	358.41	19.09	133.61	128.98	73.68	4.42	339.33	357.77
2005	31.65	25.42	18.37	0.34	77.43	362.10	19.69	136.00	128.18	75.17	5.65	342.41	361.26
2006	34.92†	23.78	16.92	0.32	77.81†	360.75†	21.04†	150.67†	116.26	69.24	3.89	339.72†	360.43†
2006 Mar	3.96	1.60	1.75	0.02	7.66	34.99	2.21	17.15	8.22	7.18	0.27	32.78	34.66
Apr	2.46	190.00†	1.55	0.03	6.02	28.28	1.57	10.86	9.19	6.34	0.37	26.71	28.83
May	2.49	1.79	1.52	0.02	5.93	27.58	1.62	10.74	8.71	6.23	0.30	25.96	28.00
Jun	2.10	2.01	1.38	0.01	5.59	26.37	1.53	9.32	9.74	5.63	0.18	24.84	26.23
Jul	2.36	1.97	1.43	0.01	5.88	27.48	1.71	10.31	9.52	5.84	0.11	25.77	27.17
Aug	2.09	1.95	1.52	0.01	5.64	26.55	1.58	9.03	9.65	6.21	0.11	24.97	26.62
Sep	2.12	2.26	1.27	0.02	5.75	27.13	1.53	9.10	11.03	5.19	0.27	25.60	27.14
Oct	2.47	2.59	0.99	0.03	6.25	29.10	1.58	10.72	12.36	4.04	0.38	27.52	29.31
Nov	3.56	2.15	1.05	0.04	6.97	31.73	1.76	15.16	9.98	4.32	0.54	29.96	31.94
Dec	3.64	2.17	1.20	0.05	7.20	33.46	1.83	15.46	10.65	4.90	0.68	31.63	33.59†
2007 Jan	3.62	2.19	1.23	0.05	7.24	34.05	1.84	15.56	10.99†	5.03	0.69	32.21	34.11
Feb	2.75	2.48	1.10	0.04	6.50	30.39	1.60	11.65	12.26	4.49	0.45	28.79	30.25

1 Fuel used and electricity generated by major power producers(National Power , PowerGen, Nuclear Electric, National Grid Company, Scottish Power, Hydro Electric, Scottish Nuclear, NIGEN, Coolkeeragh Power Ltd, Ballyumford Power Ltd, Midlands Electricity, South Western Electricity, Teeside Power Ltd, Lakeland Power Ltd, Fibropower Ltd, Corby Power Ltd, Peterborough Power Ltd , Fibrogen Ltd, and Regional Power Ltd) and electricity available through the grid in England and Wales and from distribution companies in Scotland and Northern Ireland.
2 Includes quantities used in the production of steam for sale.
3 Including oil used in gas turbine and diesel plant and for lighting up coal -fired boilers and orimulsion.
4 Including windpower, refuse-derived fuel, natural gas and sour gas .
5 Used in works and for pumping at pumped storage stations.
6 Coal Oil (including Orimulsion) and mixed or dual-fired (including gas).
7 Including gas turbine, diesel, wind and hydro-electric plant.

Source: Department of Trade and Industry: 020 7215 2698

8.7 Sales by the gas and public electricity supply systems

	Gas: Gigawatt hours							Electricity: Terawatt hours			
	Electricity generators[1]	Heat generation[2]	Iron and steel industry	Other industries	Domestic	Other[2]	Total	Industrial[3]	Domestic	Other[4]	Total
	BBKF	WSFM	BBKG	BBKH	BBKI	BBKJ	BBKK	FTAE	FTAG	FTAH	FTAI
2002	329 442	22 010	8 791	156 285	376 372	100 833	993 733	101.59	114.52	103.68	319.80
2003	323 926[†]	19 830	10 327[†]	155 814[†]	386 488	106 737	1 003 118[†]	103.33	115.76	105.23	324.33[†]
2004	340 516[†]	19 886	9 716	143 894	396 411	112 065	1 022 488	103.24	115.52	104.95[†]	323.72[†]
2005	333 245	20 671	8 412	140 270	381 879	106 653	991 131	105.88	116.81	106.37	329.08
2006	308 159	20 671	8 443	133 236	368 000[†]	108 289[†]	946 798	105.03[†]	117.80[†]	107.49	330.32
2002 Q4	80 858	6 416	2 121	43 313	128 269	28 654	289 631	25.57	32.57	26.72	84.87
2003 Q1	79 391	6 582	2 678	50 535	157 739	35 445	332 370	26.72	34.48	27.00	88.20
Q2	76 333	4 055	2 597	36 710	62 659	22 532	204 885	25.88	25.00	25.31	76.19
Q3	82 069	3 300	2 339	27 391	34 288	12 661	162 047	25.31	22.81	24.74	72.87
Q4	86 133	5 893	2 713	41 178	131 802	36 099	303 816	25.42	33.47	28.18	87.07
2004 Q1	83 746	6 258	2 573	50 138	159 663	39 538	341 915	27.86	35.18	27.62	90.66
Q2	81 929	4 287	2 559	31 557	66 867	23 158	210 358	24.52	23.81	24.16	72.49
Q3	85 684	3 659	2 248	23 175	37 341	15 555	167 662	25.73	22.42	25.35	73.51
Q4	89 157	5 682	2 336	39 024	132 540	33 814	302 553	25.13	34.11	27.82	87.06
2005 Q1	79 412	6 408	2 392	48 909	155 265	37 505	329 890	27.41	33.80	28.28	89.49
Q2	86 111	4 513	2 307	30 364	68 004	22 312	213 612	26.67	25.87	25.22	77.77
Q3	89 410	3 854	1 785	23 154	32 854	15 174	166 232	24.94	23.87	24.57	73.39
Q4	78 312	5 896	1 928	37 843	125 756	31 662	281 397	26.86	33.27	28.30	88.43
2006 Q1	66 495	6 408	2 408	53 416	161 441	38 893	329 060	26.56	36.05	29.26[†]	91.87[†]
Q2	73 948	4 513	2 273	28 603	65 469	21 483	196 288	26.47	25.57	25.21	77.25
Q3	78 978	3 854	1 917[†]	19 603[†]	29 250[†]	15 271[†]	148 874[†]	25.43	23.76[†]	24.62	73.81
Q4	88 738	5 896	1 845	31 614	111 840	32 642	272 576	26.57[†]	32.42[†]	28.40	87.39

1 Power stations belonging to major generating companies, industrial establishments and transport undertakings generating 1 gigawatt or more a year.
2 Public administration, commerce and agriculture.

3 Manufacturing industry, construction, energy and water supply industries
4 Commercial premises, public administration, transport and agriculture.

Source: Department of Trade and Industry: 020 7215 2698

8.8 Indigenous production, refinery receipts, arrivals and shipments of oil[1]

	Million tonnes			Thousand tonnes									
	Indigenous production			Refinery receipts		Foreign trade[2] [7]							
						Net imports/ exports[6] [8]	Crude oil and NGLs		Process oils		Petroleum products		
	Crude oil	NGLs	Total[3]	Total receipts[4] [8]	Indige-nous[5]		Imports	Exports	Imports	Exports	Imports	Exports	Bunkers[7]
	BHMB	BHML	BHMA	G8GZ	BHMC	G8H2	BHMF	BHMG	BHMM	BHMH	BHMI	BHMJ	BHMK
2002	107.4	8.5	115.9	85 512	28 544	–38 720	52 042	85 028	4 926	2 116	14 900	23 444	1 913
2003	97.8	8.2	106.1	85 006	30 829	–27 571	48 589	72 526	5 588	2 372	16 472	23 323	1 764
2004	87.5	7.9	95.4	90 021	27 505	–13 712	55 858	63 412	6 659	1 091	18 545	30 270	2 085
2005	77.2	7.5	84.7	86 096	27 210	–2 424	52 211	52 106	6 675	1 992	22 511	29 722	2 055
2006	69.7	6.9	76.6	87 473	29 007	6 575	51 134	47 553	7 333	2 643	26 260	27 955	1 887
2005 Dec	6.5	0.6	7.0	6 960	2 582	–871	3 891	4 545	487	230	2 117	2 590	155
2006 Jan	6.8	0.6	7.4	7 564	3 117	149	3 875	4 341	572	182	2 262	2 038	153
Feb	5.9	0.6	6.5	6 362	2 223	192	3 735	3 650	404	180	2 097	2 214	121
Mar	6.4	0.6	7.0	7 249	2 077	100	4 672	5 270	501	173	2 486	2 115	149
Apr	6.1	0.6	6.7	7 216	2 330	393	4 256	4 395	630	373	2 232	1 956	170
May	6.0	0.6	6.5	7 570	1 807	1 357	5 047	3 882	717	193	2 090	2 422	196
Jun	5.3	0.6	5.9	6 852	2 313	–298	3 934	3 994	605	279	1 957	2 520	183
Jul	5.8	0.5	6.3	7 904	2 417	555	4 904	4 067	582	183	1 816	2 499	147
Aug	4.8	0.5	5.2	7 482	2 197	1 283	4 722	3 050	563	230	1 843	2 564	158
Sep	5.2	0.5	5.7	7 286	2 845	813	3 937	3 654	503	186	2 428	2 216	155
Oct	5.9	0.6	6.5	7 353	2 762	835	3 816	3 545	774	321	2 598	2 487	182
Nov	5.8	0.6	6.4	7 107	2 334	797	3 968	3 770	805	146	2 365	2 425	135
Dec	5.8	0.6	6.4	7 529	2 585	400	4 267	3 936	677	196	2 087	2 498	136
2007 Jan	6.0	0.6	6.6	7 266[†]	2 617	150[†]	4 019[†]	3 837[†]	630	168	1 951[†]	2 444	157
Feb	6.0	0.6	6.5	6 639	2 968	–162	3 137	3 667	533	220	2 126	2 071	111

1 The term indigenous is used in this table for convenience to include oil from the UK Continental Shelf as well as the small amounts produced on the mainland.
2 Foreign trade as recorded by the petroleum industry and may differ from figures published in the *Overseas Trade Statistics*.
3 Crude oil *plus* condensates and petroleum gases derived at onshore treatment plants.
4 Crude oil, natural gas liquids (NGLs) and process oils (i.e. partly refined oils).
5 Crude oil *plus* NGLs.

6 Net imports (+) or net exports (-) of oil and oil products.
7 From January 2000 arrivals of petroleum products and marine bunkers contain estimated additions to allow for (temporarily) missing imports data.
8 There have been some modest changes made to this table following the review announced by DTI in the June 2006 edition of *Energy Trends*. The review was aimed at improving data coherency and coverage between the different quarterly and monthly DTI tables. The 'net foreign imports' column has been replaced by 'total net imports/exports' and now covers oil 'total receipts' column for refinery receipts introduced instead.

Source: Department of Trade and Industry: 020 7215 2698

8.9 Deliveries of petroleum products for inland consumption

Thousand tonnes

	Butane and propane[1]	Other Petroleum Gases[2][6]	Naphtha (LDF)[6]	Motor Spirit[6]	Kerosene		Gas/diesel oil		Fuel oil[3]	Bitumen	Lubricating oils	Total[4]
					Aviation turbine fuel	Burning Oil[6]	Derv fuel	Other[5][6]				
	BHOB	G8GX	G8GY	BHOD	BHOE	BHOG	BHOI	BHOJ	BHOK	BHOL	BHOM	BHOA
2002	2 553	2 181	1 592	20 808	10 519	3 578	16 926	6 099	1 723	2 002	829	70 557
2003	3 019	2 114	2 332	19 919	10 764	3 567	17 712	6 326	1 540	1 959	868	71 698
2004	3 115	1 918	2 029	19 484	11 862	3 948	18 514	6 023	2 064	1 991	914	73 867
2005	3 554	2 021	1 916	18 731	12 497	3 869	19 436	6 797	1 965	1 906	750	75 375
2006	3 342†	1 988†	2 327	18 469†	12 444†	4 137†	20 499†	6 137†	2 245†	1 653	549†	75 616†
2005 Aug	312	154	175	1 501	1 244	206	1 564	606	201	183	64	6 343
Sep	288	157	191	1 584	1 136	243	1 639	568	180	171	70	6 405
Oct	320	171	206	1 497	1 054	253	1 629	549	131	162	56	6 204
Nov	329	167	114	1 590	831	471	1 774	585	159	171	60	6 364
Dec	276	173	140	1 694	1 094	505	1 579	589	183	129	51	6 622
2006 Jan	332	185†	261	1 556	837	457	1 687	559	177	108	68	6 340†
Feb	268	163	190	1 430	783	423	1 581	497	258	130	53	5 856
Mar	391	177	288	1 612	1 021	544	1 828	604	257	178	52	7 116
Apr	307	178	117	1 541	865	354	1 634	407	145	135	35	5 877
May	340	165	274	1 541	1 092	411	1 725	382	213	156	42	6 507
Jun	330†	142	180	1 462	1 329	157	1 711	490	122	169	47	6 331
Jul	308	138	136	1 594	1 112	134	1 716	548	150	109	45	6 194
Aug	210	149	133	1 553	1 272	225	1 692	570	143	138	45	6 259
Sep	193	193	172	1 552	1 130	237	1 776	578	126†	144	35	6 329
Oct	162	171	272	1 573	1 073	350	1 813	484†	235	146	52	6 460
Nov	254	167	150	1 519	971	412	1 827	527	211	131	43	6 352
Dec	248	159	171†	1 538†	960†	432†	1 508†	491	209	108†	33†	5 995
2007 Jan	322	189	226	1 424	1 102	429	1 748	497	278	97	37	6 498
Feb	268	130	233	1 390	918	438	1 615	494	178	139	39	6 052

1 Including amounts for petro-chemicals.
2 Ethane and other petroleum gases (OPG)
3 Excluding Orimulsion and refinery fuel.
4 Including other petroleum gases, aviation spirit, wide-cut gasoline, industrial and white spirits, petroleum wax, non-domestic standard burning oil and miscellaneous products, but excluding refinery fuel.
5 Includes gas oil, marine diesel oil and middle distillate feedstock.

6 There have been some modest changes made to this table following the review announced by DTI in the June 2006 edition of *Energy Trends*. The review was aimed to improve data coherency and coverage between the different quarterly and monthly DTI tables. Other petroleum gases are now shown. Middle distillate feedstock is now included with other gas/diesel oil rather than previously being combined with naphtha. Unleaded motor spirit and premier burning oil have been discontinued.

Source: Department of Trade and Industry: 020 7215 2698

9 Chemicals

9.1 Fertilisers

Thousand tonnes

| | Deliveries to UK agriculture[1] | | | | | |
| | Straight | | Compounds[2] | | | |
	Nitrogen total weight	Nitrogen[2] six monthly	Nitrogen six monthly	P_2O_5 (phosphate) six monthly	K_2O (potash) six monthly	Compounds[3] total weight
	BIAI	DMYC	DMYD	DMYE	DMYF	DMYG
2002 Jan	131.2	..	..	..	..	201.3
Feb	120.9	..	..	..	..	255.2
Mar	159.2	..	..	..	..	402.3
Apr	176.8	..	..	..	..	420.2
May	81.8	..	..	..	..	204.2
Jun	49.8	229.7	294.0	144.9	185.5	108.3
Jul	147.3	..	..	..	..	112.8
Aug	234.2	..	..	..	..	123.8
Sep	152.1	..	..	..	..	156.7
Oct	140.6	..	..	..	..	128.2
Nov	161.1	..	..	..	..	100.3
Dec	140.1	96.2	310.8	72.1	82.9	117.8
2003 Jan	180.1	..	..	..	..	190.0
Feb	175.1	..	..	..	..	280.6
Mar	213.2	..	..	..	..	416.8
Apr	152.3	..	..	..	..	339.3
May	89.5	..	..	..	..	182.5
Jun	59.2	256.5	280.7	136.7	172.1	117.2
Jul	160.0	..	..	..	..	93.3
Aug	188.5	..	..	..	..	144.6
Sep	175.5	..	..	..	..	160.6
Oct	195.9	..	..	..	..	175.3
Nov	181.7	..	..	..	..	145.2
Dec	157.3	350.2	147.1	96.6	106.5	136.8
2004 Jan	186.2	..	..	..	..	173.0
Feb	149.1	..	..	..	..	219.9
Mar	156.6	..	..	..	..	293.4
Apr	148.0	..	..	..	..	258.2
May	69.1	..	..	..	..	174.1
Jun	55.9	..	..	..	..	102.4
Jul	333.2	..	..	..	..	95.8
Aug	147.4	..	..	..	..	111.1
Sep	136.1	..	..	..	..	137.8
Oct	150.8	..	..	..	..	136.9
Nov	176.3	..	..	..	..	169.4
Dec	132.5	..	..	..	..	154.8
2005 Jan	159.0	..	..	..	..	149.1
Feb	147.3	..	..	..	..	155.4
Mar	193.9	..	..	..	..	251.4
Apr	169.7	..	..	..	..	253.1
May	73.4	..	..	..	..	182.4
Jun	53.9	..	..	..	..	140.4
Jul	288.7	..	..	..	..	87.8
Aug	210.2	..	..	..	..	127.6
Sep	179.7	..	..	..	..	143.1
Oct	188.6	..	..	..	..	126.8
Nov	169.1	..	..	..	..	116.8
Dec	119.8	..	..	..	..	108.9

1 Deliveries by F.M.A. members only for years ended 30 June.
2 Nutrient content.
3 Total weight of compound fertilisers.

Sources: HMRC;
Agricultural Industries Confederation

9.2 Sulphur and sulphuric acid

Production and consumption: monthly averages or calendar months; stocks: end of period

Thousand tonnes

| | Sulphur and other materials used for sulphuric acid manufacture | | | | Sulphuric acid (as 100 per cent acid) | |
| | Consumption | | Stocks | | | |
	Sulphur	Zinc concentrates[1]	Sulphur	Zinc concentrates[1]	Production	Consumption
	BIBA	BIBC	BIBD	BIBH	BIBF	BIBG
1998	30.9	14.6	75.6	34.0	95.4	95.6
1999	26.4	17.1	100.1	26.8	87.0	90.0
2000	27.0	13.2	113.5	21.2	88.2	88.9
2001	23.1	15.8	113.6	19.8	78.8	78.0
2002	14.2	15.7	106.7	24.7	52.7	55.6
1999 Mar	27.7	19.8	93.8	25.8	92.5	99.7
Apr	26.6	17.9	97.3	24.1	90.8	84.2
May	24.4	23.2	90.1	32.8	84.9	97.5
Jun	30.1	14.2	100.9	24.3	96.0	90.2
Jul	23.0	11.9	101.4	28.9	76.4	82.8
Aug	30.2	20.3	108.6	24.0	93.4	93.6
Sep	26.3	12.0	104.1	23.1	81.8	85.6
Oct	24.3	12.4	113.9	26.5	80.8	72.0
Nov	29.5	18.7	107.5	23.5	94.9	96.6
Dec	25.7	11.2	108.8	26.8	86.3	85.6
2000 Jan	27.6	12.0	115.0	26.3	90.3	77.6
Feb	26.1	16.0	106.7	23.8	85.1	91.5
Mar	30.2	17.0	113.4	20.7	97.7	103.0
Apr	25.2	11.3	106.7	21.2	82.7	78.0
May	27.4	16.7	114.6	19.0	89.6	100.2
Jun	27.8	13.8	107.6	19.8	92.1	94.3
Jul	25.2	13.2	113.7	21.5	84.7	87.4
Aug	28.8	13.5	120.5	19.0	90.9	93.2
Sep	29.3	11.7	114.8	19.5	93.3	92.2
Oct	28.1	11.6	115.9	19.5	91.6	84.7
Nov	26.0	10.4	119.1	20.3	83.9	85.1
Dec	22.4	10.6	114.1	24.2	75.9	79.1
2001 Jan	26.4	16.9	111.9	22.7	90.5	87.1
Feb	24.2	17.0	104.6	14.5	76.2	73.9
Mar	26.1	9.5	112.2	18.3	85.3	80.1
Apr	26.4	10.7	115.5	22.2	88.7	84.6
May	23.3	13.5	120.1	19.8	75.8	71.9
Jun	29.2	18.2	116.8	17.8	101.6	103.0
Jul	19.3	19.4	118.6	16.5	71.4	82.7
Aug	20.4	13.5	114.7	21.8	74.2	57.4
Sep	26.2	14.6	113.2	21.7	86.2	111.6
Oct	17.1	16.6	111.7	23.6	62.7	48.8
Nov	23.3	22.7	112.3	19.3	80.3	75.4
Dec	14.8	16.6	111.5	19.6	52.7	59.6
2002 Jan	12.0	17.6	107.7	24.7	50.7	55.1
Feb	13.0	14.6	106.9	24.7	49.1	60.5
Mar	21.6	11.0	107.6	24.7	73.2	63.8
Apr	23.9	12.2	107.1	24.7	79.5	92.4
May	10.7	19.7	106.3	24.7	48.2	54.8
Jun	11.7	17.4	106.4	24.7	43.8	51.4
Jul	12.8	15.5	106.6	24.7	48.0	51.0
Aug	12.6	21.7	106.9	24.7	55.1	51.6
Sep	14.0	15.4	106.2	24.7	49.7	42.2
Oct	13.0	16.5	105.9	24.7	44.7	62.3
Nov	12.4	15.0	106.2	24.7	46.1	32.1
Dec	12.7	11.7	106.4	24.7	43.8	49.5
2003 Jan	12.8	11.8	107.4	22.0	42.1	42.4
Feb	13.1	..	107.3	..	32.8	43.4
Mar	13.5	..	106.9	..	35.9	38.8
Apr	13.3	..	107.3	..	34.4	31.8
May	13.7	..	107.5	..	36.1	41.2
Jun	14.1	..	106.7	..	37.0	36.0
Jul	11.6	..	107.5	..	29.1	25.9
Aug	13.3	..	107.1	..	36.4	42.5
Sep	13.5	..	107.2	..	35.2	42.7
Oct	16.7	..	107.5	..	33.8	37.8

1 From February 2003 these data are no longer available.

Source: National Sulphuric Acid Association

9.3 Basic chemicals, pesticides and other agro-chemical products[1]
Total UK manufacturers' sales by industry

£ Thousand

	Industrial gases	Dyes & pigments	Inorganic basic chemicals	Organic basic chemicals	Fertilisers & nitrogen compounds	Plastics	Synthetic rubber in primary forms	Pesticides & other agro-chemical products
Subclass (SIC 92)	24110	24120	24130	24140	24150	24160	24170	24200
	CKOM	CKON	CKOO	CKOP	CKOQ	CKOR	CKOS	CKOT
2002	508 320	1 021 589	1 108 953	5 448 893	699 232	3 426 657	..	483 274
2003	524 737	971 120	1 080 555	5 163 343	811 258	3 473 664	..	474 365
2004	528 194	935 693	1 089 852	5 824 800	786 130	3 739 668	..	470 069
2001 Q3	132 579	258 550	289 580	1 367 720	127 572	824 128	72 462	231 030
Q4	129 962	251 056	271 589	1 210 807	115 304	832 475	69 143	164 652
2002 Q1	126 078	271 288	276 965	1 444 131	240 384	804 568	75 699	142 921
Q2	129 957	267 774	291 208	1 345 502	187 600	941 368	72 897	136 247
Q3	127 322	252 441	275 448	1 469 071	135 047	863 006	80 677	99 130
Q4	124 962	230 087	265 332	1 190 189	136 202	817 716	..	104 976
2003 Q1	129 010	257 201	272 810	1 467 524	257 992	888 288	..	133 160
Q2	130 647	258 344	274 693	1 259 769	196 925	896 333	..	129 173
Q3	134 298	235 323	273 321	1 262 444	168 185	857 837	..	107 031
Q4	130 782	220 252	259 731	1 173 606	188 155	831 206	..	105 001
2004 Q1	135 245	241 672	276 144	1 581 316	253 383	935 744	..	135 681
Q2	133 256	251 657	271 560	1 557 527	190 625	970 095	..	132 577
Q3	128 752	229 504	265 429	1 380 591	168 019	928 094	..	96 243
Q4	130 941	212 860	276 719	1 305 366	174 103	905 735	..	105 568

1 As from the end of 2004, quarterly data will not be collected for these industries. Annual results for the years 2005 onwards will be published on the ONS website at http://www.statistics.gov.uk/ as and when available.

Source: Office for National Statistics: 01633 813395

9.4 Pharmaceutical products, soaps and other cleaning preparations and perfumes[1]
Total UK manufacturers' sales by industry

£ Thousand

	Pharmaceutical products			Perfumes and essential oils	
	Basic products	Preparations	Soap & detergents, cleaning & polishing preparations	Perfumes & toilet preparations	Essential oils
Subclass (SIC 92)	24410	24420	24510	24520	24630
	CKOU	CKOV	CKOW	CKOX	CKOY
2002	867 982	8 318 855	1 886 334	2 377 369	548 137
2003	748 613	9 230 833	1 718 431	2 313 845	..
2004	733 658	8 760 908	1 804 671	2 171 087	..
2001 Q3	157 878	1 996 266	493 958	686 084	137 590
Q4	192 833	2 244 546	498 112	692 288	141 500
2002 Q1	229 737	2 066 964	494 464	550 720	135 312
Q2	216 451	2 098 634	480 091	575 818	139 684
Q3	230 131	2 123 729	493 566	605 893	..
Q4	191 663	2 029 527	418 214	644 938	..
2003 Q1	193 191	2 160 693	409 896	563 410	136 823
Q2	203 869	2 285 852	423 457	552 000	140 092
Q3	171 582	2 326 716	469 822	581 783	..
Q4	179 971	2 457 573	415 255	616 652	..
2004 Q1	224 562	2 288 169	445 503	520 673	..
Q2	174 383	2 131 549	455 364	550 685	..
Q3	163 555	2 157 741	459 350	542 423	..
Q4	171 158	2 183 449	444 454	557 306	..

1 As from the end of 2004, quarterly data will not be collected for these industries. Annaul results for the years 2005 onwards will be published on the ONS website at http://www.statistics.gov.uk/ as and when available.

Source: Office for National Statistics: 01633 813395

Chemicals

9.5 Other chemical products[1]
Total UK manufacturers' sales by industry

£ Thousand

	Paints, varnishes, & similar coatings; printing ink, mastic & sealants	Explosives	Glues & gelatines	Photographic chemical materials	Prepared unrecorded media	Other chemical products	Man made fibres
Subclass (SIC 92)	24300	24610	24620	24640	24650	24660	24700
	CKOZ	CKPA	CKPB	CKPC	CKPD	CKUX	CKUY
2002	2 725 613	..	357 805	305 373	124 354	1 941 449	601 807
2003	2 792 607	105 579	371 321	316 808	127 414	1 768 073	618 236
2004	2 775 868	109 706	400 400	249 915	75 297	1 992 133	586 931
2001 Q3	639 252	30 601	93 998	83 654	..	496 398	146 061
Q4	600 333	30 679	87 721	72 319	26 762	511 098	139 144
2002 Q1	663 064	..	91 933	73 174	28 553	503 830	152 738
Q2	700 851	23 388	88 789	77 156	32 122	491 787	166 738
Q3	717 210	21 454	91 637	76 799	28 940	492 446	154 579
Q4	644 487	25 649	85 446	78 244	34 740	453 386	127 751
2003 Q1	699 164	24 431	95 886	81 095	32 666	436 132	151 992
Q2	734 341	26 225	91 215	80 446	34 179	427 189	164 116
Q3	717 652	28 047	95 086	79 738	32 200	452 312	157 736
Q4	641 449	26 877	89 134	75 529	28 369	452 440	144 393
2004 Q1	685 386	25 221	100 975	65 487	26 612	501 207	160 128
Q2	712 036	27 150	95 564	63 485	..	497 776	145 842
Q3	731 486	27 665	105 216	61 747	..	486 379	144 281
Q4	646 960	29 670	98 645	59 196	..	506 771	136 680

1 As from the end of 2004, quarterly data will not be collected for these industries. Annual results for the years 2005 onwards will be published on the ONS website at http://www.statistics.gov.uk/ as and when available.

Source: Office for National Statistics: 01633 813395

64

10 Metals, engineering and vehicles

10.1 Iron and steel
Weekly averages   Stocks: end of period

Thousand tonnes

	Consumption of imported iron ore[2]	Iron			Stocks[1]		Crude steel production	Finished steel products	
		Production in blast furnaces[3]	Consumption in steel-making	Total stocks[4]	Consumption in steel-making	Total stocks		Net home and export deliveries	At producers' works[5]
	BJAB	BJAC	BJAD	BJAE	BJAF	BJAG	BJAH	BJAI	BJAJ
2004	306.4	195.8	192.5	29.5	97.1	242.4	264.7	256.6	1 666.1
2005	305.9	195.9	192.0	7.3	87.1	228.4	254.6	247.6	1 816.4
2006	316.4	205.7	200.8	30.8	92.5	256.7	267.4	261.7	1 665.9
2005 Jul	294.8	190.1	188.6	5.3	75.1	223.0	241.6	235.3	1 791.6
Aug	303.2	186.3	184.2	5.0	77.1	237.5	238.7	219.9	1 804.4
Sep	287.0	180.5	177.8	5.2	90.1	271.0	239.9	290.2	1 602.9
Oct	268.4	192.3	187.7	8.9	85.3	262.2	246.5	238.4	1 605.2
Nov	310.0	203.4	201.5	5.5	77.0	257.4	255.9	253.7	1 583.9
Dec	337.0	207.4	204.6	7.3	70.4	225.8	257.0	222.4	1 816.4
2006 Jan	326.9	211.7	208.3	7.5	81.7	269.3	263.4	253.0	1 712.3
Feb	326.7	210.4	204.8	8.8	90.3	245.3	269.3	265.4	1 712.3
Mar	329.0	216.8	210.8	11.8	101.5	245.0	284.1	276.7	1 708.1
Apr	319.3	207.5	203.6	7.5	106.8	237.0	282.1	277.3	1 701.4
May	319.7	204.5	202.5	4.7	99.0	246.9	277.0	261.4	1 698.0
Jun	322.1	208.8	207.3	5.1	107.9	250.1	287.8	297.4	1 615.8
Jul	297.7	200.5	197.6	9.1	98.7	292.4	269.4	251.6	1 641.1
Aug	313.4	207.2	201.5	17.1	84.5	251.1	261.2	215.9	1 953.8
Sep	314.6	202.4	195.8	21.8	81.2	272.5	253.0	288.5	1 717.1
Oct	338.1	210.4	201.4	39.3	92.9	284.5	267.1	279.2	1 629.9
Nov	288.7	184.6	181.4	29.7	84.8	295.7	242.0	255.1	1 550.9
Dec	304.8	205.8	197.0	30.8	81.1	256.7	253.8	228.5	1 665.9
2007 Jan	312.6	206.1	197.7	49.9	86.5	301.0	259.6	228.8	1 580.1†
Feb	314.0	221.1	217.4	58.0	106.6	313.0	293.6	277.8	1 559.2

1 Excludes iron foundries and refined iron works.
2 Including manganese ore.
3 Includes blast furnace ferro-alloys.

4 Includes blast furnace ferro-alloys, but excludes iron foundries and refined iron works.
5 Stocks of ingots, semi-finished and finished steel.

Source: UK Iron and Steel Statistics Bureau

10.2 Supplies and deliveries of steel
Weekly averages

Thousand tonnes (crude steel equivalent)

	Supply from home sources							
	Crude steel production							
	Total	of which: alloy	Producers' stock changes[1]	Re-usable material[2]	Total	Imports[3]	Exports[3]	Net home disposals
	BJBA	BJBB	BJBC	BJBD	BJBE	BJBF	BJBG	BJBH
2001	260.4	20.4	−2.6	–	263.0	173.6	145.1	291.5
2002	224.4	19.4	−1.1	–	225.5	185.8	141.4	269.9
2003	250.3	18.4	–	–	250.3	175.5	153.2	272.7
2004	264.7	18.4	0.7	–	264.0	187.4	163.7	287.8
2005	254.5	16.6	3.6	–	251.0	159.8	182.3	228.5
2006	267.4	14.6	−3.6	–	271.0	180.6	177.8	273.7
2004 Q1	260.1	19.2	−12.8	–	272.8	174.2	157.5	289.6
Q2	283.2	19.7	−5.5	–	288.7	182.9	171.2	300.4
Q3	261.9	18.2	17.1	–	244.8	197.1	160.8	281.2
Q4	253.7	16.6	4.0	–	249.8	195.5	165.2	280.0
2005 Q1	254.7	20.6	−5.4	–	260.1	191.3	180.7	270.7
Q2	271.1	20.8	14.9	–	256.2	175.4	194.0	237.6
Q3	238.9	12.2	−15.5	–	254.4	131.3	168.9	216.8
Q4	253.4	12.7	20.2	–	233.2	141.6	185.5	189.3
2006 Q1	273.2	13.9	−10.2	–	283.4	179.1	186.7	275.8
Q2	281.9	15.9	−8.7	–	290.6	184.0	192.0	282.6
Q3	261.2	14.0	9.6	–	251.6	177.3	156.8	272.1
Q4	253.3	14.7	−4.8	–	258.2	181.8	175.6	264.4

1 Increases in stock are shown as + and decreases in stock (ie deliveries from stock) as -.
2 Currently mainly old rails for re-rolling.
3 Derived from HM Customs statistics.

Source: UK Iron and Steel Statistics Bureau

10.3 Aluminium
Monthly averages or calendar months; stocks: end of period

Thousand tonnes

	Production		Despatches to customers				
	Primary[1]	Secondary[2]	Primary[1]	Secondary	Rolled products	Extrusions and tubes	Castings
	BJDH	BJDI	BJDJ	BJDK	BJDN	BJDO	BJDM
2000	25.4	19.8	25.1	19.8	34.9	15.4	11.2
2001	28.4	20.7	28.1	20.7	32.1	14.0	10.8
2002	28.7	17.3	29.0	17.3	26.0	13.2	10.6
2003	28.6	17.2	28.3	17.2	22.9	12.4	10.6
2004	30.0	15.5	30.6	15.5	22.2	12.3	9.2
2005	30.7	11.2	30.7	11.2	22.5	11.0	8.6
2002 Oct	28.3	17.3	30.7	17.3	26.0	14.7	10.6
Nov	27.8	17.3	27.2	17.3	26.0	13.5	10.6
Dec	31.1	17.3	25.1	17.3	26.0	8.2	10.6
2003 Jan	28.8	17.2	34.9	17.2	22.9	13.2	10.6
Feb	29.7	17.2	29.8	17.2	22.9	12.3	10.6
Mar	28.7	17.2	29.0	17.2	22.9	13.1	10.6
Apr	28.0	17.2	29.7	17.2	22.9	12.4	10.6
May	31.3	17.2	32.3	17.2	22.9	12.3	10.6
Jun	28.1	17.2	28.1	17.2	22.9	12.5	10.6
Jul	28.7	17.2	26.3	17.2	22.9	13.7	10.6
Aug	29.4	17.2	27.1	17.2	22.9	10.5	10.6
Sep	25.9	17.2	27.0	17.2	22.9	13.4	10.6
Oct	26.8	17.2	28.1	17.2	22.9	14.4	10.6
Nov	29.1	17.2	27.4	17.2	22.9	13.0	10.6
Dec	28.5	17.2	20.2	17.2	22.9	8.3	10.6
2004 Jan	29.5	15.5	34.7	15.5	22.2	12.7	11.6
Feb	27.6	15.5	29.4	15.5	22.2	12.6	11.6
Mar	29.6	15.5	31.2	15.5	22.2	14.7	11.6
Apr	28.8	15.5	30.9	15.5	22.2	12.8	11.6
May	30.1	15.5	27.5	15.5	22.2	12.1	11.6
Jun	29.6	15.5	35.6	15.5	22.2	13.1	11.6
Jul	30.7	15.5	27.8	15.5	22.2	13.7	11.6
Aug	30.9	15.5	32.2	15.5	22.2	10.9	11.6
Sep	30.2	15.5	32.1	15.5	22.2	13.2	11.6
Oct	31.1	15.5	28.9	15.5	22.2	12.4	11.6
Nov	30.2	15.5	32.2	15.5	22.2	12.2	11.6
Dec	31.4	15.5	24.5	15.5	22.2	7.2	11.6
2005 Jan	31.3	11.2	30.2	11.2	22.5	11.2	8.6
Feb	28.0	11.2	26.9	11.2	22.5	11.1	8.6
Mar	31.5	11.2	29.4	11.2	22.5	12.0	8.6
Apr	30.4	11.2	30.0	11.2	22.5	12.0	8.6
May	31.1	11.2	31.3	11.2	22.5	11.6	8.6
Jun	30.4	11.2	30.3	11.2	22.5	11.8	8.6
Jul	31.5	11.2	29.8	11.2	22.5	10.8	8.6
Aug	31.2	11.2	34.2	11.2	22.5	10.8	8.6
Sep	30.5	11.2	30.3	11.2	22.5	11.9	8.6
Oct	31.1	11.2	32.1	11.2	22.5	11.3	8.6
Nov	30.4	11.2	31.8	11.2	22.5	11.1	8.6
Dec	30.8	11.2	31.8	11.2	22.5	6.9	8.6
2006 Jan	30.9	..	31.5	..	..	10.8	..
Feb	27.9	..	28.3	..	..	10.8	..
Mar	31.1	..	31.7	..	..	12.6	..
Apr	30.0	..	28.4	..	..	10.0	..
May	30.1	..	33.3	..	..	11.8	..
Jun	29.7	..	31.9	..	..	11.6	..
Jul	31.2	..	29.0	..	..	11.0	..
Aug	31.2	..	30.7	..	..	10.3	..
Sep	28.7	..	31.6	..	..	11.2	..

1 Including the pure content of primary alloys.
2 Including the primary content used in the production of secondary metal.

Source: Aluminium Federation: 0121 456 1103

10.4 Total engineering
Total turnover of UK - based manufacturers[1,2,3]
Standard Industrial Classification 2003

£ millions

		2005	2006	2005 Q3	2005 Q4	2006 Q1	2006 Q2	2006 Q3	2006 Q4
Division Description									
Division 29 : Manufacture of machinery and equipment not elsewhere classified									
2911 Manufacture of engines and turbines except aircraft, vehicle & cycle engines	MXVO	1 847	1 952	448	467	443	483	511	515
2912 Manufacture of pumps and compressors	MXXO	2 872	3 191[†]	720	745	767	798[†]	829	797
2913 Manufacture of taps and valves	MXZH	1 231	1 196[†]	319	290	301	302	308	285[†]
2914 Manufacture of bearings, gears, gearing and driving elements	MYCT	947	1 037[†]	224	238	257	259	259	262[†]
2922 Manufacture of lifting and handling equipment	MYLS	3 542	3 916	844	932	991	963	987	976[†]
2923 Manufacture of non-domestic cooling and ventilation equipment	MYPT	3 393	3 779[†]	873	873	853	966	986	974[†]
2924 Manufacture of other general purpose machinery not elsewhere classified	MYRM	3 027	2 975[†]	745	702	752	769	731	723
2941 Manufacture of metalworking machine tools	MYWY	730	848	183	208	198	214	211	225
2949 Manufacture of other machine tools	MYYP	699	766	185	182	175	198	204	191
2952 Manufacture of machinery for mining, quarrying and construction	MZCE	3 098	3 234[†]	801	824	798	846[†]	768	822
2953 Manufacture of machinery for food, beverage and tobacco processing	MZFS	942	963	232	219	236	237	246	243
2954 Manufacture of machinery for textile, apparel and leather production	MZJP	123	127[†]	30	29	28	32	32[†]	35
2956 Manufacture of other special purpose machinery not elsewhere classified	MZQF	2 262	2 187[†]	576	593	543	546	542	557[†]
2971 Manufacture of electric domestic appliances	MZTZ	2 642	2 733[†]	637	737	654	635	687	758[†]
Division 30 : Manufacture of electrical and optical equipment									
3001 Manufacture of office machinery	MZXQ	889	1 235	215	226	327	320	296	292
3002 Manufacture of computers and other information processing equipment	VBCE	4 234	2 999[†]	1 077	1 080	886	776	733[†]	603
Division 31 : Manufacture of electrical machinery and apparatus not elsewhere classified									
3110 Manufacture of electric motors, generators and transformers	VBEB	2 348	2 574[†]	591	571	642	605[†]	647	680
3120 Manufacture of electricity distribution and control apparatus	VBFU	3 459	3 678[†]	891	860	929	957	914[†]	879
3130 Manufacture of insulated wire and cable	VBHW	959	1 349[†]	237	245	301	326	354[†]	368
3140 Manufacture of accumulators, primary cells and primary batteries	VBJW	440	354	111	119	87	85	86	96
3150 Manufacture of lighting equipment and electric lamps	VBLP	1 331	1 389[†]	336	311	332	322	361[†]	374
3161 Manufacture of other electrical equipment for engines and vehicles not otherwise classified	VBNI	1 004	946[†]	239	248	242	243	223	238
3162 Manufacture of other electrical equipment not elsewhere classified	VBPK	2 694	2 762[†]	685	659	702	666	713	681[†]
Division 32 : Manufacture of radio, television and communication equipment and apparatus									
3210 Manufacture of electronic valves and tubes and other electronic components	VBRI	3 917	3 846[†]	975	1 006	996	953	973	924[†]
3220 Manufacture of television and radio transmitters and apparatus for line telephony and line telegraphy	VBTF	3 610	4 075	942	956	1 053	1 059	879	1 084
3230 Manufacture of television and radio receivers, sound or video recording or reproducing apparatus and associated goods	VBVJ	3 229	3 711	732	963	896	915	832	1 067
Division 33 : Manufacture of medical, precision and optical instruments, watches and clocks									
3310 Manufacture of medical and surgical equipment and orthopaedic appliances	VBXH	3 749	3 607[†]	956	879	974	900	845	887[†]
3320 Manufacture of instruments and applicances for measuring, checking, testing, navigating and other purposes, except industrial process control equipment	VBZF	6 853	6 766[†]	1 668	1 732	1 580	1 622[†]	1 665	1 898
3340 Manufacture of optical instruments and photographic equipment	VCCV	1 060	1 091[†]	274	253	277	277	261	276[†]

1 The figures shown represent the output of UK - based manufacturers classified to Subsections DK and DL of the Standard Industrial Classification 2003. The figures shown are derived from the monthly production inquiry (MPI) and include estimates for non-responders and for establishments which are not sampled.

2 Orders on hand figures are given for the end of the period to which they relate.
3 The data on this table are not seasonally adjusted.

Source: Office for National Statistics: 01633 813351

10.5 Manufacture of machinery and equipment not elsewhere classified
Values at current prices

£ million

	Total			Home			Export		
	Orders[1] on Hand	New[2] Orders	Turnover	Orders[1] on Hand	New[2] Orders	Turnover	Orders[1] on Hand	New[2] Orders	Turnover
	JGZP	JGVN	JGWL	JGZX	JGVV	JGWT	JHAF	JGWD	JGXB
2002	11 715.9	30 144.6	29 383.8	8 120.8	19 675.5	19 069.3	3 595.1	10 469.1	10 314.5
2003	13 079.3	31 586.1	30 222.9	9 819.4	20 890.5	19 192.0	3 259.9	10 695.5	11 030.8
2004	12 520.3	31 337.8	31 896.6	9 246.9	19 377.2	19 949.7	3 273.4	11 960.4	11 946.8
2005	12 299.9	33 289.8	33 510.3	8 487.0	19 914.9	20 674.7	3 812.9	13 375.1	12 835.6
2006	12 487.4	35 622.8	35 435.3	8 249.6	21 429.0	21 666.4	4 237.8	14 193.9	13 769.0
2004 Q3	13 090.1	7 187.8	7 849.4	9 604.1	4 541.0	4 900.1	3 486.0	2 646.7	2 949.2
Q4	12 520.3	7 981.4	8 551.2	9 246.9	5 070.1	5 427.4	3 273.4	2 911.2	3 123.8
2005 Q1	13 194.4	8 707.5	8 033.5	9 360.4	5 177.6	5 064.0	3 833.9	3 529.9	2 969.4
Q2	13 344.1	8 485.4	8 335.7	9 339.6	5 138.4	5 159.1	4 004.5	3 347.0	3 176.5
Q3	12 661.4	7 740.3	8 423.0	8 907.8	4 717.7	5 149.5	3 753.6	3 022.7	3 273.5
Q4	12 299.9	8 356.6	8 718.1	8 487.0	4 881.2	5 302.1	3 812.9	3 475.5	3 416.2
2006 Q1	12 580.1	8 732.6	8 452.3	8 338.7	4 966.0	5 114.3	4 241.4	3 766.6	3 338.1
Q2	13 028.3	9 345.8	8 897.6	8 664.1	5 745.2	5 419.8	4 364.2	3 600.6	3 477.9
Q3	12 885.1	8 756.0	8 899.3	8 583.6	5 435.9	5 516.4	4 301.5	3 320.2	3 382.8
Q4	12 487.4	8 788.4	9 186.1	8 249.6	5 281.9	5 615.9	4 237.8	3 506.5	3 570.2
2005 Jul	13 293.1	2 648.8	2 699.8	9 296.5	1 655.8	1 698.9	3 996.6	993.0	1 000.9
Aug	13 293.9	2 591.1	2 590.2	9 320.6	1 652.6	1 628.5	3 973.3	938.5	961.7
Sep	12 661.4	2 500.4	3 133.0	8 907.8	1 409.3	1 822.1	3 753.6	1 091.2	1 310.9
Oct	12 766.2	2 938.9	2 834.1	9 085.1	1 933.5	1 756.2	3 681.0	1 005.4	1 078.0
Nov	12 678.8	2 935.5	3 022.9	8 982.0	1 721.5	1 824.7	3 696.8	1 214.1	1 198.3
Dec	12 299.9	2 482.2	2 861.1	8 487.0	1 226.2	1 721.2	3 812.9	1 256.0	1 139.9
2006 Jan	12 401.4	2 638.4	2 536.9	8 304.8	1 344.2	1 526.3	4 096.6	1 294.2	1 010.6
Feb	12 645.5	2 899.6	2 655.5	8 493.0	1 808.0	1 619.9	4 152.5	1 091.6	1 035.7
Mar	12 580.1	3 194.6	3 259.9	8 338.7	1 813.8	1 968.1	4 241.4	1 380.8	1 291.8
Apr	12 842.3	2 945.6	2 683.4	8 454.7	1 748.9	1 632.9	4 387.6	1 196.7	1 050.6
May	12 977.7	3 142.9	3 007.4	8 536.2	1 900.2	1 818.7	4 441.5	1 242.7	1 188.7
Jun	13 028.3	3 257.3	3 206.8	8 664.1	2 096.1	1 968.2	4 364.2	1 161.2	1 238.6
Jul	13 050.9	2 930.2	2 907.5	8 693.6	1 830.4	1 800.9	4 357.4	1 099.8	1 106.6
Aug	12 996.0	2 719.8	2 774.8	8 739.0	1 817.7	1 772.3	4 257.0	902.2	1 002.5
Sep	12 885.1	3 106.0	3 217.0	8 583.6	1 787.8	1 943.2	4 301.5	1 318.2	1 273.7
Oct	12 828.8	2 991.4	3 047.6	8 559.2	1 824.4	1 848.8	4 269.6	1 166.9	1 198.8
Nov	12 622.4	2 984.9	3 191.3	8 303.9	1 705.8	1 961.1	4 318.5	1 279.1	1 230.2
Dec	12 487.4	2 812.1	2 947.2	8 249.6	1 751.7	1 806.0	4 237.8	1 060.5	1 141.2
2007 Jan	12 020.6	2 390.7	2 857.4	8 058.8	1 528.4	1 719.3	3 961.8	862.2	1 138.2
Feb	12 103.0	2 988.2	2 905.8	8 195.0	1 912.2	1 775.9	3 908.0	1 076.1	1 129.9

Note: From this edition, current prices are shown instead of constant prices.
1 For Orders on Hand the percentage compares the level at the end of the
latest period shown with the corresponding level of the earlier period.
The Orders on Hand value represents the value at the end of the
period, rather than the average value for that period.
2 Net of cancellations.

10.6 Manufacture of electrical and optical equipment
Values at current prices

£ million

	Total			Home			Export		
	Orders[1] on Hand	New[2] Orders	Turnover	Orders[1] on Hand	New[2] Orders	Turnover	Orders[1] on Hand	New[2] Orders	Turnover
	JGZV	JGVT	JGWR	JHAD	JGWB	JGWZ	JHAL	JGWJ	JGXJ
2002	14 833.1	47 421.0	48 959.3	10 758.5	27 882.7	28 692.5	4 074.6	19 538.4	20 266.8
2003	13 516.6	43 434.3	44 750.6	9 753.5	25 679.3	26 684.5	3 763.2	17 755.0	18 066.5
2004	12 980.4	42 749.2	43 285.4	9 447.1	25 606.6	25 912.9	3 533.3	17 142.8	17 372.6
2005	14 359.2	42 136.1	40 757.4	10 445.4	26 135.1	25 136.8	3 913.8	16 000.9	15 620.6
2006	14 494.7	41 481.5	41 346.1	10 236.1	24 908.8	25 117.8	4 258.5	16 572.9	16 228.1
2004 Q3	13 004.4	10 159.6	10 629.1	9 303.1	5 993.9	6 355.0	3 701.3	4 165.7	4 274.2
Q4	12 980.4	11 207.3	11 231.3	9 447.1	6 975.1	6 831.1	3 533.3	4 232.3	4 400.3
2005 Q1	12 988.6	10 109.0	10 100.9	9 393.4	6 202.3	6 256.1	3 595.2	3 906.5	3 844.8
Q2	13 146.7	10 250.2	10 092.1	9 357.2	6 165.4	6 201.5	3 789.6	4 085.0	3 890.6
Q3	14 018.7	11 064.2	10 192.3	9 972.0	6 920.1	6 305.2	4 046.7	4 144.1	3 886.9
Q4	14 359.2	10 712.7	10 372.1	10 445.4	6 847.3	6 374.0	3 913.8	3 865.3	3 998.3
2006 Q1	14 383.0	10 502.6	10 478.8	10 519.2	6 415.5	6 341.7	3 863.8	4 087.2	4 137.2
Q2	14 743.1	10 622.3	10 262.3	10 680.4	6 424.1	6 262.8	4 062.6	4 198.3	3 999.4
Q3	14 877.3	10 137.9	10 003.6	10 622.0	6 196.8	6 255.1	4 255.3	3 941.1	3 748.4
Q4	14 494.7	10 218.7	10 601.4	10 236.1	5 872.4	6 258.2	4 258.5	4 346.3	4 343.1
2005 Jul	13 372.2	3 438.7	3 213.2	9 344.6	1 970.2	1 982.7	4 027.6	1 468.5	1 230.4
Aug	13 936.0	3 880.3	3 316.6	9 909.4	2 640.7	2 075.9	4 026.6	1 239.6	1 240.6
Sep	14 018.7	3 745.2	3 662.5	9 972.0	2 309.2	2 246.6	4 046.7	1 436.0	1 415.9
Oct	13 965.9	3 312.9	3 365.7	9 943.9	2 073.7	2 101.8	4 021.9	1 239.2	1 264.0
Nov	13 828.2	3 490.3	3 627.9	9 860.7	2 162.3	2 245.5	3 967.5	1 327.9	1 382.4
Dec	14 359.2	3 909.5	3 378.5	10 445.4	2 611.3	2 026.7	3 913.8	1 298.2	1 351.9
2006 Jan	14 276.9	3 056.4	3 138.8	10 277.3	1 733.6	1 901.8	3 999.6	1 322.8	1 237.0
Feb	14 684.2	3 680.2	3 272.9	10 760.2	2 474.7	1 991.7	3 924.0	1 205.6	1 281.2
Mar	14 383.0	3 766.0	4 067.1	10 519.2	2 207.2	2 448.2	3 863.8	1 558.8	1 619.0
Apr	14 606.8	3 341.1	3 117.3	10 744.8	2 142.2	1 916.6	3 862.0	1 198.9	1 200.7
May	14 478.0	3 325.5	3 454.3	10 514.9	1 876.6	2 106.5	3 963.1	1 448.9	1 347.7
Jun	14 743.1	3 955.7	3 690.7	10 680.4	2 405.3	2 239.7	4 062.6	1 550.5	1 451.0
Jul	14 615.1	3 083.9	3 211.9	10 579.4	1 939.3	2 040.3	4 035.7	1 144.6	1 171.5
Aug	14 785.6	3 474.1	3 303.5	10 708.4	2 236.1	2 107.1	4 077.3	1 238.0	1 196.4
Sep	14 877.3	3 579.9	3 488.2	10 622.0	2 021.4	2 107.7	4 255.3	1 558.5	1 380.5
Oct	14 730.9	3 325.6	3 472.0	10 457.6	1 882.1	2 046.5	4 273.3	1 443.5	1 425.5
Nov	14 592.6	3 625.1	3 763.4	10 317.2	2 102.8	2 243.2	4 275.5	1 522.3	1 520.2
Dec	14 494.7	3 268.0	3 366.0	10 236.1	1 887.5	1 968.5	4 258.5	1 380.5	1 397.4
2007 Jan	14 349.4	2 983.3	3 128.6	10 066.7	1 724.6	1 894.0	4 282.7	1 258.7	1 234.5
Feb	14 469.8	3 244.2	3 123.9	10 160.0	1 997.2	1 903.9	4 309.8	1 247.0	1 220.0

Note: From this edition, current prices are shown instead of constant prices.
1 For Orders on Hand the percentage compares the level at the end of the latest period shown with the corresponding level of the earlier period. The Orders on Hand value represents the value at the end of the period, rather than the average value for that period.
2 Net of cancellations.

10.7 Passenger cars

Number

	Total production					Production for export				
	1000cc and under	Over 1000cc and not over 1600cc	Over 1600cc and not over 2500cc	Over 2500cc	Total	1000cc and under	Over 1000cc and not over 1600cc	Over 1600cc and not over 2500cc	Over 2500cc	Total
	GKAB	GKAD	GKAF	GKAH	JCYM	GKAC	GKAE	GKAG	GKAI	JCYL
2000	96 043	676 438	723 294	145 677	1 641 452	56 556	375 528	509 591	121 315	1 062 990
2001	93 695	632 747	634 573	131 350	1 492 365	56 426	329 944	400 648	107 236	894 254
2002	79 545	711 553	720 067	118 579	1 629 744	35 866	442 975	470 285	98 158	1 047 284
2003	23 985	750 840	740 486	142 247	1 657 558	12 380	503 950	509 050	118 379	1 143 759
2004	15 471	796 174	690 759	144 346	1 646 750	10 316	560 505	492 564	116 371	1 179 756
2005	6 111	854 687	546 744	188 155	1 595 697	4 925	625 929	405 204	148 445	1 184 503
2006	–	792 187	446 143	203 755	1 442 085	–	622 205	324 880	159 008	1 106 093
2006 Jan	–	62 453	40 296	16 373	119 122	–	45 143	28 836	12 488	86 467
Feb	–	74 048	38 871	18 274	131 193	–	53 830	27 236	14 145	95 211
Mar	–	88 834	46 000	24 154	158 988	–	67 774	32 449	19 499	119 722
Apr	–	65 103	37 156	16 313	118 572	–	52 814	28 855	13 504	95 173
May	–	74 864	39 886	17 566	132 316	–	60 704	30 835	13 901	105 440
Jun	–	78 055	42 280	18 991	139 326	–	61 508	30 749	14 566	106 823
Jul	–	66 528	37 241	14 060	117 829	–	51 223	26 995	10 692	88 910
Aug	–	35 223	23 067	14 669	72 959	–	25 963	15 333	10 810	52 106
Sep	–	67 981	37 354	16 977	122 312	–	53 839	25 365	13 083	92 287
Oct	–	66 536	35 526	14 081	116 143	–	56 995	27 157	11 620	95 772
Nov	–	68 181	38 726	21 656	128 563	–	56 623	28 557	17 085	102 265
Dec	–	44 381	29 740	10 641	84 762	–	35 789	22 513	7 615	65 917
2007 Jan	–	58 476	44 747	20 974	124 197	–	45 690	32 511	16 683	94 884
Feb	–	50 765	45 021	19 863[†]	115 649[†]	–	35 745	34 582	14 634[†]	84 961[†]
Mar	–	60 559	57 295	20 154	138 008	–	43 994	39 466	16 697	100 157

Source: Office for National Statistics: 01633 812394

10.8 Commercial motor vehicles[1]

Number

	Total production						Production for export					
	Light Commercial vehicles	Gross Vehicle Weight Trucks		Motive units	Buses, coaches and mini-buses	Total	Light Commercial vehicles	Gross Vehicle Weight Trucks		Motive units	Buses, coaches and mini-buses	Total
		Under 7.5 tonnes	Over 7.5 tonnes					Under 7.5 tonnes	Over 7.5 tonnes			
	GKDH	GKDJ	GKDL	GKCV	GKDN	JCYG	GKDI	GKDK	GKDM	GKCW	GKDO	JCYF
2000	145 655	5 160	6 849	2 673	12 105	172 442	65 636	1 032	3 059	129	6 325	76 181
2001	169 705	5 000	7 359	2 539	8 270	192 873	87 208	1 307	3 315	151	4 238	96 224
2002	168 311	4 600	7 357	1 795	9 204	191 267	104 902	1 157	3 474	70	4 631	114 234
2003	166 359	4 151	7 779	2 095	8 487	188 871	94 887	806	3 494	130	3 709	102 917
2004	178 887	4 977	8 537	2 558	14 334	209 293	113 076	659	3 626	164	10 582	128 107
2005	171 866	5 533	9 756	2 755	16 843	206 753	112 647	763	4 258	190	12 415	130 273
2006	175 713	4 418	11 447	2 230	13 896	207 704	118 632	844	5 523	179	11 041	136 219
2006 Mar	18 323	464	1 146	207	1 179	21 319	12 270	99	489	20	904	13 782
Apr	13 443	457	875	167	1 347	16 289	10 091	98	368	24	1 222	11 803
May	12 751	404	978	169	793	15 095	9 102	43	465	10	688	10 308
Jun	14 129	362	1 096	175	1 282	17 044	8 923	52	527	15	1 100	10 617
Jul	13 287	227	840	98	866	15 318	9 283	33	436	8	665	10 425
Aug	6 804	391	944	183	426	8 748	3 454	107	521	8	273	4 363
Sep	18 614	477	950	301	1 089	21 431	11 564	67	457	4	645	12 737
Oct	16 526	207	871	308	1 957	19 869	11 308	69	515	14	1 651	13 557
Nov	17 953	249	967	220	1 869	21 258	12 665	87	560	28	1 533	14 873
Dec	12 906	138	760	91	1 064	14 959	8 484	55	428	13	833	9 813
2007 Jan	16 611	343	931	165	1 544	19 594	9 575	65	384	47	1 348	11 419
Feb	14 841	320	802	193	1 335	17 491	8 449	111	365	31	1 081	10 037
Mar	17 273	264	1 020	199	1 534	20 290	10 476	85	532	41	1 212	12 346

Source: Office for National Statistics: 01633 812394

11 Textiles and other manufactures

11.1 Index numbers of textile and clothing industries
Standard Industrial Classification 2003

2003=100, seasonally adjusted

| | Textile industry (production) | | | | | | | |
	Man-made fibres	All textiles[1]	Preparation and spinning of textile fibres	Textile weaving	Manufacture of knitted and crocheted fabrics	Finishing of textiles	Manufacture of other textiles	Manufacture of made-up textile articles except apparel
SIC 2003 classification	2 470	17	171	172	176	173	175	174
	AHXI	AIMS	AIOE	AIOF	AHGJ	AHGE	AHGQ	AHGF
2003	100.0	100.0	100.0	100.0	100.0	100.0	100.0	100.0
2004	99.2	93.0	89.5	89.1	94.1	96.4	86.6	101.4
2005	80.0	91.4	66.2	89.6	85.9	91.0	87.6	101.7
2006	79.5	85.4	66.7	81.5	82.4	99.7	86.9	96.0
2004 Q4	98.3	92.5	92.5	87.2	85.7	96.5	83.1	102.7
2005 Q1	94.9	90.9	70.0	90.3	92.1	81.5	87.7	102.8
Q2	81.0	93.2	72.6	89.7	87.6	89.1	91.4	101.5
Q3	69.2	91.0	58.1	92.2	80.7	96.0	85.1	100.9
Q4	75.0	90.5	64.3	86.1	83.1	97.6	86.0	101.7
2006 Q1	71.8	86.6	70.7	85.1	87.6	104.6	83.7	95.8
Q2	76.2	85.1	65.7	87.3	80.6	98.7	85.3	94.4
Q3	85.0	85.7	66.1	81.2	80.5	100.9	89.2	95.4
Q4	84.9	84.2	64.1	72.3	80.8	94.5	89.2	98.4
2007 Q1	75.5	83.4	66.0	70.4	79.7	99.4	93.0	86.6

| | Clothing industry (production) | | | | |
	Manufacture of wearing apparel, dressing and dyeing of fur[2]	Manufacture of other outerwear	Manufacture of workwear	Manufacture of underwear[3]	Manufacture of other wearing apparel and accessories nec[3]
SIC 2003 classification	18	1822	1821	1823	1824
	AIMT	AHGU	AHGT	AHGV	AHGW
2003	100.0	100.0	100.0	100.0	100.0
2004	89.5	95.4	87.5	105.3	71.6
2005	87.9	94.1	84.7	..	..
2006	89.5	91.7	90.4	..	..
2004 Q4	85.6	89.7	89.8	107.0	65.2
2005 Q1	83.1	85.0	92.4	..	..
Q2	87.8	92.9	82.2	..	..
Q3	89.4	97.5	79.4	..	..
Q4	91.2	101.1	84.8	..	..
2006 Q1	89.0	98.4	94.3	..	..
Q2	90.8	92.8	93.5	..	..
Q3	87.8	87.4	87.0	..	..
Q4	90.3	88.4	86.7	..	..
2007 Q1	88.3	85.7	84.5	..	..

1 In addition to the sectors listed, this includes throwing, texturing, etc of continuous filament yarn; spinning and weaving of flax, hemp and ramie; jute and polypropylene yarns and fabrics, and miscellaneous textiles (ie lace; rope, twine and net; narrow fabrics and other miscellaneous textiles).
2 In addition to the sectors listed, this includes hats, caps and millinery; gloves, other dress industries (ie swimwear and foundation garments; umbrellas and miscellaneous industries).

3 For confidentiality reasons, the data for these industries have been suppressed from 2005 Q1 onwards. This suppression is required because both industries now fail ONS disclosure rules and are therefore no longer available for publication.

Source: Office for National Statistics: 01633 812319

11.2 Household textiles, non-woven products, canvas and ropes[1]
Total UK manufacturers' sales by industry

£ Thousand

	Household textiles			Non-woven excluding apparel	Canvas goods, sacks etc	Cordage rope, twine & netting
	Soft furnishings	Household textiles	Carpets & rugs			
Subclass (SIC 92)	17401	17403	17510	17530	17402	17520
	CKPE	CKPF	CKPG	CKPH	CKPI	CKPJ
2002	528 697	782 536	840 517	166 592	120 351	..
2003	592 748	732 362	750 697	153 389	112 987	87 328
2004	575 923	653 816	689 945	149 188	100 897	75 530
2001 Q3	139 992	218 937	220 282	39 120	37 494	26 665
Q4	140 519	209 244	217 960	39 987	32 045	23 132
2002 Q1	122 140	199 646	212 015	40 620	32 507	21 817
Q2	130 164	192 838	204 124	43 259	32 835	..
Q3	139 134	196 336	206 386	..	29 327	22 776
Q4	137 259	193 716	217 992	..	25 683	18 954
2003 Q1	146 353	190 581	202 480	39 756	32 422	21 392
Q2	151 610	191 622	180 666	38 773	30 294	25 864
Q3	144 138	177 868	172 041	37 299	26 868	22 499
Q4	150 647	172 292	195 510	37 561	23 404	17 574
2004 Q1	139 764	171 148	172 601	36 966	28 536	18 766
Q2	146 324	164 879	172 927	37 355	25 795	24 002
Q3	138 436	159 291	166 521	38 523	25 890	17 244
Q4	151 399	158 498	177 896	36 344	20 676	15 518

1 As from the end of 2004, quarterly data will not be collected for these industries. Annual results for the years 2005 onwards will be published on the ONS website at http://www.statistics.gov.uk/ as and when available.

Source: Office for National Statistics: 01633 813395

11.3 Knitted and crocheted products, lace and narrow fabrics[1]
Total UK manufacturers' sales by industry

£ Thousand

	Knitted and crocheted			Lace	Narrow fabrics
	Fabrics	Hosiery	Pullovers, cardigans & similar articles		
Subclass (SIC 92)	17600	17710	17720	17541	17542
	CKPK	CKPL	CKPM	CKPN	CKPO
2002	244 325	..	351 497	23 442	186 972
2003	202 657	..	312 099	17 875	160 099
2004	197 031	..	219 492	15 708	144 529
2001 Q3	..	..	127 850	6 770	47 658
Q4	..	86 485	115 043	6 386	48 669
2002 Q1	65 797	..	82 900	7 243	48 223
Q2	..	..	66 684	6 204	47 339
Q3	57 695	..	102 224	4 781	47 210
Q4	..	..	99 689	5 214	44 200
2003 Q1	52 227	..	63 284	4 797	40 789
Q2	52 505	..	57 490	4 769	39 976
Q3	..	..	98 523	3 967	39 150
Q4	..	..	92 802	4 341	40 184
2004 Q1	49 422	..	53 084	4 582	37 952
Q2	51 654	..	49 323	3 978	36 709
Q3	50 558	..	65 855	3 462	35 535
Q4	..	..	51 230	3 686	34 333

1 As from the end of 2004, quarterly data will not be collected for these industries. Annual results for the years 2005 onwards will be published on the ONS website at http://www.statistics.gov.uk/ as and when available.

Source: Office for National Statistics: 01633 813395

11.4 Wearing apparel, dressing and dying of fur, leather clothes[1]
Total UK manufacturers' sales by industry

£ Thousand

	Workwear	Outerwear		Underwear		Hats	Other & accessories	Dressing & dyeing of fur & articles of fur	Leather clothes
		Men's	Women's	Men's	Women's				
Subclass (SIC 92)	18210	18221	18222	18231	18232	18241	18249	18300	18100
	CKPP	CKPQ	CKPR	CKPS	CKPT	CKPU	CKPV	CKPW	CKPX
2002	270 898	296 498	880 357	223 664	552 991	45 156	425 260	6 297	..
2003	287 771	291 549	844 730	195 604	461 974	37 122	362 097	3 937	8 689
2004	262 704	248 638	791 793	171 319	392 406	34 712	314 667	4 467	6 678
2001 Q2	60 134	83 455	194 177	48 963	154 188	..	116 518	1 598	2 714
Q3	60 489	84 999	202 813	59 780	143 195	13 771	108 079	2 139	2 799
Q4	57 186	77 656	181 318	68 637	158 177	12 059	116 107	2 119	4 891
2002 Q1	66 362	64 310	215 242	47 365	148 329	11 851	102 330	1 907	1 997
Q2	64 937	71 555	221 890	48 950	139 487	11 212	103 520	1 980	..
Q3	66 025	80 550	225 896	60 781	126 194	11 318	110 235	1 225	2 528
Q4	73 573	80 083	217 330	66 568	138 981	10 776	109 174	1 185	3 471
2003 Q1	72 092	71 176	209 821	51 870	110 878	10 373	92 390	855	2 307
Q2	72 748	61 875	195 087	40 850	118 041	9 003	90 151	821	1 812
Q3	73 757	77 148	233 484	55 365	110 387	8 657	93 798	1 086	1 899
Q4	69 174	81 349	206 338	47 519	122 668	9 089	85 757	1 174	2 671
2004 Q1	65 211	66 356	207 891	43 589	102 862	10 902	67 798	1 008	1 435
Q2	66 093	73 748	185 842	41 275	98 446	7 465	73 161	840	1 287
Q3	62 388	62 890	210 358	45 456	98 009	8 360	86 834	1 595	1 874
Q4	69 012	45 644	187 702	40 999	93 089	7 985	86 874	1 024	2 082

1 As from the end of 2004, quarterly data will not be collected for these industries. Annual results for the years 2005 onwards will be published on the ONS website at http://www.statistics.gov.uk/ as and when available.

Source: Office for National Statistics: 01633 813395

11.5 Miscellaneous products - goods not classified elsewhere[1]
Total UK manufacturers' sales by industry

£ Thousand

	Pumps	Compressors	Taps & valves
Subclass (SIC 92)	29121	29122	29130
	CKPY	CKPZ	CKQA
2002	1 021 177	1 112 086	1 147 070
2003	1 133 685	1 142 365	1 104 915
2004	1 156 732	1 176 542	1 164 351
2001 Q2	244 232	310 975	292 890
Q3	240 094	293 727	296 275
Q4	262 583	276 820	285 859
2002 Q1	231 218	271 009	291 337
Q2	249 411	277 824	288 487
Q3	252 339	283 137	293 403
Q4	288 209	280 116	273 844
2003 Q1	258 145	299 143	267 460
Q2	292 316	289 568	283 105
Q3	280 253	273 389	286 829
Q4	302 970	280 265	267 522
2004 Q1	287 588	292 119	290 613
Q2	282 748	296 709	287 634
Q3	280 844	299 516	295 911
Q4	305 552	288 198	290 193

1 As from the end of 2004, quarterly data will not be collected for these industries. Annual results for the years 2005 onwards will be published on the ONS website at http://www.statistics.gov.uk/ as and when available.

Source: Office for National Statistics: 01633 813395

12 Construction

12.1 Volume of construction output by all agencies[1] by type of work at constant 2000 prices (seasonally adjusted)
Great Britain

£ millions

	New work							Repair and maintenance						All work (seasonally adjusted volume index numbers)
	New housing for			Other new work for				Housing		Other work for				
					Private sector									
	Public sector	Private sector	Infrastructure	Public sector	Industrial	Commercial	Total new work	Public	Private	Public sector	Private sector	Total repair and maintenance	Total all work	
	BLAC	BLAD	BAXF	BLAE	BLAF	BLAG	BLAB	BLBK	BLBL	BLAJ	BLAK	BLAH	FGAY	SFZX
2003	1 637	9 568	6 734	7 274	3 064	12 095	40 372	6 334	12 264	6 919	11 963	37 480	77 852	112.0
2004	1 972	10 791	5 851	8 062	3 371	12 757	42 804	6 845	12 418	6 643	11 534	37 441	80 245	115.0
2005	1 833	11 239	5 328	7 341	3 582	12 888	42 211	6 730	12 044	7 003	11 562	37 338	79 549	114.0
2006[2]	2 258	11 460	4 988	7 047	3 981	14 616	44 349	6 526	11 674	6 483	11 576	36 260	80 609	116.0
2004 Q1	507	2 615	1 479	2 003	818	3 085	10 507	1 889	3 165	1 843	2 988	9 884	20 391	117.0
Q2	547	2 672	1 542	2 045	818	3 245	10 870	1 627	3 093	1 529	2 779	9 028	19 898	114.0
Q3	493	2 768	1 536	2 018	841	3 211	10 867	1 626	3 099	1 615	2 850	9 191	20 058	115.0
Q4	425	2 737	1 293	1 997	894	3 216	10 560	1 704	3 061	1 656	2 917	9 338	19 898	114.0
2005 Q1	485	2 669	1 297	1 867	819	3 053	10 189	1 930	3 015	1 905	2 902	9 752	19 941	114.0
Q2	482	2 875	1 322	1 844	874	3 221	10 618	1 778	3 069	1 712	2 872	9 432	20 050	115.0
Q3	431	2 873	1 386	1 796	909	3 241	10 636	1 530	2 941	1 711	2 958	9 140	19 776	114.0
Q4	436	2 822	1 323	1 833	980	3 373	10 767	1 492	3 019	1 674	2 830	9 015	19 782	114.0
2006 Q1[3]	560	2 756	1 276	1 799	964	3 382	10 737	1 712	2 970	1 750	2 790	9 222	19 959	115.0
Q2[3]	596	2 857	1 264	1 764	959	3 552	10 992	1 587	3 019	1 619	2 837	9 063	20 055	115.0
Q3[3]	571	2 929	1 267	1 745	985	3 758	11 256	1 651	2 794	1 626	2 874	8 944	20 200	116.0
Q4[2]	531	2 917	1 181	1 739	1 074	3 924	11 365	1 576	2 891	1 488	3 075	9 031	20 396	117.0

1 Classified to construction in the *Standard Industrial Classification 1992*. Estimates of unrecorded output by small firms and self-employed workers, and output by the public sector's direct labour department are included.
2 Provisional.
3 Revised

Source: Department for Trade and Industry: 020 7215 1953

12.2 Value of new orders obtained by contractors for new work[1] at current prices
Great Britain

£ millions

	New housing[2]			Other new work						New work total
	Public and housing association	Private	Total	Infrastructure	Other public	Private industrial	Private commercial	Total		
	BLBC	BLBD	FGAU	BAWT	BAWU	BAWV	BAWW	BLBE		FHAA
2003	1 340	9 471	10 812	4 894	6 142	2 383	9 721	23 139		33 951
2004	1 697	12 153	13 850	3 772	6 847	2 593	12 026	25 238		39 089
2005	1 951	13 171	15 122	5 532	6 694	3 421	13 163	28 811		43 932
2006[3]	2 629	13 441	16 069	4 322	6 177	3 611	17 519	31 629		47 698
2004 Q1	549	3 168	3 717	964	1 643	553	3 382	6 543		10 260
Q2	444	2 893	3 338	1 164	1 834	589	2 827	6 414		9 752
Q3	335	3 234	3 569	816	1 572	717	3 099	6 203		9 773
Q4	368	2 858	3 226	828	1 797	735	2 719	6 078		9 305
2005 Q1	552	3 203	3 756	1 483	1 606	679	3 283	7 052		10 807
Q2	448	3 605	4 053	1 463	1 693	856	3 248	7 259		11 312
Q3	390	3 626	4 016	1 488	1 867	842	3 114	7 311		11 328
Q4	560	2 737	3 297	1 098	1 528	1 044	3 518	7 188		10 485
2006 Q1	833	3 333	4 166	1 025	1 625	961	4 410	8 021		12 187
Q2	586	3 704	4 290	1 279	1 375	804	5 133	8 590		12 880
Q3	696	3 317	4 014	1 089	1 672	955	4 386	8 102		12 116
Q4[3]	513	3 086	3 599	929	1 505	892	3 590	6 916		10 515
2006 Jun	154	1 558	1 711	292	547	236	1 687	2 763		4 474
Jul	205	1 112	1 316	272	669	394	1 534	2 869		4 186
Aug	203	1 054	1 257	524	580	285	1 696	3 084		4 342
Sep	289	1 151	1 440	293	424	275	1 157	2 149		3 589
Oct[4]	210	1 148	1 358	447	581	313	1 218	2 559		3 918
Nov[4]	130	1 080	1 210	279	441	310	1 416	2 447		3 657
Dec[3]	173	858	1 031	202	483	269	956	1 910		2 941
2007 Jan[3]	350	1 085	1 435	671	678	347	1 283	2 978		4 413

1 Including the value of speculative building when work starts on site.
2 Excluding orders for home improvement work.
3 Provisional.
4 Revised

Source: Department for Trade and Industry

12.3 Building materials and components
Great Britain

	Building bricks (millions)		Concrete blocks (000 sq m)		Concrete roofing tiles (000 sq m of roof covered)		Slate[1] (tonnes)		Cement[2] (tonnes)		RMX[3] (000 cu m)	Sand and gravel (000 tonnes)
	Production	Deliveries	Production	Deliveries	Production	Deliveries	Production	Deliveries	Production	Deliveries	Deliveries	Deliveries
	BLDA	QXIH	BLDM	QXII	BLDN	QXIJ	BLDQ	QXIK	QXIM	QXIL	BLDP	BLDS
1997	250	254	6 878	6 837	2 080	2 090	8 859	8 636	1 053	996	1 861	7 062
1998	250	248	7 055	7 041	2 082	2 132	8 742	8 546	1 034	988	1 915	7 148
1999	245	252	7 314	7 154	2 164	2 114	8 239	8 330	1 058	978	1 963	6 819
2000	239	241	7 518	7 377	2 230	2 087	7 155	7 495	1 038	988	1 920	7 322
2001	230	235	7 327	7 376	2 069	2 036	7 760	7 852	924	888	1 917	8 121
2002	229	235	7 623	7 612	2 085	2 033	7 913	7 972	924	897	1 883	7 126
2003	231	245	7 973	8 032	1 786	1 783	6 591	6 543	935	923	1 857	6 896
2004	239	236	8 021	7 905	1 728	1 617	..	..	950	923	1 905	6 779
2005	229	214	7 500	7 463	2 143	2 041	..	..	871	860	1 869	6 708
2006	209	200	7 292	7 251	1 978	2 010	..	..	955	935	1 919	6 491
2004 Q3	236	246	8 179	8 509	1 640	1 711	–	..	990	954	2 013	7 217
Q4	236	215	7 577	7 240	1 685	1 725	..	..	929	884	1 851	6 338
2005 Q1	238	210	7 712	7 331	1 929	1 593	..	..	848	852	1 712	6 318
Q2	242	236	7 943	8 129	2 501	2 135	..	..	1 008	995	1 998	7 392
Q3	226	220	7 616	7 818	2 045	2 368	..	..	980	974	1 973	7 107
Q4	210	190	6 729	6 573	2 098	2 067	..	..	903	847	1 794	6 017
2006 Q1	206	189	7 052	6 940	2 264	2 262	..	..	882	912	1 815	5 930
Q2	219	213	7 478	7 520	2 001	1 903	..	..	994	965	1 998	7 179
Q3	213	216	7 538	7 870	2 210	2 124	..	..	997†	972	2 016	6 905
Q4	199	182	7 102	6 674	1 830	1 929	..	..	950†	891	1 847	5 952
2005 Mar	264	224	8 189	7 548	..	..	..	..	965	943	..	..
Apr	237	224	7 984	8 082	..	..	..	..	1 014	991	..	..
May	230	225	7 511	8 060	..	..	..	..	1 018	972	..	..
Jun	260	260	8 333	8 244	..	..	..	..	992	1 023	..	..
Jul	213	219	7 669	7 875	..	..	..	..	1 028	946	..	..
Aug	207	208	7 128	7 720	..	..	..	..	954	951	..	..
Sep	259	233	8 050	7 859	..	..	..	..	958	1 026	..	..
Oct	228	217	7 525	7 442	..	..	..	..	1 013	911	..	..
Nov	219	185	7 207	6 904	..	..	..	..	925	939	..	..
Dec	182	169	5 454	5 374	..	..	..	..	770	690	..	..
2006 Jan	144	169	6 221	6 527	..	..	..	..	743	810	..	..
Feb	210	183	6 788	6 726	..	..	..	..	891	902	..	..
Mar	264	216	8 146	7 568	..	..	..	..	1 013	1 025	..	..
Apr	211	187	6 333	6 489	..	..	..	..	942	868	..	..
May	211	206	7 679	7 623	..	..	..	..	1 018	994	..	..
Jun	235	246	8 424	8 447	..	..	..	..	1 021	1 044	..	..
Jul	201	210	7 567	7 836	..	..	..	..	1 042	949	..	..
Aug	194	208	7 313	7 864	..	..	..	..	986	977	..	..
Sep	244	230	7 650	7 786	..	..	..	..	962	991	..	..
Oct	210	196	7 823	7 566	..	..	..	..	1 030	985	..	..
Nov	220	198	7 906	7 447	..	..	..	..	1 011	1 021†	..	..
Dec	166	152	5 575	5 010	..	..	..	..	801	666	..	..
2007 Jan	176	157	6 929	6 203	..	..	..	..	762	835	..	..
Feb	196	175	7 012	6 624	..	..	..	..	..	..	..	..

1 Excluding slate residue used as fill.
2 United Kingdom; Great Britain from January 2002.
3 United Kingdom; RMX stands for ready mixed concrete.

Source: Department of Trade and Industry: 020 7215 1555

12.4 Permanent dwellings started and completed

Number

	Starts				Completions			
	Private enterprise	Registered social landlords[1]	Local Authorities	All dwellings	Private enterprise	Registered social landlords[1]	Local Authorities	All dwellings
United Kingdom								
	LMDB	LMDD	LMDE	LMDF	LMDG	LMDW	LMDY	LMDZ
2001/02	178 035	17 292	192	195 519	153 438	21 678	225	175 341
2002/03	179 042	16 342	185	195 569	164 139	19 586	301	184 026
2003/04	193 272	18 771	289	212 332	171 843	18 375	207	190 425
2004/05	204 879	20 665	239	225 783	183 932	22 716	131	206 779
2005/06	210 939	24 166	255	235 360	188 998	24 393	326	213 717
2003 Q4	43 256	3 098	74	46 428	50 502	4 294	59	54 855
2004 Q1	50 607	7 344	39	57 990	37 660	5 293	36	42 989
Q2	55 743	4 378	143	60 264	46 849	4 413	51	51 313
Q3	54 196	3 811	13	58 020	47 426	5 447	19	52 892
Q4	46 928	4 664	9	51 601	50 264	5 891	27	56 182
2005 Q1	48 012	7 812	74	55 898	39 393	6 965	34	46 392
Q2	56 562	4 563	74	61 199	48 403	5 437	138	53 978
Q3	51 507	4 614	6	56 127	43 898	5 811	12	49 721
Q4	47 968	5 537	37	53 542	53 552	5 863	54	59 469
2006 Q1	54 902	9 452	138	64 492	43 145	7 282	122	50 549
England								
	BLHC	BLHM	BAEP	BLHA	BLHK	BLHO	BAEX	BLHI
2001/02	139 117	11 061	118	150 296	115 827	14 102	63	129 992
2002/03	139 952	10 906	159	151 017	124 695	13 083	199	137 977
2003/04	148 769	12 347	275	161 391	130 096	13 671	191	143 958
2004/05	159 947	14 391	205	174 543	139 132	16 661	100	155 893
2005/06	167 432	17 226	248	184 906	144 937	18 162	299	163 398
2004 Q3	42 351	3 020	2	45 373	36 124	3 764	19	39 907
Q4	36 804	4 040	1	40 845	37 812	5 017	25	42 854
2005 Q1	36 977	3 349	74	40 400	29 469	4 299	5	33 773
Q2	44 995	4 145	74	49 214	36 712	4 096	114	40 922
Q3	40 755	4 020	5	44 780	33 545	4 372	9	37 926
Q4	38 379	4 325	31	42 735	42 011	4 768	54	46 833
2006 Q1	43 303	4 736	138	48 177	32 669	4 926	122	37 717
Q2	43 011	4 134	93	47 238	38 221	4 872	52	43 145
Q3	36 266	3 862	26	40 154	32 278	5 288	57	37 623
Q4	42 042	5 501	31	47 574	36 176	5 527	46	41 749
Wales								
	BLIC	BLIM	BAEQ	BLIA	BLIK	BLIO	BAEY	BLII
2001/02	8 375	715	6	9 096	7 494	711	68	8 273
2002/03	9 014	497	11	9 522	7 522	782	6	8 310
2003/04	9 480	566	14	10 060	7 863	417	16	8 296
2004/05	9 095	381	34	9 510	7 986	475	31	8 492
2005/06	8 613	359	1	8 973	7 883	347	27	8 257
2004 Q2	1 970	149	15	2 134	2 116	146	–	2 262
Q3	2 571	66	11	2 648	1 972	143	–	2 115
Q4	2 141	66	8	2 215	2 424	114	2	2 540
2005 Q1	2 413	100	–	2 513	1 474	72	29	1 575
Q2	2 215	104	–	2 319	1 975	81	24	2 080
Q3	2 328	62	1	2 391	1 877	79	3	1 959
Q4	1 683	124	–	1 807	2 085	80	–	2 165
2006 Q1	2 387	69	–	2 456	1 946	107	–	2 053
Q2	2 529	87	–	2 616	2 089	71	–	2 160
Q3	2 316	74	12	2 402	2 172	88	–	2 260

12.4
continued

Permanent dwellings started and completed

	Starts				Completions			
	Private enterprise	Registered social landlords[1]	Local Authorities	All dwellings	Private enterprise	Registered social landlords[1]	Local Authorities	All dwellings
Scotland								
	BLFC	BLFM	BAER	BLFA	BLFK	BLFO	BAEZ	BLFI
2001/02	18 478	4 744	43	23 265	18 045	5 479	65	23 589
2002/03	18 503	4 270	15	22 788	18 535	4 695	94	23 324
2003/04	22 352	4 718	–	27 070	19 933	3 727	–	23 660
2004/05	22 638	4 864	–	27 502	21 874	4 752	–	26 626
2005/06	20 939	5 352	6	26 297	19 550	5 102	–	24 652
2004 Q1	5 749	3 112	–	8 861	4 440	747	–	5 187
Q2	6 356	186	–	6 542	5 449	619	–	6 068
Q3	6 058	557	–	6 615	5 800	1 411	–	7 211
Q4	4 882	524	–	5 406	5 689	706	–	6 395
2005 Q1	5 342	3 597	–	8 939	4 936	2 016	–	6 952
Q2	5 480	311	–	5 791	5 211	1 157	–	6 368
Q3	4 832	478	–	5 310	4 764	1 170	–	5 934
Q4	4 902	867	6	5 775	5 122	888	–	6 010
2006 Q1	5 725	3 696	–	9 421	4 453	1 887	–	6 340
Q2	8 830	127	28	8 985	5 626	654	–	6 280
Northern Ireland								
	BLGC	BLGM	BAES	BLGA	BLGK	BLGO	BAFA	BLGI
2001/02	12 065	772	25	12 862	12 072	1 386	29	13 487
2002/03	11 573	669	–	12 242	13 387	1 026	2	14 415
2003/04	12 671	1 140	–	13 811	13 951	560	–	14 511
2004/05	13 199	1 029	–	14 228	14 940	828	–	15 768
2005/06	13 955	1 229	–	15 184	16 628	782	–	17 410
2004 Q2	3 602	61	–	3 663	3 557	67	–	3 624
Q3	3 216	168	–	3 384	3 530	129	–	3 659
Q4	3 101	34	–	3 135	4 339	54	–	4 393
2005 Q1	3 280	766	–	4 046	3 514	578	–	4 092
Q2	3 872	3	–	3 875	4 505	103	–	4 608
Q3	3 592	54	–	3 646	3 712	190	–	3 902
Q4	3 004	221	–	3 225	4 334	127	–	4 461
2006 Q1	3 487	951	–	4 438	4 077	362	–	4 439
Q2	3 901	69	–	3 970	–	–	–	–
Q3	3 554	52	–	3 606	..	..	..	..

1 Includes non-registered social landlords.

Sources: Department for Communities and Local Government;
0117 372 8055;
National Assembly for Wales;
Scottish Development Department;
Department for Social Development (Northern Ireland)

13.1 Motor vehicles: new registrations in Great Britain

Thousands

	Private and light goods (PLG)	PLG: Bodytype cars	PLG: Others (mainly light goods)	Motorcycles	Other goods vehicles	Public transport vehicles	Agriculture machines	Other licensed vehicles	Vehicles exempt from tax	All vehicles	Of which bodytype cars
	BMAK	BMAA	BMAE	BMAL	BBJY	BBJZ	BBKA	BBKB	BBKC	BBKD	BBKE
2001	2 704.2	2 426.4	278.0	177.5	49.0	7.1	19.9	8.2	170.9	3 136.6	2 579.4
2002	2 815.6	2 528.9	286.9	162.3	44.9	7.7	23.1	8.5	167.2	3 229.5	2 682.1
2003	2 820.7	2 497.1	323.5	157.3	48.4	8.4	24.1	9.5	163.5	3 231.9	2 646.0
2004	2 784.9	2 437.5	347.2	133.7	48.0	8.1	25.0	8.5	177.2	3 185.3	2 599.0
2005	2 603.7	2 266.2	337.0	132.1	51.3	8.9	23.5	9.2	193.2	3 021.4	2 443.5
2005 Mar	464.8	414.8	49.9	15.2	5.2	1.1	3.2	0.8	27.0	517.3	440.4
Apr	192.7	164.0	28.7	14.1	4.4	0.8	2.7	0.9	16.5	232.0	178.9
May	201.2	174.2	27.0	13.1	4.6	0.9	2.4	0.8	16.5	239.4	189.2
Jun	241.6	210.6	30.9	15.3	4.7	1.0	2.3	0.8	17.2	282.8	226.3
Jul	185.9	161.6	24.3	13.2	4.3	0.7	2.6	0.8	15.2	222.7	175.3
Aug	90.2	74.2	16.0	10.5	3.5	0.4	1.8	0.8	11.3	118.5	84.2
Sep	441.6	395.0	46.6	15.7	5.5	1.1	2.1	0.8	24.0	490.8	417.6
Oct	163.8	138.4	25.4	9.3	4.4	0.6	1.5	0.8	16.8	197.3	153.9
Nov	172.4	146.1	26.2	8.4	4.8	0.7	1.4	0.8	15.9	204.3	160.8
Dec	170.8	147.5	23.2	6.2	3.5	0.5	1.0	0.6	12.7	195.3	159.2
2006 Jan	164.6	142.7	22.0	6.4	3.4	0.5	1.2	0.6	12.5	189.2	154.0
Feb	81.4	66.8	14.6	4.9	3.0	0.5	1.3	0.6	9.2	100.9	74.8
Mar	462.4	409.8	52.6	16.8	5.5	1.4	3.2	0.8	24.7	514.8	432.9
Apr	173.5	149.0	24.5	12.1	10.5	1.0	2.5	1.0	15.0	215.6	163.0
May	202.0	173.7	28.3	13.8	1.5	0.6	2.6	0.8	16.6	237.8	189.0
Jun	232.7	201.7	31.0	14.3	2.4	0.5	2.4	0.8	17.5	270.7	217.9
Jul	177.8	153.2	24.6	13.5	2.8	0.4	2.6	0.8	17.2	215.3	169.2
Aug	82.9	66.2	16.6	10.6	2.9	0.3	1.8	0.8	12.8	112.1	77.8
Sep	439.0	392.8	46.2	14.7	7.5	0.8	2.1	0.9	23.8	488.8	415.4
Oct	165.1	137.9	27.3	9.7	2.4	0.6	1.6	0.8	16.4	196.6	153.1
Nov	170.8	142.4	28.4	8.3	3.6	0.5	1.6	1.0	15.8	201.5	157.2
Dec	146.8	124.4	22.4	6.6	2.4	0.4	1.3	0.6	12.2	170.3	135.7
2007 Jan	170.3	148.4	21.8	6.7	2.3	0.6	1.4	0.8	14.8	197.0	100.9
Feb	76.9	62.7	14.4	5.1	1.9	0.4	1.3	0.7	10.6	96.9	49.3

Source: Department for Transport

13.2 Motor vehicles currently licensed as at 31 December[1]

Thousands

	Private cars	Other vehicles	Motor-cycles, scooters and mopeds	Public transport vehicles[1]	Goods vehicles[2]	Special concession group[3]	Other vehicles[4]	Crown and exempt vehicles	All vehicles
	BMBJ	BMBK	BMBB	BMBE	BMBD	BMBC	BMBF	BMBL	BMBI
1995	20 505	2 217	594	74	421	274	115†	1 169	25 369
1996	21 172	2 267	609	77	413	254	86	1 424	26 302
1997	21 681	2 317	626	79	414	249	86	1 522	26 974
1998	22 115	2 362	684	80	412	243	84	1 558	27 538
1999	22 785	2 427	760	84	415	241	83	1 573	28 368
2000	23 196	2 469	825	86	418	233	81	1 590	28 898
2001	23 899	2 544	882	89	422	233	76	1 602	29 747
2002	24 543	2 622	941	92	425	243[5]	79	1 855[5]	30 557
2003	24 985	2 730	1 005	96	426	258[5]	78	1 887[5]	31 207
2004	25 754	2 900	1 060	100	434	275[5]	82	1 929[5]	32 259
2005	26 208	3 019	1 075	103	433	283[5]	81	1 978[5]	32 897
2006	26 508	3 137	1 094	107	446	289[5]	86	1 991[5]	33 369

1 Taxation group now restricted to only vehicles with 9 or more seats.
2 Includes agricultural vans and lorries and showman's goods vehicles licensed to draw trailers.
3 Includes combine harvesters, mowing machines, digging machines, mobile cranes and works trucks. Taxation group subject to revision from 1st July 1995, formerly termed the "agricultural and special machines" group.
4 Includes three-wheelers, pedestrian controlled vehicles and showman's haulage.
5 Vehicles in this taxation class are exempt from duty and form part of the "Crown and Exempt" taxation class with effect from January 2002.

Source: Department for Transport

13.3 Index numbers of road traffic and goods transport by road

	Index of vehicle kilometres travelled on roads in Great Britain								Index of tonne-kilo-metres of road goods transport[3,4]
	Motor traffic							Pedal cycles	
						Other goods vehicles			
	All motor traffic	Two-wheeled motor vehicles	Cars	Buses and coaches	Light vans[1]	Total	Articulated[2]		
	BLUV	BMCO	BMCJ	BMCP	BMCK	BMCL	BMCQ	BMCM	BMCN
1998	107	110	106	107	114	110	114	96	106
1999	109	120	107	108	116	111	115	98	104
2000[5]	109	122	107	105	117	111	115	100	105
2001	110	130†	109	106†	121†	111	115	102	104
2002	113	138	112	106	124	111†	116	107†	104
2003	114†	151	112	110	130	112	..	110	106
2004	116	141	113	106	137	116	..	102	106
2005	116	146	113	106	141	114	..	107	106
Seasonally adjusted									
2003 Q1	121†	..	118†	..	151†	100†	..	101	105
Q2	112	..	109	..	145	96	..	106	107
Q3	109	..	106	..	144	94	..	113	105
Q4	115	..	113	..	152	96	..	90	105
2004 Q1	123	..	120	..	159	103	..	101	105
Q2	114	..	111	..	153	100	..	106	106
Q3	109	..	106	..	151	96	..	113	104
Q4	118	..	115	..	160	99	..	90	109
2005 Q1	122	..	119	..	166	101	..	101	105
Q2	115	..	111	..	158	99	..	106	107
Q3	110	..	106	..	154	95	..	113	107
Q4	117	..	114	..	163	96	..	90	105

1 Not exceeding 3.5 tonnes gross vehicle weight. Includes all car based vans and those of the next larger capacity such as transit vans.
2 Goods vehicles up to 3.5 tonnes gross vehicle weight.
3 The figures for road goods transport are estimated from a continuing sample enquiry; excluding estimates of work done by vehicles under 3.5 tonnes gross vehicle weight. The quarterly figures relate to 13-week periods and not three calendar months.
4 From 2004 onwards, figures are provisional.
5 Figures affected by September 2000 fuel protest.

Source: Department for Transport: 020 7944 3095

13.4 Road casualties in Great Britain

	Total casualties		Severity			All severities			
	All ages	Under 16 years	Killed	Seriously injured	Slightly injured	Pedestrians	Pedal cyclists	Motor cyclists and their passengers[1]	Other drivers and their passengers
	BMDA	BMDB	BMDC	BMDD	BMDE	BMDF	BMDG	BMDH	BMDI
1999	320 310	42 051	3 423	39 122	277 765	42 888	22 840	26 192	228 390
2000	320 283	39 715	3 409	38 155	278 719	42 033	20 612	28 212	229 426
2001	313 309	38 269	3 450	37 110	272 749	40 577	19 114	28 810	224 808
2002	302 605	34 689	3 431	35 976	263 198	38 784	17 107	28 353	218 361
2003	290 607	31 988	3 508	33 707	253 392	36 405	17 033	28 411	208 758
2004	280 840	31 000	3 221	31 130	246 489	34 881	16 648	25 641	203 670
2005	271 017	28 126	3 201	28 954	238 862	33 281	16 561	24 824	196 351
2003 Q3	74 681	8 888	937	8 778	64 966	8 655	5 356	8 641	52 029
Q4	76 888	7 299	900	8 563	67 425	9 732	3 813	6 520	56 823
2004 Q1	65 814	6 853	703	7 096	58 015	8 833	3 168	4 794	49 019
Q2	69 430	8 616	825	8 184	60 421	8 531	4 752	7 287	48 860
Q3	70 743	8 400	801	7 968	61 974	7 969	5 031	7 518	50 225
Q4	74 853	7 131	892	7 882	66 079	9 548	3 697	6 042	55 566
2005 Q1	62 037	6 066	740	6 301	54 996	8 097	2 884	4 692	46 364
Q2	67 547	7 787	727	7 322	59 498	8 549	4 527	7 006	47 465
Q3	68 616	7 646	818	7 598	60 200	7 618	5 249	7 304	48 445
Q4	72 817	6 627	916	7 733	64 168	9 017	3 901	5 822	54 077
2006 Q1[2]	59 610	5 640	710	6 280	52 620	7 530	3 010	4 080	44 990
Q2[2]	63 050	7 000	750	7 130	55 170	7 560	4 300	6 290	44 900
Q3[2]	67 470	7 410	840	7 630	59 010	7 280	5 190	7 260	47 740

1 Includes riders and passengers of mopeds, motor scooters and combinations.
2 Provisional data

Source: Department for Transport: 020 7890 6595

13.5 Local (stage) bus services: vehicle kilometres and passenger journeys
Great Britain

Millions

	London[1]	English metropolitan areas	English shire counties	England	Scotland	Wales	All Great Britain	All outside London	All outside London and English metropolitan areas
Vehicle kilometres[2]									
	BAJO	BAJP	BAJQ	BAJR	BAJS	BAJT	BAJU	BAJV	BAJW
1998/99	358	684	1 123	2 165	358	118	2 642	2 284	1 600
1999/00	366	661	1 160	2 186	363	123	2 673	2 307	1 646
2000/01	373	656	1 134	2 164	369	126	2 659	2 286	1 630
2001/02	379	647	1 102	2 128	368	126	2 622	2 243	1 596
2002/03	406	631	1 082	2 119	374	123	2 616	2 210	1 579
2003/04	474	596	1 063	2 133	369	113	2 615	2 141	1 545
2004/05	470	575	1 088	2 133	366	116	2 614	2 144	1 569
2005/06	465	547	1 086	2 098	357	115	2 570	2 105	1 558
Passenger journeys[2]									
	BAJX	BAJY	BAJZ	BAKA	BAKB	BAKC	BAKD	BAKE	BAKF
1998/99	1 266	1 195	1 242	3 702	413	116	4 231	2 965	1 770
1999/00	1 294	1 178	1 250	3 722	442	114	4 278	2 984	1 806
2000/01	1 347	1 166	1 247	3 761	443	116	4 319	2 972	1 806
2001/02	1 422	1 154	1 222	3 798	449	104	4 352	2 930	1 776
2002/03	1 527	1 145	1 210	3 882	452	110	4 444	2 917	1 772
2003/04	1 692	1 114	1 189	3 995	457	111	4 564	2 872	1 758
2004/05	1 782	1 083	1 167	4 032	465	113	4 609	2 827	1 744
2005/06	1 810	1 117	1 198	4 125	477	118	4 719	2 909	1 792

1 Passenger journey statistics for London may not be consistent with those published by Transport for London.
2 There have been revisions to kilometres and journeys based on new data from bus operators and local authorities.

Source: Department for Transport: 020 7944 3076

13.6 Local (stage) bus services: fare indices
Great Britain

1995=100

	London	English metropolitan areas	English shire counties	England	Scotland	Wales	All Great Britain	All outside London	All outside London and English metropolitan areas
1998/99[1]	113.7	118.7	116.7	116.5	121.8	116.3	117.1	118.2	117.8
1999/00[1]	117.2	124.6	122.0	121.5	125.3	122.2	122.0	123.4	122.8
2000/01[1]	117.2	129.9	128.6	125.9	129.9	127.5	126.4	129.2	128.9
2001/02[1]	115.5	137.4	135.1	130.3	131.8	133.5	130.6	135.3	134.4
2002/03[1]	114.8	142.7	141.7	134.2	134.5	139.5	134.5	140.8	139.9
2003/04[1]	116.9	148.0	148.5	139.1	136.8	145.5	139.1	146.3	145.4
2004/05[1]	126.8	154.2	155.7	146.2	140.4	152.4	145.7	152.5	151.4
2005/06[1]	139.7	167.0	165.9	159.2	144.6	160.2	156.3	162.4	160.3
	BAKG	BAKH	BAKI	BAKJ	BAKK	BAKL	BAKM	BAKN	BAKO
2002 Q3	114.7	142.2	141.2	133.9	133.3	138.9	134.0	140.1	139.3
Q4	114.7	143.6	142.2	134.7	135.9	140.3	135.0	141.5	140.6
2003 Q1	115.1	144.3	143.7	135.6	136.1	141.2	135.9	142.6	141.7
Q2	115.1	145.6	146.1	136.8	136.4	142.1	137.0	144.1	143.4
Q3	115.1	147.2	147.5	137.8	136.6	144.1	137.9	145.4	144.6
Q4	115.1	148.2	148.9	138.6	137.0	147.6	138.8	146.7	146.0
2004 Q1	122.2	151.3	151.4	143.0	137.3	148.3	142.5	148.9	147.6
Q2	122.2	152.2	153.1	143.9	139.7	149.5	143.6	150.4	149.4
Q3	122.2	152.8	154.2	144.5	139.7	151.9	144.2	151.3	150.4
Q4	122.2	154.6	157.0	146.0	140.8	153.7	145.7	153.4	152.2
2005 Q1	140.7	157.0	158.5	150.4	141.3	154.3	149.4	155.0	153.4
Q2	140.7	161.3	160.2	152.2	142.6	157.1	151.1	157.5	155.0
Q3[2]	131.7	163.9	162.2	152.8	143.3	158.0	151.8	159.4	156.6
Q4	131.7	166.7	166.5	153.5	144.0	159.5	152.6	162.5	159.8
2006 Q1	148.7	172.8	161.7	162.1	146.3	164.4	160.4	167.3	164.1
Q2	148.6	167.2	158.5	155.6	149.3	164.5	155.3	160.3	156.4
Q3	147.6	166.3	155.1	153.8	149.3	164.6	153.7	158.5	154.2
Q4	145.7	166.3	158.1	154.3	149.3	164.6	154.2	162.0	166.3

1 Owing to rounding financial year data may differ slightly from that published by DfT.
2 London bus fares reduced overall in Q3 owing to TfL's free travel scheme for children, introduced in September 2005.

Source: Department for Transport: 020 7944 3076

13.7 National Rail and London Underground

Millions

	National Rail: passenger kilometres by ticket type			London Underground: passenger journeys[1,2]		
	Ordinary fares	Season tickets	Total	Full and reduced fares	Season tickets	Total
1999/00	28 030	10 443	38 472	477	450	927
2000/01	27 245	10 933	38 179	486	484	970
2001/02	28 149	10 992	39 141	491	462	953
2002/03	28 394	11 284	39 678	495	446	942
2003/04	29 003	11 908	40 911	491	457	948
2004/05	29 487	12 275	41 762	486	490	976
2005/06	30 405	12 805	43 211	460	510	970
	BMGB	BMGD	BMGA	BMGF	BMGG	BMGE
2003 Q1	6 662	3 030	9 691	113	112	225
Q2	7 204	2 831	10 036	120	111	231
Q3	7 674	2 752	10 426	127	106	233
Q4	7 143	3 078	10 221	127	119	246
2004 Q1	6 983	3 247	10 229	117	121	238
Q2	7 250	2 927	10 177	120	119	239
Q3	7 747	2 818	10 565	124	117	241
Q4	7 463	3 296	10 759	127	125	252
2005 Q1	7 027	3 233	10 260	115	129	244
Q2	7 720	3 112	10 832	120	131	251
Q3	7 632	2 940	10 572	107	127	234
Q4	7 721	3 354	11 075	121	119	240
2006 Q1	7 332	3 399	10 731	113	133	246
Q2	8 008	3 087	11 095	119	126	245
Q3	8 515	2 932	11 447	125	125	250
Q4	8 360	3 386	11 746	128	129	256

1 The annual figures are greater than the the the sum of the four quarters owing to year end revision by Transport for London.
2 London Underground data partly estimated.

Sources: Office of Rail Regulation: www.rail-reg.gov.uk;
Department for Transport: 020 7944 3076

13.8 National Rail: freight traffic

	National Rail[1]			Freight moved
	Freight lifted: million tonnes			
	Coal and coke	Other traffic	Total	Billion net tonne kilometres
	BMHB	BMHD	BMHA	BMHE
2001	46.9	48.5	95.4	19 200
2002	41.1	46.4	87.5	18 634
2003	42.4	46.9	89.3	18 748
2004	48.8	49.9	98.7	20 175
2005	53.5	49.3	102.8	21 689
2003 Q1	9.5	13.6	23.1	4 752
Q2	8.7	13.2	21.9	4 618
Q3	8.6	13.8	22.4	4 737
Q4	8.9	13.0	21.9	4 641
2004 Q1	9.0	13.7	22.6	4 878
Q2[2]	10.6	14.4	25.0	4 994
Q3	10.7	14.3	25.0	5 153
Q4	11.7	14.3	26.1	5 149
2005 Q1	12.0	13.8	25.8	5 278
Q2[3]	11.2	14.5	25.7	5 504
Q3	10.6	13.9	24.6	5 388
Q4	13.0	15.0	27.9	5 519
2006 Q1	12.8	14.3	27.1	5 698
Q2	13.0	15.1	28.1	5 654
Q3	11.4	14.6	26.1	5 399
Q4	12.5	14.4	26.9	5 495

1 Freight train traffic only.
2 There is a break in the series between 2004 Q1 and 2004 Q2, due to a change in the method of data collection.
3 There is a further break in the series between 2005 Q1 and 2005 Q2, since the 2005 Q2 figures onwards include some of the tonnes lifted by and additional Freight Operating Company.

Note: The freight lifted series has been revised. Previously the coal figure for one of the freight operating companies included iron ore. Iron ore has now been correctly assigned to the 'other' category. This revision did not affect the total figures, but caused a reduction in the coal and coke figures and an increase in the 'other' category.

Source: Office of Rail Regulation: www.rail-reg.gov.uk

13.9 UK airlines: aircraft kilometres flown, passengers and cargo uplifted[1]
Tonne-kilometres and seat kilometres used on scheduled services

Monthly averages or calendar months: thousands or tonnes

	All services			Domestic services			International services		
	Aircraft kilometres flown (000's)	Passengers uplifted (000's)	Cargo uplifted (tonnes)	Aircraft kilometres flown (000's)	Passengers uplifted (000's)	Cargo uplifted (tonnes)	Aircraft kilometres flown (000's)	Passengers uplifted (000's)	Cargo uplifted (tonnes)
	BMIA	BMIB	BMIC	BMID	BMIE	BMIF	BMIG	BMIH	BMII
2000	1 012 008	70 066.50	897 864	120 270	17 987.90	24 361	891 738	50 120.80	873 512
2001	1 054 939	70 034.40	741 623	128 125	18 331.60	19 560	920 814	51 703.10	722 061
2002	1 047 400	72 708.90	769 519	125 758	19 992.70	16 800	921 643	52 717.60	752 713
2003	1 082 392	76 207.10	799 406	121 260	20 730.90	17 158	964 140	55 476.30	782 232
2004	1 204 698	86 048.90	905 622	138 790	22 539.70	14 928	1 065 908	63 508.60	890 720
2005	1 324 222	93 602.90	921 406	147 468	23 128.40	10 012	1 177 063	70 474.70	911 405
2006	1 400 167	97 543.37	946 267	149 582	22 852.81	8 399	1 582 588	70 330.50	940 321
2002 Jul	92 652	7 296.20	65 039	11 335	1 998.60	1 502	81 318	5 297.60	63 536
Aug	92 358	6 974.10	61 077	11 069	1 904.60	1 384	81 289	5 069.50	59 692
Sep	89 175	6 612.00	62 876	10 687	1 769.20	1 375	78 488	4 842.80	61 501
Oct	90 789	6 490.50	68 992	10 585	1 772.90	1 712	80 204	4 717.60	67 279
Nov	85 508	5 564.00	70 269	10 458	1 675.90	1 449	75 050	3 888.10	68 820
Dec	84 826	5 488.00	63 633	9 901	1 589.00	1 330	74 925	3 900.60	62 303
2003 Jan	85 332	5 182.70	57 971	10 038	1 463.60	1 326	75 294	3 719.10	56 645
Feb	78 501	5 339.90	61 203	8 758	1 396.70	1 241	69 743	3 943.20	59 962
Mar	87 376	5 957.40	67 861	9 772	1 570.40	1 315	77 604	4 387.00	66 546
Apr	86 156	6 093.30	61 770	9 720	1 725.60	1 238	76 436	4 367.70	60 533
May	90 575	6 401.70	66 677	10 212	1 760.60	1 263	80 363	4 641.20	65 414
Jun	91 856	6 839.10	65 786	9 676	1 799.00	1 451	82 188	5 040.10	64 317
Jul	96 889	7 218.40	63 722	10 563	1 911.90	1 852	86 326	5 306.50	61 870
Aug	97 406	7 439.60	64 416	10 359	1 958.30	1 305	87 047	5 481.30	63 112
Sep	91 047	6 979.00	67 516	10 147	1 868.10	1 676	83 900	5 110.90	65 841
Oct	97 142	6 893.00	73 931	11 365	1 905.60	1 455	85 777	4 987.40	72 476
Nov	91 188	6 082.70	76 014	10 671	1 761.80	1 649	80 517	4 320.90	74 364
Dec	88 924	5 780.30	72 539	9 979	1 609.30	1 387	78 945	4 171.00	71 152
2004 Jan	92 746	5 637.40	66 296	10 547	1 507.30	1 360	82 199	4 130.20	64 937
Feb	88 947	6 028.90	72 876	10 421	1 678.80	1 328	78 526	4 350.20	71 548
Mar	96 622	6 784.00	81 275	11 550	1 853.30	1 524	85 072	4 930.10	79 751
Apr	97 529	7 063.00	71 670	11 554	1 898.00	1 402	85 975	5 165.00	70 267
May	103 598	7 270.90	77 514	11 336	1 822.30	995	92 262	5 448.60	76 518
Jun	103 317	7 893.40	73 777	11 883	1 971.00	1 209	91 434	5 922.50	72 562
Jul	106 835	8 326.10	75 298	11 741	2 098.00	1 208	95 094	6 228.00	74 090
Aug	105 970	8 234.70	71 329	11 984	2 073.60	1 341	93 986	6 161.10	69 989
Sep	111 635	7 848.40	74 822	12 730	1 997.50	1 253	98 905	5 850.90	73 570
Oct	103 048	7 602.00	79 973	11 868	1 976.10	1 559	91 180	5 625.80	78 415
Nov	96 562	6 665.70	80 749	12 000	1 875.10	858	84 562	4 790.60	79 891
Dec	97 889	6 694.40	80 043	11 176	1 788.70	891	86 713	4 905.60	79 182
2005 Jan	100 014	6 375.30	71 101	11 494	1 590.70	646	88 828	4 784.60	70 455
Feb	92 589	6 291.80	72 159	10 815	1 654.40	773	81 774	4 637.30	71 387
Mar	104 148	7 559.20	80 413	11 880	1 904.80	908	92 268	5 654.40	79 506
Apr	107 874	7 646.60	74 458	12 240	1 914.80	782	95 634	5 731.80	73 676
May	115 294	8 073.20	75 346	12 700	1 970.20	806	102 594	6 103.00	74 548
Jun	115 219	8 560.30	74 797	11 537	2 003.50	1 259	103 682	6 556.90	73 538
Jul	121 204	9 098.20	76 106	13 472	2 145.50	930	107 732	6 952.80	75 176
Aug	119 731	9 009.40	69 614	13 136	2 109.20	820	106 595	6 900.20	68 794
Sep	117 645	8 738.10	76 595	12 972	2 067.50	806	104 673	6 670.70	75 789
Oct	118 905	8 367.90	83 404	12 983	2 045.70	781	105 922	6 322.20	82 624
Nov	105 519	6 982.00	83 838	12 641	1 920.00	806	92 879	5 062.00	83 032
Dec	106 080	6 900.90	83 575	11 598	1 802.10	695	94 482	5 098.80	82 880
2006 Jan	109 075	6 609.20	77 962	12 233	1 623.60	605	96 842	4 985.60	80 358
Feb	100 291	6 663.50	73 672	11 511	1 679.70	733	420 780	4 983.90	72 939
Mar	112 867	7 766.20	87 093	12 942	1 923.80	785	99 928	5 842.30	86 308
Apr	115 300	8 344.60	78 401	12 287	1 934.90	667	103 013	6 409.80	77 734
May	123 296	8 610.70	78 236	13 276	1 997.00	673	110 020	6 613.60	77 562
Jun	122 920	9 022.30	78 635	13 388	2 026.20	824	109 532	6 996.10	77 811
Jul	127 129	9 560.00	78 551	12 358	2 110.60	733	114 771	7 449.30	77 818
Aug	125 321	9 130.70	72 886	12 664	1 985.20	706	112 657	7 145.50	72 180
Sep	122 265	8 884.61	78 162	12 372	1 963.90	735	109 893	2 560.70	77 426
Oct	122 796	8 547.26	80 873	12 833	1 998.20	696	109 963	6 549.10	80 178
Nov	109 734	7 278.19	82 498	12 746	1 909.17	661	96 988	5 369.00	81 836
Dec	109 173	7 126.11	79 298	10 972	1 700.54	581	98 201	5 425.60	78 171
2007 Jan	112 520	6 777.62	69 074	12 226	1 603.85	552	100 294	5 173.77	68 521

13.9 UK airlines: aircraft kilometres flown, passengers and cargo uplifted[1]
Tonne-kilometres and seat kilometres used on scheduled services

continued

Monthly averages or calendar months: thousands or tonnes

	All services (thousand tonne-kilometres)				Domestic services (thousand tonne-kilometres)				International services (thousand tonne-kilometres)			
	Mail	Freight	Passenger	Seat kilometres used (millions)	Mail	Freight	Passenger	Seat kilometres used (millions)	Mail	Freight	Passenger	Seat kilometres used (millions)
	BMIJ	BMIK	BMIL	BMIM	BMIN	BMIO	BMIP	BMIQ	BMIR	BMIS	BMIT	BMIU
2000	179 239	5 160 794	16 495 712	170 323.5	3 647	5 712	636 636	7 843.8	175 522	5 155 082	15 857 076	162 800.6
2001	101 886	4 548 053	15 264 370	158 717.7	3 539	4 089	649 744	7 658.1	98 347	4 544 144	14 614 626	151 059.6
2002	56 551	4 940 528	15 042 639	156 582.0	2 797	3 605	703 521	8 330.2	53 754	4 936 923	14 339 173	148 252.0
2003	55 082	5 250 490	15 376 586	166 445.2	3 067	3 480	737 791	8 991.9	52 015	5 247 010	14 638 795	157 453.4
2004	80 859	5 698 327	16 480 406	182 728.0	2 619	2 621	780 832	9 530.6	78 240	5 695 706	15 699 574	173 196.7
2005	89 299	5 998 434	14 980 897	200 333.0	277	2 652	783 849	9 789.5	90 022	5 995 782	14 197 048	190 543.3
2006	99 322	6 215 021	15 095 677	213 335.6	85	2 285	772 537	9 798.3	99 237	6 213 036	15 322 905	203 537.1
2002 Jul	3 590	418 248	1 372 205	14 320.0	239	324	66 976	791.5	3 351	417 924	1 305 229	13 528.5
Aug	3 578	398 948	1 402 147	14 579.9	227	290	67 382	797.1	3 351	398 658	1 334 765	13 782.8
Sep	3 271	406 311	1 322 762	13 784.6	223	284	63 078	744.5	3 048	406 027	1 259 684	13 040.1
Oct	3 558	444 868	1 292 158	13 530.0	257	413	62 963	745.4	3 301	444 455	1 229 195	12 784.6
Nov	4 930	459 477	1 168 848	12 176.8	241	305	59 379	705.3	4 689	459 172	1 109 469	11 471.5
Dec	6 728	403 994	1 215 863	12 534.3	234	267	56 925	672.2	6 494	403 727	1 158 993	11 862.0
2003 Jan	3 533	369 564	1 172 313	12 041.0	242	243	52 215	617.5	3 291	369 321	1 120 098	11 423.5
Feb	3 085	397 296	1 052 275	11 693.1	224	265	49 328	612.8	2 861	397 031	1 002 947	11 080.2
Mar	4 598	533 143	1 166 617	14 960.3	248	294	56 243	740.2	4 350	532 849	1 110 374	14 220.0
Apr	3 988	406 914	1 156 061	12 905.8	238	261	62 030	764.1	3 750	406 653	1 094 031	12 141.8
May	3 817	440 143	1 208 511	13 560.2	211	292	62 484	792.5	3 606	439 851	1 146 027	12 767.6
Jun	3 798	421 332	1 347 807	14 704.8	258	330	63 998	812.9	3 540	421 002	1 283 809	13 892.0
Jul	3 819	401 962	1 440 374	15 096.7	275	344	68 416	812.4	3 544	401 618	1 371 958	14 284.4
Aug	4 239	409 606	1 496 153	15 650.2	257	235	69 041	819.3	3 982	409 371	1 427 112	14 831.0
Sep	4 072	439 999	1 381 055	14 470.8	290	323	66 310	788.1	3 782	439 676	1 314 745	13 682.7
Oct	4 943	480 572	1 376 472	14 477.7	224	342	67 791	805.5	4 719	480 230	1 308 681	13 672.2
Nov	5 942	494 564	1 281 768	13 435.3	296	293	62 346	742.8	5 646	494 271	1 219 422	12 692.5
Dec	9 248	455 395	1 297 180	13 449.3	304	258	57 589	683.8	8 944	455 137	1 239 591	12 765.5
2004 Jan	5 761	414 252	1 267 150	13 135.4	253	239	53 713	637.9	5 508	414 013	1 213 437	12 497.5
Feb	5 471	460 557	1 217 118	12 803.9	269	255	59 429	708.8	5 202	460 302	1 157 689	12 095.2
Mar	5 777	517 345	1 401 143	14 742.4	303	284	65 862	784.2	5 474	517 061	1 335 281	13 958.2
Apr	6 703	458 300	1 424 524	15 126.0	257	280	67 361	805.6	6 446	458 020	1 357 163	14 320.3
May	7 198	498 549	1 433 682	15 158.5	229	173	64 696	769.1	6 969	498 376	1 368 986	14 389.4
Jun	6 319	453 879	1 467 827	16 431.9	249	213	67 354	835.6	6 070	453 666	1 400 473	15 596.4
Jul	5 769	475 814	1 561 267	17 455.4	243	171	72 371	892.5	5 526	475 643	1 488 896	16 562.7
Aug	5 375	452 747	1 534 320	17 127.3	218	144	71 348	874.3	5 157	452 603	1 462 972	16 253.0
Sep	6 133	454 903	1 436 946	16 150.1	236	245	67 842	841.6	5 897	454 658	1 369 104	15 308.0
Oct	6 272	500 028	1 353 461	15 680.3	242	262	67 378	838.0	6 030	499 766	1 286 083	14 842.3
Nov	7 895	513 126	1 170 601	14 220.2	46	182	63 090	789.4	7 849	512 944	1 107 511	13 430.7
Dec	12 186	498 827	1 212 367	14 696.6	74	173	60 388	753.6	12 112	498 654	1 151 979	13 943.0
2005 Jan	8 289	454 494	1 094 967	14 699.2	21	155	53 344	670.1	8 268	454 339	1 041 623	14 029.1
Feb	8 020	447 848	966 971	13 593.9	52	194	55 423	696.1	7 968	447 654	911 548	12 897.8
Mar	7 579	509 500	1 220 722	16 298.2	61	211	63 589	803.1	7 518	509 289	1 157 133	15 495.1
Apr	7 218	491 439	1 217 590	16 194.3	33	188	64 716	809.8	7 185	491 251	1 152 874	15 384.5
May	6 788	494 285	1 255 675	16 670.6	16	223	66 491	833.9	6 772	494 062	1 189 184	15 836.7
Jun	6 316	473 969	1 346 995	17 990.4	16	297	67 803	848.8	6 300	473 672	1 279 192	17 141.6
Jul	6 007	492 762	1 443 304	19 205.0	17	258	73 143	916.0	5 990	492 504	1 370 161	18 289.0
Aug	5 372	461 964	1 408 459	18 659.9	18	232	71 931	893.5	5 354	461 732	1 336 528	17 766.4
Sep	5 278	509 140	1 371 706	18 258.1	15	226	70 309	876.8	6 263	508 914	1 301 397	17 381.2
Oct	6 827	561 179	1 330 099	17 735.2	7	240	69 946	869.6	6 820	560 939	1 260 153	16 865.6
Nov	8 307	551 188	1 146 070	15 396.4	10	237	65 479	809.4	8 297	550 951	1 080 591	14 587.0
Dec	13 298	550 666	1 178 339	15 631.8	11	191	61 675	762.4	13 287	550 475	1 116 664	14 869.3
2006 Jan	7 171	511 467	111 055	15 538.5	7	154	55 749	686.1	7 164	511 313	1 054 801	14 852.4
Feb	6 279	479 895	1 092 572	14 402.3	6	189	57 906	712.9	6 273	479 706	1 034 666	13 689.4
Mar	7 034	576 299	1 277 807	16 981.8	9	193	65 822	813.3	7 025	576 106	1 211 985	16 168.5
Apr	7 156	518 472	1 384 501	18 179.9	5	158	65 911	819.6	7 151	518 314	1 318 590	17 360.3
May	6 964	517 240	1 387 018	18 215.0	7	178	68 700	850.1	6 957	517 062	1 318 318	17 364.8
Jun	7 307	521 956	1 484 171	19 469.5	6	223	72 245	862.4	7 301	521 733	1 411 926	18 607.2
Jul	6 799	519 585	1 561 182	20 625.5	6	212	65 463	900.8	6 793	519 373	1 495 719	19 724.7
Aug	7 192	486 701	1 495 475	19 719.7	8	216	64 117	836.3	7 184	486 485	1 431 628	18 883.3
Sep	8 425	513 291	1 437 492	19 028.6	8	216	64 181	833.1	8 417	513 075	1 373 311	18 195.5
Oct	9 063	518 126	1 390 842	18 405.3	8	193	66 096	853.3	9 055	517 933	1 324 746	17 551.9
Nov	10 505	549 794	1 223 173	16 204.4	7	194	66 688	860.7	10 498	549 600	1 156 485	15 343.7
Dec	15 427	502 195	1 250 389	16 565.1	8	159	59 659	769.7	15 419	502 336	1 190 730	15 795.4
2007 Jan	9 453	441 725	1 217 261	16 168.3	6	155	56 883	729.5	9 447	441 570	1 160 378	15 438.8

1 The annual figures are the sum of the monthly figures provided by the CAA. All kilometre statistics are based on standard (Great Circle) distance. Including weight of freight and mail, excess baggage and diplomatic bags, but excluding passengers' and crews' permitted baggage.

Source: Civil Aviation Authority

13.10 Merchant vessels registered in the United Kingdom (500 gross tons and over)[1]

	Bulk, tanker and dry			Other			Total		
	Number	Grt million	Dwt million	Number	Grt million	Dwt million	Number	Grt million	Dwt million
	BMJG	BMJH	BMJI	BMJJ	BMJK	BMJL	BMJM	BMJN	BMJO
2000	167	4.8	8.6	304	4.7	3.4	471	9.5	12.0
2001	194	5.5	9.6	340	5.2	4.0	534	10.7	13.6
2002	229	6.0	10.3	381	6.5	5.3	610	12.5	15.6
2003	262	7.7	12.7	461	8.3	7.0	723	16.0	19.7
2004	293	8.5	14.0	461	8.4	7.5	754	16.9	21.6
2005	323	9.9	16.7	472	8.9	8.2	795	18.8	24.9
2006	331	10.4	17.3	483	9.4	8.7	814	19.8	26.1
End Quarter									
2002 Q1	196	5.3	9.4	353	5.5	4.2	549	10.8	13.6
Q2	203	5.6	9.8	360	5.7	4.3	563	11.2	14.1
Q3	225	5.9	10.2	368	6.1	4.8	593	12.0	15.0
Q4	229	6.0	10.3	381	6.5	5.3	610	12.5	15.6
2003 Q1	236	6.4	11.0	392	6.7	5.5	628	13.1	16.4
Q2	246	7.0	11.5	431	7.4	6.2	677	14.4	17.7
Q3	250	7.2	11.8	442	7.7	6.5	692	14.9	18.4
Q4	262	7.7	12.7	461	8.3	7.0	723	16.0	19.7
2004 Q1	268	8.1	13.4	475	8.9	7.7	743	17.0	21.1
Q2	279	8.3	13.8	470	9.0	7.8	749	17.3	21.6
Q3	295	8.5	14.1	465	8.7	7.7	760	17.2	21.8
Q4	293	8.5	14.0	461	8.4	7.5	754	16.9	21.6
2005 Q1	306	9.1	15.2	459	8.4	7.7	765	17.5	23.0
Q2	311	9.4	15.8	472	8.6	7.9	783	18.0	23.8
Q3	315	9.8	16.5	474	8.8	8.0	789	18.5	24.5
Q4	323	9.9	16.7	472	8.9	8.2	795	18.8	24.9
2006 Q1	326	9.8	16.4	466	8.7	7.9	792	18.5	24.3
Q2	335	10.3	17.2	467	9.0	8.3	802	19.2	25.5
Q3	334	10.4	17.3	478	9.4	8.7	812	19.8	26.0
Q4	331	10.4	17.3	483	9.4	8.7	814	19.8	26.1

1 Covers vessels registered within the United Kingdom, the Channel Isles and the Isle of Man.

Source: Department for Transport

13.11 UK passenger movement by sea and air[1]

Thousands

Inward

| | Sea | | | | | | Air | | | | |
	Irish Republic	Other EU	Rest of Europe and Mediterranean Sea area	Rest of world	Pleasure cruises[2]	Total	Irish Republic	Other EU	Rest of Europe and Mediterranean Sea area	Rest of world	Total[3]
	BMKC	BMKD	BMKE	BMKF	BMKG	BMKB	BMKI	BMKJ	BMKK	BMKL	BMKH
2004	1 808	10 950	119	19	384	13 279	5 423	41 729	11 215	24 903	83 268
2005	1 664†	10 040†	103†	27	461	12 295†	5 898	43 522	13 640	25 891	88 951
2006	1 574	10 006	79	..	..		6 191	44 457	15 280	26 653	92 582
2004 Q1	263	1 664	20	–	5	1 953	1 225	7 459	2 025	5 739	16 447
Q2	517	3 116	36	10	154	3 831	1 368	11 060	2 806	6 368	21 602
Q3	713	3 981	44	6	165	4 909	1 485	14 072	3 749	6 907	26 213
Q4	315	2 189	19	3	60	2 586	1 345	9 138	2 635	5 889	19 006
2005 Q1	278	1 548	18	..	11	1 854†	1 310	8 072	2 644	6 004	18 030
Q2	444	2 752	34	14	151	3 395	1 502	11 633	3 471	6 693	23 299
Q3	653	3 696	41	7	221	4 618	1 627	14 446	4 439	7 167	27 679
Q4	289	2 044	10	6	78	2 428	1 459	9 371	3 086	6 027	19 943
2006 Q1	224	1 568	11	..	..	1 803	1 412	8 109	3 082	6 128	18 731
Q2	441	2 844	25	..	..	..	1 627	12 071	3 940	7 017	24 655
Q3	620	3 603	33	..	..	..	1 674	14 733	4 893	7 341	28 642
Q4	289	1 991	10	..	..	..	1 478	9 544	3 365	6 167	20 554

Outward

| | Sea | | | | | | Air | | | | |
	Irish Republic	Other EU	Rest of Europe and Mediterranean Sea area	Rest of world	Pleasure cruises[2]	Total	Irish Republic	Other EU	Rest of Europe and Mediterranean Sea area	Rest of world	Total[3]
	BMKO	BMKP	BMKQ	BMKR	BMKS	BMKN	BMKU	BMKV	BMKW	BMKX	BMKT
2004	1 848	10 955	119	22	384†	13 327	5 403	41 584	11 155	24 880	83 021
2005	1 715	10 067†	104	24	474	12 384†	5 894	43 400	13 556	25 788	88 637
2006	1 647	10 084	76	..	..		6 166	44 304	15 138	26 591	92 201
2004 Q1	255	1 597	20	–	8	1 879	1 199	7 353	1 951	5 581	16 083
Q2	527	3 181	35	12	138	3 894	1 347	11 505	2 874	5 928	21 654
Q3	731	3 930	44	5	169	4 879	1 507	13 864	3 712	7 030	26 113
Q4	335	2 247	20	4	69	2 675	1 350	8 862	2 618	6 341	19 171
2005 Q1	290	1 539	19	–	7	1 855†	1 300	8 102	2 589	5 924	17 915
Q2	448	2 740	33	11	163	3 395	1 472	11 918	3 490	6 091	22 971
Q3	675	3 672	41	6	223	4 618	1 656	14 288	4 405	7 276	27 624
Q4	302	2 116	11	7	81	2 516	1 466	9 092	3 072	6 497	20 127
2006 Q1	239	1 508	10	..	..	1 756	1 401	7 984	2 937	5 981	18 303
Q2	458	2 919	25	..	..	..	1 600	12 550	4 001	6 479	24 631
Q3	639	3 568	32	..	..	..	1 691	14 486	4 825	7 445	28 447
Q4	311	2 089	9	..	..	..	1 474	9 284	3 375	6 686	20 820

Note: Sea and Air passenger numbers are seasonal, which should be taken into account when comparing figures within a year.

1 Excluding movement by land across the frontier between the Irish Republic and Northern Ireland, passengers travelling between the Channel Islands and Great Britain, passengers carried in aircraft chartered by British government departments and as far as possible, passengers travelling by sea on day trips and HM and other Armed Forces travelling in the course of their duties.

2 Passengers on pleasure cruises beginning or ending at UK seaports (excluding scheduled voyages between Southampton and New York which are included in rest of world).

3 Excluding oil rigs.

*Sources: Department for Transport;
Civil Aviation Authority*

13.12 UK passenger movement by sea and air
Analysis of countries of landing and of embarkation

Thousands

		2005	2006	2005 Q2	2005 Q3	2005 Q4	2006 Q1	2006 Q2	2006 Q3	2006 Q4
European continent and Mediterranean Sea area										
By sea[1]										
Belgium	BMLB	778	748	198	241	187	145	193	222	187
France	BMLC	16 834†	16 925	4 614	6 294	3 415	2 550	4 890	6 134	3 352
Netherlands	BMLD	1 847†	1 897	503	588	419	323	533	605	436
Irish Republic	BMDJ	3 379†	3 221	892	1 328	591	463	899	1 258	600
Germany	BMDK	98†	1	30	37	13	..	..	..	..
Denmark	BMDL	92†	89	25	34	18	14	23	34	17
Sweden	BMDM	78†	59	24	29	15	6	19	28	7
Spain	BMDN	378	372	98	145	92	37	105	148	81
Norway	BMDO	200	149	65	79	19	20	48	62	18
Other Europe	BMLE	8	6	2	3	2	..	2	2	1
Total	A4N3	23 693	23 465	6 451	8 778	4 772	3 559	6 712	8 494	4 700
By air										
Austria	BMLH	1 797	1 788	416	483	344	546	409	454	379
Belgium	BMLI	1 711	1 626	443	439	428	401	439	389	397
Denmark	BMLJ	2 255	2 306	576	639	559	493	601	624	588
Eastern Europe[2]	BMLM	7 871	9 593	1 945	2 372	1 950	1 978	2 442	2 912	2 261
Finland	BMLK	799	930	172	175	289	173	204	210	343
France	BMLL	11 009	11 570	2 883	3 265	2 348	2 584	3 113	3 414	2 459
Germany	BMLN	10 912	11 504	2 779	2 971	2 664	2 442	3 060	3 187	2 815
Greece	BMLO	5 598	5 520	1 656	3 008	710	206	1 623	2 995	696
Irish Republic	BMLP	11 791	12 357	2 974	3 282	2 925	2 813	3 227	3 365	2 952
Italy	BMLQ	10 715	10 572	2 885	3 411	2 226	2 074	2 917	3 348	2 233
Malta	BMLR	1 110	1 055	295	395	234	183	286	349	237
Netherlands	BMLS	7 887	8 255	2 053	2 081	1 956	1 813	2 173	2 185	2 084
Norway	BMLT	1 753	1 892	454	456	443	435	483	514	460
Portugal	BMLU	4 088	4 295	1 183	1 464	826	623	1 267	1 548	857
Spain	BMLV	27 302	27 569	7 749	10 035	5 425	4 128	8 040	10 119	5 282
Sweden	BMLW	2 321	2 290	616	607	562	496	624	601	569
Switzerland	BMLX	4 502	4 958	1 024	1 068	978	1 558	1 172	1 146	1 082
Turkey	BMLY	3 551	3 407	1 004	1 746	598	206	938	1 692	571
Yugoslavia	BMLZ	150	166	38	50	33	32	45	53	36
Other countries[3]	BMMA	1 484	1 727	418	526	308	250	492	622	363
Total	BMLG	118 607	123 382	31 564	38 474	25 805	23 435	33 555	39 729	26 663
Mediterranean area										
By air										
Cyprus	BMMC	2 990	3 008	867	1 182	617	309	913	1 191	595
Near East[4]	BMMD	1 056	1 022	270	312	243	232	283	270	237
North Africa[5]	BMME	2 776	3 465	680	765	733	793	866	927	879
Total	BMMB	6 822	7 495	1 817	2 259	1 593	1 334	2 061	2 388	1 712
Rest of World										
By sea										
Other long sea journeys	RVCO	52	..	25	13	13	..	..	..	..
Pleasure cruises[6]	LUQZ	935	..	314	444	159	..	..	..	..
Total	A4N4	986	..	339	457	172	..	..	..	..
By air										
Australia and New Zealand	BMMP	1 397	1 384	336	352	340	350	323	350	361
Canada	BMMQ	3 610	3 634	974	1 356	690	606	1 026	1 317	685
Canary Islands	BMMR	7 261	7 311	1 670	1 893	1 866	1 794	1 752	1 901	1 864
Caribbean[7]	BMMS	1 824	1 893	423	406	467	527	442	433	491
Central Africa[8]	BMMT	67	69	18	18	16	15	18	19	17
Central America[9]	BMMU	1 271	1 353	341	425	278	259	370	429	295
East Africa[10]	BMMV	736	774	152	222	181	187	170	224	193
Far East[11]	BMMW	4 787	5 020	1 191	1 294	1 174	1 205	1 237	1 354	1 224
Indian Continent[12]	BMMX	2 691	3 475	590	642	765	954	789	834	898
Japan	BMMY	1 185	1 086	294	314	287	272	278	289	247
Middle East[13]	BMMZ	3 774	4 158	868	1 052	905	946	970	1 215	1 027
Southern Africa[14]	BMNA	1 733	1 771	373	416	457	480	381	425	485
South America[15]	BMNB	379	361	83	97	99	102	93	75	91
United States of America	BMNC	18 310	18 074	4 874	5 252	4 323	3 720	4 966	5 144	4 244
West Africa[16]	BMND	916	985	195	236	245	249	222	252	262
Other countries[17]	BMNE	852	849	199	229	216	208	206	222	213
Oil rigs	BMNF	627	712	158	172	163	154	176	188	194
Total	BMMO	51 420	52 909	12 738	14 376	12 471	12 027	13 419	14 671	12 792

Note: Sea and Air passenger numbers are seasonal, which should be taken into account when comparing figures within a year.

1 This represents ferry passengers as cruise passengers are shown seperately. Includes hovercraft.
2 Including Albania, Bulgaria, Czech Republic, Hungary, Poland, Romania and Commonwealth of Independent States.
3 Including Faroes, Gibraltar, Iceland, Luxembourg, Croatia, Slovenia and Bosnia-Herzegovina.
4 Including Jordan, Lebanon, Israel and Syria.
5 Including Algeria, Egypt, Libya, Morocco and Tunisia.
6 Passengers on journeys beginning and ending at UK seaports.
7 Including Bahamas, Barbados, Bermuda, Cayman Islands, French Antilles, Jamaica, Leeward Islands, Netherlands Antilles, Puerto Rico, Trinidad and Tobago, Turks and Caicos Islands, US Virgin Islands and Windward Islands.
8 Including Angola, Central African Republic, Chad, Congo, Democratic Republic of Congo, Malawi and Zambia.
9 Including Belize, Costa Rica, Cuba, Dominican Republic, El Salvador, Guatemala, Haiti, Honduras, Mexico, Nicaragua and Panama.
10 Including Burundi, Djibouti, Ethiopia, Kenya, Rwanda, Somali Republic, Sudan, Tanzania and Uganda.
11 Including Bandar Seri Begawan, Burma, China, Hong Kong, Indonesia, Kampuchea, Korea, Laos, Malaysia, Nepal, Philippines, Singapore, Taiwan, Thailand and Vietnam.
12 Including Afghanistan, Bangladesh, India, Pakistan and Sri Lanka.
13 Including Iran, Iraq, Kuwait, Persian Gulf States, Republic of North Yemen, Republic of South Yemen, Saudi Arabia and United Arab Emirates.
14 Including Botswana, Lesotho, Mozambique, Namibia, South African Republic, Swaziland and Zimbabwe.
15 Including Argentina, Bolivia, Brazil, Chile, Colombia, Ecuador, Guyana, Paraguay, Peru, Uruguay and Venezuela.
16 Including Benin, Cameroon, Equatorial Guinea, Gabon, Gambia, Ghana, Guinea, Guinea Bissau, Ivory Coast, Liberia, Mali, Mauritania, Niger, Nigeria, Senegal, Sierra Leone, Togo, Upper Volta and Western Sahara.
17 Atlantic Ocean Islands, Indian Ocean Islands and Pacific Ocean Islands and Madeira.

Sources: Department for Transport;
Civil Aviation Authority

14 Retailing

14.1 Index numbers of retail sales[1]

Sales: weekly average 2000=100, seasonally adjusted

			Volume									Value					
		Predominantly non-food stores									Predominantly non-food stores						
	All retailers	Predominantly food stores	Total	Non-specialised stores	Textile, clothing and footwear stores	House-hold goods stores	Other stores	Non-store and repair	All retailers	Predominantly food stores	Total	Non-specialised stores	Textile, clothing and footwear stores	House-hold goods stores	Other stores	Non-store retailing and repair
Sales in 2000 (£m)	207 149	89 041	106 359	18 781	27 880	27 699	31 999	11 749	207 149	89 041	106 359	18 781	27 880	27 699	31 999	11 749
	EAPS	EAPT	EAPV	EAPU	EAPX	EAPY	EAPW	EAPZ	EAQV	EAQW	EAQY	EAQX	EARA	EARB	EAQZ	EARC
2002	112.2	108.2	116.2	110.5	123.8	117.8	111.6	106.5	110.6	110.4	111.8	107.4	114.9	113.1	110.5	100.5
2003	116.3	111.9	121.3	113.8	129.6	122.3	117.5	105.4	113.7	114.8	114.8	109.2	118.9	113.4	115.6	96.2
2004	123.3	116.5	129.6	118.0	139.4	130.8	127.0	117.1	118.8	119.6	119.9	111.2	124.8	117.2	123.0	102.7
2005	125.8	119.7	131.9	119.3	144.2	131.1	129.1	118.0	119.9	123.6	119.1	110.8	126.7	112.8	123.0	99.1
2006	129.9	122.7	136.6	124.0	151.3	137.6	130.2	124.1	123.4	128.3	121.7	113.9	132.1	114.1	123.7	101.1
2006 Q2	129.8	122.3	137.0	125.3	150.4	138.7	130.6	121.3	123.1	127.3	122.1	115.0	131.3	115.3	124.2	99.0
Q3	130.8	123.5	137.3	125.5	152.1	138.3	130.6	126.4	124.4	129.6	122.4	115.2	132.9	114.7	124.3	103.0
Q4	132.6	123.6	140.2	126.0	155.7	142.6	132.7	131.9	125.8	130.6	124.0	115.5	135.9	115.2	126.2	106.0
2007 Q1	133.1	124.0	140.4	125.9	155.4	143.4	133.3	135.4	126.3	131.4	124.1	115.0	134.9	117.7	125.7	108.0
2006 Aug	131.2	122.5	138.5	126.4	152.5	141.5	130.8	131.4	124.7	128.6	123.4	116.0	133.3	117.3	124.5	107.2
Sep	130.5	123.5	136.8	124.5	151.2	137.8	130.7	125.7	124.5	130.1	122.2	114.5	132.1	114.7	124.7	102.7
Oct	131.9	123.4	139.3	127.2	155.1	139.2	132.8	128.7	125.3	130.2	123.6	116.5	135.7	113.7	125.8	103.3
Nov	132.0	123.2	139.4	125.4	155.8	140.4	132.6	132.1	125.5	130.2	123.7	114.9	136.1	114.6	125.8	106.2
Dec	133.5	124.0	141.4	125.6	156.2	147.2	132.8	134.3	126.5	131.2	124.6	115.1	136.0	116.8	127.0	108.0
2007 Jan	131.5	123.9	137.4	125.9	149.5	142.4	129.3	135.1	124.6	130.8	121.2	114.8	130.0	115.8	122.0	108.3
Feb	133.6†	124.0†	141.2†	125.5†	157.2†	143.3†	134.4†	138.4†	126.7†	131.2	124.7†	114.6†	136.4†	117.7†	126.6†	110.8†
Mar	134.0	124.2	142.3	126.1	158.7	144.2	135.7	133.2	127.4	132.1	125.9	115.5	137.7	119.1	127.8	105.5

1 Great Britain only. The motor trades are excluded. Information for periods earlier than those shown is available from ONS Newport (tel. 01633 812713).

Source: Office for National Statistics

14.2 Index numbers of retail sales[1]
Value of retail sales at current prices

Sales: weekly average 2000=100, not seasonally adjusted

		Predominantly food stores			
	All retailing	Total value of sales	Non-specialised stores	Specialist food stores	Alcoholic drinks, other beverages and tobacco
Sales in 2000 (£m)	207 149	89 041	76 846	6 393	5 801
	EAFY	EAFS	EAGB	CY3X	CY45
2002	110.6	110.4	112	101	95
2003	113.7	114.8	118	100	87
2004	118.8	119.6	124	101	82
2005	119.9	123.6	129	103	78
2006	123.4	128.3	134	101	76
2006 Q2	118.9	127.2	133	102	76
Q3	119.1	127.0	133	96	77
Q4	144.9	139.3	146	111	84
2007 Q1	115.7	124.7	132	90	68
2006 Aug	118.5	125.7	132	99	77
Sep	118.0	125.6	132	92	74
Oct	124.2	127.4	133	100	77
Nov	137.3	134.1	141	105	77
Dec	167.6	152.9	160	126	94
2007 Jan	111.6	118.7	126	83	64
Feb	115.1†	125.6	133	91†	68
Mar	119.4	128.9	136	94	72

Retailing

14.2 continued Index numbers of retail sales[1]
Value of retail sales at current prices

Sales: weekly average 2000=100, not seasonally adjusted

| | Predominantly non-food stores | | | | | | | | | |
| | | | Textile, clothing and footwear stores | | | | Household goods stores | | | |
	Total	Non-specialised stores	Total	Retail of textiles	Retail sale of clothing	Retail sale of footwear and leather goods	Total	Retail sale of furniture, lighting, etc	Retail sale of electrical household appliances	Retail sale of hardware, paint and glass
Sales in 2000 (£m)	106 359	18 781	27 880	915	23 725	3 240	27 699	8 706	10 966	8 027
	EAFT	EAGE	EAFU	EAPG	EAGH	EAPH	EAFV	EAPI	EAPJ	EAPK
2002	111.8	107.4	114.9	122	116	101	113.1	113	109	119
2003	114.8	109.2	118.9	114	120	109	113.4	110	107	125
2004	119.9	111.2	124.8	115	127	113	117.2	116	108	132
2005	119.1	110.8	126.7	101	129	114	112.8	111	103	129
2006	121.7	113.9	132.1	94	136	113	114.1	115	105	126
2006 Q2	114.7	100.3	125.3	91	128	114	109.6	107	90	139
Q3	114.9	102.6	127.0	87	130	116	108.4	111	93	127
Q4	152.1	157.6	169.1	104	177	133	130.7	126	139	124
2007 Q1	109.7	97.5	113.9	100	117	92	113.0	119	101	124
2006 Aug	114.7	103.5	123.6	88	126	114	109.7	112	95	127
Sep	113.6	99.7	124.5	84	127	114	109.7	114	95	125
Oct	122.8	113.1	138.6	96	142	122	114.7	123	102	123
Nov	140.5	145.2	154.0	108	161	114	125.0	131	120	126
Dec	184.8	203.0	205.4	106	216	156	148.2	126	185	122
2007 Jan	107.6	98.6	110.3	94	113	98	118.1	115	118	122
Feb	107.5	93.7†	109.9†	113†	113	86†	110.5†	117†	96	123
Mar	113.2	99.6	119.9	95	125	91	110.9	123	91	126

| | Predominantly non-food stores | | | | | | | | |
| | Other specialised non-food stores | | | | | | Non-store retail and repair | | |
	Total	Pharmaceutical medical cosmetic and toilet goods	Retail sale of books, newspapers and periodicals	Retail sale of floor coverings	Photographic, optical & precision equipment, office supplies	Other retail sale in specialist stores nes including secondhand	Total	Retail sale via mail order houses	Non-store retail excepting mail order
Sales in 2000 (£m)	31 999	3 553	5 022	1 788	4 167	17 470	11 749	8 819	2 930
	EAFW	EAPQ	EAPL	EAPM	EAWH	CY4B	EAFX	EAPN	CY4H
2002	110.5	97	106	116	110	114	100.5	97	110
2003	115.6	103	102	110	102	126	96.2	93	105
2004	123.0	105	104	116	131	131	102.7	100	110
2005	123.0	104	104	114	136	130	99.1	98	103
2006	123.7	100	94	124	131	135	101.1	100	103
2006 Q2	118.4	95	79	118	127	132	93.8	90	105
Q3	117.4	95	85	126	128	128	97.5	94	107
Q4	152.5	124	121	129	145	172	123.6	127	115
2007 Q1	110.5	96	78	131	136	115	100.5	100	102
2006 Aug	117.8	94	83	130	130	128	98.1	94	111
Sep	115.7	93	91	128	123	124	100.6	97	110
Oct	121.8	97	97	133	134	130	113.1	114	110
Nov	139.3	107	107	150	147	152	133.4	138	120
Dec	187.8	159	151	109	153	220	124.2	127	115
2007 Jan	101.4	91	75	124	126	103	94.6	94	98
Feb	111.0	97†	79†	131†	134	116†	104.0†	101†	112†
Mar	117.4	100	79	136	145	123	102.4	104	98

1 Great Britain only. The motor trades are excluded. Information for periods earlier than those shown is available from ONS Newport (tel. 01633 812713).

Source: Office for National Statistics

88

15 External trade in goods

15.1 Values of United Kingdom total trade in goods

£ million BOP basis seasonally adjusted

	Total trade in goods			Total excluding oil			Total excluding oil and erratics[1]		
	Exports	Imports	Balance	Exports	Imports	Balance	Exports	Imports	Balance
	BOKG	BOKH	BOKI	ELBM	ENXP	BQKH	BPBL	BQBG	BPAP
2001	189 093	230 305	−41 212	174 278	220 780	−46 502	162 591	206 231	−43 640
2002	186 524	234 229	−47 705	172 203	225 016	−52 813	160 967	210 840	−49 873
2003	188 320	236 927	−48 607	173 712	225 695	−51 983	161 431	212 703	−51 272
2004	190 877	251 770	−60 893	174 677	236 463	−61 786	162 467	224 251	−61 784
2005	211 616	280 399	−68 783	191 821	258 411	−66 590	179 363	245 401	−66 038
2006	244 542	328 233	−83 691	221 418	301 419	−80 001	209 249	286 136	−76 887
2002 Q1	46 382	57 754	−11 372	43 106	55 678	−12 572	40 409	52 716	−12 307
Q2	49 102	60 104	−11 002	44 956	57 713	−12 757	41 706	53 888	−12 182
Q3	46 608	58 624	−12 016	43 252	56 216	−12 964	40 443	52 696	−12 253
Q4	44 432	57 747	−13 315	40 889	55 409	−14 520	38 409	51 540	−13 131
2003 Q1	48 666	59 528	−10 862	44 404	56 652	−12 248	41 386	53 304	−11 918
Q2	46 697	58 242	−11 545	43 350	55 674	−12 324	40 430	52 601	−12 171
Q3	46 338	58 640	−12 302	42 843	55 714	−12 871	39 808	52 222	−12 414
Q4	46 619	60 517	−13 898	43 115	57 655	−14 540	39 807	54 576	−14 769
2004 Q1	46 079	60 026	−13 947	42 393	57 040	−14 647	39 419	54 090	−14 671
Q2	47 137	62 384	−15 247	43 397	58 577	−15 180	40 540	55 514	−14 974
Q3	48 218	63 747	−15 529	44 145	59 699	−15 554	40 900	56 514	−15 614
Q4	49 443	65 613	−16 170	44 742	61 147	−16 405	41 608	58 133	−16 525
2005 Q1	48 483	64 747	−16 264	43 980	60 572	−16 592	40 907	57 345	−16 438
Q2	50 986	67 210	−16 224	46 298	62 194	−15 896	43 407	59 226	−15 819
Q3	54 613	72 603	−17 990	49 486	65 949	−16 463	46 185	62 556	−16 371
Q4	57 534	75 839	−18 305	52 057	69 696	−17 639	48 864	66 274	−17 410
2006 Q1	64 500	85 652	−21 152	58 700	78 891	−20 191	55 796	75 143	−19 347
Q2	66 683	89 213	−22 530	60 283	82 385	−22 102	57 028	78 593	−21 565
Q3	57 487	77 305	−19 818	51 571	70 046	−18 475	48 800	66 201	−17 401
Q4	55 872	76 063	−20 191	50 864	70 097	−19 233	47 625	66 199	−18 574
2007 Q1	55 134	75 869	−20 735	50 475	70 084	−19 609	47 528	66 172	−18 644
2004 Mar	15 894	20 259	−4 365	14 508	19 298	−4 790	13 410	18 187	−4 777
Apr	15 741	20 791	−5 050	14 524	19 520	−4 996	13 574	18 482	−4 908
May	15 485	20 564	−5 079	14 192	19 319	−5 127	13 285	18 373	−5 088
Jun	15 911	21 029	−5 118	14 681	19 738	−5 057	13 681	18 659	−4 978
Jul	15 919	21 258	−5 339	14 592	19 886	−5 294	13 566	18 840	−5 274
Aug	15 915	21 152	−5 237	14 460	19 981	−5 521	13 379	18 907	−5 528
Sep	16 384	21 337	−4 953	15 093	19 832	−4 739	13 955	18 767	−4 812
Oct	16 239	21 835	−5 596	14 686	20 348	−5 662	13 644	19 245	−5 601
Nov	16 399	21 821	−5 422	14 913	20 196	−5 283	13 933	19 315	−5 382
Dec	16 805	21 957	−5 152	15 143	20 603	−5 460	14 031	19 573	−5 542
2005 Jan	16 163	21 685	−5 522	14 620	20 288	−5 668	13 591	19 279	−5 688
Feb	15 884	21 204	−5 320	14 633	19 882	−5 249	13 584	18 895	−5 311
Mar	16 436	21 858	−5 422	14 727	20 402	−5 675	13 732	19 171	−5 439
Apr	16 658	22 565	−5 907	15 128	20 853	−5 725	14 281	19 838	−5 557
May	16 562	22 055	−5 493	15 018	20 443	−5 425	14 013	19 593	−5 580
Jun	17 766	22 590	−4 824	16 152	20 898	−4 746	15 113	19 795	−4 682
Jul	17 607	23 298	−5 691	15 752	21 348	−5 596	14 623	20 238	−5 615
Aug	18 211	24 465	−6 254	16 718	22 257	−5 539	15 621	21 038	−5 417
Sep	18 795	24 840	−6 045	17 016	22 344	−5 328	15 941	21 280	−5 339
Oct	19 024	24 580	−5 556	17 036	22 343	−5 307	16 006	21 463	−5 457
Nov	19 036	25 453	−6 417	17 361	23 363	−6 002	16 267	22 031	−5 764
Dec	19 474	25 806	−6 332	17 660	23 990	−6 330	16 591	22 780	−6 189
2006 Jan	20 400	27 293	−6 893	18 566	24 817	−6 251	17 593	23 547	−5 954
Feb	21 306	28 738	−7 432	19 549	26 780	−7 231	18 533	25 525	−6 992
Mar	22 794	29 621	−6 827	20 585	27 294	−6 709	19 670	26 071	−6 401
Apr	22 253	29 245	−6 992	20 148	27 235	−7 087	19 078	26 048	−6 970
May	22 683	31 251	−8 568	20 613	28 805	−8 192	19 572	27 439	−7 867
Jun	21 747	28 717	−6 970	19 522	26 345	−6 823	18 378	25 106	−6 728
Jul	19 157	25 951	−6 794	16 945	23 486	−6 541	16 029	22 130	−6 101
Aug	19 512	26 046	−6 534	17 664	23 519	−5 855	16 755	22 272	−5 517
Sep	18 818	25 308	−6 490	16 962	23 041	−6 079	16 016	21 799	−5 783
Oct	18 581	25 069	−6 488	16 788	23 015	−6 227	15 694	21 787	−6 093
Nov	18 675	25 433	−6 758	17 090	23 322	−6 232	15 964	21 968	−6 004
Dec	18 616	25 561	−6 945	16 986	23 760	−6 774	15 967	22 444	−6 477
2007 Jan	18 273[†]	25 012[†]	−6 739[†]	16 772[†]	22 998[†]	−6 226[†]	15 781[†]	21 784[†]	−6 003[†]
Feb	17 962	24 910	−6 948	16 488	23 215	−6 727	15 568	21 730	−6 162
Mar	18 899	25 947	−7 048	17 215	23 871	−6 656	16 179	22 658	−6 479

1 These are defined as ships, North Sea installations, aircraft, precious stones and silver.

Source: Office for National Statistics: 020 7533 6064

89

15.2 Volume and Price index numbers

Indices 2003=100 BOP basis

	Volume (seasonally adjusted)						Price index (not seasonally adjusted)							
	Total trade in goods		Total excluding oil		Total excluding oil and erratics[1]		Total trade in goods			Total excluding oil			Total excluding oil & erratics[1]	
	Exports	Imports	Exports	Imports	Exports	Imports	Exports	Imports	Terms of trade[2]	Exports	Imports	Terms of trade[2]	Exports	Imports
	BQKU	BQKV	BQKI	BQKJ	BOMA	ELAL	BQKR	BQKS	BQKT	BQKK	BQKL	BQKM	BQAK	ELBA
2001	101.5	93.8	100.8	93.5	103.3	93.1	98.3	103.3	95.2	98.8	104.4	94.6	97.3	103.9
2002	100.3	98.2	99.9	98.6	101.8	98.2	98.2	100.7	97.5	98.7	101.1	97.6	97.7	100.9
2003	100.0	100.0	100.0	100.0	100.0	100.0	100.0	100.0	100.0	100.0	100.0	100.0	100.0	100.0
2004	101.5	106.9	102.0	106.3	102.0	106.8	100.3	99.5	100.8	98.9	98.7	100.2	99.0	99.0
2005	110.9	114.8	112.5	114.6	113.2	115.4	104.7	103.7	101.0	100.6	100.6	100.0	100.8	100.7
2006	127.9	131.2	130.8	131.6	133.1	132.6	107.8	107.4	100.4	101.8	103.0	98.8	102.1	103.1
2002 Q1	99.7	95.7	99.2	95.8	101.7	96.5	98.4	101.5	96.9	99.7	102.6	97.2	98.6	102.3
Q2	104.8	100.2	103.9	100.6	105.0	100.0	99.3	101.5	97.8	99.6	101.8	97.8	98.7	101.6
Q3	100.5	99.0	100.6	99.5	102.6	99.1	98.1	100.2	97.9	98.2	100.3	97.9	97.3	100.2
Q4	96.1	97.9	95.8	98.4	98.1	97.2	97.1	99.6	97.5	97.2	99.8	97.4	96.3	99.7
2003 Q1	103.2	100.2	102.8	100.8	103.4	100.7	99.9	100.3	99.6	99.0	99.7	99.3	99.0	99.7
Q2	99.2	98.5	99.3	98.3	99.6	98.6	100.3	99.9	100.4	101.0	100.3	100.7	101.0	100.4
Q3	98.0	98.7	98.1	98.4	98.2	97.9	100.4	100.3	100.1	100.6	100.4	100.2	100.5	100.2
Q4	99.5	102.6	99.7	102.5	98.8	102.8	99.3	99.6	99.7	99.4	99.7	99.7	99.5	99.8
2004 Q1	100.1	103.6	100.0	103.4	99.8	103.7	98.1	97.7	100.4	98.0	97.8	100.2	98.1	98.1
Q2	101.4	106.4	102.2	105.5	102.7	105.9	99.5	99.1	100.4	98.6	98.6	100.0	98.7	98.9
Q3	101.8	107.4	102.9	107.1	102.5	107.3	100.9	100.4	100.5	98.8	99.1	99.7	99.0	99.3
Q4	102.7	110.1	103.1	109.4	103.1	110.1	102.7	100.7	102.0	100.3	99.3	101.0	100.4	99.5
2005 Q1	101.5	108.0	101.7	107.9	101.7	108.2	102.7	101.5	101.2	100.6	99.8	100.8	100.8	100.0
Q2	107.4	111.3	108.7	110.9	109.5	112.0	103.3	102.2	101.1	100.0	99.8	100.2	100.2	99.9
Q3	114.2	117.5	116.7	117.1	117.1	117.7	106.2	105.2	101.0	100.4	100.9	99.5	100.7	101.0
Q4	120.6	122.4	123.0	122.5	124.3	123.6	106.6	105.8	100.8	101.3	102.0	99.3	101.5	102.0
2006 Q1	135.8	136.6	139.3	137.2	142.8	138.8	108.3	107.3	100.9	102.6	102.9	99.7	102.7	102.8
Q2	141.0	143.1	144.8	144.5	147.7	146.5	109.4	108.1	101.2	102.5	103.0	99.5	102.7	103.0
Q3	118.2	122.6	120.6	122.5	122.8	122.7	108.5	108.0	100.5	101.6	103.0	98.6	101.9	103.2
Q4	116.5	122.4	118.6	122.4	119.3	122.3	105.1	106.4	98.8	100.6	103.0	97.7	101.0	103.3
2007 Q1	114.3	121.0	116.4	121.3	117.7	121.2	105.5	106.3	99.2	101.2	103.3	98.0	101.5	103.7
2004 Jun	102.8	107.7	103.9	106.8	104.2	106.8	99.1	98.9	100.2	98.0	98.4	99.6	98.1	98.7
Jul	102.4	108.8	103.0	107.7	103.0	108.0	99.3	99.1	100.2	98.0	98.5	99.5	98.2	98.8
Aug	100.7	106.9	101.5	107.6	101.0	107.7	101.0	100.6	100.4	98.5	99.0	99.5	98.7	99.2
Sep	102.2	106.6	104.1	106.0	103.5	106.2	102.5	101.4	101.1	100.0	99.8	100.2	100.1	100.0
Oct	100.1	109.1	101.2	109.2	101.0	109.3	104.2	102.2	102.0	100.8	99.9	100.9	101.0	100.1
Nov	101.8	109.4	102.6	108.0	103.2	109.5	103.1	100.9	102.2	100.7	99.6	101.1	100.8	99.7
Dec	106.3	111.8	105.6	110.9	105.2	111.6	100.9	99.1	101.8	99.3	98.5	100.8	99.4	98.8
2005 Jan	101.8	108.9	101.3	108.5	101.4	109.3	102.0	101.1	100.9	100.5	99.8	100.7	100.6	100.0
Feb	100.3	105.5	101.5	105.5	101.3	106.1	102.2	101.3	100.9	100.4	99.8	100.6	100.6	100.0
Mar	102.4	109.5	102.2	109.8	102.4	109.3	103.9	102.2	101.7	100.9	99.8	101.1	101.2	100.0
Apr	104.7	112.6	105.9	112.0	107.4	113.0	103.3	101.7	101.6	100.2	99.5	100.7	100.4	99.6
May	104.4	109.6	105.3	109.1	105.7	111.0	103.4	102.1	101.3	100.6	100.0	100.6	100.7	100.1
Jun	113.1	111.7	114.9	111.7	115.5	112.0	103.3	102.8	100.5	99.3	99.8	99.5	99.6	100.0
Jul	109.3	113.0	110.5	113.0	110.3	113.5	106.0	105.3	100.7	100.8	101.5	99.3	101.0	101.5
Aug	114.6	118.5	118.1	118.4	118.7	118.6	106.5	105.3	101.1	100.4	100.6	99.8	100.7	100.8
Sep	118.8	120.9	121.5	120.0	122.3	121.1	106.1	104.9	101.1	100.0	100.6	99.4	100.3	100.7
Oct	119.7	119.3	121.7	118.8	123.3	121.0	106.9	105.6	101.2	101.1	101.7	99.4	101.4	101.8
Nov	120.1	123.1	123.0	123.1	124.0	123.2	106.5	106.0	100.5	101.3	102.3	99.0	101.5	102.2
Dec	122.0	124.7	124.3	125.5	125.6	126.5	106.4	105.9	100.5	101.4	102.1	99.3	101.6	102.1
2006 Jan	128.1	130.0	131.4	129.8	134.2	130.6	107.8	106.8	100.9	102.0	102.3	99.7	102.2	102.4
Feb	135.2	138.0	139.3	139.5	142.5	141.3	108.1	107.3	100.7	102.5	103.0	99.5	102.6	102.9
Mar	144.0	141.7	147.3	142.4	151.7	144.6	109.0	107.7	101.2	103.2	103.3	99.9	103.3	103.2
Apr	141.1	140.8	145.0	142.9	148.1	145.4	110.5	109.0	101.4	103.3	103.5	99.8	103.4	103.4
May	145.6	150.8	150.0	152.0	153.5	153.9	108.7	107.3	101.3	101.9	102.4	99.5	102.1	102.5
Jun	136.4	137.8	139.4	138.5	141.4	140.2	109.0	108.0	100.9	102.2	103.1	99.1	102.5	103.2
Jul	116.3	122.7	118.1	122.9	120.2	122.9	110.1	109.2	100.8	102.4	103.6	98.8	102.7	103.8
Aug	120.8	123.4	124.0	123.3	126.4	123.7	108.6	107.9	100.6	101.1	102.5	98.6	101.5	102.7
Sep	117.5	121.7	119.7	121.2	121.7	121.5	106.7	106.8	99.9	101.2	102.9	98.3	101.5	103.1
Oct	115.4	120.9	116.9	120.6	117.4	120.8	105.4	106.7	98.8	101.0	103.4	97.7	101.3	103.6
Nov	116.9	122.3	119.4	121.8	119.7	121.3	105.0	106.4	98.7	100.7	103.2	97.6	101.1	103.5
Dec	117.2	124.1	119.6	124.8	120.7	124.9	104.9	106.0	99.0	100.2	102.4	97.9	100.6	102.7
2007 Jan	113.9†	119.9†	115.9†	119.3†	117.1†	119.6†	104.4	105.1	99.3	100.8	102.7†	98.1	101.0	103.1
Feb	111.8	119.9	114.0	120.9	115.6	119.9	105.2†	105.8†	99.4†	101.1†	102.9	98.3†	101.4†	103.2†
Mar	117.3	123.3	119.4	123.6	120.5	124.1	106.8	107.9	99.0	101.8	104.3	97.6	102.1	104.7

1 These are defined as ships, North Sea installations, aircraft, precious stones and silver. 2 Export price index as a percentage of the import price index.

Source: Office for National Statistics: 020 7533 6064

15.3 United Kingdom trade in goods, by commodity group[1]

£ million BOP basis seasonally adjusted

	Food, beverages and tobacco (SITC 0+1)			Basic materials (SITC 2+4)			Fuels (SITC 3)			Semi-manufactures (SITC 5+6)			Finished manufactures (SITC 7+8)		
	Exports	Imports	Balance	Exports	Imports	Balance	Exports	Imports	Balance	Exports	Imports	Balance	Exports	Imports	Balance
	BOPL	BQAR	ELBE	BOPM	BQAS	ELBF	BOPN	BQAT	ELBG	BOPO	BQAU	ELBH	BOPP	BQAV	ELBI
2001	9 630	18 485	−8 855	2 571	6 442	−3 871	16 386	10 795	5 591	50 295	52 910	−2 615	109 188	140 409	−31 221
2002	9 993	19 375	−9 382	2 855	5 958	−3 103	16 000	10 279	5 721	50 223	52 722	−2 499	106 380	144 445	−38 065
2003	10 879	21 187	−10 308	3 335	6 139	−2 804	16 558	12 311	4 247	54 492	56 045	−1 553	102 193	139 641	−37 448
2004	10 578	22 147	−11 569	3 771	6 340	−2 569	17 885	17 547	338	56 466	60 226	−3 760	101 296	143 703	−42 407
2005	10 645	23 696	−13 051	3 980	6 769	−2 789	21 497	25 920	−4 423	59 883	62 677	−2 794	114 490	159 497	−45 007
2006	11 067	25 149	−14 082	4 909	7 920	−3 011	25 242	31 727	−6 485	65 174	69 581	−4 407	136 847	191 830	−54 983
2002 Q1	2 388	4 758	−2 370	647	1 489	−842	3 656	2 329	1 327	12 359	12 919	−560	27 118	35 870	−8 752
Q2	2 469	4 837	−2 368	712	1 512	−800	4 537	2 705	1 832	12 845	13 305	−460	28 222	37 391	−9 169
Q3	2 603	4 802	−2 199	741	1 477	−736	3 722	2 653	1 069	12 578	13 018	−440	26 654	36 323	−9 669
Q4	2 533	4 978	−2 445	755	1 480	−725	4 085	2 592	1 493	12 441	13 480	−1 039	24 386	34 861	−10 475
2003 Q1	2 821	5 129	−2 308	842	1 510	−668	4 714	3 100	1 614	13 240	13 472	−232	26 814	35 944	−9 130
Q2	2 634	5 270	−2 636	813	1 506	−693	3 912	2 837	1 075	13 823	14 194	−371	25 293	34 049	−8 756
Q3	2 759	5 310	−2 551	848	1 491	−643	4 018	3 155	863	13 594	14 204	−610	24 927	34 084	−9 157
Q4	2 665	5 478	−2 813	832	1 632	−800	3 914	3 219	695	13 835	14 175	−340	25 159	35 564	−10 405
2004 Q1	2 563	5 384	−2 821	867	1 572	−705	4 028	3 500	528	13 888	14 361	−473	24 523	34 768	−10 245
Q2	2 741	5 549	−2 808	921	1 563	−642	4 170	4 263	−93	13 829	14 506	−677	25 280	36 051	−10 771
Q3	2 611	5 585	−2 974	995	1 598	−603	4 603	4 626	−23	14 229	15 514	−1 285	25 573	35 998	−10 425
Q4	2 663	5 629	−2 966	988	1 607	−619	5 084	5 158	−74	14 520	15 845	−1 325	25 920	36 886	−10 966
2005 Q1	2 663	5 784	−3 121	957	1 601	−644	4 865	4 950	−85	14 646	15 627	−981	25 139	36 350	−11 211
Q2	2 713	5 963	−3 250	985	1 658	−673	5 198	5 688	−490	14 707	15 491	−784	27 172	37 901	−10 729
Q3	2 666	5 932	−3 266	1 031	1 773	−742	5 558	7 512	−1 954	15 299	15 574	−275	29 778	41 389	−11 611
Q4	2 603	6 017	−3 414	1 007	1 737	−730	5 876	7 770	−1 894	15 231	15 985	−754	32 401	43 857	−11 456
2006 Q1	2 679	6 213	−3 534	1 109	1 862	−753	6 296	8 426	−2 130	15 821	16 721	−900	38 218	51 884	−13 666
Q2	2 734	6 177	−3 443	1 213	1 912	−699	7 001	7 796	−795	16 317	17 022	−705	39 106	55 797	−16 691
Q3	2 803	6 289	−3 486	1 226	1 966	−740	6 550	8 356	−1 806	16 341	17 505	−1 164	30 257	42 727	−12 470
Q4	2 851	6 470	−3 619	1 361	2 180	−819	5 395	7 149	−1 754	16 695	18 333	−1 638	29 266	41 422	−12 156
2007 Q1	2 948	6 483	−3 535	1 288	2 104	−816	4 963	7 097	−2 134	17 021	18 123	−1 102	28 550	41 532	−12 982
2004 Apr	943	1 893	−950	320	547	−227	1 327	1 426	−99	4 610	4 822	−212	8 477	11 946	−3 469
May	883	1 825	−942	305	493	−188	1 433	1 380	53	4 357	4 702	−345	8 440	12 006	−3 566
Jun	915	1 831	−916	296	523	−227	1 410	1 457	−47	4 862	4 982	−120	8 363	12 099	−3 736
Jul	914	1 862	−948	323	549	−226	1 501	1 582	−81	4 656	5 071	−415	8 450	12 038	−3 588
Aug	825	1 830	−1 005	339	526	−187	1 641	1 337	304	4 667	5 266	−599	8 381	12 060	−3 679
Sep	872	1 893	−1 021	333	523	−190	1 461	1 707	−246	4 906	5 177	−271	8 742	11 900	−3 158
Oct	857	1 839	−982	327	516	−189	1 682	1 654	28	4 774	5 400	−626	8 531	12 272	−3 741
Nov	910	1 910	−1 000	340	547	−207	1 617	1 906	−289	4 855	5 130	−275	8 588	12 154	−3 566
Dec	896	1 880	−984	321	544	−223	1 785	1 598	187	4 891	5 315	−424	8 801	12 460	−3 659
2005 Jan	885	1 979	−1 094	294	519	−225	1 647	1 683	−36	4 849	5 022	−173	8 437	12 339	−3 902
Feb	894	1 914	−1 020	307	551	−244	1 348	1 603	−255	4 955	5 302	−347	8 294	11 680	−3 386
Mar	884	1 891	−1 007	356	531	−175	1 870	1 664	206	4 842	5 303	−461	8 408	12 331	−3 923
Apr	894	2 047	−1 153	331	544	−213	1 681	1 945	−264	4 787	5 217	−430	8 892	12 651	−3 759
May	891	1 968	−1 077	324	546	−222	1 750	1 823	−73	4 849	5 063	−214	8 686	12 462	−3 776
Jun	928	1 948	−1 020	330	568	−238	1 767	1 920	−153	5 071	5 211	−140	9 594	12 788	−3 194
Jul	872	1 967	−1 095	311	567	−256	1 986	2 203	−217	4 913	5 258	−345	9 446	13 142	−3 696
Aug	885	2 001	−1 116	367	600	−233	1 612	2 510	−898	5 262	5 274	−12	9 987	13 944	−3 957
Sep	909	1 964	−1 055	353	606	−253	1 960	2 799	−839	5 124	5 042	82	10 345	14 303	−3 958
Oct	870	2 026	−1 156	321	577	−256	2 124	2 706	−582	4 949	5 050	−101	10 588	14 073	−3 485
Nov	848	1 968	−1 120	320	582	−262	1 786	2 549	−763	5 147	5 226	−79	10 834	14 954	−4 120
Dec	885	2 023	−1 138	366	578	−212	1 966	2 515	−549	5 135	5 709	−574	10 979	14 830	−3 851
2006 Jan	895	2 112	−1 217	325	609	−284	1 989	2 957	−968	5 228	5 536	−308	11 859	15 907	−4 048
Feb	886	2 039	−1 153	373	609	−236	1 913	2 508	−595	5 290	5 695	−405	12 723	17 708	−4 985
Mar	898	2 062	−1 164	411	644	−233	2 394	2 961	−567	5 303	5 490	−187	13 636	18 269	−4 633
Apr	902	2 067	−1 165	385	591	−206	2 287	2 356	−69	5 409	5 691	−282	13 173	18 361	−5 188
May	907	2 054	−1 147	401	655	−254	2 309	2 752	−443	5 495	5 675	−180	13 457	19 953	−6 496
Jun	925	2 056	−1 131	427	666	−239	2 405	2 688	−283	5 413	5 656	−243	12 476	17 483	−5 007
Jul	908	2 071	−1 163	413	628	−215	2 466	2 795	−329	5 138	5 751	−613	10 132	14 543	−4 411
Aug	948	2 124	−1 176	403	671	−268	2 029	2 901	−872	5 688	5 845	−157	10 346	14 349	−4 003
Sep	947	2 094	−1 147	410	667	−257	2 055	2 660	−605	5 515	5 909	−394	9 779	13 835	−4 056
Oct	924	2 132	−1 208	469	714	−245	1 936	2 375	−439	5 587	5 904	−317	9 567	13 773	−4 206
Nov	979	2 185	−1 206	493	698	−205	1 711	2 581	−870	5 617	6 224	−607	9 772	13 578	−3 806
Dec	948	2 153	−1 205	399	768	−369	1 748	2 193	−445	5 491	6 205	−714	9 927	14 071	−4 144
2007 Jan	981[†]	2 188[†]	−1 207[†]	405[†]	660[†]	−255[†]	1 610[†]	2 454[†]	−844[†]	5 743[†]	5 868[†]	−125[†]	9 418[†]	13 655[†]	−4 237[†]
Feb	983	2 140	−1 157	446	712	−266	1 554	2 112	−558	5 516	6 021	−505	9 340	13 754	−4 414
Mar	984	2 155	−1 171	437	732	−295	1 799	2 531	−732	5 762	6 234	−472	9 792	14 123	−4 331

1 More commodity detail is available on a seasonally adjusted *BOP* basis in tables B1 to B11 inclusive, and C1 to C4 inclusive, of the *Monthly Review of External Trade Statistics*.

Source: *Office for National Statistics: 020 7533 6064*

91

15.4 Volume index numbers, by commodity group[1]

2003=100 BOP basis seasonally adjusted

	Food, beverages and tobacco (SITC 0+1)		Basic materials (SITC 2+4)		Fuels (SITC 3)		Semi-manufactures (SITC 5+6)		Finished manufactures (SITC 7+8)		Total manufactures (SITC 5 to 8)	
	Exports	Imports	Exports	Imports	Exports	Imports	Exports	Imports	Exports	Imports	Exports	Imports
	BPEM	BQBK	BAFB	BQBL	BAFC	BQBM	BAHA	BQBN	BAHY	ELAB	BOGT	ELAJ
2001	92	90	81	109	107	102	91	91	108	94	102	94
2002	96	94	90	101	103	91	94	95	103	101	101	99
2003	100	100	100	100	100	100	100	100	100	100	100	100
2004	99	106	105	100	93	123	104	106	101	106	102	106
2005	98	110	106	102	90	131	108	106	117	118	114	115
2006	100	114	121	110	90	136	117	112	143	142	134	134
2002 Q1	92	91	83	102	103	94	93	93	104	97	100	96
Q2	95	95	90	103	113	92	96	96	110	103	105	101
Q3	100	94	93	101	96	91	95	94	104	103	101	100
Q4	96	95	94	99	102	89	94	98	96	99	96	99
2003 Q1	106	98	102	100	105	89	98	98	105	103	103	101
Q2	95	100	97	99	100	101	101	100	99	97	99	98
Q3	101	99	101	97	98	104	99	101	97	98	98	99
Q4	98	103	100	104	96	106	102	101	99	103	100	102
2004 Q1	96	104	100	100	98	117	104	104	99	103	100	103
Q2	104	106	103	99	90	125	103	103	102	106	102	105
Q3	98	107	109	101	89	122	105	108	102	106	103	107
Q4	99	108	109	100	93	130	105	109	103	109	104	109
2005 Q1	99	108	102	100	96	122	106	107	100	108	102	107
Q2	101	110	107	100	92	128	107	105	111	113	110	111
Q3	98	110	109	106	83	133	111	106	123	123	118	118
Q4	96	111	107	101	87	143	109	107	135	130	126	123
2006 Q1	97	114	112	105	90	144	113	109	160	152	144	140
Q2	98	112	117	108	95	126	117	110	167	165	150	149
Q3	101	114	121	109	90	138	117	112	125	127	122	123
Q4	103	117	134	117	87	137	120	117	120	124	120	122
2007 Q1	104	115	127	112	84	136	123	115	115	123	118	121
2004 Jun	105	105	101	99	90	126	109	106	101	107	104	107
Jul	104	107	112	105	95	139	104	107	102	107	103	107
Aug	92	105	109	99	92	100	104	111	101	107	102	108
Sep	97	108	107	99	80	126	107	107	104	105	105	106
Oct	95	106	106	96	84	110	104	113	101	108	102	110
Nov	101	111	109	103	88	144	104	105	102	108	103	107
Dec	101	107	112	102	108	136	107	110	106	111	106	111
2005 Jan	98	112	95	98	103	132	105	103	101	109	102	107
Feb	99	107	101	102	82	122	107	108	99	103	102	104
Mar	99	106	110	99	103	111	105	109	101	111	102	110
Apr	100	115	108	100	89	135	104	106	108	114	107	111
May	99	109	105	99	96	127	105	103	106	111	106	109
Jun	103	107	109	101	91	121	111	107	119	114	116	112
Jul	95	108	101	101	91	120	106	107	116	116	112	114
Aug	98	111	115	108	71	130	114	108	124	124	120	119
Sep	100	110	112	108	87	148	112	103	129	128	123	121
Oct	96	113	105	102	91	156	107	101	133	125	124	118
Nov	94	108	103	102	80	141	111	105	135	132	126	124
Dec	98	112	113	99	90	133	110	114	136	132	127	127
2006 Jan	97	116	101	104	85	149	112	110	148	140	136	131
Feb	96	112	114	102	84	128	113	111	160	155	144	143
Mar	98	114	121	110	101	154	113	107	173	160	152	145
Apr	98	113	111	101	92	109	115	110	169	162	150	147
May	98	112	118	112	94	135	119	110	174	177	155	157
Jun	99	111	123	112	98	134	116	109	158	155	144	142
Jul	98	112	119	105	96	131	109	110	125	129	120	124
Aug	102	115	122	112	83	139	122	113	128	128	126	124
Sep	103	114	122	109	91	145	119	113	122	125	121	122
Oct	100	115	135	115	93	135	120	113	117	124	118	121
Nov	106	119	142	112	83	153	122	119	120	122	121	121
Dec	103	118	124	125	84	122	119	119	123	127	122	125
2007 Jan	106	117†	120†	108	85†	149†	125	112	113†	121	117†	119†
Feb	104†	114	130	113†	80	120	119†	115†	113	123†	115	121
Mar	103	114	130	114	86	140	125	118	119	126	121	124

1 Commodity volumes are shown in more detail on a seasonally adjusted BOP basis in tables C1 toC3 inclusive, and D1 to D3 inclusive, of the *Monthly Review of External Trade Statistics.*

Source: Office for National Statistics: 020 7533 6064

15.5 Price index numbers, by commodity group[1]

2003=100 BOP basis not seasonally adjusted

	Food, beverages and tobacco (SITC 0+1)		Basic materials (SITC 2+4)		Fuels (SITC 3)		Semi-manufactures (SITC 5+6)		Finished manufactures (SITC 7+8)		Total manufactures (SITC 5 to 8)	
	Exports	Imports	Exports	Imports	Exports	Imports	Exports	Imports	Exports	Imports	Exports	Imports
	BPAI	ELAN	BPAW	ELAO	BPDU	ELAP	BQAA	ELAQ	BQAB	ELAR	BQAI	ELAY
2001	96	96	94	96	93	85	100	104	99	106	99	105
2002	96	97	95	96	93	92	97	99	100	103	99	102
2003	100	100	100	100	100	100	100	100	100	100	100	100
2004	99	98	108	103	117	118	99	102	98	97	99	98
2005	100	103	115	108	151	168	101	107	99	97	100	100
2006	103	105	123	117	176	199	103	112	100	97	101	102
2002 Q1	96	98	94	94	85	82	97	99	101	105	100	103
Q2	96	96	96	96	95	95	98	99	101	104	100	103
Q3	96	96	96	95	97	96	98	99	99	102	98	101
Q4	97	98	96	97	96	95	97	98	97	101	97	100
2003 Q1	99	98	98	98	109	112	99	99	99	100	99	100
Q2	101	100	100	100	94	91	101	101	101	100	101	101
Q3	100	101	100	100	99	98	100	100	101	100	101	100
Q4	100	101	101	102	98	99	99	100	99	99	99	100
2004 Q1	99	98	104	103	99	100	98	99	98	97	98	98
Q2	99	99	108	104	112	112	98	101	98	97	98	98
Q3	98	98	108	103	126	128	99	103	98	97	98	99
Q4	100	99	112	103	133	133	101	104	99	97	100	99
2005 Q1	100	101	113	104	126	140	102	106	99	96	100	99
Q2	100	103	114	108	140	153	101	106	99	96	100	99
Q3	100	103	116	108	170	192	101	106	99	97	100	100
Q4	101	103	119	110	169	187	102	108	99	98	100	101
2006 Q1	102	102	120	114	176	200	103	110	100	98	101	102
Q2	103	105	124	115	187	212	103	112	100	97	101	102
Q3	102	106	124	117	185	208	102	114	99	97	100	101
Q4	102	106	122	121	157	178	102	114	98	97	100	102
2007 Q1	103	106	122	120	155	170	101	114	99	97	100	102
2004 Apr	99	98	109	105	105	105	98	100	98	97	98	98
May	99	99	109	105	117	118	99	101	98	98	99	99
Jun	98	99	105	103	113	113	98	101	98	97	98	98
Jul	98	98	105	103	115	115	98	102	97	97	98	98
Aug	98	98	109	103	130	135	99	102	98	97	98	99
Sep	99	99	111	103	132	135	100	104	99	98	99	99
Oct	100	99	113	104	145	149	101	104	99	98	100	99
Nov	100	98	113	103	133	132	102	104	99	97	100	99
Dec	99	100	110	102	121	117	100	104	98	95	99	98
2005 Jan	100	101	112	103	119	132	102	106	99	97	100	99
Feb	100	101	112	104	123	135	101	106	99	96	100	99
Mar	100	102	115	105	136	153	102	106	100	96	101	99
Apr	99	102	116	107	138	149	101	106	99	95	100	99
May	100	103	114	108	134	145	102	107	99	96	100	99
Jun	100	103	113	108	147	164	100	105	98	96	99	99
Jul	101	105	114	110	163	185	102	107	99	98	100	100
Aug	100	102	116	108	173	199	101	106	99	97	100	100
Sep	100	102	117	107	174	193	100	106	98	97	99	100
Oct	101	102	120	109	172	186	102	108	99	98	100	101
Nov	101	103	118	111	168	186	102	108	99	98	100	101
Dec	101	104	118	111	167	188	102	108	99	98	100	101
2006 Jan	102	102	118	113	176	201	102	109	100	98	101	101
Feb	102	102	120	114	175	199	103	111	100	98	101	102
Mar	103	103	122	115	176	199	104	111	101	99	102	102
Apr	104	104	124	115	192	222	104	112	101	98	102	102
May	103	104	123	115	185	208	102	112	100	97	101	101
Jun	103	106	125	116	184	207	103	112	100	97	101	102
Jul	103	107	125	117	195	220	103	114	100	98	101	102
Aug	102	106	123	117	192	216	102	113	99	96	100	101
Sep	102	106	123	118	168	187	102	114	99	97	100	101
Oct	102	107	123	121	156	176	102	114	99	97	100	102
Nov	102	106	123	121	155	176	102	114	98	97	100	102
Dec	102	105	121	120	159	182	101	113	98	96	99	101
2007 Jan	102	105	121	117	148	159†	101	113	99	97	100	101
Feb	103†	106	122†	120†	153	169	101	113	99	97	100	101
Mar	104	108	124	124	164	183	102	115	100	98	101	103

1 Commodity price indices are shown in more detail on a not seasonally adjusted BOP basis in tables C4 to C6 inclusive, and D4 to D6 inclusive, of the Monthly Review of External Trade Statistics.

Source: Office for National Statistics: 020 7533 6064

15.6 United Kingdom exports, by commodity[1]

£ million BOP-consistent basis seasonally adjusted

		2005	2006	2006 Q3	2006 Q4	2007 Q1	2006 Oct	2006 Nov	2006 Dec	2007 Jan	2007 Feb	2007 Mar
0. Food and live animals	BOGG	6 550	6 826	1 742	1 731	1 862	569	593	569	610[†]	609	643
Of which:												
01. Meat and meat preparations	BOGS	729	770	203	208	199	76	67	65	66[†]	66	67
02. Dairy products and eggs	BQMS	718	722	176	181	202	58	63	60	61[†]	69	72
04 & 08. Cereals and animal feeding stuffs	BQMT	1 555	1 606	406	414	438	139	137	138	141[†]	145	152
05. Vegetables and fruit	BQMU	514	584	147	148	155	49	50	49	49[†]	54	52
1. Beverages and tobacco	BQMZ	4 095	4 241	1 061	1 120	1 086	355	386	379	371[†]	374	341
11. Beverages	BQNB	3 481	3 728	931	1 005	998	316	347	342	335	341[†]	322
12. Tobacco	BQOW	614	513	130	115	88	39	39	37	36[†]	33	19
2. Crude materials	BQOX	3 745	4 634	1 153	1 289	1 220	447	469	373	384[†]	423	413
Of which:												
24. Wood, lumber and cork	BQOY	131	148	37	39	38	13	12	14	13	12	13
25. Pulp and waste paper	BQOZ	283	339	83	98	101	32	36	30	29	35	37
26. Textile fibres	BQPA	516	545	135	132	132	45	48	39	39	43[†]	50
28. Metal ores	BQPB	1 713	2 433	603	721	657	257	274	190	211[†]	232	214
3. Fuels	BOPN	21 497	25 242	6 550	5 395	4 963	1 936	1 711	1 748	1 610[†]	1 554	1 799
33. Petroleum and petroleum products	ELBL	19 795	23 124	5 916	5 008	4 659	1 793	1 585	1 630	1 501[†]	1 474	1 684
32, 34 and 35. Coal, gas and electricity	BOQI	1 702	2 118	634	387	304	143	126	118	109[†]	80	115
4. Animal and vegetable oils and fats	BQPI	235	275	73	72	68	22	24	26	21	23	24
5. Chemicals	ENDG	33 389	37 385	9 460	9 381	9 743	3 125	3 169	3 087	3 270[†]	3 149	3 324
Of which:												
51. Organic chemicals	BQPJ	6 703	8 055	2 174	1 935	2 020	678	655	602	717[†]	656	647
52. Inorganic chemicals	BQPK	1 555	2 157	514	572	597	153	203	216	185[†]	211	201
53. Colouring materials	CSCE	1 635	1 624	400	394	419	138	133	123	136	144[†]	139
54. Medicinal products	BQPL	12 321	13 787	3 379	3 452	3 626	1 149	1 167	1 136	1 217[†]	1 140	1 269
55. Toilet preparations	CSCF	3 219	3 481	878	911	933	302	312	297	309[†]	308	316
57 & 58. Plastics	BQQA	4 298	4 490	1 117	1 141	1 165	394	366	381	374[†]	374	417
6. Manufactures classified chiefly by material	BQQB	26 494	27 789	6 881	7 314	7 278	2 462	2 448	2 404	2 473	2 367[†]	2 438
Of which:												
63. Wood and cork manufactures	BQQC	255	275	65	65	73	22	21	22	24	25[†]	24
64. Paper and paperboard manufactures	BQQD	2 044	2 041	518	519	522	174	173	172	167[†]	173	182
65. Textile manufactures	BQQE	2 645	2 704	664	657	681	212	226	219	220[†]	224	237
67. Iron and steel	BQQF	5 184	5 138	1 278	1 368	1 440	487	459	422	491[†]	470	479
68. Non-ferrous metals	BQQG	3 863	4 868	1 239	1 350	1 383	448	459	443	513[†]	428	442
69. Metal manufactures	BQQH	4 067	4 549	1 245	1 139	1 113	385	375	379	362[†]	373	378
7. Machinery and transport equipment[2]	BQQI	89 382	110 643	23 936	22 600	21 881	7 399	7 540	7 661	7 252[†]	7 207	7 422
71 - 716, 72, 73 & 74. Mechanical machinery	BQQK	25 797	28 373	7 138	6 988	7 344	2 315	2 324	2 349	2 475[†]	2 445	2 424
716, 75, 76 & 77. Electrical machinery	BQQL	37 120	55 458	10 339	8 968	7 902	2 899	2 953	3 116	2 592[†]	2 572	2 738
78. Road vehicles	BQQM	19 440	19 430	4 704	4 734	4 875	1 557	1 559	1 618	1 608[†]	1 658	1 609
79. Other transport equipment	BQQN	7 025	7 382	1 755	1 910	1 760	628	704	578	577[†]	532	651
8. Miscellaneous manufactures[2]	BQQO	25 108	26 204	6 321	6 666	6 669	2 168	2 232	2 266	2 166[†]	2 133	2 370
Of which:												
84. Clothing	CSCN	2 712	2 890	712	737	762	235	245	257	257[†]	255	250
85. Footwear	CSCP	471	522	131	144	131	47	50	47	47[†]	44	40
87 & 88. Scientific and photographic	BQQQ	7 245	7 417	1 805	1 836	1 819	593	615	628	592[†]	596	631
9. Other commodities and transactions	BOQL	1 121	1 303	310	304	364	98	103	103	116	123[†]	125
TOTAL UK EXPORTS	BOKG	211 616	244 542	57 487	55 872	55 134	18 581	18 675	18 616	18 273[†]	17 962	18 899

1 The numbers on the left hand side of the table refer to the code numbers of the *Standard International Trade Classification,* Revision 3, which was introduced in January 1988.

2 Sections 7 and 8 are shown by broad economic category in table G2 of the *Monthly Review of External Trade Statistics.*

Source: Office for National Statistics: 020 7533 6064

15.7 United Kingdom imports, by commodity[1]

£ million BOP-consistent basis seasonally adjusted

		2005	2006	2006 Q3	2006 Q4	2007 Q1	2006 Oct	2006 Nov	2006 Dec	2007 Jan	2007 Feb	2007 Mar
0. Food and live animals	BQQR	18 594	19 930	4 995	5 165	5 145	1 701	1 750	1 714	1 744†	1 686	1 715
Of which:												
01. Meat and meat preparations	BQQS	3 618	3 835	981	1 013	991	339	342	332	330†	330	331
02. Dairy products and eggs	BQQT	1 700	1 816	462	471	451	162	154	155	152†	152	147
04 & 08. Cereals and animal feeding stuffs	BQQU	2 364	2 515	630	657	670	219	220	218	215†	217	238
05. Vegetables and fruit	BQQV	5 447	5 848	1 500	1 515	1 509	494	512	509	512†	498	499
1. Beverages and tobacco	BQQW	5 102	5 219	1 294	1 305	1 338	431	435	439	444	454†	440
11. Beverages	EGAT	3 625	3 718	917	925	973	306	306	313	322	332	319
12. Tobacco	EMAI	1 477	1 501	377	380	365	125	129	126	122	122†	121
2. Crude materials	ENVB	6 128	7 135	1 778	1 976	1 912	643	628	705	596†	649	667
Of which:												
24. Wood, lumber and cork	ENVC	1 357	1 456	362	417	424	131	130	156	138†	143	143
25. Pulp and waste paper	EQAH	477	513	126	123	120	42	39	42	42†	36	42
26. Textile fibres	EQAP	314	299	72	82	75	29	27	26	25	26	24
28. Metal ores	EHAA	1 999	2 679	685	763	744	258	254	251	208†	263	273
3. Fuels	BQAT	25 920	31 727	8 356	7 149	7 097	2 375	2 581	2 193	2 454†	2 112	2 531
33. Petroleum and petroleum products	ENXO	21 988	26 814	7 259	5 966	5 785	2 054	2 111	1 801	2 014†	1 695	2 076
32, 34 and 35. Coal, gas and electricity	BPBI	3 932	4 913	1 097	1 183	1 312	321	470	392	440†	417	455
4. Animal and vegetable oils and fats	EHAB	641	785	188	204	192	71	70	63	64†	63	65
5. Chemicals	ENGA	29 208	31 927	7 847	8 506	8 273	2 754	2 848	2 904	2 626†	2 784	2 863
Of which:												
51. Organic chemicals	EHAC	7 183	7 739	1 816	2 233	2 119	727	761	745	677†	709	733
52. Inorganic chemicals	EHAE	1 507	2 121	460	623	494	191	261	171	136†	160	198
53. Colouring materials	CSCR	1 073	1 122	284	289	286	96	92	101	90†	93	103
54. Medicinal products	EHAF	8 503	9 210	2 310	2 364	2 383	761	760	843	750†	826	807
55. Toilet preparations	CSCS	3 035	3 350	833	849	845	272	274	303	278†	279	288
57 & 58. Plastics	EHAG	5 037	5 439	1 396	1 400	1 390	460	449	491	445†	473	472
6. Manufactures classified chiefly by material	EHAH	33 469	37 654	9 658	9 827	9 850	3 150	3 376	3 301	3 242†	3 237	3 371
Of which:												
63. Wood and cork manufactures	EHAI	1 506	1 581	403	418	432	137	137	144	143†	142	147
64. Paper and paperboard manufactures	EHAJ	4 820	5 051	1 254	1 314	1 277	429	433	452	418†	419	440
65. Textile manufactures	EHAK	3 844	4 043	1 011	1 043	1 012	342	353	348	335	337†	340
67. Iron and steel	EHAL	4 402	4 957	1 305	1 406	1 463	446	465	495	481†	502	480
68. Non-ferrous metals	EHAM	3 923	6 193	1 703	1 569	1 599	490	547	532	546†	510	543
69. Metal manufactures	EHAN	5 355	5 845	1 504	1 512	1 617	490	509	513	511†	520	586
7. Machinery and transport equipment[2]	EHAO	117 321	146 751	31 544	29 969	29 872	9 954	9 824	10 191	9 878†	9 978	10 016
71 - 716, 72, 73 & 74. Mechanical machinery	EHAQ	21 851	22 771	5 673	5 801	6 060	1 923	1 947	1 931	2 016†	2 015	2 029
716, 75, 76 & 77. Electrical machinery	EHAR	55 736	81 701	15 231	13 401	11 941	4 480	4 365	4 556	3 966†	4 009	3 966
78. Road vehicles	EHAS	31 434	32 955	8 273	8 293	9 342	2 752	2 698	2 843	3 140†	2 922	3 280
79. Other transport equipment	EHAT	8 300	9 324	2 367	2 474	2 529	799	814	861	756†	1 032	741
8. Miscellaneous manufactures[2]	EHAU	42 176	45 079	11 183	11 453	11 660	3 819	3 754	3 880	3 777†	3 776	4 107
Of which:												
84. Clothing	CSDR	11 297	11 856	2 907	2 982	2 961	979	1 001	1 002	941†	989	1 031
85. Footwear	CSDS	2 563	2 705	662	671	675	218	224	229	216†	228	231
87 & 88. Scientific and photographic	EHAW	7 415	7 704	1 884	1 938	1 843	648	651	639	604†	615	624
9. Other commodities and transactions	BQAW	1 840	2 026	462	509	530	171	167	171	187†	171	172
TOTAL UK IMPORTS	BOKH	280 399	328 233	77 305	76 063	75 869	25 069	25 433	25 561	25 012†	24 910	25 947

1 The numbers on the left hand side of the table refer to the code numbers of the *Standard International Trade Classification,* Revision 3, which was introduced in January 1988.

2 Sections 7 and 8 are shown by broad economic category in table G2 of the *Monthly Review of External Trade Statistics.*

Source: Office for National Statistics: 020 7533 6064

15.8 United Kingdom exports, by area

£ million BOP-consistent basis seasonally adjusted

		2005	2006	2006 Q3	2006 Q4	2007 Q1	2006 Oct	2006 Nov	2006 Dec	2007 Jan	2007 Feb	2007 Mar
European Union:[1]	LGCK	121 494	153 589	35 639	34 242	32 790	11 324	11 234	11 684	10 954[†]	10 780	11 056
EMU members:	QAKW	108 918	135 686	31 828	30 510	29 127	10 089	9 949	10 472	9 757[†]	9 561	9 809
Austria	CHMY	1 332	1 697	372	376	358	129	130	117	116[†]	122	120
Belgium & Luxembourg	CHNQ	11 396	14 885	3 689	3 406	3 247	1 162	1 086	1 158	1 039[†]	1 082	1 126
Finland	CHMZ	1 514	1 858	484	452	500	155	158	139	193[†]	148	159
France	ENYL	19 933	29 251	6 137	5 678	4 859	1 948	1 836	1 894	1 682[†]	1 588	1 589
Germany	ENYO	23 026	27 456	6 654	6 721	6 329	2 121	2 156	2 444	2 069[†]	2 056	2 204
Greece	CHNT	1 367	1 494	375	392	373	128	127	137	126[†]	122	125
Irish Republic	CHNS	16 297	17 516	4 459	4 487	4 417	1 475	1 504	1 508	1 469[†]	1 451	1 497
Italy	CHNO	8 791	9 624	2 397	2 350	2 407	756	771	823	818[†]	781	808
Netherlands	CHNP	12 718	16 749	3 861	3 665	3 443	1 240	1 194	1 231	1 130[†]	1 132	1 181
Portugal	CHNU	1 697	2 360	573	400	421	119	156	125	139[†]	165	117
Spain	CHNV	10 678	12 597	2 789	2 522	2 721	831	813	878	961[†]	898	862
Non-EMU members:[1]	BQIA	12 576	17 903	3 811	3 732	3 663	1 235	1 285	1 212	1 197[†]	1 219	1 247
Of which:												
Czech Rep	FKML	1 080	1 581	354	346	368	111	120	115	118[†]	121	129
Denmark	CHNR	2 314	3 886	808	639	557	206	221	212	200[†]	190	167
Hungary	QALC	834	858	212	225	237	73	75	77	79[†]	79	79
Poland	ERDR	1 653	2 806	547	608	584	194	219	195	200[†]	195	189
Sweden	CHNA	4 586	5 224	1 278	1 242	1 270	404	422	416	393[†]	426	451
Other Western Europe:	HCJD	9 730	9 105	2 015	2 177	2 095	764	719	694	688[†]	662	745
Of which:												
Iceland	EPLW	179	188	45	46	38	15	17	14	11	11	16
Norway	EPLX	2 211	2 094	490	528	538	169	192	167	160	157	221
Switzerland	EPLV	4 985	4 105	819	926	814	358	279	289	241	281	292
Turkey	EOBA	2 160	2 423	585	607	654	210	198	199	263[†]	197	194
North America:	HBZQ	35 006	36 776	9 045	8 610	9 142	2 839	2 937	2 834	3 019[†]	2 907	3 216
Of which:												
Canada	EOBC	3 277	3 879	852	907	940	294	302	311	333[†]	312	295
Mexico	EPJX	638	747	195	216	185	70	78	68	61	65	59
USA	EOBB	30 912	31 960	7 957	7 441	7 978	2 461	2 538	2 442	2 616[†]	2 518	2 844
Other OECD countries:	HCII	8 577	8 709	2 141	2 210	2 158	711	777	722	669	708[†]	781
Of which:												
Australia	EPMA	2 580	2 479	602	648	663	204	206	238	202[†]	224	237
Japan	EOBD	3 900	4 111	982	998	956	310	356	332	318	308	330
New Zealand	EPMB	415	373	91	85	109	29	30	26	38[†]	34	37
South Korea	ERDM	1 677	1 746	466	479	430	168	185	126	111	142	177
Oil exporting countries:	HDII	10 850	9 057	2 001	2 084	2 179	625	768	691	653[†]	690	836
Of which:												
Brunei	QALF	43	79	41	12	24	7	3	2	2	20	2
Dubai	QALI	4 656	2 827	457	428	527	120	175	133	163[†]	173	191
Indonesia	FKMR	366	312	64	74	70	21	31	22	17	26	27
Kuwait	QATB	426	438	109	115	117	30	33	52	28	52	37
Nigeria	QATE	799	820	201	200	210	62	68	70	48[†]	65	97
Saudi Arabia	ERDI	1 559	1 644	414	437	410	123	159	155	132	125[†]	153
Rest of the World	HCHW	25 959	27 306	6 646	6 549	6 770	2 318	2 240	1 991	2 290[†]	2 215	2 265
Of which:												
Brazil	FKMO	836	918	195	256	289	94	81	81	86[†]	77	126
China	ERDN	2 811	3 268	816	905	775	308	302	295	225	251	299
Egypt	QALL	543	578	139	178	156	49	61	68	40	44	72
Hong Kong	ERDG	3 087	2 863	671	709	564	232	229	248	156	176	232
India	ERDJ	2 798	2 696	580	796	632	232	307	257	231[†]	194	207
Israel	ERDL	1 352	1 307	252	342	309	112	122	108	105	103[†]	101
Malaysia	ERDK	1 088	877	208	236	210	84	77	75	62[†]	74	74
Pakistan	FKMU	461	488	115	103	113	33	36	34	36	34[†]	43
Philippines	FKMX	279	242	64	60	64	20	22	18	15	24	25
Russia	ERDQ	1 869	2 051	524	574	617	194	211	169	207[†]	190	220
Singapore	ERDH	2 078	2 320	498	603	572	210	183	210	159	208	205
South Africa	EPME	2 073	2 182	489	534	548	190	173	171	188[†]	189	171
Taiwan	ERDP	939	911	219	237	246	78	82	77	85	81[†]	80
Thailand	ERDO	638	567	147	153	145	48	60	45	44	56	45

1 Includes the ten countries which joined the EU on 1 May 2004; Cyprus, Czech Republic, Estonia, Hungary, Latvia, Lithuania, Malta, Poland, Slovakia, Slovenia.

Source: Office for National Statistics: 020 7533 6064

15.9 United Kingdom imports, by area

£ million BOP-consistent basis seasonally adjusted

		2005	2006	2006 Q3	2006 Q4	2007 Q1	2006 Oct	2006 Nov	2006 Dec	2007 Jan	2007 Feb	2007 Mar
European Union:[1]	LGDC	158 365	191 175	43 042	41 709	41 729	13 759	13 642	14 308	13 961†	13 627	14 141
EMU members	QAKX	139 299	163 909	37 564	36 279	36 398	11 942	11 852	12 485	12 169†	11 826	12 403
Austria	CHNB	2 463	2 912	691	611	622	216	196	199	218†	197	207
Belgium & Luxembourg	CHNY	15 153	18 858	4 576	3 877	3 759	1 313	1 260	1 304	1 208†	1 242	1 309
Finland	CHNC	2 432	2 862	750	727	645	237	239	251	229†	208	208
France	ENYP	22 185	30 535	6 377	5 784	5 765	1 977	1 883	1 924	1 955†	1 899	1 911
Germany	ENYS	39 171	42 764	10 430	10 573	11 172	3 323	3 498	3 752	3 701†	3 621	3 850
Greece	CHOB	702	756	165	178	171	59	57	62	59†	60	52
Irish Republic	CHOA	10 410	10 737	2 569	2 761	2 653	918	894	949	913†	856	884
Italy	CHNW	12 675	13 287	3 203	3 205	3 104	1 044	1 057	1 104	1 064†	1 006	1 034
Netherlands	CHNX	20 437	23 660	5 405	5 413	5 411	1 798	1 787	1 828	1 808†	1 713	1 890
Portugal	CHOC	2 018	3 611	661	518	416	181	162	175	146†	130	140
Spain	CHOD	11 452	13 638	2 652	2 573	2 605	854	800	919	839†	870	896
Non-EMU members:[1]	BQIB	19 066	27 266	5 478	5 430	5 331	1 817	1 790	1 823	1 792†	1 801	1 738
Of which:												
Czech Rep	FKMM	1 883	2 575	614	651	717	208	200	243	242†	235	240
Denmark	CHNZ	4 395	6 247	1 141	1 034	981	347	341	346	328†	311	342
Hungary	QALD	1 859	2 102	461	538	564	170	178	190	182†	197	185
Poland	ERED	2 318	4 093	746	731	733	272	257	202	255†	249	229
Sweden	CHND	5 461	6 340	1 510	1 471	1 418	482	496	493	483	467†	468
Other Western Europe:	HBTS	20 072	23 419	6 132	5 255	5 661	1 659	1 812	1 784	1 826†	1 916	1 919
Of which:												
Iceland	EPMW	346	402	98	96	93	35	32	29	26	34†	33
Norway	EPMX	12 078	14 440	3 894	2 987	3 215	879	1 057	1 051	1 024†	1 035	1 156
Switzerland	EPMV	3 882	4 380	1 084	1 099	1 189	396	388	315	407†	423	359
Turkey	EOBU	3 511	3 952	991	1 013	1 110	326	316	371	350†	407	353
North America:	HCRB	27 128	31 596	7 560	8 186	7 867	2 693	2 761	2 732	2 585†	2 765	2 517
Of which:												
Canada	EOBW	4 155	5 012	1 197	1 228	1 242	413	408	407	349†	463	430
Mexico	EPJY	446	452	98	108	100	35	47	26	37	27	36
USA	EOBV	22 184	25 852	6 184	6 788	6 442	2 221	2 282	2 285	2 167†	2 253	2 022
Other OECD countries:	HDJQ	14 426	13 759	3 405	3 348	3 474	1 099	1 141	1 108	1 107†	1 157	1 210
Of which:												
Australia	EPNA	2 100	2 126	525	530	521	158	211	161	193	147	181
Japan	EOBX	8 670	7 932	1 958	1 899	2 039	645	624	630	637†	698	704
New Zealand	EPNB	592	607	161	160	168	58	54	48	57†	57	54
South Korea	ERDY	3 064	3 094	761	759	746	238	252	269	220	255†	271
Oil exporting countries:	HCPC	6 017	7 021	1 847	1 672	1 507	563	615	494	432†	515	560
Of which:												
Brunei	QALG	25	71	30	12	20	5	–	7	19	–	1
Dubai	QALJ	643	683	153	166	167	53	54	59	59†	59	49
Indonesia	FKMS	839	960	226	241	242	79	78	84	81†	84	77
Kuwait	QATC	367	746	227	119	157	55	41	23	21	81	55
Nigeria	QATF	152	206	77	25	35	3	15	7	18	8	9
Saudi Arabia	ERDU	1 714	1 235	360	247	209	96	77	74	51	44	114
Rest of the World	HCIF	54 391	61 263	15 319	15 893	15 631	5 296	5 462	5 135	5 101†	4 930	5 600
Of which:												
Brazil	FKMP	1 739	1 904	456	524	457	171	183	170	166†	132	159
China	ERDZ	12 963	15 330	3 734	4 038	4 777	1 330	1 350	1 358	1 393†	1 553	1 831
Egypt	QALM	350	666	139	203	160	43	76	84	52	56†	52
Hong Kong	ERDS	6 601	7 384	1 792	1 834	1 749	613	625	596	583	576†	590
India	ERDV	2 783	3 140	783	766	846	252	254	260	299	270†	277
Israel	ERDX	1 002	971	239	240	272	83	79	78	84†	107	81
Malaysia	ERDW	1 814	1 905	457	477	464	160	153	164	153	159	152
Pakistan	FKMV	487	515	128	124	127	44	40	40	41†	38	48
Philippines	FKMY	712	745	180	166	184	50	58	58	50	74	60
Russia	EREC	5 009	5 770	1 618	1 273	1 097	440	479	354	343	349†	405
Singapore	ERDT	3 829	3 781	747	1 196	1 062	408	461	327	361	275†	426
South Africa	EPNE	3 938	3 927	799	844	761	219	347	278	286	174†	301
Taiwan	EREB	2 225	2 355	574	590	611	196	199	195	196†	210	205
Thailand	EREA	1 719	1 935	474	471	453	159	159	153	152	149†	152

1 Includes the ten countries which joined the EU on 1 May 2004; Cyprus, Czech Republic, Estonia, Hungary, Latvia, Lithuania, Malta, Poland, Slovakia, Slovenia.

Source: Office for National Statistics: 020 7533 6064

15.10 Import penetration and export sales ratios for products of manufacturing industry[1]
Standard Industrial Classification 1992

Per cent

			2002	2003	2004	2003 Q1	2003 Q2	2003 Q3	2003 Q4	2004 Q1	2004 Q2	2004 Q3	2004 Q4
Ratio 1 Imports/Home Demand													
Description		*SIC Division*											
Total of divisions below	BAZI			80	86	87	80	88	89	87	83	85	89	91
Textiles	BAZJ	*17*	70	73	77	68	71	78	76	73	73	81	80
Wearing apparel; dressing and dyeing of fur	BAZK	*18*	93	97	100	95	97	100	97	101	96	104	99
Chemicals and chemical products	BAZL	*24*	80	86	87	79	91	90	87	83	85	89	93
Ratio 2 Imports/Home Demand plus exports													
Description													
Total of divisions below	BAZM			48	50	51	48	49	50	50	49	49	52	52
Textiles	BAZN	*17*	52	53	55	50	51	56	55	53	53	58	56
Wearing apparel; dressing and dyeing of fur	BAZO	*18*	76	78	80	78	78	78	78	80	80	81	81
Chemicals and chemical products	BAZP	*24*	42	44	45	43	45	44	45	44	44	46	46
Ratio 3 Exports/Sales													
Description													
Total of divisions below	BAZQ			77	84	85	76	87	88	84	81	82	87	90
Textiles	BAZR	*17*	53	59	63	53	57	64	62	58	60	69	67
Wearing apparel; dressing and dyeing of fur	BAZS	*18*	77	90	100	82	88	101	89	103	85	115	96
Chemicals and chemical products	BAZT	*24*	81	88	88	80	92	91	88	83	86	89	94
Ratio 4 Exports/Sales plus imports													
Description													
Total of divisions below	BAZU			40	42	42	39	44	44	42	41	42	42	43
Textiles	BAZV	*17*	26	28	28	26	28	28	28	27	28	29	29
Wearing apparel; dressing and dyeing of fur	BAZW	*18*	19	20	20	18	19	22	19	21	17	22	19
Chemicals and chemical products	BAZX	*24*	47	49	48	46	51	51	49	47	48	48	50

1 As from the end of 2004, quarterly data will not be collected for these industries. Annual results for the years 2005 onwards will be published on the ONS website at http://www.statistics.gov.uk/ as usual with various omissions.

Source: Office for National Statistics: 01633 812921

16 UK Balance of payments

16.1 Balance of payments
Summary

£ million

	Seasonally adjusted (balances)					Not seasonally adjusted			
	Trade in goods and services	Income	Current transfers	Current balance	Capital balance	Current balance	Capital balance	Net financial transactions	Net errors and omissions[1]
	IKBJ	HBOJ	IKBP	HBOP	FNVQ	HBOG	FKMJ	HBNT	HHDH
1997	1 764	3 314	−5 918	−840	958	−840	958	−8 771	8 653
1998	−7 141	12 320	−8 374	−3 195	489	−3 195	489	9 922	−7 216
1999	−15 454	1 270	−7 533	−21 717	747	−21 717	747	21 416	−446
2000	−19 361	4 540	−10 012	−24 833	1 703	−24 833	1 703	12 604	10 526
2001	−26 789	11 664	−6 759	−21 884	1 318	−21 884	1 318	17 503	3 063
2002	−30 875	23 443	−9 081	−16 513	932	−16 513	932	7 202	8 379
2003	−29 445	24 646	−10 122	−14 921	1 466	−14 921	1 466	20 507	−7 052
2004	−34 975	26 596	−10 949	−19 328	2 063	−19 328	2 063	5 641	11 624
2005	−44 474	27 416	−12 107	−29 165	1 491	−29 165	1 491	30 305	−2 631
2006	−54 086	22 801	−12 104	−43 389	713	−43 389	713	33 726	8 950
1996 Q3	−320	−433	−893	−1 646	430	−1 849	430	3 716	−2 297
Q4	173	−197	−1 270	−1 294	279	−211	279	2 453	−2 521
1997 Q1	1 253	362	−1 726	−111	369	−112	335	−3 363	3 140
Q2	333	1 741	−1 354	720	59	−255	80	747	−572
Q3	759	1 686	−1 719	726	193	505	205	1 979	−2 689
Q4	−581	−475	−1 119	−2 175	337	−978	338	−8 134	8 774
1998 Q1	−1 066	1 700	−2 190	−1 556	30	−2 649	−2	828	1 823
Q2	−1 362	1 841	−1 600	−1 121	−65	−2 029	−39	2 502	−434
Q3	−1 776	4 854	−1 788	1 290	219	1 919	230	−1 610	−539
Q4	−2 937	3 925	−2 796	−1 808	305	−436	300	8 202	−8 066
1999 Q1	−4 467	−70	−2 039	−6 576	−1	−6 836	−29	1 188	5 677
Q2	−2 994	−110	−1 644	−4 748	205	−6 066	229	1 620	4 217
Q3	−3 110	792	−2 020	−4 338	244	−3 550	254	4 751	−1 455
Q4	−4 883	658	−1 830	−6 055	299	−5 265	293	13 857	−8 885
2000 Q1	−4 516	1 407	−1 863	−4 972	248	−4 539	222	4 677	−360
Q2	−3 889	464	−2 247	−5 672	656	−6 373	677	1 686	4 010
Q3	−5 420	2 545	−2 791	−5 666	401	−5 473	417	−3 054	8 110
Q4	−5 536	124	−3 111	−8 523	398	−8 448	387	9 295	−1 234
2001 Q1	−4 931	2 545	−1 867	−4 253	240	−2 913	221	−2 437	5 129
Q2	−6 502	3 074	−2 720	−6 148	569	−7 780	594	3 118	4 068
Q3	−9 205	3 620	26	−5 559	212	−4 822	225	3 538	1 059
Q4	−6 151	2 425	−2 198	−5 924	297	−6 369	278	13 284	−7 193
2002 Q1	−7 426	5 283	−2 298	−4 441	154	−2 990	130	−10 393	13 253
Q2	−7 368	4 270	−2 557	−5 655	158	−7 917	184	−64	7 797
Q3	−7 237	6 924	−1 519	−1 832	160	−1 305	174	3 423	−2 292
Q4	−8 844	6 966	−2 707	−4 585	460	−4 301	444	14 236	−10 379
2003 Q1	−6 132	7 932	−2 364	−564	236	535	202	−7 851	7 114
Q2	−6 582	5 098	−2 926	−4 410	208	−6 719	237	11 603	−5 121
Q3	−7 600	4 688	−2 479	−5 391	329	−4 636	348	4 628	−340
Q4	−9 131	6 928	−2 353	−4 556	693	−4 101	679	12 127	−8 705
2004 Q1	−8 067	5 825	−2 686	−4 928	735	−4 045	697	−5 552	8 900
Q2	−8 407	6 377	−2 439	−4 469	601	−6 699	634	9 386	−3 321
Q3	−9 036	4 954	−2 807	−6 889	266	−7 432	283	1 662	5 487
Q4	−9 465	9 440	−3 017	−3 042	461	−1 152	449	145	558
2005 Q1	−10 272	7 119	−3 531	−6 684	773	−6 986	732	−168	6 422
Q2	−9 348	9 520	−2 620	−2 448	667	−3 272	700	575	1 997
Q3	−13 493	6 527	−3 022	−9 988	358	−10 526	373	18 754	−8 601
Q4	−11 361	4 250	−2 934	−10 045	−307	−8 381	−314	11 144	−2 449
2006 Q1	−13 775	6 141	−3 069	−10 703	550	−11 510	493	1 912	9 105
Q2	−15 390	8 766	−2 916	−9 540	−764	−8 793	−725	8 471	1 047
Q3	−12 716	4 735	−2 504	−10 485	463	−11 664	484	9 983	1 197
Q4	−12 205	3 159	−3 615	−12 661	464	−11 422	461	13 360	−2 399

1 This series represents net errors and omissions in the balance of payments accounts. It is the converse of the current and capital balances (HBOG and FKMJ) and net financial account transactions (HBNT) and is required to balance these three accounts, not seasonally adjusted.

Source: Office for National Statistics: 020 7533 6078

16.2 Balance of payments
Current account balances (seasonally adjusted)

£ million

	Trade in goods and services			Income			Current transfers				
	Trade in goods	Trade in services	Total trade	Compensation of employees	Investment income	Total income	Central government	Other sectors	Total current transfers	Current balance	Current balance as % of GDP [1]
	BOKI	IKBD	IKBJ	IJAJ	HBOM	HBOJ	FNSV	FNTC	IKBP	HBOP	AA6H
1997	−12 342	14 106	1 764	83	3 231	3 314	−3 087	−2 831	−5 918	−840	−0.1
1998	−21 813	14 672	−7 141	−10	12 330	12 320	−5 020	−3 354	−8 374	−3 195	−0.4
1999	−29 051	13 597	−15 454	201	1 069	1 270	−3 940	−3 593	−7 533	−21 717	−2.4
2000	−32 976	13 615	−19 361	150	4 390	4 540	−5 550	−4 462	−10 012	−24 833	−2.6
2001	−41 212	14 423	−26 789	66	11 598	11 664	−2 593	−4 166	−6 759	−21 884	−2.2
2002	−47 705	16 830	−30 875	67	23 376	23 443	−5 633	−3 448	−9 081	−16 513	−1.6
2003	−48 607	19 162	−29 445	59	24 587	24 646	−6 976	−3 146	−10 122	−14 921	−1.3
2004	−60 893	25 918	−34 975	71	26 525	26 596	−8 304	−2 645	−10 949	−19 328	−1.6
2005	−68 783	24 309	−44 474	65	27 351	27 416	−9 449	−2 658	−12 107	−29 165	−2.4
2006	−83 691	29 605	−54 086	58	22 743	22 801	−9 968	−2 136	−12 104	−43 389	−3.4
1996 Q3	−3 089	2 769	−320	−16	−417	−433	−486	−407	−893	−1 646	−0.9
Q4	−3 041	3 214	173	−26	−171	−197	−539	−731	−1 270	−1 294	−0.7
1997 Q1	−2 303	3 556	1 253	1	361	362	−806	−920	−1 726	−111	−0.1
Q2	−3 140	3 473	333	18	1 723	1 741	−1 088	−266	−1 354	720	0.4
Q3	−2 777	3 536	759	22	1 664	1 686	−843	−876	−1 719	726	0.4
Q4	−4 122	3 541	−581	42	−517	−475	−350	−769	−1 119	−2 175	−1.0
1998 Q1	−4 734	3 668	−1 066	75	1 625	1 700	−1 319	−871	−2 190	−1 556	−0.7
Q2	−4 977	3 615	−1 362	−27	1 868	1 841	−843	−757	−1 600	−1 121	−0.5
Q3	−5 782	4 006	−1 776	−29	4 883	4 854	−1 279	−509	−1 788	1 290	0.6
Q4	−6 320	3 383	−2 937	−29	3 954	3 925	−1 579	−1 217	−2 796	−1 808	−0.8
1999 Q1	−7 934	3 467	−4 467	33	−103	−70	−1 022	−1 017	−2 039	−6 576	−3.0
Q2	−6 598	3 604	−2 994	89	−199	−110	−824	−820	−1 644	−4 748	−2.1
Q3	−6 598	3 488	−3 110	47	745	792	−948	−1 072	−2 020	−4 338	−1.9
Q4	−7 921	3 038	−4 883	32	626	658	−1 146	−684	−1 830	−6 055	−2.6
2000 Q1	−7 480	2 964	−4 516	13	1 394	1 407	−1 276	−587	−1 863	−4 972	−2.1
Q2	−7 405	3 516	−3 889	82	382	464	−1 227	−1 020	−2 247	−5 672	−2.4
Q3	−8 844	3 424	−5 420	30	2 515	2 545	−1 219	−1 572	−2 791	−5 666	−2.4
Q4	−9 247	3 711	−5 536	25	99	124	−1 828	−1 283	−3 111	−8 523	−3.5
2001 Q1	−9 180	4 249	−4 931	−53	2 598	2 545	−1 037	−830	−1 867	−4 253	−1.7
Q2	−11 080	4 578	−6 502	65	3 009	3 074	−1 379	−1 341	−2 720	−6 148	−2.5
Q3	−10 481	1 276	−9 205	29	3 591	3 620	967	−941	26	−5 559	−2.2
Q4	−10 471	4 320	−6 151	25	2 400	2 425	−1 144	−1 054	−2 198	−5 924	−2.3
2002 Q1	−11 372	3 946	−7 426	8	5 275	5 283	−1 065	−1 233	−2 298	−4 441	−1.7
Q2	−11 002	3 634	−7 368	19	4 251	4 270	−1 310	−1 247	−2 557	−5 655	−2.2
Q3	−12 016	4 779	−7 237	23	6 901	6 924	−1 317	−202	−1 519	−1 832	−0.7
Q4	−13 315	4 471	−8 844	17	6 949	6 966	−1 941	−766	−2 707	−4 585	−1.7
2003 Q1	−10 862	4 730	−6 132	15	7 917	7 932	−1 600	−764	−2 364	−564	−0.2
Q2	−11 545	4 963	−6 582	23	5 075	5 098	−1 960	−966	−2 926	−4 410	−1.6
Q3	−12 302	4 702	−7 600	11	4 677	4 688	−1 639	−840	−2 479	−5 391	−1.9
Q4	−13 898	4 767	−9 131	10	6 918	6 928	−1 777	−576	−2 353	−4 556	−1.6
2004 Q1	−13 947	5 880	−8 067	15	5 810	5 825	−1 962	−724	−2 686	−4 928	−1.7
Q2	−15 247	6 840	−8 407	32	6 345	6 377	−1 906	−533	−2 439	−4 469	−1.5
Q3	−15 529	6 493	−9 036	17	4 937	4 954	−2 151	−656	−2 807	−6 889	−2.3
Q4	−16 170	6 705	−9 465	7	9 433	9 440	−2 285	−732	−3 017	−3 042	−1.0
2005 Q1	−16 264	5 992	−10 272	7	7 112	7 119	−2 725	−806	−3 531	−6 684	−2.2
Q2	−16 224	6 876	−9 348	29	9 491	9 520	−2 273	−347	−2 620	−2 448	−0.8
Q3	−17 990	4 497	−13 493	17	6 510	6 527	−2 221	−801	−3 022	−9 988	−3.3
Q4	−18 305	6 944	−11 361	12	4 238	4 250	−2 230	−704	−2 934	−10 045	−3.2
2006 Q1	−21 152	7 377	−13 775	4	6 137	6 141	−2 359	−710	−3 069	−10 703	−3.4
Q2	−22 530	7 140	−15 390	24	8 742	8 766	−2 331	−585	−2 916	−9 540	−3.0
Q3	−19 818	7 102	−12 716	8	4 727	4 735	−2 309	−195	−2 504	−10 485	−3.2
Q4	−20 191	7 986	−12 205	22	3 137	3 159	−2 969	−646	−3 615	−12 661	−3.8

1 Using series YBHA: GDP at current market prices.

Source: Office for National Statistics: 020 7533 6078

16.3 Balance of payments
Summary of financial account

£ million

	Investment in the UK				UK investment abroad						Net transactions				
	Direct investment	Portfolio investment	Other investment	Total	Direct investment	Portfolio investment	Financial derivatives	Other investment	Reserve assets	Total	Direct investment	Portfolio investment	Other investment	Reserve assets	Total
	HJYU	HHZF	XBMN	HBNS	-HJYP	-HHZC	-ZPNN	-XBMM	-LTCV	-HBNR	HJYV	HHZD	HHYR	LTCV	HBNT
1997	22 900	26 786	196 670	246 356	37 302	51 941	−1 156	169 420	−2 380	255 127	−14 402	−25 155	27 250	2 380	−8 771
1998	45 054	20 853	67 640	133 547	73 786	32 073	3 043	14 887	−164	123 625	−28 732	−11 220	52 753	164	9 922
1999	55 066	114 106	55 469	224 641	125 602	21 390	−2 685	59 557	−639	203 225	−70 536	92 716	−4 088	639	21 416
2000	80 566	164 543	267 030	512 139	155 582	65 563	−1 553	276 028	3 915	499 535	−75 016	98 980	−8 998	−3 915	12 604
2001	37 348	48 148	223 969	309 465	42 827	86 551	−8 417	174 086	−3 085	291 962	−5 479	−38 403	49 883	3 085	17 503
2002	16 782	51 010	71 187	138 979	35 041	1 011	−1 001	97 185	−459	131 777	−18 259	49 999	−25 998	459	7 202
2003	16 776	95 222	245 370	357 368	40 889	36 267	5 401	255 863	−1 559	336 861	−24 113	58 955	−10 493	1 559	20 507
2004	42 416	87 247	404 321	533 984	53 831	140 853	7 875	325 588	196	528 343	−11 415	−53 606	78 733	−196	5 641
2005	107 794	125 639	520 741	754 174	50 002	166 109	2 451	504 651	656	723 869	57 792	−40 470	16 090	−656	30 305
2006	75 840	173 608	440 432	689 880	43 184	194 091	14 339	404 966	−426	656 154	32 656	−20 483	35 466	426	33 726
1996 Q3	5 259	9 048	28 891	43 198	2 966	24 541	−393	13 279	−911	39 482	2 293	−15 493	15 612	911	3 716
Q4	3 921	19 044	51 288	74 253	6 196	13 913	−332	50 523	1 500	71 800	−2 275	5 131	765	−1 500	2 453
1997 Q1	8 798	8 031	76 114	92 943	8 815	13 891	−490	75 548	−1 458	96 306	−17	−5 860	566	1 458	−3 363
Q2	4 803	9 191	49 657	63 651	4 304	36 374	70	21 931	225	62 904	499	−27 183	27 726	−225	747
Q3	3 430	9 499	20 085	33 014	18 189	−2 663	−232	15 405	336	31 035	−14 759	12 162	4 680	−336	1 979
Q4	5 869	65	50 814	56 748	5 994	4 339	−504	56 536	−1 483	64 882	−125	−4 274	−5 722	1 483	−8 134
1998 Q1	11 004	−911	41 997	52 090	5 484	23 977	−626	23 425	−998	51 262	5 520	−24 888	18 572	998	828
Q2	8 055	−9 451	49 236	47 840	7 107	9 160	595	28 167	309	45 338	948	−18 611	21 069	−309	2 502
Q3	13 199	841	19 228	33 268	20 212	−17 831	1 531	30 653	313	34 878	−7 013	18 672	−11 425	−313	−1 610
Q4	12 796	30 374	−42 821	349	40 983	16 767	1 543	−67 358	212	−7 853	−28 187	13 607	24 537	−212	8 202
1999 Q1	12 832	19 069	68 198	100 099	8 149	15 377	−1 519	77 741	−837	98 911	4 683	3 692	−9 543	837	1 188
Q2	5 262	84 215	61 300	150 777	84 661	12 107	441	51 746	202	149 157	−79 399	72 108	9 554	−202	1 620
Q3	12 863	6 224	−29 530	−10 443	11 589	9 965	535	−36 524	−759	−15 194	1 274	−3 741	6 994	759	4 751
Q4	24 109	4 598	−44 499	−15 792	21 203	−16 059	−2 142	−33 406	755	−29 649	2 906	20 657	−11 093	−755	13 857
2000 Q1	14 601	91 753	139 095	245 449	112 991	−13 178	492	142 932	−2 465	240 772	−98 390	104 931	−3 837	2 465	4 677
Q2	22 735	29 873	60 168	112 776	34 299	45 177	−926	31 994	546	111 090	−11 564	−15 304	28 174	−546	1 686
Q3	43 931	12 932	29 864	86 727	5 849	19 518	−526	63 410	1 530	89 781	38 082	−6 586	−33 546	−1 530	−3 054
Q4	−701	29 985	37 903	67 187	2 443	14 046	−593	37 692	4 304	57 892	−3 144	15 939	211	−4 304	9 295
2001 Q1	16 426	20 888	214 849	252 163	21 156	37 299	−2 331	201 075	−2 599	254 600	−4 730	−16 411	13 774	2 599	−2 437
Q2	12 210	7 969	−20 847	−668	11 835	30 083	1 473	−47 214	37	−3 786	375	−22 114	26 367	−37	3 118
Q3	5 518	8 173	−549	13 142	8 648	11 046	−5 843	−3 749	−498	−3 786	−3 130	−2 873	3 200	498	3 538
Q4	3 194	11 118	30 516	44 828	1 188	8 123	−1 716	23 974	−25	31 544	2 006	2 995	6 542	25	13 284
2002 Q1	−6 050	9 049	24 262	27 261	18 143	−6 575	−340	26 954	−528	37 654	−24 193	15 624	−2 692	528	−10 393
Q2	15 376	22 727	−7 367	30 736	16 315	42 400	−1 968	−25 969	22	30 800	−939	−19 673	18 602	−22	−64
Q3	1 061	2 789	−5 335	−1 485	15 331	−36 798	1 855	14 022	682	−4 908	−14 270	39 587	−19 357	−682	3 423
Q4	6 395	16 445	59 627	82 467	−14 748	1 984	−548	82 178	−635	68 231	21 143	14 461	−22 551	635	14 236
2003 Q1	3 656	16 431	112 428	132 515	20 994	15 526	7 677	97 795	−1 626	140 366	−17 338	905	14 633	1 626	−7 851
Q2	5 771	12 864	122 701	141 336	14 213	25 426	−2 302	93 043	−647	129 733	−8 442	−12 562	29 658	647	11 603
Q3	1 186	41 115	−5 094	37 207	7 323	−3 958	1 348	26 563	1 303	32 579	−6 137	45 073	−31 657	−1 303	4 628
Q4	6 163	24 812	15 335	46 310	−1 641	−727	−1 322	38 462	−589	34 183	7 804	25 539	−23 127	589	12 127
2004 Q1	9 292	49 901	208 542	267 735	17 558	45 902	4 504	205 848	−525	273 287	−8 266	3 999	2 694	525	−5 552
Q2	7 558	12 011	71 679	91 248	13 609	−198	3 967	65 079	−595	81 862	−6 051	12 209	6 600	595	9 386
Q3	9 141	16 471	63 115	88 727	19 421	47 649	1 278	18 771	−54	87 065	−10 280	−31 178	44 344	54	1 662
Q4	16 425	8 864	60 985	86 274	3 243	47 500	−1 874	35 890	1 370	86 129	13 182	−38 636	25 095	−1 370	145
2005 Q1	19 365	54 314	200 148	273 827	24 064	28 239	−269	222 494	−533	273 995	−4 699	26 075	−22 346	533	−168
Q2	16 660	27 460	131 422	175 542	3 899	54 436	1 155	114 950	527	174 967	12 761	−26 976	16 472	−527	575
Q3	71 249	8 250	121 729	201 228	11 673	49 262	1 574	119 589	376	182 474	59 576	−41 012	2 140	−376	18 754
Q4	520	35 615	67 442	103 577	10 366	34 172	−9	47 618	286	92 433	−9 846	1 443	19 824	−286	11 144
2006 Q1	30 478	44 580	307 690	382 748	17 972	50 800	5 968	306 561	−465	380 836	12 506	−6 220	1 129	465	1 912
Q2	20 149	26 848	10 731	57 728	−3 058	42 249	2 915	7 361	−210	49 257	23 207	−15 401	3 370	210	8 471
Q3	18 718	55 771	60 511	135 000	6 887	26 686	4 035	87 024	385	125 017	11 831	29 085	−26 513	−385	9 983
Q4	6 495	46 409	61 500	114 404	21 383	74 356	1 421	4 020	−136	101 044	−14 888	−27 947	57 480	136	13 360

Source: Office for National Statistics: 020 7533 6078

17 Government finance

17.1 Public sector finances

£ millions[1]

	Public sector surplus on current budget	Public sector net investment	Net Borrowing					Public sector net debt[2]	Public sector net debt as percentage of GDP
			Central government	Local government	General government	Public corporations	Public sector		
	ANMU	-ANNW	-NMFJ	-NMOE	-NNBK	-CPCM	-ANNX	RUTN	RUTO
2000	21 991[†]	4 472[†]	−17 500[†]	768[†]	−16 732[†]	−787	−17 519[†]	321.9	33.0
2001	19 896	9 048	−11 151	−262	−11 413	565	−10 848	324.2	31.8
2002	−7 103	11 228	18 525	−1 935	16 590	1 741	18 331	351.6	32.7
2003	−19 865	16 607	38 668	−3 590	35 078	1 394	36 472	383.3	33.5
2004	−20 127	17 407	37 092	−277	36 815	719	37 534	425.8	35.4
2005	−19 161	21 837	36 091	1 984	38 075	2 923[†]	40 998	467.1	37.3
2006	−9 217	23 932	35 576	−866	34 710	−1 561	33 149	503.4	38.1[†]
2000/01	24 146	4 043	−19 891	−110	−20 001	−102	−20 103	312.4	31.7
2001/02	11 086	11 053	−404	36	−368	335	−33	317.6	30.7
2002/03	−11 437	13 314	24 804	−2 427	22 377	2 374	24 751	349.1	32.0
2003/04	−18 086	15 460	35 970	−2 928	33 042	504	33 546	384.4	33.1
2004/05	−18 841	20 271	37 420	192	37 612	1 500	39 112	424.1	34.9
2005/06	−15 300	22 697	32 822	3 291	36 113	1 884	37 997	463.4	36.4
2006/07	−8 758	24 876	34 587	21	34 608	−974	33 634	501.0	37.4
2001 Q1	18 345[†]	2 869[†]	−15 154[†]	−688[†]	−15 842[†]	366	−15 476[†]	312.4	31.7
Q2	−2 431	1 304	4 509	−793	3 716	19	3 735	319.7	32.1
Q3	5 069	1 990	−3 939	889	−3 050	−29	−3 079	313.6	31.1
Q4	−1 087	2 885	3 433	330	3 763	209	3 972	324.2	31.8
2002 Q1	9 535	4 874	−4 407	−390	−4 797	136	−4 661	317.6	30.7
Q2	−9 082	1 021	10 701	−725	9 976	127	10 103	324.2	30.9
Q3	−486	2 651	3 676	−681	2 995	142	3 137	328.2	30.9
Q4	−7 070	2 682	8 555	−139	8 416	1 336	9 752	351.6	32.7
2003 Q1	5 201	6 960	1 872	−882	990	769	1 759	349.1	32.0
Q2	−11 631	2 415	15 774	−1 944	13 830	216	14 046	357.7	32.2
Q3	−3 778	3 494	7 170	−100	7 070	202	7 272	362.9	32.2
Q4	−9 657	3 738	13 852	−664	13 188	207	13 395	383.3	33.5
2004 Q1	6 980	5 813	−826	−220	−1 046	−121	−1 167	384.4	33.1
Q2	−11 646	3 264	16 268	−1 610	14 658	252	14 910	397.4	33.8
Q3	−5 615	3 623	8 353	666	9 019	219	9 238	403.4	33.9
Q4	−9 846	4 707	13 297	887	14 184	369	14 553	425.8	35.4
2005 Q1	8 266	8 677	−498	249	−249	660[†]	411	424.1	34.9[†]
Q2	−11 451	2 236	11 556	−1 532	10 024	3 663	13 687	439.5	35.9
Q3	−3 723	4 704	7 303	1 877	9 180	−753	8 427	447.1	36.1
Q4	−12 253	6 220	17 730	1 390	19 120	−647	18 473	467.1	37.3
2006 Q1	12 127	9 537	−3 767	1 556	−2 211	−379	−2 590	463.4	36.4
Q2	−11 877	4 638	21 887	−5 099	16 788	−273	16 515	485.5	37.6
Q3	−1 372	4 766	5 504	941	6 445	−307	6 138	488.6	37.4
Q4	−8 095	4 991	11 952	1 736	13 688	−602	13 086	503.4	38.1
2007 Q1	12 586	10 481	−4 756	2 443	−2 313	208	−2 105	501.0	37.4
2005 Mar	−5 208[†]	2 924[†]	6 691[†]	1 172[†]	7 863	269	8 132	424.1	34.9[†]
Apr	1 551	243	−5 270	−395	−5 665[†]	4 357[†]	−1 308[†]	422.8	34.7
May	−7 841	1 027	11 297	−2 035	9 262	−394	8 868	427.9	35.0
Jun	−5 161	966	5 529	898	6 427	−300	6 127	439.5	35.9
Jul	3 394	1 279	−3 509	1 376	−2 133	18	−2 115	431.2	35.0
Aug	−3 819	1 705	6 062	61	6 123	−599	5 524	436.8	35.4
Sep	−3 298	1 720	4 750	440	5 190	−172	5 018	447.1	36.1
Oct	1 143	1 826	−924	1 110	186	497	683	443.1	35.6
Nov	−8 150	2 383	11 688	−276	11 412	−879	10 533	451.9	36.2
Dec	−5 246	2 011	6 966	556	7 522	−265	7 257	467.1	37.3
2006 Jan	13 502	2 696	−13 109	1 690	−11 419	613	−10 806	445.3	35.3
Feb	1 670	3 313	3 473	−1 297	2 176	−533	1 643	447.7	35.4
Mar	−3 045	3 528	5 869	1 163	7 032	−459	6 573	463.4	36.4
Apr	104	1 948	3 945	−3 481	464	1 380	1 844	462.3	36.2
May	−6 991	1 480	10 629	−1 399	9 230	−759	8 471	470.1	36.6
Jun	−4 990	1 210	7 313	−219	7 094	−894	6 200	485.5	37.6
Jul	8 174	1 875	−6 355	140	−6 215	−84	−6 299	472.2	36.5
Aug	−5 697	1 129	6 145	799	6 944	−118	6 826	476.7	36.7
Sep	−3 849	1 762	5 714	2	5 716	−105	5 611	488.6	37.4
Oct	3 726	1 019	−3 595	958	−2 637	−70	−2 707	480.7	36.7
Nov	−7 853	1 763	9 790	366	10 156	−540	9 616	489.2	37.1
Dec	−3 968	2 209	5 757	412	6 169	8	6 177	503.4	38.1
2007 Jan	14 276	3 116	−12 353	1 163	−11 190	30	−11 160	481.8	36.3
Feb	2 863	3 435	36	869	905	−333	572	483.7[†]	36.2
Mar	−4 553	3 930	7 561	411	7 972	511	8 483	501.0	37.4

1 Unless otherwise stated.
2 £ billion

Source: Office for National Statistics: 020 7533 5991

17.2 Central government transactions and fiscal balances

£ million

Current receipts

| | Taxes on production | of which | Taxes on income and wealth | | | | Compulsory social contributions | Interest and dividends | Other receipts[3] | |
	Total	VAT	Total	Income and capital gains tax[1]	Other[2]	Other taxes				Total
	NMBY	NZGF	NMCU	LIBR	LIBP	LIQR	AIIH	LIQP	LIQQ	ANBV
2000/01	129 123	60 736	144 263	110 324	33 939	8 559	62 068	9 064	7 187	360 264
2001/02	132 882	64 730	145 180	111 688	33 492	9 419	63 162	7 862	7 468	365 973
2002/03	139 640	69 081	143 238	112 373	30 865	9 538	63 529	7 998	7 640	371 583
2003/04	148 534	76 627	145 488	115 233	30 255	10 172	75 148	7 847	7 494	394 683
2004/05	154 755	79 960	160 979	124 977	36 002	10 798	80 209	7 485	7 824	422 050
2005/06	159 105	81 445	180 292	135 271	45 021	11 586	85 404	7 709	8 066	452 162
2006/07	168 797	86 425	194 714	146 985	47 729	12 129	90 463	7 782	8 328	482 213
2005 Jun	12 995†	6 660†	10 078†	8 784†	1 294	867†	6 995	566†	672	32 173†
Jul	13 492	6 965	20 485	13 030	7 455	1 029	6 936	490	654	43 086
Aug	13 248	6 676	11 849	10 777	1 072	1 031	6 663	548	659	33 998
Sep	13 669	7 081	11 359	9 036	2 323	1 072	6 942	790	664	34 496
Oct	13 737	7 185	17 733	9 296	8 437	948	6 813	608	678	40 517
Nov	13 665	6 961	10 004	8 875	1 129	832	6 858	715	684	32 758
Dec	13 461	6 857	12 246	10 114	2 132	894	7 348	587	684	35 220
2006 Jan	12 812	6 566	31 089	20 129	10 960	927	7 461	641	675	53 605
Feb	12 624	6 221	16 426	14 993	1 433	920	7 689	546	678	38 883
Mar	13 217	6 799	13 999	12 211	1 788	1 110	8 425	1 034	682	38 467
Apr	13 845	7 162	15 844	10 016	5 828	960	6 986†	560	691	38 886
May	13 736	7 041	10 612	9 245	1 367	996	6 973	681	687	33 685
Jun	14 010	7 073	11 015	9 652	1 363	1 084	7 140	599	687	34 535
Jul	13 959	7 215	24 818	14 721	10 097	940	7 121	554	690	48 082
Aug	14 139	7 116	12 712	11 215	1 497	1 033	6 833	540	695	35 952
Sep	14 652	7 800	12 457	10 016	2 441	1 027	7 211	630	691	36 668
Oct	14 807	7 773	19 630	9 658	9 972	1 060	7 043	823	692	44 055
Nov	14 474	7 372	10 754	9 280	1 474	977	7 054	731	695	34 685
Dec	14 506	7 367	13 831	11 189	2 642	978	7 909	589	698	38 511
2007 Jan	13 516	7 019	30 666	22 075	8 591†	958	8 230	615	700	54 685
Feb	13 167	6 450	18 677	17 096	1 581	977	8 316	503	701	42 341
Mar	13 986	7 037	13 698	12 822	876	1 139	9 647	957	701	40 128

Current expenditure

	Interest	Net Social Benefits	Other	Total	Saving, gross plus capital taxes	Depreciation	Surplus on current budget	Net investment	Net borrowing
	NMFX	GZSJ	LIQS	ANLP	ANPM	NSRN	ANLV	-ANNS	-NMFJ
2000/01	25 989	96 016	205 188	327 193	33 071	5 133	27 938	8 047	−19 891
2001/02	22 099	105 207	220 548	347 854	18 119	5 122	12 997	12 593	−404
2002/03	20 942	108 950	244 845	374 737	−3 154	5 287	−8 441	16 363	24 804
2003/04	22 333	116 857	267 396	406 586	−11 903	5 524	−17 427	18 543	35 970
2004/05	23 971	122 252	287 416	433 639	−11 589	5 782	−17 371	20 049	37 420
2005/06	25 804	128 354	306 170	460 328	−8 166	6 119	−14 285	18 537	32 822
2006/07	27 500	132 290	324 658	484 448	−2 235	6 564	−8 799	25 788	34 587
2005 Jun	1 871	10 258	23 801†	35 930†	−3 757†	504	−4 261†	1 268†	5 529†
Jul	2 505	10 525	24 702	37 732	5 354	493	4 861	1 352	−3 509
Aug	2 449	10 561	24 977	37 987	−3 989	497	−4 486	1 576	6 062
Sep	1 202	10 463	25 496	37 161	−2 665	500	−3 165	1 585	4 750
Oct	2 348	10 687	23 890	36 925	3 592	516	3 076	2 152	−924
Nov	2 455	13 526	25 659	41 640	−8 882	520	−9 402	2 286	11 688
Dec	2 122	10 934	26 485	39 541	−4 321	522	−4 843	2 123	6 966
2006 Jan	2 618	10 478	24 399	37 495	16 110	520	15 590	2 481	−13 109
Feb	2 186	9 981	26 854	39 021	−138	522	−660	2 813	3 473
Mar	1 597	10 649	28 720	40 966	−2 499	524	−3 023	2 846	5 869
Apr	2 216	10 210†	27 439	39 865	−979	533	−1 512	2 433	3 945
May	2 252	10 889	28 758	41 899	−8 214	533	−8 747	1 882	10 629
Jun	1 827	10 644	27 216	39 687	−5 152	534	−5 686	1 627	7 313
Jul	2 656†	10 812	25 946	39 414	8 668	541	8 127	1 772	−6 355
Aug	2 395	11 094	26 904	40 393	−4 441	544	−4 985	1 160	6 145
Sep	1 365	11 258	27 431	40 054	−3 386	545	−3 931	1 783	5 714
Oct	2 497	10 940	25 297	38 734	5 321	549	4 772	1 177	−3 595
Nov	2 671	12 864	26 480	42 015	−7 330	551	−7 881	1 909	9 790
Dec	2 291	10 999	28 029	41 319	−2 808	554	−3 362	2 395	5 757
2007 Jan	3 041	11 185	25 124	39 350	15 335	558	14 777	2 424	−12 353
Feb	2 704	10 145	26 063	38 912	3 429	560	2 869	2 905	36
Mar	1 585	11 250	29 971	42 806	−2 678	562	−3 240	4 321	7 561

1 Includes capital gains tax paid by households. Includes income tax and capital gains tax paid by corporations.
2 Mainly comprises corporation tax and petroleum revenue tax.
3 Includes receipts from the spectrum.

Source: Office for National Statistics: 020 7533 5991

Government finance

17.3 Public sector aggregates[1]

£ millions, not seasonally adjusted

	Surplus on current budget[2]		Net investment[3]		Net borrowing[4]		Net cash requirement[5]	
	General Government	Public Sector	General Government	Public Sector	General Government	Public Sector	General Government	Public Sector
Calendar years								
	ANLW	ANMU	-ANNV	-ANNW	-NNBK	-ANNX	RUUS	RURQ
2000	22 851†	21 991†	6 763†	4 472†	-16 732†	-17 519†	-38 840	-36 870
2001	19 879	19 896	10 088	9 048	-11 413	-10 848	-3 768	-1 928
2002	-6 145	-7 103	11 132	11 228	16 590	18 331	16 421	19 310
2003	-17 958	-19 865	18 435	16 607	35 078	36 472	38 214	38 521
2004	-18 239	-20 127	19 575	17 407	36 815	37 534	41 321	42 324
2005	-18 995	-19 161	20 599	21 837	38 075	40 998	41 870	40 951
2006	-13 693	-9 217	23 125	23 932	34 710	33 149	36 693	33 055†
Financial years								
2000/01	25 191	24 146	5 827	4 043	-20 001	-20 103	-37 862	-36 323
2001/02	10 640	11 086	11 555	11 053	-368	-33	2 943	3 637
2002/03	-9 734	-11 437	13 406	13 314	22 377	24 751	21 499	25 221
2003/04	-16 611	-18 086	18 005	15 460	33 042	33 546	40 005	39 732
2004/05	-17 878	-18 841	21 238	20 271	37 612	39 112	38 737	38 571
2005/06	-17 482	-15 300	18 693	22 697	36 113	37 997	40 075	40 022
2006/07	..	-8 758	..	24 876	34 608	33 634	36 879	35 137
Quarterly								
1999 Q2	-5 046†	-5 033†	593†	201†	5 545†	5 234†	5 318	5 306
Q3	5 077	4 857	1 535	881	-3 679	-3 976	-3 154	-3 215
Q4	5 544	5 157	1 779	948	-3 914	-4 209	2 223	2 167
2000 Q1	16 536	16 190	4 219	3 298	-12 573	-12 892	-14 072	-12 231
Q2	-1 638	-1 882	-205	-542	1 504	1 340	-12 221	-11 819
Q3	5 289	5 149	965	465	-4 508	-4 684	-16 734	-16 486
Q4	2 664	2 534	1 784	1 251	-1 155	-1 283	4 187	3 666
2001 Q1	18 876	18 345	3 283	2 869	-15 842	-15 476	-13 094	-11 684
Q2	-2 748	-2 431	1 520	1 304	3 716	3 735	6 246	6 352
Q3	4 871	5 069	2 251	1 990	-3 050	-3 079	-6 322	-6 101
Q4	-1 120	-1 087	3 034	2 885	3 763	3 972	9 402	9 505
2002 Q1	9 637	9 535	4 750	4 874	-4 797	-4 661	-6 383	-6 119
Q2	-8 898	-9 082	1 297	1 021	9 976	10 103	7 126	7 045
Q3	-313	-486	2 983	2 651	2 995	3 137	-145	1 329
Q4	-6 571	-7 070	2 102	2 682	8 416	9 752	15 823	17 055
2003 Q1	6 048	5 201	7 024	6 960	990	1 759	-1 305	-208
Q2	-11 115	-11 631	3 135	2 415	13 830	14 046	16 404	16 266
Q3	-3 392	-3 778	4 033	3 494	7 070	7 272	6 036	5 903
Q4	-9 499	-9 657	4 243	3 738	13 188	13 395	17 079	16 560
2004 Q1	7 395	6 980	6 594	5 813	-1 046	-1 167	486	1 003
Q2	-10 936	-11 646	3 800	3 264	14 658	14 910	11 577	11 690
Q3	-5 068	-5 615	4 279	3 623	9 019	9 238	6 968	7 370
Q4	-9 630	-9 846	4 902	4 707	14 184	14 553	22 290	22 261
2005 Q1	7 756	8 266	8 257	8 677	-249	411	-2 098	-2 750
Q2	-10 488	-11 451	2 269	2 236	10 024	13 687	15 944	16 254
Q3	-3 888	-3 723	4 716	4 704	9 180	8 427	8 463	8 181
Q4	-12 375	-12 253	5 357	6 220	19 120	18 473	19 561	19 266
2006 Q1	9 269	12 127	6 351	9 537	-2 211	-2 590	-3 893	-3 679†
Q2	-11 385	-11 877	3 617	4 638	16 788	16 515	19 337	18 972
Q3	-2 607	-1 372	4 548	4 766	6 445	6 138	5 592	5 453
Q4	-9 112	-8 095	4 864	4 991	13 688	13 086	15 657	12 309
2007 Q1	..	12 586	..	10 481	-2 313	-2 105	-3 707	-1 597

1 National accounts entities as defined under the European System of Accounts 1995 (ESA95).
2 Net saving, plus capital taxes.
3 Gross capital formation, plus payments less receipts, of investment grants less depreciation.
4 Net borrowing = net investment minus surplus on current budget
5 Previously called Public Sector Borrowing Requirement (PSBR).

Source: Office for National Statistics: 020 7533 5984

17.4 Selected financial statistics[1]

£ million

	Building societies		Unit trusts[3]	Net equity of households in life assurance and pension funds' reserves
	Advances			
	Not seasonally adjusted	Seasonally adjusted		

Amount outstanding as at 31 Dec

	AHIF		AGXB	
2006	242 498		410 124	

Transactions

	AAMN	AHHU	AGXE	NBYD
2003	23 816	23 711[†]	9 753	34 654
2004	22 078	21 822	5 718	40 582
2005	20 419	20 389	12 030	55 994
2006	27 057	27 070	20 678	61 544
2006 Q1	5 021	6 234[†]	7 562	16 933
Q2	7 205	7 166	4 191	14 859
Q3	7 514	5 831	4 721	13 962
Q4	7 317	7 839	4 204	15 790
2006 Mar	2 120	2 147[†]	3 436	..
Apr	1 212	1 794	2 339	..
May	1 781	1 904	298	..
Jun	4 212	3 468	1 554	..
Jul	1 495	925	454	..
Aug	3 383	2 453	1 653	..
Sep	2 636	2 453	2 614	..
Oct	4 627	5 323	1 665	..
Nov	3 152	2 706	632	..
Dec	−462	−190	1 907	..
2007 Jan	2 966	3 488	681[†]	..
Feb	1 441	2 205	973	..

	Banks[4]				Consumer credit[5]		of which Credit cards[5]	
	UK private sector deposits		Lending to the private sector					
	Sterling (Not seasonally adjusted)	Other currencies	Sterling (Not seasonally adjusted)	Other currencies	Not seasonally adjusted	Seasonally adjusted	Not seasonally adjusted	Seasonally adjusted

Amount outstanding as at 31 Dec

	AEAS	AGAK	AECE	AECK	VZRD	VZRI	VZRE	VZRJ
2006	1 285 627[†]	299 474[†]	1 622 353[†]	396 343[†]	212 859[†]	212 714[†]	55 797	54 756[†]

Transactions

					Net lending	Net lending	Net lending	Net lending
	AEAT	AEAZ	AECF		VZQC	RLMH	VZQS	VZQX
2003	60 629	40 328	103 591		22 401	22 703[†]	8 710	8 857[†]
2004	86 098	27 697	133 774		25 337	25 439	9 998	9 957
2005	137 238[†]	39 719[†]	137 554[†]		19 666	19 756	6 166	6 144
2006	151 933[†]	58 369[†]	191 037[†]		13 017[†]	13 137	1 951	1 997
2006 Q2	51 017[†]	−11 136	75 602		4 065[†]	3 167[†]	1 205	524[†]
Q3	36 470	23 456[†]	42 351[†]		3 019	3 029	240	172
Q4	32 364	12 158	24 875		3 396	3 318	1 359	343
2007 Q1	..	..	..		1 651	2 652	−1 416	298
2006 Apr	12 216[†]	6 388	25 278		1 561	1 022[†]	725	238[†]
May	6 582	−2 407	15 039		1 496[†]	1 176	294	194
Jun	32 219	−15 117	35 285		1 008	969	186	92
Jul	−2 848	15 874[†]	16 445[†]		1 228	1 151	125	152
Aug	6 955	7 180	11 644		401	702	−111	−266
Sep	32 363	402	14 262		1 390	1 176	225	286
Oct	7 083	6 808	2 349		1 270	1 166	−158	113
Nov	8 087	7 939	15 277		913	1 117	343	92
Dec	17 194	−2 589	7 249		1 212	1 035	1 175	137
2007 Jan	−8 989	16 590	31 771		1 241	727	−770[†]	−50
Feb	13 957	5 404	13 389		145	1 041	−296[†]	124
Mar	..	..	..		265	885	−350	223

1 For further details see *Financial Statistics*, Tables 1.2E, 3.2B, 4.2A, 4.3A, 4.3B, 5.2D, 6.2A, 10.5D.
2 Total administered by the Department for National Savings.
3 Including open ended investment companies (OEICs).
4 Monthly figures relate to calendar months.
5 Data have been revised back to February 2003 due to the inclusion of some additional other specialist lenders and the removal of some non-resident based securitisation vehicles.

Sources: Office for National Statistics;
Department for National Savings;
Building Societies Commission;
Association of Unit Trusts and Investment Funds;
Bank of England;
Department of Trade and Industry

17.5 Monetary aggregates

£ million

| | Amount outstanding | | | | | |
| | Notes and coin in circulation outside the Bank of England | | Retail deposits and cash in M4 | | M4 | |
	Not seasonally adjusted	Seasonally adjusted	Not seasonally adjusted	Seasonally adjusted	Not seasonally adjusted	Seasonally adjusted
	AVAA	AVAB	VQXV	VQWU	AUYM	AUYN
2003	38 807	38 832	777 347	777 066	1 081 299	1 081 618†
2004	41 147	41 177	845 654	845 860	1 179 192	1 179 198
2005	43 034	42 991	922 687	923 495	1 328 318	1 328 444
2006	45 214	45 200	995 063	996 154	1 496 356†	1 496 556
2004 Q3	41 376	41 429	827 059	828 366	1 148 480	1 152 556†
Q4	42 719	42 061†	845 654	845 860	1 179 192	1 179 198
2005 Q1	42 202	42 501	862 159	862 574	1 216 923	1 218 145
Q2	42 346	42 721	885 405	883 184	1 250 541	1 245 051
Q3	43 230	43 265	903 201	904 739	1 277 129	1 281 428
Q4	44 359	43 477	922 687	923 495	1 328 318	1 328 444
2006 Q1	43 943	44 426	945 295	944 985	1 365 316†	1 366 391
Q2	44 877	45 062	962 876	960 431	1 419 744	1 413 985
Q3	45 474	45 497	973 931	976 004	1 459 181	1 463 840
Q4	46 563	45 814	995 063	996 154	1 496 356	1 496 556
2006 Feb	43 554	44 438†	924 466	934 924†	1 335 174†	1 346 617†
Mar	43 894	44 715	945 295	941 874	1 365 316	1 359 254
Apr	45 004	44 912	954 294	948 932	1 378 999	1 376 131
May	44 822	45 006	953 226	952 528	1 385 927	1 384 839
Jun	44 804	45 269	962 876	957 165	1 419 744	1 405 398
Jul	45 307	45 431	961 231	961 709	1 417 776	1 419 114
Aug	45 695	45 490	965 932	966 528	1 426 236	1 432 864
Sep	45 421	45 570	973 931	971 924	1 459 181	1 456 582
Oct	45 517	45 810	976 476	978 099	1 467 725	1 468 927
Nov	45 997	45 912	987 309	985 085	1 477 701	1 476 294
Dec	48 175	45 719	995 063	991 062	1 496 356	1 490 115
2007 Jan	46 150	46 063	984 209	995 696	1 488 723	1 503 404
Feb	45 356	46 260	990 567	1 002 687	1 503 281	1 516 428

Source: Bank of England

17.6 Selected interest rates, exchange rates and security prices[1]

	Selected retail banks' base rate	Average discount rate for 91 day Treasury bills	Inter bank 3 months bid rate	Inter bank 3 months offer rate	British government securities 20 years yield[2]	Exchange rate US spot
	ZCMG	AJNB	HSAJ	HSAK	AJLX	LUSS
2005 Sep	4.50	4.40	4.52	4.55	4.26	1.7688
Oct	4.50	4.42	4.54	4.56	4.36	1.7700
Nov	4.50	4.40	4.55	4.58	4.25	1.7304
Dec	4.50	4.43	4.57	4.59	4.14	1.7166
2006 Jan	4.50	4.40	4.52	4.54	3.81	1.7775
Feb	4.50	4.39	4.51	4.53	3.96	1.7511
Mar	4.50	4.41	4.54	4.56	4.15	1.7345
Apr	4.50	4.45	4.60	4.63	4.32	1.8179
May	4.50	4.51	4.66	4.68	4.43	1.8712
Jun	4.50	4.54	4.71	4.73	4.46	1.8494
Jul	4.50	4.58	4.73	4.74	4.45	1.8671
Aug	4.75	4.77	4.94	4.95	4.42	1.9018
Sep	4.75	4.87	5.02	5.05	4.29	1.8682
Oct	4.75	4.98	5.14	5.16	4.35	1.9073
Nov	5.00	5.04	5.20	5.22	4.27	1.9670
Dec	5.00	5.11	5.26	5.29	4.33	1.9570
2007 Jan	5.25	5.37	5.54	5.55	4.51	1.9574
Feb	5.25	5.31	5.48	5.50	4.59	1.9600
Mar	5.25	5.38	5.56	5.58	4.52	1.9613
Apr	5.25	..	..	..	..	..

1 As from December 2003 *The Financial Times* Actuaries indices have been removed as The Bank of England are no longer able to provide these data
2 Average of working days.

Source: Bank of England

18 Prices and wages

18.1 Consumer Prices Index[1]: Detailed figures by division[2]

Index level (2005=100)

COICOP Division	Food and non-alcoholic beverages 01	Alcoholic beverages and tobacco 02	Clothing and footwear 03	Housing, water, electricity, gas & other fuels 04	Furniture, household equipment & routine maintenance 05	Health[3] 06	Transport 07	Communication 08	Recreation and culture 09	Education[3] 10	Restaurants and hotels 11	Miscellaneous goods and services[3] 12	CPI (overall index)
	CHZR	CHZS	CHZT	CHZU	CHZV	CHZW	CHZX	CHZY	CHZZ	CJUU	CJUV	CJUW	CHZQ
Weights 2007	103	43	62	115	68	24	152	24	153	18	138	100	1 000
	D7BU	D7BV	D7BW	D7BX	D7BY	D7BZ	D7C2	D7C3	D7C4	D7C5	D7C6	D7C7	D7BT
2005 Mar	100.8	98.7	101.3	97.7	100.7	98.9	98.0	100.4	100.2	98.7	98.7	98.8	99.3
Apr	99.9	99.8	100.9	99.6	99.3	99.5	98.5	100.5	100.7	98.7	99.5	99.3	99.7
May	100.6	100.2	101.0	99.8	100.1	99.7	99.5	100.1	100.4	98.7	99.8	99.4	100.0
Jun	100.6	100.3	100.6	100.0	100.4	99.8	99.6	100.3	100.3	98.7	99.9	99.6	100.0
Jul	99.4	100.6	96.5	100.4	99.4	100.6	102.1	99.5	99.8	98.7	100.3	100.4	100.1
Aug	99.6	100.5	98.2	100.4	99.6	100.8	103.3	99.9	99.3	98.7	100.6	100.6	100.4
Sep	99.7	100.3	99.9	100.7	100.2	100.7	102.2	99.8	99.6	100.8	100.8	100.8	100.6
Oct	99.5	100.7	99.9	101.7	99.4	101.0	102.0	99.5	99.7	103.3	101.2	101.2	100.7
Nov	100.1	100.7	100.5	102.3	100.5	101.0	100.4	99.6	99.5	103.3	101.2	101.4	100.7
Dec	100.7	100.2	100.1	102.8	102.8	100.3	100.7	99.4	99.5	103.3	101.4	101.5	101.0
2006 Jan	100.4	101.0	96.0	103.3	97.8	101.0	101.2	100.9	98.6	103.3	101.5	102.0	100.5
Feb	101.0	100.8	95.9	103.6	98.5	101.1	101.4	101.0	99.4	103.3	101.9	102.1	100.9
Mar	100.4	101.1	96.5	104.5	100.3	101.0	101.4	100.9	98.9	103.3	102.2	102.4	101.1
Apr	100.2	102.3	96.5	107.3	98.5	102.2	102.9	100.9	99.1	103.3	102.5	103.3	101.7
May	101.7	102.5	97.2	108.8	99.3	102.6	103.5	99.7	98.9	103.3	103.0	103.4	102.2
Jun	102.4	103.6	96.7	109.7	100.2	102.5	103.5	100.0	98.7	103.3	103.1	103.9	102.5
Jul	102.6	103.4	92.2	110.5	98.1	103.0	105.5	99.8	98.4	103.3	103.5	104.0	102.5
Aug	103.0	103.8	94.4	110.9	99.1	103.4	105.8	99.2	98.4	103.3	103.6	104.5	102.9
Sep	103.6	103.7	96.4	111.5	100.6	103.6	102.9	99.6	98.6	107.9	103.8	104.7	103.0
Oct	104.2	103.9	96.6	112.7	99.0	104.2	101.5	100.4	98.6	117.8	104.2	105.0	103.2
Nov	105.1	103.4	97.2	113.7	100.0	104.1	101.1	100.3	98.7	117.8	104.5	105.0	103.4
Dec	105.4	103.0	96.0	114.5	103.3	104.2	102.8	99.9	99.2	117.8	104.7	104.9	104.0
2007 Jan	104.4	104.5	92.0	114.9	98.3	104.8	102.1	99.0	98.3	117.8	104.9	105.1	103.2
Feb	105.4	105.1	91.9	115.1	99.6	104.9	102.8	98.1	98.4	117.8	105.2	105.8	103.7
Mar	106.0	105.6	92.8	115.0	102.9	104.8	103.1	98.1	98.2	117.8	105.7	106.2	104.2

Percentage change on a year earlier

	D7G8	D7G9	D7GA	D7GB	D7GC	D7GD	D7GE	D7GF	D7GG	D7GH	D7GI	D7GJ	D7G7
2005 Mar	1.7	2.2	−5.1	5.8	−	2.6	4.0	−2.9	−0.7	5.0	2.8	3.6	1.9
Apr	1.0	2.0	−5.3	6.5	−1.0	2.7	3.8	−3.2	−0.6	5.0	3.3	4.3	1.9
May	1.4	2.3	−5.5	6.4	−1.0	2.8	3.3	−3.6	−0.5	5.0	3.3	4.3	1.9
Jun	2.2	2.3	−4.8	6.4	−0.6	2.7	3.4	−2.9	−1.2	5.0	3.2	4.6	2.0
Jul	1.7	2.2	−4.8	6.7	0.6	3.4	4.6	−2.5	−1.5	5.0	3.4	5.2	2.3
Aug	2.2	1.8	−4.4	6.3	0.2	3.7	5.4	−2.1	−2.0	5.0	3.5	5.1	2.4
Sep	2.0	1.4	−5.3	6.5	−0.2	3.1	6.0	−1.2	−1.6	4.7	3.7	5.1	2.5
Oct	1.5	1.9	−5.3	6.5	−0.2	3.0	5.8	−1.6	−1.5	4.7	3.7	4.2	2.3
Nov	1.7	2.5	−5.1	6.5	0.1	2.9	4.1	−1.2	−1.5	4.7	3.5	4.3	2.1
Dec	1.7	2.5	−4.2	6.4	−	2.4	2.8	−1.0	−1.7	4.7	3.5	4.2	1.9
2006 Jan	1.2	2.3	−4.7	6.3	−0.8	2.3	5.1	0.5	−2.1	4.7	3.4	3.5	1.9
Feb	1.1	1.6	−4.7	6.4	−0.5	2.3	4.2	0.4	−0.8	4.7	3.5	3.6	2.0
Mar	−0.4	2.5	−4.7	7.0	−0.4	2.1	3.5	0.5	−1.4	4.7	3.6	3.7	1.8
Apr	0.3	2.5	−4.4	7.7	−0.8	2.7	4.4	0.3	−1.6	4.7	3.0	4.0	2.0
May	1.1	2.2	−3.7	9.0	−0.8	2.9	4.0	−0.4	−1.6	4.7	3.2	4.1	2.2
Jun	1.8	3.3	−3.9	9.8	−0.1	2.7	3.9	−0.3	−1.6	4.7	3.2	4.4	2.5
Jul	3.2	2.8	−4.5	10.0	−1.3	2.4	3.3	0.3	−1.4	4.7	3.2	3.6	2.4
Aug	3.4	3.3	−3.9	10.5	−0.5	2.6	2.4	−0.7	−0.9	4.7	3.0	3.9	2.5
Sep	4.0	3.4	−3.5	10.7	0.3	2.8	0.6	−0.2	−1.0	7.1	2.9	3.9	2.4
Oct	4.7	3.2	−3.3	10.8	−0.4	3.1	−0.5	0.9	−1.1	14.0	3.0	3.8	2.4
Nov	5.0	2.7	−3.2	11.1	−0.5	3.1	0.8	0.7	−0.7	14.0	3.2	3.5	2.7
Dec	4.6	2.7	−4.1	11.4	0.6	3.9	2.1	0.5	−0.3	14.0	3.2	3.3	3.0
2007 Jan	3.9	3.5	−4.1	11.2	0.5	3.8	0.9	−1.8	−0.3	14.0	3.3	3.1	2.7
Feb	4.4	4.2	−4.2	11.1	1.2	3.7	1.4	−2.8	−1.0	14.0	3.3	3.6	2.8
Mar	5.6	4.4	−3.9	10.1	2.7	3.7	1.6	−2.8	−0.7	14.0	3.4	3.7	3.1

Note: Further information on the consumer prices index is available from the National Statistics website: www.statistics.gov.uk/cpi

1 Prior to 10 December 2003, the consumer prices index (CPI) was published in the UK as the harmonised index of consumer prices (HICP).
2 Inflation rates prior to 1997 and index levels prior to 1996 are estimated. Further details are given in *Economic Trends No. 541 December 1998.* These details are also available on the National Statistics website: http://www.statistics.gov.uk/cci/article.asp?ID=31&Pos=3&Col-Rank=2&Rank=720

3 The coverage of these categories was extended in January 2000; further extensions to coverage came into effect in January 2001 for health and miscellaneous goods and services; the coverage of miscellaneous goods and services was further extended with effect from January 2002 (details are given in a series of Economic Trends articles available on the National Statistics website:www.statistics.gov.uk/cpi)

Source: Office for National Statistics: 020 7533 5874

18.2 Consumer Prices Index[1]: Detailed figures by divisions, groups and classes

	Weights	Index (2005=100)						Percentage change over 12 months					
	2007	2006 Oct	2006 Nov	2006 Dec	2007 Jan	2007 Feb	2007 Mar	2006 Oct	2006 Nov	2006 Dec	2007 Jan	2007 Feb	2007 Mar
CPI (overall index)	*1 000*	103.2	103.4	104.0	103.2	103.7	104.2	*2.4*	*2.7*	*3.0*	*2.7*	*2.8*	*3.1*
01 Food and non-alcoholic beverages	*103*	104.2	105.1	105.4	104.4	105.4	106.0	*4.7*	*5.0*	*4.6*	*3.9*	*4.4*	*5.6*
02 Alcoholic beverages and tobacco	*43*	103.9	103.4	103.0	104.5	105.1	105.6	*3.2*	*2.7*	*2.7*	*3.5*	*4.2*	*4.4*
03 Clothing and footwear	*62*	96.6	97.2	96.0	92.0	91.9	92.8	*−3.3*	*−3.2*	*−4.1*	*−4.1*	*−4.2*	*−3.9*
04 Housing, water, electricity, gas and other fuels	*115*	112.7	113.7	114.5	114.9	115.1	115.0	*10.8*	*11.1*	*11.4*	*11.2*	*11.1*	*10.1*
05 Furniture, household equipment and maintenance	*68*	99.0	100.0	103.3	98.3	99.6	102.9	*−0.4*	*−0.5*	*0.6*	*0.5*	*1.2*	*2.7*
06 Health	*24*	104.2	104.1	104.2	104.8	104.9	104.8	*3.1*	*3.1*	*3.9*	*3.8*	*3.7*	*3.7*
07 Transport	*152*	101.5	101.1	102.8	102.1	102.8	103.1	*−0.5*	*0.8*	*2.1*	*0.9*	*1.4*	*1.6*
08 Communication	*24*	100.4	100.3	99.9	99.0	98.1	98.1	*0.9*	*0.7*	*0.5*	*−1.8*	*−2.8*	*−2.8*
09 Recreation and culture	*153*	98.6	98.7	99.2	98.3	98.4	98.2	*−1.1*	*−0.7*	*−0.3*	*−0.3*	*−1.0*	*−0.7*
10 Education	*18*	117.8	117.8	117.8	117.8	117.8	117.8	*14.0*	*14.0*	*14.0*	*14.0*	*14.0*	*14.0*
11 Restaurants and hotels	*138*	104.2	104.5	104.7	104.9	105.2	105.7	*3.0*	*3.2*	*3.2*	*3.3*	*3.3*	*3.4*
12 Miscellaneous goods and services	*100*	105.0	105.0	104.9	105.1	105.8	106.2	*3.8*	*3.5*	*3.3*	*3.1*	*3.6*	*3.7*
All goods	*547*	101.8	102.3	103.0	101.5	102.0	102.8	*1.5*	*1.8*	*2.3*	*2.0*	*2.0*	*2.5*
All services	*453*	104.8	104.8	105.4	105.3	105.7	105.8	*3.6*	*3.7*	*3.8*	*3.6*	*3.8*	*3.7*
01.1 Food	*90*	103.9	105.0	105.2	104.3	105.2	105.8	*4.5*	*4.9*	*4.5*	*4.0*	*4.3*	*5.5*
01.1.1 Bread and cereals	*15*	102.5	103.3	104.0	103.2	103.9	105.5	*2.4*	*2.7*	*2.9*	*2.3*	*2.6*	*4.4*
01.1.2 Meat	*21*	103.5	103.7	104.3	103.5	104.2	104.5	*4.0*	*2.6*	*3.6*	*3.1*	*3.5*	*5.0*
01.1.3 Fish	*4*	113.7	113.0	114.9	113.8	116.5	116.0	*12.2*	*11.4*	*12.2*	*10.9*	*12.8*	*12.6*
01.1.4 Milk, cheese and eggs	*12*	102.8	103.0	103.3	102.7	102.2	104.6	*1.5*	*1.6*	*1.8*	*1.2*	*0.0*	*5.3*
01.1.5 Oils and fats	*2*	107.6	108.4	108.3	108.4	107.7	108.0	*8.9*	*10.4*	*9.9*	*11.2*	*9.9*	*6.6*
01.1.6 Fruit	*9*	104.3	108.0	107.2	100.4	101.1	99.0	*4.5*	*5.5*	*4.9*	*2.8*	*3.6*	*1.9*
01.1.7 Vegetables including potatoes and tubers	*14*	103.1	107.1	106.4	107.3	110.1	110.8	*9.3*	*13.3*	*8.1*	*8.6*	*9.6*	*10.2*
01.1.8 Sugar, jam, syrups, chocolate and confectionery	*11*	104.5	104.5	104.5	105.0	105.6	105.8	*3.4*	*3.3*	*3.4*	*3.4*	*3.6*	*3.6*
01.1.9 Food products nec[2]	*2*	100.6	99.6	100.0	99.3	100.3	100.9	*1.3*	*0.4*	*1.2*	*0.2*	*1.4*	*1.9*
01.2 Non-alcoholic beverages	*13*	106.3	105.7	106.2	104.9	107.0	107.4	*6.4*	*5.8*	*5.2*	*3.7*	*4.9*	*6.0*
01.2.1 Coffee, tea and cocoa	*3*	110.1	108.4	110.1	106.5	108.8	109.6	*9.6*	*6.9*	*8.7*	*5.7*	*6.8*	*10.2*
01.2.2 Mineral waters, soft drinks and juices	*10*	105.0	104.8	105.0	104.3	106.3	106.5	*5.3*	*5.4*	*4.1*	*3.0*	*4.1*	*4.5*
02.1 Alcoholic beverages	*18*	101.3	100.1	99.0	100.3	100.9	101.9	*1.1*	*0.7*	*0.8*	*0.3*	*1.3*	*1.7*
02.1.1 Spirits	*5*	101.1	98.4	96.9	98.8	100.0	101.7	*0.7*	*0.1*	*0.3*	*−1.2*	*−0.2*	*1.1*
02.1.2 Wine	*9*	101.8	101.3	99.8	101.5	102.0	102.7	*1.3*	*1.1*	*0.7*	*1.1*	*2.2*	*2.2*
02.1.3 Beer	*4*	100.3	99.2	99.6	99.0	99.3	99.9	*0.7*	*0.3*	*1.5*	*0.1*	*1.3*	*1.2*
02.2 Tobacco	*25*	105.8	105.8	105.9	107.7	108.1	108.2	*4.7*	*4.0*	*4.1*	*5.7*	*6.2*	*6.2*
03.1 Clothing	*54*	96.6	97.3	96.2	91.8	91.6	92.6	*−3.3*	*−3.2*	*−4.2*	*−4.4*	*−4.4*	*−4.1*
03.1.2 Garments	*50*	96.2	96.9	95.7	91.1	90.9	91.9	*−3.7*	*−3.6*	*−4.7*	*−4.8*	*−4.9*	*−4.6*
03.1.3 Other clothing and clothing accessories	*3*	101.4	102.4	102.3	99.8	98.8	99.8	*1.2*	*1.3*	*1.1*	*0.4*	*0.6*	*0.9*
03.1.4 Cleaning, repair and hire of clothing	*1*	105.7	105.8	106.1	106.4	106.6	106.7	*4.6*	*4.3*	*4.3*	*4.3*	*4.1*	*4.0*
03.2 Footwear including repairs	*8*	96.5	96.6	94.7	93.1	93.8	94.1	*−3.1*	*−3.0*	*−3.4*	*−2.6*	*−2.2*	*−2.0*
04.1 Actual rentals for housing	*49*	104.0	104.2	104.3	104.7	104.6	104.6	*3.0*	*3.2*	*3.2*	*3.4*	*3.2*	*3.1*
04.3 Regular maintenance and repair of the dwelling	*17*	102.4	102.7	103.5	104.4	104.9	104.9	*2.3*	*2.8*	*3.3*	*3.4*	*4.1*	*3.9*
04.3.1 Materials for maintenance and repair	*10*	100.2	100.6	101.7	102.0	102.9	102.7	*1.1*	*1.9*	*2.6*	*2.5*	*3.7*	*3.3*
04.3.2 Services for maintenance and repair	*7*	105.6	105.8	106.1	107.8	..	..	*4.1*	*4.0*	*4.1*	*4.6*	*4.6*	*4.7*
04.4 Water supply and misc. services for the dwelling	*10*	108.2	108.2	108.2	108.2	108.2	108.2	*5.5*	*5.5*	*5.5*	*5.5*	*5.5*	*5.5*
04.4.1 Water supply	*5*	109.0	109.0	109.0	109.0	109.0	109.0	*5.7*	*5.7*	*5.7*	*5.7*	*5.7*	*5.7*
04.4.3 Sewerage collection	*5*	107.5	107.5	107.5	107.5	107.5	107.5	*5.2*	*5.2*	*5.2*	*5.2*	*5.2*	*5.2*
04.5 Electricity, gas and other fuels	*39*	134.6	137.6	139.9	140.1	140.7	140.3	*29.9*	*30.0*	*30.2*	*29.2*	*28.6*	*24.9*
04.5.1 Electricity	*19*	130.5	133.0	134.6	135.2	135.7	135.7	*27.3*	*27.0*	*27.3*	*26.7*	*25.7*	*22.5*
04.5.2 Gas	*18*	145.4	150.1	152.9	153.3	153.8	152.6	*40.6*	*39.9*	*39.8*	*39.0*	*38.8*	*33.5*
04.5.3 Liquid fuels	*1*	104.5	99.8	104.5	97.2	99.5	102.9	*−12.0*	*−5.7*	*−4.7*	*−13.1*	*−12.7*	*−10.6*
04.5.4 Solid fuels	*1*	112.4	113.7	113.7	113.9	114.2	114.3	*8.0*	*8.3*	*8.0*	*8.0*	*8.2*	*8.3*
05.1 Furniture, furnishings and carpets	*28*	99.3	100.7	108.3	97.7	99.3	106.6	*0.2*	*−0.3*	*1.9*	*0.0*	*1.2*	*3.9*
05.1.1 Furniture and furnishings	*22*	98.9	101.0	109.8	97.7	99.0	108.5	*0.3*	*0.1*	*2.3*	*0.4*	*1.5*	*5.1*
05.1.2 Carpets and other floor coverings	*6*	101.0	99.9	102.9	97.5	100.4	99.4	*0.3*	*−1.5*	*−0.1*	*−1.7*	*−0.2*	*−0.6*
05.2 Household textiles	*8*	93.8	95.8	95.8	91.5	93.8	93.1	*−4.1*	*−4.0*	*−4.2*	*−2.5*	*−2.8*	*−3.6*
05.3 Household appliances, fitting and repairs	*8*	95.1	95.0	95.0	93.5	94.4	96.4	*−4.9*	*−4.8*	*−4.7*	*−4.1*	*−2.7*	*2.3*
05.3.1/2 Major appliances and small electric goods	*7*	94.3	94.2	94.2	92.3	93.4	95.7	*−5.5*	*−5.5*	*−5.4*	*−4.8*	*−3.2*	*2.5*
05.3.3 Repair of household appliances	*1*	101.4	101.6	101.8	102.4	102.6	102.6	*0.7*	*1.1*	*1.2*	*1.0*	*1.2*	*1.2*
05.4 Glassware, tableware and household utensils	*7*	98.8	99.7	99.9	97.3	98.7	99.1	*−0.9*	*−1.0*	*−1.0*	*0.2*	*1.1*	*0.9*
05.5 Tools and equipment for house and garden	*6*	101.9	101.7	101.9	102.0	102.4	102.0	*2.6*	*2.5*	*2.3*	*1.7*	*1.7*	*1.0*
05.6 Goods and services for routine maintenance	*11*	105.2	105.3	105.6	106.5	106.8	107.5	*4.1*	*4.5*	*3.7*	*4.7*	*4.0*	*4.2*
05.6.1 Non-durable household goods	*5*	104.0	104.5	104.6	104.6	105.1	106.2	*3.0*	*4.4*	*2.9*	*3.8*	*2.7*	*3.3*
05.6.2 Domestic services and household services	*6*	106.2	105.9	106.4	108.2	108.2	108.6	*5.0*	*4.4*	*4.3*	*5.4*	*5.0*	*5.0*
06.1 Medical products, appliances and equipment	*10*	100.0	99.7	99.9	100.2	100.3	100.0	*−0.4*	*−0.4*	*1.2*	*1.0*	*0.9*	*0.9*
06.1.1 Pharmaceutical products	*5*	101.1	100.7	101.3	101.5	101.5	100.8	*0.6*	*0.8*	*3.2*	*2.0*	*1.6*	*1.5*
06.1.2/3 Other medical and therapeutic equipment	*5*	99.2	98.9	98.7	99.3	99.5	99.6	*−1.0*	*−1.4*	*−0.5*	*0.3*	*0.4*	*0.6*

18.2

continued

Consumer Prices Index[1]: Detailed figures by divisions, groups and classes

	Weights	Index (2005=100)						Percentage change over 12 months					
	2007	2006 Oct	2006 Nov	2006 Dec	2007 Jan	2007 Feb	2007 Mar	2006 Oct	2006 Nov	2006 Dec	2007 Jan	2007 Feb	2007 Mar
06.2 Out-patient services	5	105.7	106.0	106.1	106.9	107.0	107.0	4.5	4.6	4.3	4.3	4.1	4.0
06.2.1/3 Medical services and paramedical services	3	104.2	104.4	104.2	104.7	104.8	104.8	3.4	3.3	2.6	2.2	1.6	1.5
06.2.2 Dental services	2	107.2	107.6	107.9	109.2	109.3	109.4	5.6	5.9	5.9	6.5	6.7	6.6
06.3 Hospital services	9	109.0	109.1	109.2	110.0	110.0	110.1	6.9	6.9	7.0	7.0	6.9	7.0
07.1 Purchase of vehicles	49	99.4	99.4	99.4	99.7	100.1	99.9	−0.2	0.1	0.2	0.1	0.5	0.3
07.1.1A New cars	27	101.2	101.5	101.5	101.5	101.9	102.0	0.7	1.4	1.3	1.3	1.4	1.5
07.1.1B Second hand cars	19	96.1	95.8	95.4	96.4	96.7	96.0	−1.9	−2.1	−1.8	−2.2	−1.5	−2.1
07.1.2/3 Motorcycles and bicycles	3	99.3	98.9	99.7	98.7	100.2	99.8	−0.1	−0.5	0.4	0.1	1.4	1.3
07.2 Operation of personal transport equipment	72	103.2	103.3	104.6	104.4	103.9	105.5	−1.1	0.3	2.9	1.1	0.4	1.8
07.2.1 Spare parts and accessories	6	103.2	103.4	103.3	103.3	102.5	102.1	2.5	2.3	2.2	1.8	0.7	0.0
07.2.2 Fuels and lubricants	36	99.8	99.3	101.6	100.5	99.7	102.2	−7.6	−4.6	0.8	−2.0	−3.4	−0.9
07.2.3 Maintenance and repairs	24	107.7	108.6	109.0	109.5	109.7	110.1	6.1	6.2	6.2	5.0	5.1	5.3
07.2.4 Other services	6	104.7	105.0	105.3	107.4	107.2	109.5	2.1	2.2	2.1	3.7	3.6	5.6
07.3 Transport services	31	101.1	99.1	104.6	101.1	104.6	102.9	0.3	2.4	3.2	1.6	5.1	3.3
07.3.1 Passenger transport by railway	8	103.6	104.6	104.1	108.0	109.2	108.8	3.2	3.8	3.6	5.0	5.4	5.1
07.3.2 Passenger transport by road	14	103.0	103.6	103.9	105.8	106.1	106.4	1.3	2.0	1.8	1.5	1.9	1.8
07.3.3 Passenger transport by air	7	90.5	83.3	103.6	81.5	89.1	84.9	−10.0	−5.2	0.5	−6.3	4.4	1.4
07.3.4 Passenger transport by sea and inland waterway	2	107.8	98.5	103.6	98.4	112.8	104.9	10.6	6.7	13.2	7.2	16.6	3.9
08.1 Postal services	1	114.3	114.3	114.3	114.3	114.3	114.3	13.1	13.1	13.1	13.1	13.1	13.1
08.2/3 Telephone and telefax equipment and services	23	99.8	99.7	99.3	98.3	97.4	97.3	0.4	0.2	0.0	−2.5	−3.4	−3.4
09.1 Audio-visual equipment and related products	29	86.7	87.2	88.0	86.2	84.7	83.3	−10.0	−7.8	−7.5	−9.1	−9.2	−8.8
09.1.1 Reception and reproduction of sound and pictures	6	84.1	84.6	84.3	83.1	82.0	80.0	−9.8	−8.8	−8.9	−9.0	−10.6	−11.3
09.1.2 Photographic, cinematographic and optical equipment	4	74.6	73.2	71.7	66.2	64.7	66.0	−19.5	−14.5	−17.0	−21.4	−22.2	−15.0
09.1.3 Data processing equipment	7	81.9	82.6	83.1	82.2	80.6	76.8	−14.5	−13.0	−13.0	−11.6	−14.0	−14.8
09.1.4 Recording media	11	94.6	96.3	99.4	98.1	96.3	95.7	−4.7	−2.2	−0.1	−3.6	−1.0	−2.4
09.1.5 Repair of audio-visual equipment & related products	1	104.9	104.8	105.0	106.3	106.3	106.5	3.1	3.0	3.2	4.3	4.2	4.5
09.2 Other major durables for recreation and culture	9	101.0	100.9	100.9	100.5	100.4	100.4	0.8	0.5	0.5	1.8	1.6	1.6
09.2.1/2 Major durables for in/outdoor recreation	9	101.0	100.9	100.9	100.5	100.4	100.4	0.8	0.5	0.5	1.8	1.6	1.6
09.3 Other recreational items, gardens and pets	37	97.2	97.0	97.5	97.5	97.4	97.8	−2.9	−2.9	−1.9	−0.1	−3.0	−2.1
09.3.1 Games, toys and hobbies	21	94.5	93.9	94.5	94.9	93.8	94.6	−5.8	−6.1	−4.1	−1.0	−6.4	−4.7
09.3.2 Equipment for sport and open-air recreation	4	98.5	98.2	98.0	97.9	97.1	97.6	−1.1	0.3	−0.8	1.5	0.3	0.1
09.3.3 Gardens, plants and flowers	5	98.3	99.8	100.5	100.3	102.5	102.0	−0.8	0.3	0.3	−0.3	1.0	1.6
09.3.4/5 Pets, related products and services	7	104.4	104.4	104.6	103.6	105.4	105.3	3.5	3.3	3.3	2.0	3.5	3.2
09.4 Recreational and cultural services	32	106.6	106.5	107.0	105.8	106.3	106.8	5.1	4.5	4.4	4.2	4.7	5.1
09.4.1 Recreational and sporting services	10	107.2	107.3	107.3	107.3	107.4	107.5	4.8	4.6	4.5	4.4	4.5	4.4
09.4.2 Cultural services	22	106.4	106.2	106.9	105.2	105.8	106.5	5.2	4.5	4.4	4.1	4.7	5.3
09.5 Books, newspapers and stationery	17	104.1	104.7	105.5	102.3	105.3	104.8	3.6	3.6	4.7	2.0	2.4	2.3
09.5.1 Books	5	102.6	103.8	105.8	96.5	105.6	104.4	1.8	3.4	7.2	0.1	1.4	1.6
09.5.2 Newspapers and periodicals	7	108.1	108.6	108.8	108.5	108.8	109.1	7.3	5.8	5.5	4.5	4.9	4.7
09.5.3/4 Misc. printed matter, stationery, drawing materials	5	100.1	100.2	100.6	99.6	99.5	98.9	0.2	0.6	0.9	−0.2	−0.4	−0.8
09.6 Package holidays	29	99.3	99.7	99.7	100.1	100.1	100.0	0.0	0.7	0.8	1.5	1.3	1.3
10.0 Education	18	117.8	117.8	117.8	117.8	117.8	117.8	14.0	14.0	14.0	14.0	14.0	14.0
11.1 Catering services	119	103.9	104.3	104.6	104.8	105.1	105.5	2.9	3.2	3.2	3.4	3.4	3.5
11.1.1 Restaurants & cafes	106	104.0	104.3	104.6	104.7	104.9	105.4	3.0	3.1	3.2	3.3	3.2	3.3
11.1.2 Canteens	13	103.4	104.9	104.9	105.7	106.2	106.6	2.4	3.5	3.3	3.8	4.6	4.6
11.2 Accommodation services	19	106.2	105.6	105.5	105.8	106.3	106.7	3.6	3.6	3.1	3.1	2.5	2.8
12.1 Personal care	31	102.8	102.7	102.2	102.3	104.1	104.9	2.8	2.7	2.1	1.4	2.8	3.6
12.1.1 Hairdressing and personal grooming establishments	8	104.5	104.8	105.1	105.6	105.8	106.1	3.4	3.6	3.5	3.6	3.6	3.7
12.1.2/3 Appliances and products for personal care	23	102.1	101.9	101.1	101.1	103.4	104.5	2.6	2.4	1.7	0.7	2.6	3.6
12.3 Personal effects nec[2]	10	104.3	104.3	104.2	103.5	104.4	104.7	3.9	3.5	3.4	5.0	4.0	3.9
12.3.1 Jewellery, clocks and watches	7	106.7	106.8	106.4	105.8	106.8	107.1	6.1	6.1	5.9	6.3	5.0	4.9
12.3.2 Other personal effects	3	100.4	100.2	100.6	99.7	100.5	100.8	0.4	−0.8	−0.8	2.6	2.2	2.1
12.4 Social protection	12	107.2	107.7	108.0	109.1	109.2	109.4	5.2	5.4	5.6	5.7	5.7	5.8
12.5 Insurance	8	102.4	103.5	103.0	104.5	104.8	104.9	2.3	2.7	2.8	4.3	6.5	4.7
12.5.2 House contents insurance	2	103.3	102.9	102.5	103.2	103.9	103.6	2.8	2.2	1.5	3.4	7.4	7.1
12.5.3 Health insurance	2	110.0	110.0	110.0	112.0	112.0	112.0	8.3	8.3	8.3	8.6	8.6	8.6
12.5.4 Transport insurance	4	99.3	101.3	100.5	102.3	102.6	102.8	−0.2	0.8	1.1	3.0	5.4	2.4
12.6 Financial services nec[2]	28	105.7	105.0	105.0	105.0	104.9	105.1	3.2	2.5	2.5	2.0	1.9	2.1
12.6.2 Other financial services nec[2]	28	105.7	105.0	105.0	105.0	104.9	105.2	3.2	2.5	2.5	2.0	1.9	2.1
12.7 Other services nec[2]	11	108.0	108.2	108.6	109.1	109.2	109.2	6.2	5.9	5.8	5.0	4.9	4.8

1 Prior to 10 December 2003, the consumer prices index (CPI) was published in the UK as the harmonised index of consumer prices (HICP).
2 nec - not elsewhere covered

Source: Office for National Statistics: 020 7533 5874

18.3 Retail Prices Index

13 January 1987=100

| | ALL ITEMS (RPI) | All items excluding | | | | | Food and catering | Alcohol and tobacco | Housing and household expenditure | Personal expenditure | Travel and leisure | Consumer durables | All items excluding mortgage interest payments & indirect taxes (RPIY)[3] |
		mortgage interest payments (RPIX)	mortgage interest payments and depreciation[1]	housing	food	seasonal food[2]							
Weights													
	CZGU	CZGY	DOGZ	CZGX	CZGV	CZGW	CBVV	CBVW	CBVX	CBVY	CBVZ	CBWA	
1998	1 000	955	923	803	870	982	178	105	359	95	263	121	
1999	1 000	958	928	807	872	980	179	100	358	95	268	127	
2000	1 000	960	924	805	882	982	170	95	355	101	279	126	
2001	1 000	954	914	795	884	982	169	97	362	96	276	125	
2002	1 000	964	924	801	886	980	166	99	363	94	278	126	
2003	1 000	961	919	797	891	983	160	98	365	92	285	126	
2004	1 000	961	914	791	889	981	160	97	367	93	283	121	
2005	1 000	950	901	776	890	981	159	96	387	89	269	122	
2006	1 000	950	906	778	895	983	155	96	392	90	267	117	
2007	1 000	945	895	762	895	981	152	95	408	83	262	109	
Annual averages													
	CHAW	CHMK	CHON	CHAZ	CHAY	CHAX	CHBS	CHBT	CHBU	CHBV	CHBW	CHBY	CBZW
1997	157.5	156.5	156.4	152.9	160.5	158.5	150.4	183.2	158.4	137.7	159.0	117.3	151.5
1998	162.9	160.6	160.3	156.2	166.5	163.8	153.4	192.3	166.2	139.9	162.8	115.9	154.5
1999	165.4	164.3	163.6	158.9	169.4	166.5	155.4	202.6	167.7	139.6	165.6	112.3	157.1
2000	170.3	167.7	166.4	161.3	175.1	171.4	156.7	210.3	176.2	137.2	170.3	108.0	159.9
2001	173.3	171.3	169.5	163.7	178.0	174.3	162.2	216.9	180.0	135.7	172.0	105.0	163.7
2002	176.2	175.1	172.5	166.0	181.1	177.2	164.8	222.3	184.6	133.2	174.2	101.9	167.5
2003	181.3	180.0	176.2	168.9	186.7	182.4	167.9	228.0	194.3	133.2	177.0	99.8	172.0
2004	186.7	184.0	179.1	170.9	192.8	187.9	170.0	233.6	207.4	131.5	178.1	97.7	175.5
2005	192.0	188.2	182.6	173.7	198.7	193.3	172.9	239.8	219.4	131.0	179.2	95.3	179.4
2006	198.1	193.7	187.8	178.3	205.2	199.5	176.9	247.1	231.8	131.7	181.1	94.0	184.8
Monthly figures													
2004 Mar	184.6	182.5	178.1	170.4	190.2	185.7	170.2	231.2	201.9	132.1	177.4	98.5	174.3
Apr	185.7	183.6	179.1	170.8	191.6	186.9	170.2	233.4	204.5	132.2	177.8	98.2	174.9
May	186.5	184.3	179.7	171.4	192.4	187.6	170.6	233.8	205.8	132.3	178.5	98.6	175.6
Jun	186.8	184.2	179.5	171.2	193.0	188.1	169.8	234.2	207.4	131.7	178.5	98.5	175.6
Jul	186.8	183.8	178.9	170.5	193.1	188.2	169.2	234.7	208.3	129.0	178.8	95.6	175.1
Aug	187.4	184.3	179.3	170.9	193.8	188.8	169.1	235.2	209.3	130.1	179.1	96.4	175.7
Sep	188.1	184.7	179.4	171.1	194.6	189.5	169.3	235.3	211.3	132.0	178.1	97.7	176.1
Oct	188.6	185.1	179.8	171.3	195.1	189.9	169.9	235.5	212.5	132.2	177.9	97.2	176.6
Nov	189.0	185.4	180.1	171.6	195.5	190.3	170.4	235.0	213.4	132.6	177.9	97.6	176.9
Dec	189.9	186.4	180.9	172.5	196.4	191.2	171.2	234.7	215.6	131.8	178.6	99.1	177.9
2005 Jan	188.9	185.2	179.8	171.2	195.2	190.1	171.6	236.0	214.3	129.4	177.1	94.5	176.7
Feb	189.6	185.9	180.4	171.9	195.9	190.8	172.4	236.9	214.9	130.2	177.6	95.0	177.4
Mar	190.5	186.8	181.4	173.0	196.8	191.6	173.4	236.8	216.3	131.4	178.1	96.7	178.3
Apr	191.6	187.8	182.4	173.3	198.2	192.9	172.7	239.4	218.3	131.4	179.3	95.6	179.0
May	192.0	188.2	182.7	173.7	198.6	193.2	173.7	240.2	219.0	131.4	179.1	95.9	179.4
Jun	192.2	188.3	182.8	173.8	198.8	193.4	173.6	240.5	219.7	131.4	178.9	95.8	179.5
Jul	192.2	188.3	182.7	173.5	199.1	193.7	172.4	241.0	220.2	128.8	180.2	94.0	179.5
Aug	192.6	188.6	183.0	173.8	199.5	194.1	172.7	241.0	220.5	130.3	180.2	94.1	179.8
Sep	193.1	189.3	183.7	174.6	200.0	194.5	172.7	241.1	220.7	131.6	181.0	95.1	180.5
Oct	193.3	189.5	183.8	174.7	200.4	194.8	172.7	241.8	221.4	131.8	180.8	94.7	180.7
Nov	193.6	189.7	184.0	174.9	200.5	195.0	173.4	241.9	222.5	132.2	179.6	95.4	180.9
Dec	194.1	190.2	184.5	175.5	201.0	195.5	174.1	241.6	224.5	131.9	179.0	97.0	181.5
2006 Jan	193.4	189.4	183.7	174.5	200.3	194.8	174.1	242.5	223.0	129.1	179.4	92.4	180.7
Feb	194.2	190.1	184.4	175.2	201.0	195.6	174.9	242.8	224.0	130.0	179.9	93.5	181.4
Mar	195.0	190.8	185.2	176.0	202.0	196.4	174.3	243.8	225.8	131.1	180.0	95.1	182.2
Apr	196.5	192.3	186.7	177.0	203.8	198.0	174.2	245.8	228.3	131.7	181.6	93.6	183.2
May	197.7	193.6	187.8	178.2	204.9	199.1	176.1	246.8	230.0	132.7	182.1	94.3	184.5
Jun	198.5	194.2	188.4	178.9	205.7	199.8	176.8	248.3	231.6	132.6	181.9	94.7	185.2
Jul	198.5	194.2	188.3	178.7	205.6	199.9	177.1	248.3	231.5	129.4	183.3	91.8	185.2
Aug	199.2	194.9	188.9	179.3	206.4	200.7	177.6	249.1	232.6	131.3	183.3	93.0	186.0
Sep	200.1	195.3	189.2	179.6	207.4	201.5	178.1	249.2	235.9	133.0	181.2	94.8	186.4
Oct	200.4	195.5	189.3	179.7	207.5	201.7	179.1	249.7	237.3	133.4	179.6	93.7	186.7
Nov	201.1	196.2	190.0	180.4	208.2	202.4	180.2	249.6	238.7	133.7	179.8	94.5	187.5
Dec	202.7	197.4	191.2	181.7	210.1	204.1	180.6	249.4	242.7	132.9	181.0	96.7	188.6
2007 Jan	201.6	196.1	189.8	180.0	208.9	203.0	180.0	251.3	240.6	130.1	180.8	91.1	187.3
Feb	203.1	197.1	190.7	181.1	210.4	204.4	181.2	252.4	243.0	131.3	181.4	92.1	188.4
Mar	204.4	198.3	191.9	182.4	211.7	205.7	182.1	253.8	245.3	132.5	181.6	95.1	189.5

Note: Further information on the RPI is available from the National Statistics Website: www.statistics.gov.uk/rpi.

1 This series has been constructed using the index for all items excluding mortgage interest payments prior to February 1995.

2 Seasonal food is defined as items of food the prices of which show significant seasonal variations. These are fresh fruit and vegetables, fresh fish, eggs and home-killed lamb.

3 There are no weights available for RPIY.

Source: Office for National Statistics: 020 7533 5874

18.4 Retail Prices Index[1]
Detailed figures for various groups, sub-groups and sections

13 January 1987=100

		Group and sub-group weights in 2007	2006 Apr	2006 May	2006 Jun	2006 Jul	2006 Aug	2006 Sep	2006 Oct	2006 Nov	2006 Dec	2007 Jan	2007 Feb	2007 Mar
ALL ITEMS (RPI)	CHAW	1000	196.5	197.7	198.5	198.5	199.2	200.1	200.4	201.1	202.7	201.6	203.1	204.4
All items excluding:														
mortgage interest payments (RPIX)	CHMK	950	192.3	193.6	194.2	194.2	194.9	195.3	195.5	196.2	197.4	196.1	197.1	198.3
mortgage interest payments and depreciation	CHON	906	186.7	187.8	188.4	188.3	188.9	189.2	189.3	190.0	191.2	189.8	190.7	191.9
mortgage interest payments and council tax	DQAD	911	189.3	190.6	191.3	191.2	192.0	192.4	192.6	193.3	194.5	193.2	194.2	195.5
housing	CHAZ	778	177.0	178.2	178.9	178.7	179.3	179.6	179.7	180.4	181.7	180.0	181.1	182.4
food	CHAY	895	203.8	204.9	205.7	205.6	206.4	207.4	207.5	208.2	210.1	208.9	210.4	211.7
seasonal food	CHAX	983	198.0	199.1	199.8	199.9	200.7	201.5	201.7	202.4	204.1	203.0	204.4	205.7
All items excluding mortgage interest payments and indirect taxes (RPIY)[2]	CBZW		183.2	184.5	185.2	185.2	186.0	186.4	186.7	187.5	188.6	187.3	188.4	189.5
Food	CHBA	105	154.1	156.3	157.1	157.3	157.7	158.4	159.3	160.6	160.8	159.9	161.4	162.3
Bread	DOAA	4	163.7	163.3	162.9	163.6	165.1	166.8	166.8	169.4	170.5	170.2	171.0	174.9
Cereals	DOAB	3	143.5	142.5	143.7	144.3	144.0	144.9	143.7	144.8	145.8	143.3	145.4	146.7
Biscuits and cakes	DOAC	6	167.4	168.9	169.0	168.8	169.5	169.0	169.0	170.4	171.4	171.4	171.8	174.5
Beef	DOAD	4	134.3	137.1	137.3	142.1	140.1	141.7	143.3	142.4	141.7	143.4	141.7	143.1
Lamb	DOAE	2	183.9	188.9	190.0	190.0	189.9	189.6	188.9	188.3	190.4	189.4	188.7	190.1
of which home-killed lamb	DOAF	1	185.0	193.7	196.7	193.5	195.3	191.8	189.5	191.3	194.4	193.4	188.6	190.3
Pork	DOAG	1	155.2	157.1	157.7	159.9	158.9	155.6	159.7	156.1	156.8	159.2	157.5	157.4
Bacon	DOAH	2	174.7	177.2	180.4	183.2	185.1	184.6	187.1	189.8	190.0	189.8	190.0	188.5
Poultry	DOAI	4	108.5	108.7	109.9	111.4	110.5	106.8	109.6	108.5	109.8	107.0	112.4	110.9
Other meat	DOAJ	7	144.6	146.1	145.9	146.4	148.0	148.0	147.9	148.4	149.8	148.4	149.0	150.1
Fish	DOAK	4	160.5	159.2	162.4	164.8	166.9	167.6	169.1	168.9	169.9	170.2	173.6	173.5
of which fresh fish	DOAL	2	167.5	167.2	172.5	176.8	178.6	180.6	183.0	182.1	180.6	178.8	186.2	186.1
Butter	DOAM	1	168.1	168.6	169.0	169.6	173.8	173.5	173.7	173.8	174.1	173.9	173.8	173.9
Oils and fats	DOAN	1	138.6	143.7	144.9	144.9	145.6	143.3	144.8	145.8	145.7	146.0	144.5	144.8
Cheese	DOAO	3	175.7	176.0	176.0	175.1	176.4	175.9	175.7	176.0	176.4	176.5	174.0	176.8
Eggs	DOAP	1	158.2	158.9	162.0	162.3	166.8	168.1	169.6	170.5	179.0	178.7	179.0	181.1
Milk, fresh	DOAQ	5	174.9	173.2	178.2	187.9	188.4	188.2	188.9	188.8	189.0	188.9	188.3	192.0
Milk products	DOAR	4	144.1	146.0	145.5	147.2	147.5	147.8	147.1	147.8	147.1	145.1	145.1	148.7
Tea	DOAS	1	146.9	154.6	158.7	157.9	161.1	162.4	162.5	161.4	161.5	157.3	160.6	161.2
Coffee and other hot drinks	DOAT	1	116.4	116.5	116.0	116.1	123.3	125.0	125.2	123.6	125.9	122.4	124.7	125.7
Soft drinks	DOAU	10	191.2	192.1	192.3	192.2	191.0	193.6	193.9	193.7	193.9	193.0	196.4	197.3
Sugar and preserves	DOAV	1	154.8	156.1	156.3	156.4	156.8	158.4	158.5	159.9	160.6	161.3	163.0	162.1
Sweets and chocolates	DOAW	10	190.7	192.3	192.7	192.1	193.8	193.9	193.3	193.1	193.3	194.2	195.7	196.3
Potatoes	DOAX	4	151.5	153.2	156.9	153.7	151.0	151.7	154.7	161.1	162.0	159.0	166.1	167.8
of which unprocessed potatoes	DOAY	1	139.2	147.1	151.0	149.4	138.7	141.4	144.3	150.7	152.0	150.7	156.2	159.9
Vegetables other than potatoes	DOAZ	8	129.8	137.5	138.8	137.5	135.0	136.3	138.8	144.1	142.4	146.2	148.5	149.4
of which fresh vegetables	DOBA	6	116.4	125.5	126.9	125.4	121.9	122.4	124.1	129.8	127.6	131.9	134.4	135.3
Fruit	DOBB	7	140.5	149.0	148.5	142.3	144.7	150.1	152.0	158.2	157.1	147.4	147.8	144.8
of which fresh fruit	DOBC	6	136.3	146.1	145.5	138.6	141.5	147.4	148.9	156.6	155.3	144.0	144.4	140.9
Other foods	DOBD	11	149.3	150.4	150.4	150.0	151.3	150.7	152.5	151.7	151.6	150.8	151.8	152.8
Catering	CHBC	50	243.7	244.7	245.3	245.9	246.4	246.6	247.8	248.5	249.2	249.7	250.1	250.9
Restaurant meals	DOBE	27	238.7	239.7	240.2	240.7	241.1	240.8	242.1	242.8	243.6	244.1	244.3	245.2
Canteen meals	DOBF	4	297.8	298.2	298.2	298.5	298.3	301.6	302.7	305.0	304.7	307.1	308.2	309.0
Take-aways and snacks	DOBG	19	233.2	234.3	234.9	235.8	236.5	237.0	237.9	238.3	239.1	239.3	239.9	240.3
Alcoholic drink	CHBD	67	211.7	212.6	213.2	213.2	214.0	214.1	214.7	214.5	214.3	215.1	216.0	217.6
Beer	DOBH	36	230.5	232.1	232.2	232.7	233.1	233.3	234.0	234.6	235.1	234.8	235.7	237.6
Beer on sales	DOBI	31	249.4	251.1	251.5	252.1	252.6	252.8	253.5	254.3	255.0	254.9	255.9	257.9
Beer off sales	DOBJ	5	148.1	148.8	147.7	147.8	147.8	148.1	149.1	148.4	148.4	147.5	147.9	149.0
Wines and spirits	DOBK	31	186.9	187.2	188.2	187.7	189.0	189.0	189.4	188.4	187.6	189.3	190.2	191.5
Wines and spirits on sales	DOBL	17	233.9	235.2	235.5	235.8	236.6	237.1	237.7	238.3	238.8	239.2	239.8	240.6
Wines and spirits off sales	DOBM	14	156.5	155.9	157.6	156.4	158.2	157.8	157.9	155.8	153.6	156.6	157.8	159.7
Tobacco	CHBE	29	340.9	342.2	346.9	347.1	347.5	347.7	347.9	348.0	348.1	354.0	355.5	355.7
Cigarettes	DOBN	26	348.5	349.7	354.5	354.7	355.2	355.4	355.6	355.6	355.8	361.7	363.2	363.4
Other tobacco	DOBO	3	271.1	272.1	276.5	276.5	276.7	276.7	276.9	276.8	276.9	282.0	283.7	283.6

18.4 Retail Prices Index[1]

Detailed figures for various groups, sub-groups and sections

continued

13 January 1987 = 100

		Group and sub-group weights in 2007	2006 Apr	2006 May	2006 Jun	2006 Jul	2006 Aug	2006 Sep	2006 Oct	2006 Nov	2006 Dec	2007 Jan	2007 Feb	2007 Mar
Housing	CHBF	222	298.7	299.8	300.7	302.1	303.6	307.8	308.9	310.0	313.8	315.7	319.4	320.4
Rent	DOBP	45	278.0	278.3	278.5	280.5	280.6	280.6	280.8	281.3	281.5	282.5	282.6	282.5
Mortgage interest payments	DOBQ	50	304.3	306.3	308.1	310.1	312.5	327.8	330.3	332.8	347.6	351.7	365.7	368.6
Depreciation (Jan 1995 = 100)	CHOO	44	263.4	265.8	267.9	269.8	273.0	276.2	278.3	279.5	281.1	282.8	285.6	287.2
Council tax and Rates	DOBR	39	280.6	280.7	280.7	280.7	280.7	280.7	280.7	280.7	280.7	280.7	280.7	280.7
Water and other charges	DOBS	12	354.1	354.1	354.1	354.1	354.1	354.1	354.1	354.1	354.1	354.1	354.1	354.1
Repairs and maintenance charges	DOBT	12	310.5	311.3	311.9	313.4	314.3	315.4	317.1	317.6	318.9	324.1	324.8	325.6
Do-it-yourself materials	DOBU	13	158.5	157.9	158.2	158.4	159.7	161.0	160.7	161.1	162.4	162.8	164.1	164.1
Dwelling insurance and ground rent	DOBV	7	280.7	281.4	278.6	278.5	280.0	280.5	279.2	280.1	279.5	281.5	283.0	281.2
Fuel and light	CHBG	33	188.4	197.2	201.8	204.1	205.6	208.2	214.5	219.0	222.7	222.6	223.6	223.1
Coal and solid fuels	DOBW	1	185.7	187.6	183.9	183.7	185.3	187.6	197.3	199.5	199.5	199.8	200.2	200.5
Electricity	DOBX	15	176.1	183.5	187.9	189.9	191.3	193.7	198.8	202.6	205.0	206.0	206.7	206.7
Gas	DOBY	14	192.5	204.4	210.4	212.6	215.1	220.3	231.1	238.7	243.3	243.9	244.8	242.8
Oil and other fuels	DOBZ	3	275.4	277.0	276.6	285.4	280.0	267.3	249.3	240.0	249.4	235.2	240.1	247.1
Household goods	CHBH	71	145.1	146.5	148.4	145.2	146.2	148.9	146.1	147.9	154.6	144.3	147.1	153.8
Furniture	DOCA	26	162.1	164.5	169.9	162.4	163.6	169.4	164.0	168.5	187.7	162.4	165.0	185.8
Furnishings	DOCB	11	157.8	160.4	159.6	155.9	159.1	158.2	158.1	158.4	162.5	154.0	160.1	158.5
Electrical appliances	DOCC	8	74.1	74.5	74.4	75.6	76.1	79.0	74.7	74.2	73.3	71.2	72.6	74.2
Other household equipment	DOCD	5	140.8	141.6	142.5	137.4	140.0	141.5	140.3	142.5	141.8	139.0	142.6	143.1
Household consumables	DOCE	14	159.8	159.8	160.8	159.8	159.6	160.2	160.1	160.8	161.2	161.5	162.4	163.2
Pet care	DOCF	7	168.9	169.9	170.0	170.5	169.6	171.2	171.4	171.4	171.8	170.4	172.7	172.8
Household services	CHBI	66	189.0	188.4	189.3	189.5	189.5	191.5	196.6	196.2	196.3	196.3	196.0	196.5
Postage	DOCG	1	188.9	188.9	188.9	188.9	188.9	200.2	200.2	200.2	200.2	200.2	200.2	200.2
Telephones, telemessages, etc	DOCH	24	89.7	88.4	88.6	88.5	87.9	87.8	88.6	88.4	88.2	87.7	86.8	86.9
Domestic services	DOCI	12	286.1	287.3	289.1	290.9	291.9	293.7	295.0	295.7	296.6	300.2	300.3	301.1
Fees and subscriptions	DOCJ	29	268.6	269.1	270.9	271.2	272.2	277.8	291.8	290.7	291.1	291.0	292.1	293.1
Clothing and footwear	CHBJ	49	94.8	95.7	95.3	91.5	93.6	95.5	95.9	96.3	95.0	91.3	92.4	93.8
Men's outerwear	DOCK	10	96.7	97.5	96.6	93.5	94.8	97.8	97.5	98.2	97.5	92.5	94.0	95.3
Women's outerwear	DOCL	17	70.1	70.8	70.4	65.2	67.8	69.8	70.6	70.6	69.0	65.2	66.1	68.0
Children's outerwear	DOCM	6	87.6	89.3	89.4	88.0	89.4	89.0	89.7	90.5	90.8	87.4	87.2	87.3
Other clothing	DOCN	7	147.5	148.4	148.3	146.1	148.9	150.4	149.6	151.1	150.9	148.1	149.2	149.7
Footwear	DOCO	9	108.8	109.7	109.3	107.5	108.3	110.3	110.3	110.4	108.3	106.8	108.3	109.2
Personal goods and services	CHBQ	41	208.3	209.3	210.0	208.6	209.9	210.8	211.2	211.3	211.9	211.8	213.1	213.8
Personal articles	DOCP	12	133.4	134.6	135.9	134.0	135.8	137.2	136.9	137.0	138.1	136.5	138.0	139.5
Chemists goods	DOCQ	16	190.8	190.7	190.6	189.4	190.2	190.7	191.3	191.1	190.8	191.0	192.3	192.3
Personal services	DOCR	13	353.3	356.0	356.6	356.6	357.4	357.6	359.1	360.0	360.7	364.0	364.4	364.8
Motoring expenditure	CHBK	140	188.1	189.5	189.2	190.5	190.2	186.6	183.5	183.8	184.6	185.4	185.1	186.0
Purchase of motor vehicles	DOCS	56	106.9	106.8	106.4	106.1	105.6	105.5	105.2	104.9	104.5	105.5	105.8	105.0
Maintenance of motor vehicles	DOCT	20	290.4	291.5	292.9	294.4	295.2	296.4	298.0	300.3	301.4	303.8	303.9	304.8
Petrol and oil	DOCU	40	273.1	282.1	279.6	284.7	286.2	268.6	254.4	253.2	259.0	256.2	253.1	259.8
Vehicle tax and insurance	DOCV	24	285.0	280.8	283.5	286.9	283.7	283.3	282.3	286.9	285.3	289.1	289.9	290.4
Fares and other travel costs	CHBR	19	230.2	227.6	228.9	238.4	240.2	229.0	228.1	226.1	234.4	229.6	236.4	234.8
Rail fares	DOCW	5	252.0	251.3	250.5	251.8	254.1	248.0	247.6	250.9	249.4	257.4	261.9	260.6
Bus and coach fares	DOCX	4	256.8	253.4	253.6	254.0	254.8	257.3	259.3	261.4	262.3	270.0	271.1	272.2
Other travel costs	DOCY	10	201.8	198.9	201.3	216.2	218.0	201.3	199.4	194.2	208.2	195.0	203.5	201.3
Leisure goods	CHBL	41	92.4	91.9	91.9	91.5	91.6	91.9	91.2	91.6	92.2	91.0	91.6	91.1
Audio-visual equipment	DOCZ	9	17.7	17.3	17.2	17.1	17.2	17.2	16.8	16.9	16.9	16.7	16.5	15.9
CDs and tapes	DODA	4	99.8	100.9	100.1	99.3	96.4	97.3	97.4	99.2	101.8	101.3	99.9	99.8
Toys, photographic and sports goods	DODB	12	90.8	90.3	90.0	89.1	90.1	89.7	89.6	89.1	89.4	88.9	88.2	89.1
Books and newspapers	DODC	10	245.9	246.4	247.4	249.4	249.0	252.6	251.9	253.2	254.5	247.1	256.9	256.5
Gardening products	DODD	6	143.8	143.9	145.4	144.1	143.9	143.6	142.7	144.2	145.3	144.9	148.3	146.8
Leisure services	CHBM	67	265.8	266.2	265.8	267.3	267.4	269.1	270.5	270.8	271.4	271.8	272.4	272.7
Television licences and rentals	DODE	12	164.0	164.0	164.1	164.7	164.7	164.7	166.1	166.1	166.2	166.1	166.1	166.1
Entertainment and other recreation	DODF	17	349.9	348.6	348.7	351.4	348.4	358.7	361.3	360.1	362.3	359.6	363.2	364.7
Foreign holidays (Jan 1993 = 100)	CHMQ	30	168.0	168.5	167.9	168.7	169.3	169.1	169.5	170.3	170.4	171.5	171.5	171.4
UK holidays (Jan 1994 = 100)	CHMS	8	162.4	163.3	163.6	164.9	165.8	165.5	166.2	166.3	166.8	167.5	167.5	168.0

Note: Indices are given to one decimal place to provide as much information as is available but precision is greater at higher levels of aggregation, ie at sub-group and group levels. Further information on the RPI is available from the National Statistics Website: www.statistics.gov.uk/rpi.

2 The taxes excluded are council tax, VAT, duties, vehicle excise duty, insurance tax and airport tax. There are no weights available for RPIY.

Source: Office for National Statistics: 020 7533 5874

1 *Retail Prices Index 1914-1990* contains group and sub-group indices and weights back to 1956, group indices back to 1947, together with cost of living indices as far back as 1914.

18.5 Retail Prices Index (All Items)

	Annual average	Jan	Feb	Mar	Apr	May	Jun	Jul	Aug	Sep	Oct	Nov	Dec
January 1962=100													
1962	101.6	100.0	100.1	100.5	101.9	102.2	102.9	102.5	101.6	101.5	101.4	101.8	102.3
1963	103.6	102.7	103.6	103.7	104.0	103.9	103.9	103.3	103.0	103.3	103.7	104.0	104.2
1964	107.0	104.7	104.8	105.2	106.1	107.0	107.4	107.4	107.8	107.8	107.9	108.8	109.2
1965	112.1	109.5	109.5	109.9	112.0	112.4	112.7	112.7	112.9	113.0	113.1	113.6	114.1
1966	116.5	114.3	114.4	114.6	116.0	116.8	117.1	116.6	117.3	117.1	117.4	118.1	118.3
1967	119.4	118.5	118.6	118.6	119.5	119.4	119.9	119.2	118.9	118.8	119.7	120.4	121.2
1968	125.0	121.6	122.2	122.6	124.8	124.9	125.4	125.5	125.7	125.8	126.4	126.7	128.4
1969	131.8	129.1	129.8	130.3	131.7	131.5	132.1	132.1	131.8	132.2	133.2	133.5	134.4
1970	140.2	135.5	136.2	137.0	139.1	139.5	139.9	140.9	140.8	141.5	143.0	144.0	145.0
1971	153.4	147.0	147.8	149.0	152.2	153.2	154.3	155.2	155.3	155.5	156.4	157.3	158.1
1972	164.3	159.0	159.8	160.3	161.8	162.6	163.7	164.2	165.5	166.4	168.7	169.3	170.2
1973	179.4	171.3	172.4	173.4	176.7	178.0	178.9	179.7	180.2	181.8	185.4	186.8	188.2
1974	..	191.8	..	..	..	..	..	..	..	..	..	..	..
January 1974=100													
1974	108.5	100.0	101.7	102.6	106.1	107.6	108.7	109.7	109.8	111.0	113.2	115.2	116.9
1975	134.8	119.9	121.9	124.3	129.1	134.5	137.1	138.5	139.3	140.5	142.5	144.2	146.0
1976	157.1	147.9	149.8	150.6	153.5	155.2	156.0	156.3	158.5	160.6	163.5	165.8	168.0
1977	182.0	172.4	174.1	175.8	180.3	181.7	183.6	183.8	184.7	185.7	186.5	187.4	188.4
1978	197.1	189.5	190.6	191.8	194.6	195.7	197.2	198.1	199.4	200.2	201.1	202.5	204.2
1979	223.5	207.2	208.9	210.6	214.2	215.9	219.6	229.1	230.9	233.2	235.6	237.7	239.4
1980	263.7	245.3	248.8	252.2	260.8	263.2	265.7	267.9	268.5	270.2	271.9	274.1	275.6
1981	295.0	277.3	279.8	284.0	292.2	294.1	295.8	297.1	299.3	301.0	303.7	306.9	308.8
1982	320.4	310.6	310.7	313.4	319.7	322.0	322.9	323.0	323.1	322.9	324.5	326.1	325.5
1983	335.1	325.9	327.3	327.9	332.5	333.9	334.7	336.5	338.0	339.5	340.7	341.9	342.8
1984	351.8	342.6	344.0	345.1	349.7	351.0	351.9	351.5	354.8	355.5	357.7	358.8	358.5
1985	373.2	359.8	362.7	366.1	373.9	375.6	376.4	375.7	376.7	376.5	377.1	378.4	378.9
1986	385.9	379.7	381.1	381.6	385.3	386.0	385.8	384.7	385.9	387.8	388.4	391.7	393.0
1987	..	394.5	..	..	..	..	..	..	..	..	..	..	..
January 1987=100													
1991	133.5	130.2	130.9	131.4	133.1	133.5	134.1	133.8	134.1	134.6	135.1	135.6	135.7
1992	138.5	135.6	136.3	136.7	138.8	139.3	139.3	138.8	138.9	139.4	139.9	139.7	139.2
1993	140.7	137.9	138.8	139.3	140.6	141.1	141.0	140.7	141.3	141.9	141.8	141.6	141.9
1994	144.1	141.3	142.1	142.5	144.2	144.7	144.7	144.0	144.7	145.0	145.2	145.3	146.0
1995	149.1	146.0	146.9	147.5	149.0	149.6	149.8	149.1	149.9	150.6	149.8	149.8	150.7
1996	152.7	150.2	150.9	151.5	152.6	152.9	153.0	152.4	153.1	153.8	153.8	153.9	154.4
1997	157.5	154.4	155.0	155.4	156.3	156.9	157.5	157.5	158.5	159.3	159.5	159.6	160.0
1998	162.9	159.5	160.3	160.8	162.6	163.5	163.4	163.0	163.7	164.4	164.5	164.4	164.4
1999	165.4	163.4	163.7	164.1	165.2	165.6	165.6	165.1	165.5	166.2	166.5	166.7	167.3
2000	170.3	166.6	167.5	168.4	170.1	170.7	171.1	170.5	170.5	171.7	171.6	172.1	172.2
2001	173.3	171.1	172.0	172.2	173.1	174.2	174.4	173.3	174.0	174.6	174.3	173.6	173.4
2002	176.2	173.3	173.8	174.5	175.7	176.2	176.2	175.9	176.4	177.6	177.9	178.2	178.5
2003	181.3	178.4	179.3	179.9	181.2	181.5	181.3	181.3	181.6	182.5	182.6	182.7	183.5
2004	186.7	183.1	183.8	184.6	185.7	186.5	186.8	186.8	187.4	188.1	188.6	189.0	189.9
2005	192.0	188.9	189.6	190.5	191.6	192.0	192.2	192.2	192.6	193.1	193.3	193.6	194.1
2006	198.1	193.4	194.2	195.0	196.5	197.7	198.5	198.5	199.2	200.1	200.4	201.1	202.7
2007	..	201.6	203.1	204.4	..	..	..	..	..	..	..	..	..

Note: Further information on the RPI is available from the National Statistics Website: www.statistics.gov.uk/rpi.

Source: Office for National Statistics: 020 7533 5874

18.6 Harmonised Indices of Consumer Prices (HICPs) - International comparisons : EU countries

percentage changes over 12 months

Per cent

		2004	2005	2006	2006 Mar	2006 Apr	2006 May	2006 Jun	2006 Jul	2006 Aug	2006 Sep	2006 Oct	2006 Nov	2006 Dec	2007 Jan	2007 Feb	2007 Mar
European Union countries																	
United Kingdom[1]	D7G7	1.3	2.1	2.3	1.8	2.0	2.2	2.5	2.4	2.5	2.4	2.4	2.7	3.0	2.7	2.8	3.1
Austria	D7SK	2.0	2.1	1.7	1.3	2.1	2.1	1.9	2.0	2.1	1.3	1.3	1.6	1.6	1.7	1.7†	1.9
Belgium	D7SL	1.9	2.5	2.3	2.2	2.6	2.8	2.5	2.4	2.3	1.9	1.7	2.0	2.1	1.7	1.8	1.8
Bulgaria	GHY8	6.1	6.0	7.4	9.1	8.5	9.0	8.4	7.8	7.0	5.4	5.2	5.9	6.1	6.8	4.6	4.4
Cyprus	D7RO	1.9	2.0	2.2	2.6	2.5	2.5	2.6	2.8	2.7	2.2	1.7	1.3	1.5	1.4	1.2	1.4
Czech Republic	D7RP	2.6	1.6	2.1	2.4	2.3	2.8	2.3	2.4	2.6	2.2	0.8	1.0	1.5	1.4	1.7	2.1
Denmark	D7SM	0.9	1.7	1.9	1.8	1.8	2.1	2.1	2.0	1.9	1.5	1.4	1.8	1.7	1.8	1.9	1.9
Estonia	D7RQ	3.0	4.1	4.4	4.0	4.3	4.6	4.4	4.5	5.0	3.8	3.8	4.7	5.1	5.0	4.6	5.6
Finland	D7SN	0.1	0.8	1.3	1.2	1.5	1.7	1.5	1.4	1.3	0.8	0.9	1.3	1.2	1.3	1.2	1.6
France	D7SO	2.3	1.9	1.9	1.7	2.0	2.4	2.2	2.2	2.1	1.5	1.2	1.6	1.7	1.4	1.2	1.2
Germany	D7SP	1.8	1.9	1.8	1.9	2.3	2.1	2.0	2.1	1.8	1.0	1.1	1.5	1.4	1.8	1.9	2.0
Greece	D7SQ	3.0	3.5	3.3	3.3	3.5	3.3	3.4	3.9	3.4	3.1	3.1	3.2	3.2	3.0	3.0	2.8
Hungary	D7RR	6.8	3.5	4.0	2.4	2.4	2.9	2.9	3.2	4.7	5.9	6.3	6.4	6.6	8.4	9.0	9.0
Ireland	D7SS	2.3	2.2	2.7	2.8	2.7	3.0	2.9	2.9	3.2	2.2	2.2	2.4	3.0	2.9	2.6	2.9
Italy	D7ST	2.3	2.2	2.2	2.2	2.3	2.3	2.3	2.4	2.3	2.4	1.9	2.0	2.1	1.9	2.1	2.1
Latvia	D7RS	6.2	6.9	6.6	6.6	6.1	7.1	6.3	6.9	6.8	5.9	5.6	6.3	6.8	7.1	7.2	8.5
Lithuania	D7RT	1.2	2.7	3.8	3.1	3.4	3.6	3.7	4.4	4.3	3.3	3.7	4.4	4.5	4.0	4.4	4.8
Luxembourg	D7SU	3.2	3.8	3.0	3.7	3.5	3.6	3.9	3.4	3.1	2.0	0.6	1.8	2.3	2.3	1.8	2.4
Malta	D7RU	2.7	2.5	2.6	2.9	3.5	3.5	3.3	3.6	3.0	3.1	1.7	0.9	0.8	1.2	0.8	0.5
Netherlands	D7SV	1.4	1.5	1.7	1.4	1.8	1.8	1.8	1.7	1.9	1.5	1.3	1.6	1.7	1.2	1.4	1.9
Poland	D7RV	3.6	2.2	1.3	0.9	1.2	1.5	1.5	1.4	1.7	1.4	1.1	1.3	1.4	1.6	1.9	2.4
Portugal	D7SX	2.5	2.1	3.0	3.8	3.7	3.7	3.5	3.0	2.7	3.0	2.6	2.4	2.5	2.6	2.3	2.4
Romania	GHY7	11.9	9.1	6.6	8.5	7.0	7.3	7.2	6.2	6.1	5.5	4.8	4.7	4.9	4.1	3.9	3.7
Slovakia	D7RW	7.5	2.8	4.3	4.3	4.4	4.8	4.5	5.0	5.0	4.5	3.1	3.7	3.7	2.2	2.0	2.1
Slovenia	D7RX	3.7	2.5	2.5	2.0	2.8	3.4	3.0	1.9	3.1	2.5	1.5	2.4	3.0	2.8	2.3	2.6
Spain	D7SY	3.1	3.4	3.6	3.9	3.9	4.1	4.0	4.0	3.8	2.9	2.6	2.7	2.7	2.4	2.5	2.5
Sweden	D7SZ	1.0	0.8	1.5	1.5	1.8	1.9	1.9	1.8	1.6	1.2	1.2	1.5	1.4	1.6	1.7	1.6
EICP[2] EU 25 average[3]	D7RY	2.0	2.2	2.2	2.1	2.3	2.4	2.4	2.4	2.3	1.9	1.8	2.1	2.1	..	..	..
EICP[2] EU 27 average[3]	GJ2E	..	..	..	..	..	..	..	..	..	..	..	..	..	2.1	2.1	2.2

Note: Further information on HICP is available from the National Statistics Website: www.statistics.gov.uk/hicp.

1 Published as the Consumer Prices Index (CPI) in the UK. (UK 2005=100, others 1996=100)
2 The EICP (European Index of Consumer Prices)is the official EU aggregate. It covers 15 member states until April 2004, 25 member states from May 2004, and 27 members from Jan 2007, the new member states being integrated using a chain index formula. The EU 25 annual average for 2004 is calculated from the EU 15 average from January to April and the EU 25 average from May to December.

3 The coverage of the European Union was extended to include Cyprus, Czech Republic, Estonia, Hungary, Latvia, Lithuania, Malta, Poland, Slovakia and Slovenia from 1 May 2004 and Bulgaria and Romania from 1 Jan 2007.

Source: Statistical Office of the European Communities (Eurostat)

18.7 Internal purchasing power of the pound (based on RPI)[1]

Pence

	1987	1988	1989	1990	1991	1992	1993	1994	1995	1996	1997	1998	1999	2000	2001	2002	2003	2004	2005	2006
	BAMT	BAMU	BAMV	BAMW	BASX	CZVM	CBXX	DOFX	DOHR	DOLM	DTUL	CDQG	JKZZ	ZMHO	IKHI	FAUI	SEZH	C687	E9AO	GB4Y
1987	100	105	113	124	131	136	138	141	146	150	155	160	162	167	170	173	178	183	188	194
1988	95	100	108	118	125	130	132	135	139	143	147	152	155	159	162	165	170	175	180	185
1989	88	93	100	109	116	120	122	125	129	133	137	141	144	148	150	153	157	162	167	172
1990	81	85	91	100	106	110	112	114	118	121	125	129	131	135	137	140	144	148	152	157
1991	76	80	86	94	100	104	105	108	112	114	118	122	124	128	130	132	136	140	144	148
1992	74	77	83	91	96	100	102	104	108	110	114	118	119	123	125	127	131	135	139	143
1993	72	76	82	90	95	98	100	102	106	109	112	116	118	121	123	125	129	133	136	141
1994	71	74	80	88	93	96	98	100	103	106	109	113	115	118	120	122	126	130	133	137
1995	68	72	77	85	90	93	94	97	100	102	106	109	111	114	116	118	122	125	129	133
1996	67	70	75	83	87	91	92	94	98	100	103	107	108	112	113	115	119	122	126	130
1997	65	68	73	80	85	88	89	92	95	97	100	103	105	108	110	112	115	119	122	126
1998	63	66	71	77	82	85	86	88	92	94	97	100	102	105	106	108	111	115	118	122
1999	62	65	70	76	81	84	85	87	90	92	95	98	100	103	105	107	110	113	116	120
2000	60	63	68	74	78	81	83	85	88	90	92	96	97	100	102	103	106	110	113	116
2001	59	62	66	73	77	80	81	83	86	88	91	94	95	98	100	102	105	108	111	114
2002	58	61	65	72	76	79	80	82	85	87	89	92	94	97	98	100	103	106	109	112
2003	56	59	64	70	74	76	78	79	82	84	87	90	91	94	96	97	100	103	106	109
2004	55	57	62	68	72	74	75	77	80	82	84	87	89	91	93	94	97	100	103	106
2005	53	56	60	66	70	72	73	75	78	80	82	85	86	89	90	92	94	97	100	103
2006	51	54	58	64	67	70	71	73	75	77	80	82	83	86	87	89	92	94	97	100

Year in which purchasing power was 100p

1 To find the purchasing power of the pound in 2000, given that it was 100 pence in 1990, select the column headed 1990 and look at the 2000 row. The result is 74 pence. These figures are calculated by taking the inverse ratio of the respective annual averages of the Retail Prices Index (RPI).

Note: Further information on the RPI is available from the National Statistics Website: www.statistics.gov.uk/rpi.

Source: Office for National Statistics: 020 7533 5874

18.8 Tax and Price Index

| | | Tax and Price Index: January 1987 = 100 | | | | | | | | | | | | | |
| | | | | | | | DQAB | | | | | | | | |
	1993	1994	1995	1996	1997	1998	1999	2000	2001	2002	2003	2004	2005	2006	2007
January	128.7	132.1	137.2	141.6	143.6	147.1	150.5	152.7	156.7	156.5	161.4	166.9	172.1	175.9	183.3
February	129.6	132.9	138.2	142.3	144.2	147.9	150.8	153.7	157.6	157.0	162.3	167.6	172.8	176.7	184.8
March	130.2	133.4	138.8	143.0	144.6	148.4	151.2	154.6	157.8	157.7	163.0	168.4	173.7	177.4	186.1
April	131.3	135.3	140.3	141.7	143.8	149.7	151.2	155.7	156.3	158.6	164.9	168.9	174.1	178.3	..
May	131.8	135.8	141.0	142.0	144.4	150.6	151.7	156.3	157.4	159.1	165.2	169.7	174.5	179.5	..
June	131.7	135.8	141.2	142.1	145.0	150.5	151.7	156.7	157.6	159.1	165.0	170.0	174.7	180.3	..
July	131.4	135.1	140.4	141.5	145.0	150.1	151.1	156.1	156.5	158.8	165.0	170.0	174.7	180.3	..
August	132.1	135.8	141.3	142.2	146.0	150.8	151.5	156.1	157.2	159.3	165.4	170.6	175.1	181.0	..
September	132.7	136.1	142.0	143.0	146.9	151.5	152.3	157.3	157.8	160.6	166.3	171.3	175.6	181.9	..
October	132.6	136.4	141.2	143.0	147.1	151.6	152.6	157.2	157.5	160.9	166.4	171.8	175.8	182.2	..
November	132.4	136.5	141.2	143.1	147.2	151.5	152.8	157.7	156.8	161.2	166.5	172.2	176.1	182.8	..
December	132.7	137.2	142.1	143.6	147.6	151.5	153.4	157.8	156.6	161.5	167.3	173.1	176.6	184.4	..

| | | Retail Prices Index: January 1987 = 100 | | | | | | | | | | | | | |
| | | | | | | | CHAW | | | | | | | | |
	1993	1994	1995	1996	1997	1998	1999	2000	2001	2002	2003	2004	2005	2006	2007
January	137.9	141.3	146.0	150.2	154.4	159.5	163.4	166.6	171.1	173.3	178.4	183.1	188.9	193.4	201.6
February	138.8	142.1	146.9	150.9	155.0	160.3	163.7	167.5	172.0	173.8	179.3	183.8	189.6	194.2	203.1
March	139.3	142.5	147.5	151.5	155.4	160.8	164.1	168.4	172.2	174.5	179.9	184.6	190.5	195.0	204.4
April	140.6	144.2	149.0	152.6	156.3	162.6	165.2	170.1	173.1	175.7	181.2	185.7	191.6	196.5	..
May	141.1	144.7	149.6	152.9	156.9	163.5	165.6	170.7	174.2	176.2	181.5	186.5	192.0	197.7	..
June	141.0	144.7	149.8	153.0	157.5	163.4	165.6	171.1	174.4	176.2	181.3	186.8	192.2	198.5	..
July	140.7	144.0	149.1	152.4	157.5	163.0	165.1	170.5	173.3	175.9	181.3	186.8	192.2	198.5	..
August	141.3	144.7	149.9	153.1	158.5	163.7	165.5	170.5	174.0	176.4	181.6	187.4	192.6	199.2	..
September	141.9	145.0	150.6	153.8	159.3	164.4	166.2	171.7	174.6	177.6	182.5	188.1	193.1	200.1	..
October	141.8	145.2	149.8	153.8	159.5	164.5	166.5	171.6	174.3	177.9	182.6	188.6	193.3	200.4	..
November	141.6	145.3	149.8	153.9	159.6	164.4	166.7	172.1	173.6	178.2	182.7	189.0	193.6	201.1	..
December	141.9	146.0	150.7	154.4	160.0	164.4	167.3	172.2	173.4	178.5	183.5	189.9	194.1	202.7	..

| | | | | Percentage changes on one year earlier | | | | | | | | | | |
	1994	1995	1996	1997	1998	1999	2000	2001	2002	2003	2004	2005	2006	2007
Tax and Price Index														
January	2.6	3.9	3.2	1.4	2.4	2.3	1.5	2.6	−0.1	3.1	3.4	3.1	2.2	4.2
February	2.5	4.0	3.0	1.3	2.6	2.0	1.9	2.5	−0.4	3.4	3.3	3.1	2.3	4.6
March	2.5	4.0	3.0	1.1	2.6	1.9	2.2	2.1	−0.1	3.4	3.3	3.1	2.1	4.9
April	3.0	3.7	1.0	1.5	4.1	1.0	3.0	0.4	1.5	4.0	2.4	3.1	2.4	..
May	3.0	3.8	0.7	1.7	4.3	0.7	3.0	0.7	1.1	3.8	2.7	2.8	2.9	..
June	3.1	4.0	0.6	2.0	3.8	0.8	3.3	0.6	1.0	3.7	3.0	2.8	3.2	..
July	2.8	3.9	0.8	2.5	3.5	0.7	3.3	0.3	1.5	3.9	3.0	2.8	3.2	..
August	2.8	4.1	0.6	2.7	3.3	0.5	3.0	0.7	1.3	3.8	3.1	2.6	3.4	..
September	2.6	4.3	0.7	2.7	3.1	0.5	3.3	0.3	1.8	3.5	3.0	2.5	3.6	..
October	2.9	3.5	1.3	2.9	3.1	0.7	3.0	0.2	2.2	3.4	3.2	2.3	3.6	..
November	3.1	3.4	1.3	2.9	2.9	0.9	3.2	−0.6	2.8	3.3	3.4	2.3	3.8	..
December	3.4	3.6	1.1	2.8	2.6	1.3	2.9	−0.8	3.1	3.6	3.5	2.0	4.4	..
Retail Prices Index														
January	2.5	3.3	2.9	2.8	3.3	2.4	2.0	2.7	1.3	2.9	2.6	3.2	2.4	4.2
February	2.4	3.4	2.7	2.7	3.4	2.1	2.3	2.7	1.0	3.2	2.5	3.2	2.4	4.6
March	2.3	3.5	2.7	2.6	3.5	2.1	2.6	2.3	1.3	3.1	2.6	3.2	2.4	4.8
April	2.6	3.3	2.4	2.4	4.0	1.6	3.0	1.8	1.5	3.1	2.5	3.2	2.6	..
May	2.6	3.4	2.2	2.6	4.2	1.3	3.1	2.1	1.1	3.0	2.8	2.9	3.0	..
June	2.6	3.5	2.1	2.9	3.7	1.3	3.3	1.9	1.0	2.9	3.0	2.9	3.3	..
July	2.3	3.5	2.2	3.3	3.5	1.3	3.3	1.6	1.5	3.1	3.0	2.9	3.3	..
August	2.4	3.6	2.1	3.5	3.3	1.1	3.0	2.1	1.4	2.9	3.2	2.8	3.4	..
September	2.2	3.9	2.1	3.6	3.2	1.1	3.3	1.7	1.7	2.8	3.1	2.7	3.6	..
October	2.4	3.2	2.7	3.7	3.1	1.2	3.1	1.6	2.1	2.6	3.3	2.5	3.7	..
November	2.6	3.1	2.7	3.7	3.0	1.4	3.2	0.9	2.6	2.5	3.4	2.4	3.9	..
December	2.9	3.2	2.5	3.6	2.8	1.8	2.9	0.7	2.9	2.8	3.5	2.2	4.4	..

Note: For further information on the TPI refer to the *Annual Supplement* in the January edition of *Monthly Digest*.

Source: Office for National Statistics: 020 7533 5874

18.9 Index numbers of producer prices

2000=100[1]

	Materials and fuels purchased (input prices) SIC 1992						
	Materials & fuel purchased by manu-facturing industry[5]	Materials	Fuel[5]	Materials & fuel purchased by manufacturing industry (SA)[5]	Materials & fuel purchased by manu-facturing ind. except food, beverages, tobacco & petrol (NSA)[5]	Materials & fuel purchased by manu-facturing ind. except food, beverages, tobacco & petrol (SA)[5]	Materials purchased by manufacturing industry, other than food, drink and tobacco
1992 SIC							
	D				D excl DA/DF		DA
	RNNK	PLKX	RNNL	RNPE	RNNQ	RNPF	RWCJ
2000	100.0	100.0	100.0	100.0	100.0	100.0	100.0
2001	98.8	98.1	107.1	98.8	98.7	98.7	98.1
2002	94.4	93.7	103.4	94.4	94.0	94.0	93.2
2003	95.7	95.2	102.1	95.7	93.7	93.7	93.0
2004	99.5	98.7	109.9	99.5	95.4	95.4	94.2
2005	111.1	108.1	152.1	111.1	103.0	103.0	98.9
2006	121.8	116.1	198.7	121.7†	111.1	111.1†	103.8
2003 Oct	96.3	95.7	103.8	96.9	93.8	94.1	93.0
Nov	96.8	95.7	112.0	96.8	94.5	94.0	93.1
Dec	97.0	95.7	114.3	96.7	94.5	93.5	92.8
2004 Jan	95.6	94.2	114.0	95.4	93.3	92.8	91.6
Feb	95.2	93.8	112.1	94.8	92.8	92.3	91.2
Mar	97.2	96.4	107.7	96.5	93.9	93.4	92.8
Apr	97.3	97.0	101.3	97.2	94.0	93.8	93.4
May	99.6	99.6	99.8	100.2	94.7	94.8	94.3
Jun	97.7	97.6	99.3	98.3	94.0	94.8	93.5
Jul	98.7	98.7	98.3	98.5	94.4	94.9	94.1
Aug	100.8	101.0	98.7	100.3	95.3	96.2	95.0
Sep	102.5	102.2	106.5	103.1	96.9	97.8	96.1
Oct	105.0	104.1	117.0	105.8	98.2	98.6	96.6
Nov	103.4	101.5	128.6	103.3	99.1	98.3	96.6
Dec	101.3	98.7	135.8	101.0	98.5	97.4	95.4
2005 Jan	104.9	102.4	139.2	104.6	100.4	99.8	97.2
Feb	105.5	103.0	140.3	105.2	100.5	99.9	97.2
Mar	107.9	105.7	138.2	107.2	101.0	100.3	97.9
Apr	107.1	105.2	132.7	106.9	100.6	100.4	97.9
May	107.0	105.2	131.7	107.8	100.9	101.0	98.3
Jun	109.3	107.5	133.2	110.1	100.8	101.8	98.1
Jul	112.7	110.9	137.3	112.2	102.5	103.1	99.6
Aug	113.9	112.0	140.1	113.1	102.3	103.4	99.2
Sep	113.2	111.3	138.4	113.9	102.2	103.4	99.3
Oct	114.4	111.1	159.5	115.2	105.1	105.5	100.5
Nov	117.5	111.1	204.8	117.4	108.8	107.7	100.7
Dec	119.6	111.5	229.3	119.1	110.5	109.2	100.6
2006 Jan	121.4	113.7	225.7	121.1	110.8	110.1	101.2
Feb	121.3	114.0	219.9	121.4	111.2	110.6	102.1
Mar	121.7	115.1	211.7	121.0†	111.1	110.4†	102.7
Apr	123.4	118.3	191.9	123.2	110.5	110.4	103.7
May	121.5	117.1	181.0	122.5	109.5	109.7	103.5
Jun	121.4	117.5	174.9	122.3	109.5	110.7	103.9
Jul	124.7	120.5	181.7	124.0	111.0	111.6	105.1
Aug	123.0	118.6	181.8	122.2	110.2	111.5	104.2
Sep	119.1	114.8	176.5	119.7	109.6	110.6	103.9
Oct	119.7	114.0	196.8	120.6	111.7	111.9	104.6
Nov	121.8	114.5	219.5	121.3	114.3	112.8	105.5
Dec	122.6	115.1	223.2	121.6	114.1	112.4	104.9p
2007 Jan	118.8†	112.0†	210.4†	118.5	112.6	111.9	104.3p
Feb	119.8p	113.4p	206.1p	120.3p	112.6p	112.1p	104.8p†
Mar	122.5p	116.4p	204.1p	121.8p	113.8p	113.1p	106.2p

18.9 Index numbers of producer prices

continued

2000=100[1]

					Materials and fuel purchased by selected sub-sections of manufacturing industry						
	Textiles	Leather	Wood and wood products	Pulp, paper and paper products	Coke, refined petroleum products and nuclear fuel	Chemicals and chemical products	Rubber products	Plastic products	Other non-metallic mineral products	Manufacture of basic metals	Machinery and equipment not elsewhere classified
1992 SIC											
	DB	DC	DD	DE	DF	DG	DH	DH	DI	DJ	DK
	RBBR	RBBS	RBBT	RABL	RAUW	RBBW	RAZZ	RBAC	RBBY	RBBZ	RBCA
2000	100.0	100.0	100.0	100.0	100.0	100.0	100.0	100.0	100.0	100.0	100.0
2001	100.5	101.9	99.2	100.7	92.0	101.1	100.4	98.8	100.5	98.5	98.9
2002	98.4	100.0	96.5	97.5	89.3	99.4	98.8	97.4	99.6	96.6	97.1
2003	99.2	101.1	96.8	96.5	95.4	103.0	101.8	99.1	100.7	99.8	97.8
2004	99.6	102.0	99.5	96.9	109.1	105.5	105.5	102.0	103.0	111.8	102.4
2005	103.3	105.7	104.1	100.7	150.9	114.4	113.2	110.4	111.8	123.0	109.3
2006	106.4	109.5	109.2	106.5	175.6	120.6	120.0	115.6	120.0	137.3	116.7
2003 Oct	98.9	101.4	97.0	96.3	95.0	103.5	102.4	99.2	101.0	100.8	98.1
Nov	99.2	101.5	97.5	96.8	92.5	104.0	103.2	99.6	101.8	102.0	98.6
Dec	99.2	101.6	97.3	96.7	93.0	104.2	103.7	99.9	101.5	102.8	98.8
2004 Jan	98.9	100.8	98.1	96.1	89.8	103.0	103.3	99.3	101.3	104.4	98.9
Feb	98.7	100.4	97.8	95.7	90.1	102.8	103.4	99.6	100.9	105.7	99.1
Mar	98.9	101.0	98.1	96.2	97.7	103.1	103.9	99.9	101.4	107.9	100.0
Apr	98.8	101.2	98.2	96.3	97.6	102.7	103.8	99.9	101.3	109.0	100.8
May	98.9	101.4	98.8	96.6	110.7	104.0	104.1	100.3	101.7	108.9	101.3
Jun	98.5	101.3	99.2	96.4	102.6	104.0	104.1	100.4	101.9	108.6	101.2
Jul	98.8	101.4	100.0	96.4	107.8	105.1	104.8	100.9	102.0	111.7	102.5
Aug	99.5	101.9	100.2	96.6	121.2	106.2	105.3	101.5	102.4	113.7	103.2
Sep	100.1	102.8	100.6	97.3	124.3	107.6	106.3	102.7	103.6	115.0	104.1
Oct	101.1	103.5	100.8	97.8	137.6	108.6	107.9	105.2	105.2	118.6	105.4
Nov	101.6	104.1	101.2	98.4	121.5	109.6	109.1	106.6	106.8	119.7	106.1
Dec	101.3	104.2	101.4	98.5	108.3	109.7	109.7	107.8	106.9	118.3	106.0
2005 Jan	102.3	104.9	102.0	99.4	120.9	112.0	111.5	108.9	108.8	120.5	107.6
Feb	102.3	104.9	102.1	99.6	124.8	112.6	111.8	109.3	109.0	121.1	107.7
Mar	102.4	105.1	102.2	99.6	138.8	113.3	112.0	109.4	109.5	121.5	107.9
Apr	102.1	104.9	103.1	99.3	137.8	112.7	111.6	109.1	109.7	122.7	108.3
May	102.1	105.1	103.1	99.1	133.1	112.9	111.7	109.1	109.7	121.5	108.3
Jun	101.9	104.7	103.2	99.2	149.6	112.4	110.8	108.0	109.2	120.8	108.6
Jul	103.0	105.4	103.8	100.0	164.5	113.4	112.0	108.3	110.8	122.0	109.4
Aug	103.0	105.3	103.7	99.7	175.9	113.7	112.5	109.8	111.0	122.5	109.2
Sep	103.1	105.7	104.2	100.0	172.9	113.8	112.9	110.3	110.6	123.2	109.2
Oct	104.3	106.3	106.2	101.6	165.9	116.1	114.9	112.9	113.0	123.9	110.4
Nov	106.4	107.8	107.4	104.6	162.0	119.1	118.0	114.9	118.7	127.1	111.9
Dec	107.2	108.6	108.1	106.2	164.1	120.5	119.2	115.1	121.8	129.0	112.8
2006 Jan	107.2	108.5	108.5	106.9	176.4	121.2	119.2	114.9	122.3	130.0	113.4
Feb	107.1	108.5	108.5	107.5	172.9	121.5	119.3	115.0	122.4	131.1	113.9
Mar	107.0	108.5	108.3	107.2	176.1	121.4	119.6	115.1	121.8	132.0	114.3
Apr	106.4	108.9	108.2	106.2	191.5	120.7	119.3	115.1	119.7	134.4	115.1
May	105.3	108.6	107.8	105.1	184.9	119.5	118.7	114.4	117.8	136.1	115.7
Jun	105.4	109.3	108.1	104.9	182.7	119.6	119.0	114.8	117.3	136.8	116.3
Jul	106.0	110.0	108.7	105.8	196.5	120.7	119.9	115.6	118.8	139.4	117.8
Aug	105.8	109.9	108.8	105.6	190.2	120.6	119.5	115.6	118.2	139.0	117.8
Sep	105.6	109.7	109.3	105.4	164.1	119.5	119.8	115.5	117.5	139.7	117.9
Oct	106.4	110.2	110.5	106.8	156.9	120.1	120.8	116.4	119.7	142.3	119.0
Nov	107.4	111.0	111.6	108.1	154.7	121.2	122.2	117.3	122.2	144.0	120.0
Dec	107.4	111.3	111.7	108.2	160.5p	121.3	122.1	117.0p	122.5	143.2	119.7
2007 Jan	106.8	110.4	112.7	107.8	143.9p	120.4[†]	121.3p[†]	116.5p	121.8[†]	142.3	119.3
Feb	107.0p[†]	110.7p	113.5p	108.1p[†]	149.6p[†]	120.3p	121.4p	116.7p	121.9p	143.3p[†]	119.7p[†]
Mar	107.8p	111.3p	113.9p	108.5p	160.4p	121.0p	122.1p	117.4p	122.7p	146.2p	120.8p

18.9 Index numbers of producer prices
continued

2000=100[1]

	Materials and fuel				Products of manufacturing industries except food, beverages, tobacco & petroleum manufacturing (NSA)	Products of manufacturing industries except food, beverages, tobacco & petroleum manufacturing (SA)	Products of the food, beverages and tobacco manufacturing industries	Quarterly construction output price index[2]	Monthly index of average price of new dwellings - at mortgage completion stage[3]
	Electrical and optical equipment	Transport equipment	Manufact-uring not elsewhere classified	Output of manufactured products					
1992 SIC									
	DL	DM	DN	F	Part of F	2 to 4			
	RBCB	RBCC	RBCD	PLLU	PLLV	PLLW	POKH	JYYC	FCBA
2000	100.0	100.0	100.0	100.0	100.0	100.0	100.0	120	84.6
2001	97.2	99.1	99.1	99.7	99.4	99.4	101.9	124	90.3
2002	92.5	97.3	97.8	99.8	99.3	99.3	103.3	128	108.7
2003	88.8	98.1	99.9	101.3	100.6	100.6	104.6	133	126.4
2004	87.7	100.1	104.4	103.8	102.5	102.5	106.9	143	138.6
2005	90.1	105.3	109.9	106.7	104.7	104.7	108.4	150	147.6
2006	93.9	110.4	116.4	109.3	107.1	107.1	110.7	155	156.5
2003 Oct	88.0	98.4	100.4	101.6	100.8	100.8	105.1	..	132.6
Nov	88.1	98.6	100.9	101.7	100.9	101.0	105.5	..	128.8
Dec	87.6	98.7	101.1	101.9	101.2	101.2	105.7	138	132.0
2004 Jan	86.7	98.4	101.5	102.1	101.4	101.4	105.9	..	131.5
Feb	86.3	98.1	101.7	102.3	101.6	101.6	106.1	..	129.4
Mar	87.1	98.8	102.6	102.8	101.9	101.8	106.4	139	131.6
Apr	87.3	99.1	102.9	103.1	101.8	101.7	106.9	..	135.9
May	87.6	99.5	103.3	103.5	101.9	101.9	107.3	..	136.7
Jun	87.2	99.3	103.3	103.6	101.8	102.0	107.5	141	140.9
Jul	87.2	99.8	104.4	103.8	102.3	102.4	107.6	..	142.5
Aug	87.6	100.3	105.3	104.2	102.9	102.9	106.8	..	142.3
Sep	88.8	101.2	105.9	104.5	103.2	103.1	107.1	144	144.5
Oct	89.0	102.1	107.2	105.2	103.7	103.7	107.0	..	144.4
Nov	89.0	102.6	107.7	105.3	103.9	103.9	107.0	..	143.0
Dec	88.3	102.5	107.2	104.9	103.6	103.7	107.2	147	140.4
2005 Jan	89.2	104.1	108.5	104.8	104.0	103.9	107.3	..	143.9
Feb	88.9	104.2	108.6	105.1	104.1	104.1	107.7	..	144.0
Mar	89.0	104.3	108.9	105.8	104.3	104.2	108.0	148	147.4
Apr	88.9	104.4	109.3	106.5	104.5	104.3	108.3	..	144.6
May	89.2	104.7	108.9	106.3	104.4	104.4	108.3	..	146.9
Jun	89.6	104.5	108.6	106.2	104.0	104.3	108.2	149	148.0
Jul	90.5	105.5	109.5	107.0	104.6	104.7	108.5	..	149.7
Aug	90.1	105.4	109.7	107.3	104.9	104.9	108.4	..	148.8
Sep	90.1	105.4	110.2	108.0	105.4	105.3	108.7	151	148.5
Oct	91.2	106.3	111.0	107.9	105.1	105.1	108.5	..	151.1
Nov	92.1	107.3	112.2	107.7	105.3	105.3	109.2	..	146.9
Dec	92.5	107.9	112.9	107.4	105.4	105.5	109.2	151	150.9
2006 Jan	92.8	108.3	113.4	107.8	105.8	105.8	109.2	..	155.5
Feb	93.1	108.7	113.9	108.1	106.0	106.0	109.2	..	150.9
Mar	93.2	109.0	114.3	108.4	106.3	106.2	109.4	153	156.1
Apr	93.2	109.5	115.3	109.2	106.9	106.7	109.6	..	153.7
May	92.8	109.6	115.5	109.6	106.9	107.0	110.3	..	156.3
Jun	93.4	110.0	116.0	109.8	107.1	107.3	110.7	154	156.0
Jul	94.1	111.1	117.2	110.1	107.2	107.3	111.1	..	154.9
Aug	93.3	110.8	117.0	110.2	107.3	107.3	111.4	..	156.1
Sep	93.4	110.7	117.5	110.0	107.6	107.5	111.5	156	158.5
Oct	94.8	111.6	118.6	109.6	107.8	107.8	111.6	..	156.0
Nov	96.4	112.8	119.4	109.6	107.9	108.0	112.0	..	159.1
Dec	95.8	112.6	119.1	109.8	107.9	108.2	112.5	157	164.3
2007 Jan	95.2[†]	112.4[†]	119.3[†]	110.2	108.4[†]	108.5[†]	113.2	..	164.5
Feb	95.2p	112.7p	120.0p	110.6p[†]	108.9p	108.9p	113.8p[†]	..	167.7
Mar	95.4p	113.7p	121.3p	111.3p	109.4p	109.3p	114.4p	..	..

18.9 Index numbers of producer prices
continued

	Output of selected sub-sections of industry											
	Textiles and textile products[4]	Leather and leather products	Wood and wood products[4]	Pulp, paper and paper products; publishing and printing	Chemicals & chemical products; man-made fibres	Rubber and plastic products	Other non-metallic mineral products	Basic metals and fabricated metal products	Machinery and equipment not elsewhere classified[4]	Electrical and optical equipment	Transport equipment	Furniture and other manufactured goods n.e.s.
1992 SIC												
	DB	DC	DD	DE	DG(part)	DH	DI	DJ	DK	DL	DM	DN
	POKI	POKJ	POKK	POKL	POKN	POKO	POKP	POKQ	POKR	POKS	POKT	POLS
2000	100.0	100.0	100.0	100.0	100.0	100.0	100.0	100.0	100.0	100.0	100.0	100.0
2001	99.2	102.5	99.9	101.5	100.2	100.3	101.9	99.9	100.9	94.7	98.4	100.3
2002	98.8	102.7	100.0	102.1	100.5	100.4	105.0	99.5	101.8	90.0	98.8	100.9
2003	98.7	102.9	101.8	104.0	103.9	100.5	107.8	101.3	101.9	87.5	99.2	103.8
2004	98.5	102.9	105.2	106.0	106.7	101.5	109.6	108.8	103.3	86.6	100.3	104.4
2005	100.0	104.5	110.0	108.6	111.5	106.3	113.9	118.4	106.5	85.9	102.4	104.5
2006	101.2	106.5	113.0	110.7	115.8	109.8	118.3	125.4	109.2	86.8	103.9	105.7
2003 Oct	98.7	103.3	103.4	104.4	103.7	100.4	107.6	101.8	102.2	87.1	99.5	104.4
Nov	98.7	103.4	103.5	104.4	103.8	100.2	107.7	102.1	102.2	87.3	99.5	104.2
Dec	98.6	102.7	103.4	104.4	104.4	100.5	107.5	102.2	102.1	87.2	99.4	105.1
2004 Jan	98.5	102.9	103.3	104.9	104.7	100.9	107.7	103.0	102.3	86.9	99.4	105.0
Feb	98.4	102.3	103.6	105.0	104.9	101.0	108.2	103.5	102.3	86.7	99.6	104.7
Mar	98.3	102.2	103.4	105.0	105.4	100.9	109.2	104.3	102.5	86.4	99.9	104.5
Apr	98.3	101.9	103.8	105.1	105.4	101.0	109.4	105.6	102.5	86.4	100.1	104.4
May	98.3	101.9	104.7	105.3	105.7	101.0	109.6	106.5	103.1	86.4	100.1	104.4
Jun	98.3	102.5	105.0	105.4	106.2	101.1	109.7	107.9	102.9	86.4	100.0	104.7
Jul	98.4	102.8	106.1	105.7	106.5	101.2	110.2	110.3	103.0	86.5	100.2	104.6
Aug	98.5	103.2	106.4	106.9	107.0	101.4	110.2	111.0	103.5	86.4	100.4	104.1
Sep	98.6	104.2	106.7	107.1	107.5	101.6	110.2	111.8	103.8	86.8	100.8	103.8
Oct	98.7	103.6	106.2	107.3	108.4	102.1	110.1	113.5	104.9	86.6	101.1	104.1
Nov	98.7	103.8	106.5	107.5	109.1	102.5	110.5	114.0	104.3	86.7	101.0	104.2
Dec	98.8	103.7	106.7	107.4	109.8	103.7	110.4	114.7	104.4	86.7	101.1	104.2
2005 Jan	98.9	103.8	107.2	107.8	110.4	104.6	111.8	116.9	104.9	86.7	101.5	104.3
Feb	99.5	104.4	107.9	108.2	110.7	105.0	112.2	117.4	105.1	85.7	101.9	103.8
Mar	99.7	104.4	108.1	108.3	110.6	105.2	113.0	117.4	105.5	85.8	102.0	104.7
Apr	100.0	104.4	109.6	108.2	111.0	105.4	114.3	118.3	105.8	85.7	101.9	104.5
May	100.0	104.6	110.5	108.3	111.0	105.8	114.2	118.4	106.0	85.9	102.1	103.9
Jun	100.0	104.7	110.6	108.6	110.7	105.9	115.0	118.5	106.3	86.1	102.1	104.1
Jul	100.2	104.5	110.9	108.8	111.2	106.5	114.7	118.5	107.0	86.2	102.5	104.3
Aug	100.0	104.4	110.7	108.9	111.4	106.7	114.4	118.4	107.0	86.0	102.6	104.4
Sep	100.1	104.8	110.9	108.9	111.9	107.1	114.1	118.5	107.4	85.6	102.7	104.5
Oct	100.2	104.8	111.2	109.0	112.5	107.5	114.2	118.8	107.7	85.7	103.0	104.7
Nov	100.3	104.8	111.1	109.1	113.4	108.0	114.4	119.4	107.8	85.6	103.0	105.0
Dec	100.5	105.0	111.3	109.3	113.8	108.5	114.1	119.8	107.9	85.8	103.1	105.2
2006 Jan	100.7	106.0	111.5	109.6	114.9	108.8	115.8	120.6	108.1	86.3	103.3	105.0
Feb	100.6	106.1	111.4	110.1	114.5	109.2	116.3	121.1	108.3	86.3	103.4	105.3
Mar	100.8	106.2	111.6	110.3	114.7	109.4	117.6	121.6	108.5	86.4	103.7	105.4
Apr	101.0	106.8	112.0	110.4	116.0	109.4	118.0	122.9	108.8	86.3	103.6	105.6
May	101.1	106.3	112.0	110.5	115.9	109.4	118.1	124.4	109.0	86.3	103.4	106.0
Jun	101.1	106.3	112.3	110.5	115.9	109.6	118.0	124.9	109.2	87.2	103.5	105.1
Jul	101.2	106.5	112.7	110.5	115.7	109.9	118.4	126.6	109.5	87.3	103.7	105.3
Aug	101.4	106.3	113.0	110.8	116.0	110.0	118.7	127.7	109.4	87.5	103.6	105.8
Sep	101.4	106.2	113.9	111.1	116.6	110.2	119.1	128.1	109.7	87.2	104.1	106.0
Oct	101.6	107.0	114.7[†]	111.6	116.3	110.6	119.5	129.0	109.7	87.1	104.6	106.2
Nov	101.5	107.0	115.4[†]	111.5	116.5	110.3	119.9	129.4	109.9	86.9	104.7	106.4
Dec	101.6	107.0	115.8	111.4p	116.5	110.3	119.8[†]	129.0	110.0	86.8	104.8	106.3
2007 Jan	101.8	106.6	117.5	111.8p[†]	116.8	110.4	123.0	129.7p[†]	110.8	86.6[†]	105.0	106.7[†]
Feb	102.0p[†]	107.1p	119.7p	112.1p	116.9p[†]	110.4p	124.1p	130.3p	111.0p	86.5p	105.2p	106.9p
Mar	102.3p	107.2p	120.7p	112.3p	116.4p	110.7p	125.2p	131.0p	111.4p	86.5p	105.5p	107.3p

1 This month's edition contains data rebased onto 2000=100. For information the rebased back data for the headline PPI series is available under related links at www.statistics.gov.uk/ppi

2 A base weighted (1995=100) combination of the separate price indices for contractors' output in the six new work sectors. For a fuller description see *Economic Trends* No 297.

3 From February 2002, data are based on a significantly enlarged return from the Survey of Mortgage Lenders, and are calculated through improved methodology. Annual and quarterly data prior to February 2002 are from the 5% Survey of Mortgage Lenders, and have been rebased to Feb 2002=100.

4 Indicates values which are considered less reliable than the remainder currently published mainly due to the lack of market coverage.

5 The Climate Change Levy was introduced in April 2001. Further information on PPI is available from the National Statistics Website: www.statistics.gov.uk/ppi.

Sources: Office for National Statistics: Tel 01633 812106; DTI (JYYC): 020 7215 1953; DCLG (FCBA): 020 7944 3325

Prices and wages

18.10 House Price Index[1]
Analysis by Government Office Regions

Feb 2002 = 100[2]

	United Kingdom	North East	North West	Yorkshire and the Humber	East Midlands	West Midlands	East	London	South East	South West	England	Wales	Scotland	Northern Ireland
	WLPE	WLPF	WLPG	WLPH	WLPI	WLPK	WLPL	WLPM	WLPN	WLPT	WLPU	WLPV	WLPX	WLPY
2005 Jan	148.9	182.7	173.5	169.8	170.2	158.3	142.4	129.6	137.7	153.7	147.5	178.4	159.9	144.1
Feb	148.1	182.2	170.3	171.9	167.5	159.5	142.8	130.5	135.5	152.5	146.9	178.2	157.1	138.1
Mar	151.3	189.9	176.7	174.7	169.4	163.7	144.4	133.0	139.2	153.6	150.0	180.7	162.1	143.5
Apr	150.1	185.6	176.2	175.2	167.7	162.8	141.9	131.2	137.4	151.8	148.4	181.4	166.8	142.4
May	150.8	189.1	177.5	179.7	168.8	162.2	142.0	131.7	136.8	151.1	148.8	185.9	169.6	144.7
Jun	152.0	192.6	180.3	180.4	170.0	162.8	143.4	133.5	137.5	150.9	150.0	183.3	173.4	146.3
Jul	153.7	194.2	181.4	180.4	170.3	166.4	145.0	134.6	139.5	153.1	151.6	186.0	174.4	154.6
Aug	153.7	194.9	182.1	185.2	171.2	165.2	144.1	134.0	138.9	153.0	151.5	188.7	175.0	152.9
Sep[3]	154.0	192.7	182.4	183.6	171.8	164.3	145.0	134.3	140.2	153.1	151.8	186.2	175.1	158.0
Oct	152.7	196.2	181.4	184.9	171.3	163.1	142.2	131.7	138.4	152.5	150.4	188.9	173.6	154.8
Nov	153.4	195.1	181.8	182.2	170.7	164.9	144.2	133.5	138.7	153.9	151.2	186.6	173.4	158.1
Dec	153.3	197.0	183.6	184.9	170.2	164.4	142.8	133.7	137.7	153.3	151.1	187.7	174.0	158.4
2006 Jan	155.1	196.1	181.1	185.2	171.0	165.8	145.6	136.1	140.9	154.6	152.8	188.7	176.3	161.2
Feb	153.2	194.6	183.4	186.1	170.9	164.6	141.3	132.5	138.0	154.2	150.8	189.0	174.9	160.1
Mar	156.2	197.5	185.0	188.0	172.0	165.7	145.1	138.4	140.1	156.3	153.8	190.2	179.5	163.7
Apr	157.6	199.5	187.5	190.2	172.2	166.0	146.3	140.0	141.2	157.2	155.1	192.6	179.7	167.3
May	159.3	203.7	188.5	190.6	173.1	168.2	147.6	141.0	143.0	159.1	156.6	194.8	186.1	170.7
Jun	160.0	203.4	189.4	192.5	173.4	170.1	147.5	140.8	143.6	158.9	157.0	198.7	188.8	174.1
Jul	162.7	205.4	192.8	195.2	177.1	171.4	150.8	144.1	145.6	160.6	159.6	199.5	190.8	186.5
Aug	165.0	208.4	194.8	198.8	178.4	174.2	153.0	144.1	148.2	163.5	161.5	202.0	197.3	193.6
Sep	166.3	207.9	196.6	199.9	180.5	175.9	153.4	146.4	148.5	165.2	162.8	205.3	197.7	195.3
Oct	165.6	208.7	195.0	199.9	180.8	173.9	152.2	145.4	147.6	165.0	162.0	201.7	197.1	205.6
Nov	166.9	207.7	197.2	200.3	179.6	176.2	153.6	146.7	148.6	165.9	163.0	205.6	196.6	216.9
Dec	168.5	213.7	197.3	203.2	180.6	177.2	154.4	149.5	149.7	165.2	164.4	204.7	200.5	221.6
2007 Jan	172.0	212.1	201.3	204.9	184.0	178.5	157.7	154.1	153.1	169.6	167.9	207.9	204.3	229.7
Feb	171.7	212.9	198.7	202.6	182.6	177.6	158.3	154.6	153.0	168.8	167.4	209.9	203.9	236.2

Percentage change on a year earlier

	United Kingdom	North East	North West	Yorkshire and the Humber	East Midlands	West Midlands	East	London	South East	South West	England	Wales	Scotland	Northern Ireland
	WLPZ	WLQA	WLQB	WLQG	WLQH	WLQI	WLQJ	WLQK	WLQL	WLQX	WLQY	WLRE	WLRF	WLRK
2006 Jan	4.1	7.3	4.4	9.0	0.5	4.8	2.2	5.0	2.3	0.6	3.5	5.8	10.2	11.9
Feb	3.4	6.8	7.7	8.3	2.0	3.2	−1.0	1.5	1.8	1.1	2.6	6.1	11.3	15.9
Mar	3.3	4.0	4.7	7.6	1.5	1.2	0.5	4.0	0.6	1.7	2.5	5.3	10.8	14.1
Apr	5.0	7.5	6.5	8.6	2.7	2.0	3.0	6.7	2.8	3.6	4.5	6.1	7.7	17.4
May	5.7	7.7	6.2	6.0	2.5	3.7	3.9	7.1	4.5	5.3	5.2	4.8	9.7	17.9
Jun	5.3	5.6	5.1	6.7	2.0	4.4	2.9	5.5	4.5	5.3	4.6	8.5	8.9	19.1
Jul	5.9	5.8	6.3	8.2	4.0	3.0	4.0	7.0	4.4	4.9	5.3	7.3	9.4	20.6
Aug	7.4	7.0	7.0	7.3	4.2	5.5	6.2	7.6	6.7	6.9	6.6	7.0	12.7	26.6
Sep	8.0	7.9	7.8	8.9	5.1	7.1	5.8	9.0	5.9	7.9	7.2	10.3	12.9	23.6
Oct	8.5	6.4	7.5	8.1	5.5	6.6	7.0	10.4	6.7	8.1	7.7	6.8	13.6	32.9
Nov	8.8	6.5	8.4	9.9	5.2	6.8	6.5	9.9	7.1	7.8	7.8	10.2	13.4	37.2
Dec	9.9	8.4	7.4	9.9	6.1	7.8	8.1	11.8	8.7	7.7	8.9	9.1	15.2	39.9
2007 Jan	10.9	8.2	11.1	10.7	7.6	7.6	8.3	13.2	8.7	9.7	9.9	10.2	15.9	42.5
Feb	12.1	9.4	8.3	8.9	6.8	7.9	12.0	16.7	10.8	9.5	11.0	11.1	16.6	47.5

1 Series based on prices at the mortgage completion stage collected through the Survey of Mortgage Lenders. The index takes into account the mix of properties sold.
2 The series starts at February 2002 rather than January 2002 because the required volume of completions was achieved from that date only.
3 From September 2005 the index is based on the new Regulated Mortgage Survey (CML/BankSearch).

Source: Department for Communities and Local Government

18.11 Index of purchase prices of the means of agricultural production and of producer prices of agricultural products[1,2,3]

2000=100

		Weights	2005	2006 Jan	2006 Feb	2006 Mar	2006 Apr	2006 May	2006 Jun	2006 Jul	2006 Aug	2006 Sep	2006 Oct	2006 Nov	2006 Dec
Purchase prices[4]															
Goods and services															
currently consumed	BYEA	100.0	115.9	117.3	117.2	117.6	119.8	120.0	120.1	121.7	123.2	121.6	119.8	119.8	121.6
Seeds	BYEB	3.3	108.2	106.1	106.1	106.1	105.6	105.6	103.8	104.9	104.9	104.9	97.7	97.7	109.6
Energy, lubricants	BYED	8.1	137.4	142.6	144.9	150.2	161.3	165.4	159.3	156.0	157.0	143.9	138.3	133.5	137.6
Fertilizer and soil improvers	BYEE	9.1	143.3	151.5	154.6	153.8	154.5	152.5	149.7	149.7	149.1	149.6	150.0	150.7	151.0
Plant protection products	BYEF	7.2	102.9	102.4	103.3	103.8	103.8	102.9	103.2	103.5	103.4	103.1	103.4	103.8	104.2
Animal feedingstuffs	BYEG	26.4	102.9	103.6	103.8	104.8	105.1	105.3	106.7	108.0	106.9	108.9	110.9	113.4	113.4
Maintenance of plant	BYEI	7.9	130.3	135.0	135.3	135.9	136.2	136.7	137.4	138.2	138.4	139.0	139.7	140.8	141.2
Maintenance and repair of buildings	BYEJ	3.6	118.1	119.5	120.6	121.7	122.2	123.4	124.7	126.1	127.3	127.8	128.9	129.6	130.4
Veterinary services	BYEK	3.2	103.9	107.9	107.9	107.9	107.9	108.4	112.0	112.0	112.0	112.0	112.3	111.6	111.4
Other goods and services[5]	BYEL	31.2	114.5	113.2	113.2	113.8	114.9	115.2	115.8	114.8	114.4	114.8	115.6	115.8	116.5
Goods and services contributing to investment in agriculture	BYEM	100.0	108.7	109.6	110.4	111.0	111.1	111.4	111.4	111.7	111.8	112.0	112.8	113.7	113.9
Machinery and other equipment	BYEN	71.5	103.8	105.8	106.7	107.1	107.1	107.8	107.7	107.7	107.7	107.8	109.7	111.9	111.7
Buildings	BYEO	19.5	123.7	126.1	126.9	127.8	128.3	129.4	130.5	131.8	132.9	133.3	134.4	134.9	135.7
Producer prices															
All products	BYEP	100.0	109.8	110.8	111.1	114.3	115.8	113.8	115.8	113.8	117.0	117.4	116.0	118.7	119.4
All crop products	BYEQ	40.2	108.5	111.0	110.9	114.9	116.9	115.8	118.3	117.0	123.0	121.3	118.2	123.3	128.9
Cereals	BYER	13.3	99.1	100.9	102.2	103.3	104.1	106.2	109.0	106.0	105.2	113.9	121.1	124.3	127.8
Industrial crops[6]	AE6A	4.3	113.9	114.8	114.7	114.4	115.5	119.6	121.8	126.3	126.1	121.4	104.8	105.4	107.7
Forage plants	AE6B	1.9	110.4	102.7	101.3	106.5	109.7	111.4	111.4	99.0	93.0	95.6	102.7	105.1	111.7
Fresh vegetables	BYET	7.7	120.1	130.0	128.0	139.0	128.0	113.0	124.4	121.7	140.7	140.0	124.9	136.2	149.4
Fresh fruit	BYEU	1.9	120.1	123.9	119.1	124.5	141.1	143.8	111.8	115.4	128.4	117.4	109.1	117.6	124.5
Potatoes	AE6C	4.5	109.2	118.3	121.2	130.9	142.9	152.2	153.8	131.5	175.3	144.4	129.4	145.1	155.6
Flowers and plants	BYEW	5.9	105.6	109.2	108.7	107.6	107.5	107.3	106.7	106.5	106.7	106.6	110.5	110.2	111.9
Other crop products (including seeds)	BYEX	0.7	110.8	110.1	110.1	110.6	110.6	111.0	110.2	109.3	110.0	110.5	111.3	111.6	112.3
Animals and animal products	BYEY	59.8	110.8	110.7	111.2	113.9	115.2	112.5	113.9	111.7	112.1	114.2	114.6	115.1	114.5
Animals for slaughter	BYEZ	35.3	110.8	109.4	111.4	117.1	120.8	120.2	122.0	116.3	116.5	116.7	114.9	115.3	115.4
Milk	BYFA	20.2	109.0	110.2	108.4	107.0	102.5	99.3	99.4	101.5	104.0	109.0	111.2	112.3	110.5
Eggs	BYFB	3.2	121.1	128.5	128.3	128.0	124.8	123.8	123.8	124.4	125.4	124.2	132.3	132.4	132.4
Other animal products	BYFC	1.1	109.3	111.4	111.1	110.7	106.5	103.2	101.1	101.6	103.5	106.1	107.8	108.7	108.9

1 Index numbers for the years 1983 to 2003 on 1995 = 100 base and also at a more detailed level are available from the Department for Environment Food and Rural Affairs, Room 146, Kings Pool, 1-2 Peasholme Green, YO1 7PX. Tel 01904 455253.

2 The sum of the percentages of categories included in "Goods & Services consumed" and "All Products" do not add to 100% due to the exclusion of some minor categories.

3 All data and weights have been revised to be in line with Eurostat policy that the Agricultural Account and the API should be the same.

4 A revised feedstuffs index has been calculated and incorporated in this edition. Further details are available on request.

5 Formerly General expenses.

6 Primarily including Oilseeds, Linseed and Protein crops.

Source: Department for Environment, Food and Rural Affairs

18.12 Average weekly and hourly earnings and hours of full-time employees on adult rates whose pay for the period was unaffected by absence: United Kingdom
April 2000 to 2006

| | Manufacturing industries[1] | | | | All industries and services | | | |
| | | | Hourly earnings(£) | | | | Hourly earnings(£) | |
	Gross weekly earnings(£)	Total Paid Hours	Including overtime pay and overtime hours	Excluding overtime pay and overtime hours	Gross Weekly earnings(£)	Total Paid Hours	Including overtime pay and overtime hours	Excluding overtime pay and overtime hours
Total								
	C7PU	C7QL	C7PV	C7PW	C7Q5	C7QX	C7Q7	C7Q9
2000	417.2	41.3	10.10	10.00	425.2	39.7	10.71	10.71
2001	439.9	41.3	10.66	10.62	449.8	39.7	11.33	11.36
2002	455.6	41.0	11.12	11.09	472.2	39.6	11.94	11.98
2003	476.5	40.9	11.65	11.62	487.1	39.5	12.32	12.34
2004[2]	485.0	41.0	11.83	11.80	498.2	39.5	12.60	12.63
	493.1		12.03	12.01	506.1		12.80	12.84
2005	508.0	40.6	12.51	12.50	516.5	39.4	13.11	13.15
2006	528.4	40.8	12.96	12.97	537.4	37.5	13.62	13.67
Men								
	C7PX	C7QT	C7PY	C7PZ	C7QA	C7QZ	C7QC	C7QE
2000	445.6	42.0	10.62	10.54	471.8	41.0	11.50	11.53
2001	469.5	41.9	11.21	11.19	498.6	41.0	12.16	12.24
2002	482.9	41.6	11.62	11.62	523.4	40.8	12.83	12.92
2003	503.2	41.5	12.13	12.12	539.3	40.8	13.21	13.28
2004[2]	511.2	41.6	12.30	12.28	548.1	40.8	13.44	13.51
	519.4		12.50	12.49	557.4		13.67	13.76
2005	533.8	41.2	12.97	12.98	568.1	40.6	13.98	14.05
2006	554.9	41.3	13.43	13.46	591.6	40.7	14.54	14.62
Women								
	C7Q2	C7QV	C7Q3	C7Q4	C7QF	C7SA	C7QH	C7QJ
2000	312.1	38.9	8.02	7.97	344.9	37.4	9.22	9.20
2001	332.2	39.0	8.52	8.50	367.1	37.5	9.79	9.79
2002	350.8	38.8	9.04	9.03	386.8	37.5	10.32	10.32
2003	372.8	38.7	9.64	9.62	400.7	37.4	10.71	10.70
2004[2]	380.8	38.7	9.83	9.84	416.8	37.5	11.11	11.12
	388.1		10.02	10.02	422.1		11.26	11.27
2005	404.3	38.4	10.52	10.51	435.7	37.4	11.64	11.65
2006	422.6	38.6	10.94	10.97	453.6	37.6	12.08	12.11

1 Results relate to Division D (SIC) 1992.
2 In 2004 a number of supplementary surveys were introduced to improve the coverage of the Annual Survey of Hours and Earnings. Data for 2004 are presented including these supplementary surveys (top). Figures are also presented excluding supplementary surveys (bottom) to give figures comparable with earlier years.

Source: Office for National Statistics: 01633 819024

18.13 Average weekly and hourly earnings of full-time employees on adult rates by industry division: United Kingdom
April 2003 to 2006

£

Full time employees on adult rates whose pay was unaffected by absence

	Agri-culture, hunting, and forestry	Fishing	Mining and quarrying	Manufact-uring	Electric-ity, gas and water supply	Construc-tion	Wholesale and retail trade; repair of motor vehicles and personal & household goods	Hotels and restau-rants	Trans-port, storage and communic-ation	Financial intermed-iation	Real estate, renting and business activiti-es	Public administ-ration and defence, compulso-ry social security	Education	Health and social work	Other commun-ity, social and personal service activit-ies
SIC 1992 Division	A	B	C	D	E	F	G	H	I	J	K	L	M	N	O

Average gross weekly earnings

Total

	C9EG	C9EI	C9EK	C9EM	C9EO	C9EP	C9EQ	C9ER	C9ES	C9ET	C9EU	C9EV	C9EW	C9EX	C9EY
2003	340.5	392.7	657.0	476.5	561.5	489.8	414.6	311.3	476.3	660.6	568.5	469.9	481.6	446.8	486.8
2004[1]	355.8	415.7	617.1	485.0	579.2	505.1	421.3	319.1	494.4	667.5	573.9	497.6	495.9	478.9	499.5
	362.5	419.0	633.5	493.1	591.9	509.4	433.3	323.8	504.3	696.3	590.6	496.6	493.6	474.9	515.4
2005	364.7	440.6	657.9	508.0	612.2	524.6	425.2	323.5	508.0	701.3	589.3	525.0	518.6	503.2	503.8
2006	386.6	466.8	782.0	528.4	632.7	548.0	447.4	333.4	527.6	720.2	616.6	544.3	533.7	516.7	527.1

Men

	C9F2	C9F4	C9F6	C9F8	C9FA	C9FC	C9FE	C9FO	C9FQ	C9FS	C9FU	C9FW	C9FY	C9G2	C9G4
2003	356.2	391.4	671.2	503.2	595.7	503.8	464.4	351.9	493.5	832.1	636.7	522.5	528.8	581.1	562.2
2004[1]	368.8	426.6	637.1	511.2	607.9	517.8	470.3	345.9	514.0	829.8	635.3	549.0	542.2	624.3	572.8
	375.4	433.2	653.7	519.4	626.1	521.5	483.2	352.5	522.0	869.2	652.5	547.9	539.3	614.8	593.1
2005	381.9	445.7	675.4	533.8	647.3	537.6	469.5	357.2	527.7	872.4	654.9	583.6	568.4	669.5	563.6
2006	402.2	450.4	804.2	554.9	669.1	563.3	493.6	365.3	545.0	881.9	685.5	599.4	586.7	693.0	585.4

Women

	C9G6	C9G8	C9GA	C9GC	C9GE	C9GG	C9GI	C9GK	C9GM	C9HJ	C9HL	C9HN	C9HP	C9HR	C9HT
2003	270.8	–	566.5	372.8	426.0	370.8	321.6	262.2	410.0	463.7	446.4	390.9	445.9	394.0	379.1
2004[1]	290.9	–	496.3	380.8	448.4	392.8	330.9	283.8	423.1	474.1	461.0	420.8	461.8	419.7	398.4
	297.5		511.0	388.1	453.0	403.8	339.3	287.2	439.0	492.5	474.5	418.9	460.2	417.9	405.7
2005	287.6	–	552.5	404.3	490.2	411.5	343.2	282.4	432.8	500.0	472.8	440.2	484.0	440.3	417.9
2006	321.7	–	668.8	422.6	505.9	416.8	363.1	293.8	464.4	526.3	492.7	463.4	498.3	451.1	441.3

Average hourly earnings (excluding overtime)

Total

	C9HV	C9HX	C9HZ	C9I3	C9I5	C9I7	C9IA	C9IC	C9IE	C9IG	C9II	C9IK	C9IM	C9IO	C9IQ
2003	7.44	9.09	14.99	11.62	13.99	11.22	10.26	7.63	11.20	18.32	14.54	11.88	13.55	11.57	12.38
2004[1]	7.87	9.41	14.60	11.80	14.29	11.68	10.44	7.74	11.73	18.44	14.67	12.62	13.96	12.39	12.60
	8.03	9.57	14.97	12.01	14.61	11.81	10.74	7.86	11.99	19.25	15.10	12.57	13.90	12.29	13.02
2005	8.27	10.14	15.56	12.50	15.33	12.15	10.57	7.93	11.89	19.54	15.14	13.28	14.64	12.99	12.65
2006	8.68	11.10	18.86	12.97	15.37	12.66	11.10	8.13	12.57	20.00	15.73	13.80	15.06	13.41	13.29

Men

	C9IS	C9IU	C9IW	C9IY	C9J2	C9J4	C9J6	C9J8	C9JA	C9JC	C9JE	C9JG	C9JI	C9JK	C9JM
2003	7.57	8.95	14.97	12.12	14.70	11.39	11.21	8.40	11.37	23.01	15.99	12.91	14.48	14.73	14.00
2004[1]	7.96	9.26	14.80	12.28	14.82	11.83	11.38	8.23	11.97	22.88	15.94	13.62	14.88	15.82	14.14
	8.11	9.47	15.16	12.49	14.95	11.95	11.71	8.38	12.20	23.99	16.39	13.56	14.79	15.57	14.68
2005	8.46	10.13	15.72	12.98	15.96	12.30	11.42	8.56	12.12	24.19	16.52	14.43	15.64	16.91	13.83
2006	8.86	10.38	19.03	13.46	15.94	12.85	11.99	8.74	12.70	24.37	17.16	14.90	16.14	17.58	14.48

Women

	C9JO	C9JQ	C9JS	C9JU	C9JW	C9JY	C9K2	C9K4	C9K6	C9K8	C9KG	C9KI	C9KK	C9KS	C9KU
2003	6.81	–	15.17	9.62	11.17	9.69	8.38	6.64	10.51	12.88	11.83	10.28	12.83	10.30	9.98
2004[1]	7.38	–	13.31	9.84	12.17	10.25	8.60	7.07	10.80	13.10	12.22	11.07	13.26	10.97	10.39
	7.55		13.73	10.02	11.83	10.55	8.82	7.16	11.22	13.62	12.58	11.01	13.22	10.93	10.60
2005	7.35	–	14.54	10.51	13.13	10.82	8.92	7.12	10.99	14.00	12.59	11.57	13.92	11.49	10.90
2006	7.91	–	17.95	10.97	13.37	10.83	9.40	7.33	12.06	14.69	13.06	12.13	14.32	11.82	11.48

1 In 2004 a number of supplementary surveys were introduced to improve the coverage of the Annual Survey of Hours and Earnings. Data for 2004 are presented including these supplementary surveys (top). Figures are also presented excluding supplementary surveys (bottom) to give figures comparable with earlier years.

Source: Office for National Statistics: 01633 819024

18.14 Average weekly and hourly earnings of full-time employees on adult rates by age group: United Kingdom
April 2001 to 2006

£

	Full time employees on adult rates whose pay was unaffected by absence						
	18-21	22-29	30-39	40-49	50-59	60+	All ages

Average gross weekly earnings

Total

	C7MV	C7MX	C7NG	C7NI	C7NK	C7OW	C7NM
2001	239.4	373.6	483.5	498.7	457.4	..	449.7
2002	247.7	390.8	507.5	523.6	477.2	..	472.1
2003	251.2	396.9	522.1	545.0	489.8	..	487.1
2004[1]	257.6	402.3	531.0	560.1	519.0	442.3	498.2
	260.7	410.2	540.7	567.3			506.1
2005	266.0	411.0	556.3	582.8	544.4	470.4	516.4
2006	273.5	421.4	575.9	610.4	568.9	509.5	537.3

Men

	C7NO	C7NQ	C7NS	C7NU	C7O9	C7OU	C7OB
2001	256.6	401.4	520.6	560.1	510.5	..	498.6
2002	267.1	419.2	545.0	587.9	533.5	..	523.3
2003	266.3	425.0	562.5	612.0	543.4	..	539.3
2004[1]	272.4	426.4	568.8	623.9	580.6	466.6	548.2
	275.3	435.4	580.5	632.2			557.4
2005	278.9	432.8	596.4	651.2	606.8	497.3	568.0
2006	289.0	443.3	615.4	684.5	634.7	539.4	591.6

Women

	C7OD	C7OF	C7OH	C7OJ	C7OL	C7SD	C7ON
2001	219.0	339.5	412.6	389.1	353.1	..	366.9
2002	225.7	356.4	436.1	410.4	371.6	..	386.8
2003	233.6	363.6	447.8	426.5	390.1	..	400.7
2004[1]	240.1	374.2	462.5	447.8	417.9	361.4	416.8
	243.3	380.5	468.4	452.6			422.1
2005	249.8	386.2	486.0	468.8	445.8	390.3	435.6
2006	253.7	397.1	508.7	488.8	465.6	420.0	453.6

Average hourly earnings (excluding overtime)

Total

	C7OP	C7OR	C7OT	C7OV	C7OX	C7PA	C7OZ
2001	5.92	9.45	12.16	12.68	11.53	..	11.35
2002	6.13	9.93	12.83	13.35	12.11	..	11.97
2003	6.25	10.11	13.20	13.84	12.39	..	12.34
2004[1]	6.42	10.22	13.47	14.20	13.24	10.92	12.63
	6.49	10.44	13.73	14.40			12.85
2005	6.62	10.48	14.16	14.85	13.96	11.72	13.14
2006	6.80	10.72	14.67	15.54	14.55	12.70	13.67

Men

	C7P3	C7P5	C7P7	C7P9	C7PB	C7P8	C7PC
2001	6.16	9.83	12.74	13.86	12.50	..	12.24
2002	6.39	10.32	13.45	14.59	13.16	..	12.92
2003	6.40	10.48	13.85	15.12	13.35	..	13.28
2004[1]	6.57	10.48	14.05	15.40	14.38	11.29	13.52
	6.66	10.72	14.36	15.63			13.76
2005	6.75	10.68	14.77	16.13	15.10	12.10	14.05
2006	6.99	10.92	15.26	16.94	15.76	13.15	14.62

Women

	C7PJ	C7PL	C7PN	C7PP	C7PR	C7P6	C7PT
2001	5.63	8.96	10.99	10.47	9.51	..	9.79
2002	5.82	9.43	11.61	11.04	10.01	..	10.32
2003	6.06	9.65	11.95	11.44	10.52	..	10.70
2004[1]	6.22	9.91	12.35	11.97	11.26	9.59	11.12
	6.29	10.09	12.52	12.11			11.27
2005	6.46	10.24	13.02	12.59	12.05	10.48	11.65
2006	6.56	10.50	13.62	13.13	12.55	11.24	12.11

1 In 2004 a number of supplementary surveys were introduced to improve the coverage of the Annual Survey of Hours and Earnings. Data for 2004 are presented including these supplementary surveys (top). Figures are also presented excluding supplementary surveys (bottom) to give figures comparable with earlier years.

Source: Office for National Statistics: 01633 819024

18.15 Average earnings index: by industry (not seasonally adjusted)[1,2]
Great Britain

2000 = 100

Excluding bonuses

	Agriculture, forestry and fishing	Mining and quarrying	Food products, beverages and tobacco	Textiles, leather and clothing	Chemicals and man-made fibres	Basic metals and metal products	Engineering and allied industries (DK, DL,DM)	Other manufacturing (DD,DE,DF, DH,DI,DN)	Electricity, gas and water supply	Construction
SIC 1992	(A,B)	(C)	(DA)	(DB,DC)	(DG)	(DJ)			(E)	(F)
	JVUZ	JVVA	JVVB	JVVC	JVVD	JVVE	JVVF	JVVG	JVVH	JVVI
2005	125.3	123.1	121.9	119.3	120.0	120.9	121.6	120.2	114.1	124.0
2006	134.5	129.1	127.6	122.5	122.8	127.4	126.6	126.5	116.0	127.9
2004 Jul	122.5	116.1	117.8	119.6	119.0	117.3	118.3	116.3	111.4	120.4
Aug	120.5	114.6	118.0	117.2	118.9	116.7	117.5	115.2	110.9	119.7
Sep	123.4	115.9	117.4	118.4	118.1	116.7	117.2	115.9	109.5	120.7
Oct	122.5	127.3	118.1	118.5	120.4	117.6	118.6	116.2	111.3	121.4
Nov	127.2	122.5	119.6	118.5	120.2	117.1	119.0	116.8	110.9	121.9
Dec	128.2	121.3	121.9	119.4	121.2	116.3	119.3	117.2	111.1	122.2
2005 Jan	125.1	120.4	119.4	118.1	120.9	118.5	119.0	116.2	111.2	121.8
Feb	121.5	123.6	118.3	116.1	121.0	119.1	119.5	117.3	111.6	120.4
Mar	124.8	120.4	121.8	118.3	122.0	118.4	120.0	117.5	110.9	121.7
Apr	124.3	123.1	120.7	119.0	118.8	120.9	121.2	118.8	113.4	122.3
May	120.9	123.3	121.8	118.1	118.3	120.0	121.3	119.3	113.4	123.1
Jun	125.9	122.4	120.7	121.0	119.4	121.4	121.3	120.4	115.6	124.4
Jul	122.2	122.1	121.2	119.1	118.5	122.2	122.7	120.3	115.3	125.1
Aug	122.5	122.5	122.0	117.0	119.7	122.2	121.7	121.0	115.2	123.3
Sep	131.7	123.5	122.6	118.9	119.2	123.2	122.5	122.1	113.7	125.7
Oct	130.3	125.2	123.1	121.6	119.4	122.9	123.6	122.3	115.2	126.2
Nov	126.8	125.6	125.2	121.9	121.1	122.1	123.1	122.9	116.1	128.1
Dec	127.6	125.1	126.2	122.4	121.3	120.0	123.6	124.2	117.8	126.4
2006 Jan	129.0	127.4	125.0	122.1	121.3	124.0	123.0	124.1	115.7	126.6
Feb	132.0	124.9	124.3	123.1	121.6	124.5	124.7	124.7	116.3	127.6
Mar	133.0	126.1	125.2	121.4	121.1	125.7	125.2	125.1	115.2	127.0
Apr	141.3	127.6	129.4	122.5	122.1	125.2	126.4	125.2	114.2	126.6
May	140.2	128.1	128.4	123.2	122.0	126.9	126.3	125.9	118.3	127.2
Jun	141.4	128.4	127.8	124.0	123.0	129.5	126.5	126.9	118.2	127.9
Jul	137.2	128.7	128.3	122.8	121.6	128.4	126.4	126.5	118.7	128.2
Aug	139.9	129.0	128.2	120.1	122.5	127.9	126.2	127.1	116.2	126.7
Sep	135.7	131.0	128.1	122.1	124.3	129.3	127.7	127.7	114.6	128.5
Oct	130.3	131.3	128.2	122.0	125.1	129.2	128.8	127.8	113.0	129.5
Nov	123.8	131.7	127.7	122.4	123.9	129.9	129.1	128.8	116.6	130.0
Dec	130.5	134.7	130.0	124.4	125.2	127.9	128.6	128.6	114.9	129.3
2007 Jan	129.5	133.1†	126.7†	124.2†	123.2†	128.0†	129.6	128.7†	114.3	130.6†
Feb	121.7	132.8	124.9	125.6	124.9	129.5	130.8	129.6	115.1	129.7

Percentage change on the year

	JVVT	JVVU	JVVV	JVVW	JVVX	JVVY	JVVZ	JVWA	JVWB	JVWC
2005 Jul	−0.2	5.2	2.9	−0.4	−0.4	4.2	3.8	3.5	3.6	3.9
Aug	1.6	6.9	3.4	−0.2	0.7	4.7	3.6	5.0	3.9	3.1
Sep	6.8	6.5	4.5	0.4	0.9	5.5	4.5	5.3	3.9	4.1
Oct	6.4	−1.7	4.3	2.6	−0.8	4.5	4.2	5.3	3.5	3.9
Nov	−0.3	2.6	4.7	2.8	0.8	4.3	3.5	5.2	4.7	5.1
Dec	−0.4	3.2	3.5	2.5	−	3.2	3.6	6.0	6.0	3.4
2006 Jan	3.1	5.8	4.7	3.3	0.3	4.7	3.4	6.7	4.1	3.9
Feb	8.6	1.0	5.0	6.1	0.6	4.5	4.3	6.4	4.2	6.0
Mar	6.6	4.7	2.8	2.6	−0.7	6.2	4.3	6.5	3.9	4.4
Apr	13.7	3.6	7.2	2.9	2.8	3.6	4.2	5.4	0.7	3.4
May	16.0	4.0	5.5	4.4	3.1	5.8	4.1	5.5	4.4	3.3
Jun	12.3	4.8	5.9	2.5	3.0	6.7	4.2	5.4	2.3	2.8
Jul	12.2	5.5	5.8	3.1	2.6	5.1	3.0	5.1	2.9	2.4
Aug	14.2	5.3	5.1	2.7	2.3	4.7	3.7	5.1	0.8	2.8
Sep	3.0	6.1	4.5	2.7	4.3	5.0	4.2	4.6	0.8	2.2
Oct	−	4.9	4.1	0.4	4.9	5.1	4.3	4.5	−1.9	2.7
Nov	−2.4	4.8	2.0	0.4	2.3	6.4	4.9	4.8	0.4	1.5
Dec	2.2	7.6	3.0	1.6	3.2	6.6	4.0	3.5	−2.4	2.3
2007 Jan	0.4	4.5†	1.3†	1.8†	1.6†	3.3†	5.4†	3.7†	−1.2	3.1†
Feb	−7.8	6.4	0.5	2.0	2.7	4.1	4.9	3.9	−1.0	1.7

18.15
continued

Average earnings index: by industry (not seasonally adjusted)[1,2]
Great Britain

2000 = 100

	Wholesale trade	Retail trade and repairs	Hotels and restaurants	Transport, storage and communication	Financial interm-ediation	Real estate renting and business activities	Public admini-stration	Education	Health and social work	Other services
Excluding bonuses										
SIC 1992	(G:51)	(G:50,52)	(H)	(I)	(J)	(K)	(L)	(M)	(N)	(O)
	JVVJ	JVVK	JVVL	JVVM	JVVN	JVVO	JVVP	JVVQ	JVVR	JVVS
2005	117.6	116.4	126.6	123.6	120.6	122.6	124.2	124.1	132.4	117.3
2006	121.9	118.8	133.2	126.8	125.3	127.8	128.3	128.7	137.5	121.8
2004 Jul	112.8	114.8	123.5	119.1	114.9	118.4	118.2	119.5	128.3	114.1
Aug	113.0	115.4	124.2	119.8	115.2	118.2	119.7	123.2	128.1	114.3
Sep	113.7	115.1	122.7	120.3	115.1	118.2	121.7	123.3	128.6	113.2
Oct	113.5	114.4	124.9	121.5	116.5	118.3	120.7	121.6	128.7	112.8
Nov	114.0	113.2	123.9	120.8	116.7	118.9	122.1	120.6	129.2	115.0
Dec	115.6	114.7	128.4	120.6	117.3	120.1	121.7	121.9	129.2	113.9
2005 Jan	115.6	117.3	122.8	121.4	117.7	120.5	120.5	122.0	129.2	114.7
Feb	115.2	115.5	123.7	120.7	118.3	121.0	121.9	120.8	128.8	114.5
Mar	116.9	115.7	126.8	121.0	121.6	120.7	125.9	120.7	128.9	116.7
Apr	117.3	117.9	125.9	122.4	120.9	122.1	124.3	124.0	132.9	115.3
May	117.6	116.3	126.3	123.3	121.3	122.1	123.0	123.5	132.9	116.8
Jun	117.3	116.0	126.8	125.2	119.2	122.3	123.0	124.0	133.9	119.2
Jul	118.0	117.8	127.1	123.9	121.8	123.5	124.3	124.5	133.0	121.3
Aug	118.1	118.3	127.3	123.4	121.1	123.0	124.7	126.1	132.9	118.8
Sep	118.0	115.8	126.2	125.8	119.5	123.2	125.3	126.8	132.9	118.6
Oct	119.1	116.0	126.7	124.9	121.0	123.7	125.4	126.3	133.2	115.4
Nov	119.1	115.2	127.4	125.2	121.3	124.3	125.7	124.9	135.0	116.8
Dec	119.3	115.4	132.5	126.4	123.3	124.7	126.9	125.4	134.7	119.8
2006 Jan	119.8	117.9	127.2	124.9	123.9	126.3	126.0	124.8	135.3	120.0
Feb	119.8	115.8	127.8	124.6	123.1	125.4	129.5	125.0	135.9	118.8
Mar	119.8	116.6	130.9	125.3	123.9	126.2	127.5	125.8	136.2	120.2
Apr	120.9	117.9	131.8	127.2	126.4	127.3	127.9	127.8	136.5	122.0
May	120.9	120.0	133.1	127.5	126.5	127.3	127.9	127.1	137.2	122.3
Jun	122.1	118.5	132.1	127.9	125.7	128.0	128.4	127.6	138.7	124.6
Jul	122.0	119.2	134.0	126.8	125.8	128.0	128.5	128.8	138.7	123.0
Aug	122.1	120.1	134.1	126.8	125.6	128.1	127.2	131.6	137.7	122.7
Sep	122.4	120.5	134.7	128.3	124.9	128.3	128.4	132.2	137.7	121.4
Oct	123.6	120.5	136.2	127.0	126.3	129.3	128.2	131.3	137.8	121.2
Nov	124.4	118.7	136.1	127.4	125.8	129.4	128.8	130.9	139.4	122.3
Dec	125.3	119.7	139.8	128.0	125.8	130.1	131.4	131.4	139.2	123.3
2007 Jan	124.8†	122.0†	135.9†	127.7†	127.1	130.9†	129.2†	130.4†	139.8†	124.1†
Feb	124.9	119.8	137.2	127.7	127.9	131.2	129.7	130.4	139.6	123.2
Percentage change on the year										
	JVWD	JVWE	JVWF	JVYJ	JVYK	JVYL	JVYM	JVYN	JVYO	JVYP
2005 Jul	4.6	2.6	2.9	4.0	6.0	4.3	5.1	4.2	3.7	6.4
Aug	4.5	2.5	2.5	3.0	5.1	4.1	4.2	2.4	3.8	4.0
Sep	3.8	0.7	2.9	4.6	3.9	4.2	2.9	2.9	3.4	4.8
Oct	4.9	1.4	1.5	2.8	3.9	4.6	3.9	3.9	3.5	2.3
Nov	4.5	1.7	2.9	3.6	3.9	4.5	3.0	3.5	4.5	1.6
Dec	3.2	0.6	3.2	4.9	5.1	3.8	4.3	2.9	4.3	5.2
2006 Jan	3.7	0.6	3.6	2.9	5.3	4.8	4.6	2.3	4.7	4.6
Feb	4.0	0.3	3.3	3.3	4.0	3.7	6.2	3.4	5.5	3.8
Mar	2.5	0.8	3.3	3.6	1.9	4.6	1.3	4.3	5.7	3.0
Apr	3.0	–	4.6	3.9	4.5	4.3	2.9	3.0	2.7	5.8
May	2.8	3.1	5.4	3.4	4.2	4.2	4.0	2.9	3.3	4.8
Jun	4.1	2.2	4.2	2.2	5.4	4.7	4.3	3.0	3.6	4.5
Jul	3.3	1.2	5.4	2.4	3.3	3.7	3.4	3.5	4.3	1.3
Aug	3.4	1.5	5.4	2.8	3.8	4.1	2.0	4.3	3.6	3.3
Sep	3.7	4.0	6.8	1.9	4.5	4.2	2.5	4.3	3.6	2.4
Oct	3.8	3.9	7.5	1.7	4.4	4.5	2.3	3.9	3.4	5.0
Nov	4.4	3.1	6.8	1.8	3.7	4.1	2.4	4.8	3.3	4.6
Dec	5.0	3.7	5.5	1.3	2.0	4.4	3.5	4.7	3.3	2.9
2007 Jan	4.1†	3.4†	6.8†	2.2†	2.6	3.6†	2.6†	4.4	3.3	3.5†
Feb	4.2	3.4	7.3	2.5	3.8	4.6	0.1	4.4	2.7	3.7

18.15
continued

Average earnings index: by industry (not seasonally adjusted)[1,2]
Great Britain

2000 = 100

	Agriculture, forestry and fishing	Mining and quarrying	Food products, beverages and tobacco	Textiles, leather and clothing	Chemicals and man-made fibres	Basic metals and metal products	Engineering and allied industries	Other manufacturing	Electricity, gas and water supply	Construction
Including bonuses										
SIC 1992	(A,B)	(C)	(DA)	(DB,DC)	(DG)	(DJ)	(DK, DL,DM)	(DD,DE,DF, DH,DI,DN)	(E)	(F)
	JVUF	JVUG	JVUH	JVUI	JVUJ	JVUK	JVUL	JVUM	JVUN	JVUO
2005	124.5	127.2	117.3	119.5	120.4	124.2	122.2	116.8	115.5	124.3
2006	132.7	134.9	123.2	124.9	119.7	132.5	129.0	123.3	117.6	125.8
2004 Jul	122.2	114.8	112.9	116.9	117.6	120.5	118.1	112.4	109.1	119.5
Aug	118.8	114.2	111.2	113.6	115.0	115.4	116.8	109.7	108.8	116.4
Sep	122.7	118.2	113.4	114.4	113.1	115.4	117.0	110.9	106.5	118.2
Oct	121.4	127.5	110.5	115.4	116.5	120.2	118.1	111.7	108.6	119.0
Nov	126.3	123.8	112.0	114.8	114.1	117.4	119.6	112.4	108.1	124.0
Dec	125.8	125.6	120.5	120.1	121.7	120.5	122.7	115.1	108.4	124.7
2005 Jan	123.4	128.8	112.3	117.0	117.9	122.6	118.7	111.8	110.0	121.3
Feb	119.5	137.2	114.2	116.7	121.6	122.3	124.4	113.5	117.3	119.8
Mar	126.0	148.9	129.2	117.2	150.3	125.0	126.2	120.3	112.0	128.8
Apr	122.0	137.9	116.9	117.1	122.5	126.3	123.4	114.2	113.6	120.5
May	118.0	119.2	114.6	116.0	115.7	119.9	119.9	115.4	114.6	122.6
Jun	122.7	120.5	113.3	120.2	116.5	121.5	121.0	115.5	124.9	123.0
Jul	119.4	117.8	117.8	120.0	115.5	126.9	121.7	116.8	115.0	124.4
Aug	120.1	120.1	116.6	117.2	115.6	122.8	119.3	115.8	112.7	120.9
Sep	143.4	125.6	118.0	118.1	115.8	125.2	120.3	116.7	110.2	124.3
Oct	127.5	121.8	115.3	126.6	115.1	128.8	121.8	118.1	112.7	124.9
Nov	125.6	123.5	116.2	121.3	116.1	124.9	122.5	119.0	111.4	127.6
Dec	125.9	124.6	122.9	126.6	122.0	124.5	126.9	124.2	130.8	132.9
2006 Jan	126.1	130.8	117.0	123.7	117.4	127.8	123.4	120.4	113.7	123.9
Feb	129.2	131.0	120.8	123.6	121.2	125.4	132.1	121.0	115.7	125.2
Mar	130.5	160.6	132.4	125.5	146.2	130.5	135.4	127.2	118.8	130.3
Apr	138.9	150.4	127.2	124.4	121.1	132.3	130.4	121.8	116.9	122.8
May	137.3	130.3	122.0	124.4	112.9	130.2	126.7	122.3	121.3	123.0
Jun	139.0	128.8	122.5	125.6	115.4	131.8	127.0	124.1	129.6	125.8
Jul	134.5	126.8	122.5	125.4	114.8	135.2	127.4	123.6	119.2	125.1
Aug	137.2	126.6	120.4	121.8	114.7	130.4	126.3	124.0	115.6	121.6
Sep	133.0	130.6	125.1	122.7	117.8	135.6	127.6	121.9	114.4	125.1
Oct	127.6	130.2	121.6	125.1	116.5	139.6	129.6	122.6	114.3	125.1
Nov	121.2	136.8	121.4	125.5	114.5	133.2	130.5	123.4	116.5	127.8
Dec	138.2	135.7	125.7	131.2	123.5	138.2	132.3	127.3	115.1	133.8
2007 Jan	127.6	137.7†	117.9†	128.1†	116.0†	132.0†	130.7†	123.9†	114.3	126.7†
Feb	120.0	142.4	119.4	130.4	120.1	135.7	134.9	126.8	115.7	130.9
Percentage change on the year										
	JVYQ	JVYR	JVYS	JVYT	JVYU	JVYV	JVYW	JVYX	JVYY	JVYZ
2005 Jul	−2.3	2.6	4.4	2.6	−1.8	5.3	3.0	4.0	5.4	4.1
Aug	1.1	5.2	4.8	3.2	0.6	6.5	2.2	5.6	3.6	3.9
Sep	16.9	6.2	4.1	3.3	2.4	8.5	2.8	5.3	3.5	5.2
Oct	5.1	−4.5	4.4	9.7	−1.2	7.1	3.1	5.7	3.8	5.0
Nov	−0.5	−0.2	3.8	5.6	1.8	6.4	2.4	5.8	3.0	2.9
Dec	0.1	−0.8	2.0	5.4	0.2	3.4	3.5	7.9	20.7	6.5
2006 Jan	2.2	1.5	4.2	5.7	−0.4	4.2	4.0	7.7	3.4	2.1
Feb	8.1	−4.6	5.7	5.9	−0.3	2.5	6.3	6.6	−1.4	4.6
Mar	3.6	7.9	2.5	7.1	−2.8	4.4	7.3	5.8	6.0	1.2
Apr	13.8	9.1	8.8	6.2	−1.2	4.8	5.7	6.6	2.9	1.9
May	16.4	9.3	6.5	7.2	−2.4	8.6	5.7	6.0	5.9	0.3
Jun	13.3	6.9	8.1	4.5	−0.9	8.4	5.0	7.4	3.8	2.3
Jul	12.6	7.7	4.0	4.5	−0.6	6.5	4.7	5.8	3.6	0.6
Aug	14.2	5.4	3.3	3.9	−0.8	6.2	5.8	7.1	2.5	0.6
Sep	−7.3	4.0	6.0	3.9	1.7	8.3	6.0	4.5	3.8	0.6
Oct	0.1	6.9	5.4	−1.2	1.2	8.4	6.4	3.7	1.4	0.2
Nov	−3.5	10.7	4.4	3.5	−1.4	6.6	6.5	3.7	4.6	0.1
Dec	9.8	8.9	2.3	3.7	1.2	10.9	4.3	2.4	−12.1	0.7
2007 Jan	1.2	5.3†	0.8†	3.6†	−1.2†	3.3†	5.9†	3.0†	0.5	2.2†
Feb	−7.1	8.7	−1.1	5.5	−0.8	8.3	2.1	4.8	−	4.5

18.15 continued
Average earnings index: by industry (not seasonally adjusted)[1,2]
Great Britain

2000 = 100

Including bonuses

	Wholesale trade	Retail trade and repairs	Hotels and restaurants	Transport, storage and communication	Financial interm-ediation	Real estate renting and business activities	Public admini-stration	Education	Health and social work	Other services
SIC 1992	(G:51)	(G:50,52)	(H)	(I)	(J)	(K)	(L)	(M)	(N)	(O)
	JVUP	JVUQ	JVUR	JVUS	JVUT	JVUU	JVUV	JVUW	JVUX	JVUY
2005	119.3	116.6	131.5	124.6	114.4	118.4	124.1	123.8	132.5	120.3
2006	124.0	119.4	137.1	127.5	123.9	123.8	129.1	128.4	137.5	123.2
2004 Jul	114.1	114.0	126.2	117.0	92.1	114.8	117.5	119.3	128.3	116.4
Aug	113.2	114.1	126.6	116.8	90.9	112.7	121.2	123.0	128.0	115.3
Sep	113.9	114.6	125.6	117.3	90.5	111.5	121.1	122.9	128.5	115.6
Oct	114.1	113.8	128.5	118.3	96.3	112.5	120.1	121.3	128.7	116.2
Nov	116.5	112.4	127.8	118.8	93.2	113.4	121.4	120.5	129.2	120.0
Dec	123.7	114.8	135.6	121.0	101.7	117.7	122.3	121.6	129.3	119.1
2005 Jan	117.0	117.0	128.6	118.2	163.7	117.7	119.6	121.7	129.1	119.5
Feb	118.9	117.5	132.0	121.6	173.7	117.3	121.1	120.7	129.2	116.0
Mar	126.3	118.7	134.5	121.7	156.0	124.5	125.3	120.4	129.3	123.7
Apr	120.8	119.0	129.4	122.6	101.0	117.3	123.6	123.9	133.0	118.3
May	116.6	115.9	131.5	131.6	96.2	116.9	122.3	123.2	132.9	120.2
Jun	118.1	116.9	129.9	133.3	96.9	118.3	122.2	123.6	134.0	127.8
Jul	118.7	117.2	130.2	125.5	97.0	120.7	124.2	124.3	133.0	122.2
Aug	115.3	116.9	130.9	121.4	96.1	117.1	126.4	125.9	133.0	120.3
Sep	115.5	114.1	128.5	122.8	94.8	115.3	124.6	126.5	132.8	119.7
Oct	119.9	115.6	129.8	122.0	93.1	116.0	125.2	126.0	133.4	116.3
Nov	121.3	114.3	131.7	123.6	96.4	117.1	125.6	124.5	134.9	117.2
Dec	123.8	116.1	140.5	130.4	108.1	122.8	129.0	125.1	134.8	122.8
2006 Jan	121.1	118.0	129.9	123.6	168.7	120.9	125.5	124.4	135.2	121.1
Feb	121.4	115.6	134.7	124.1	209.8	121.1	129.1	124.8	135.9	121.1
Mar	129.6	122.2	136.5	125.7	175.6	129.8	127.5	125.5	137.1	123.3
Apr	121.0	119.3	134.5	124.3	105.4	122.9	127.9	127.4	136.4	123.2
May	120.2	119.7	138.4	139.0	103.4	122.3	127.7	126.8	137.0	125.4
Jun	123.0	120.8	134.7	138.2	113.2	124.7	129.1	127.3	138.5	124.9
Jul	123.9	121.3	136.5	127.5	103.4	124.9	131.2	128.7	138.5	123.9
Aug	121.3	119.0	136.9	124.6	99.3	122.2	130.1	131.3	137.4	123.2
Sep	121.9	119.6	137.6	124.6	96.7	122.3	128.6	131.9	137.4	121.6
Oct	124.6	120.2	139.4	122.9	97.7	122.6	128.6	130.9	137.6	120.6
Nov	126.6	118.0	140.7	124.4	100.4	122.7	129.1	130.7	139.2	123.5
Dec	133.9	118.9	145.5	130.8	113.5	129.5	134.7	131.2	139.2	126.7
2007 Jan	129.1	120.5[†]	139.3[†]	125.5[†]	195.0[†]	125.3[†]	128.9[†]	130.0	139.8	126.8[†]
Feb	133.9	120.1	141.3	128.1	240.6	126.6	129.7	130.1	139.7	125.2

Percentage change on the year

	JVZA	JVZB	JVZC	JVZD	JVZE	JVZF	JVZG	JVZH	JVZI	JVZJ
2005 Jul	4.0	2.8	3.2	7.3	5.3	5.1	5.6	4.2	3.7	5.0
Aug	1.8	2.4	3.4	4.0	5.8	3.9	4.3	2.3	3.9	4.3
Sep	1.5	−0.4	2.3	4.6	4.8	3.4	2.9	3.0	3.3	3.5
Oct	5.1	1.5	1.0	3.1	−3.3	3.1	4.3	3.9	3.7	0.1
Nov	4.1	1.7	3.1	4.0	3.4	3.3	3.4	3.4	4.4	−2.3
Dec	0.1	1.2	3.6	7.7	6.3	4.3	5.5	2.9	4.3	3.1
2006 Jan	3.5	0.9	1.0	4.6	3.1	2.8	4.9	2.3	4.7	1.3
Feb	2.1	−1.6	2.0	2.0	20.8	3.2	6.6	3.4	5.2	4.4
Mar	2.6	2.9	1.5	3.3	12.6	4.3	1.7	4.2	6.1	−0.3
Apr	0.2	0.2	4.0	1.4	4.3	4.8	3.5	2.9	2.6	4.2
May	3.1	3.3	5.2	5.6	7.6	4.6	4.4	3.0	3.1	4.3
Jun	4.2	3.3	3.7	3.7	16.7	5.4	5.6	3.0	3.4	−2.2
Jul	4.3	3.5	4.9	1.6	6.6	3.5	5.7	3.5	4.1	1.4
Aug	5.2	1.8	4.6	2.6	3.3	4.3	2.9	4.3	3.3	2.4
Sep	5.5	4.8	7.0	1.5	2.0	6.1	3.1	4.2	3.5	1.6
Oct	3.9	4.0	7.4	0.7	4.9	5.8	2.7	3.9	3.2	3.8
Nov	4.4	3.3	6.9	0.6	4.2	4.8	2.8	5.0	3.2	5.4
Dec	8.1	2.3	3.6	0.3	5.0	5.4	4.5	4.8	3.2	3.1
2007 Jan	6.6	2.2[†]	7.3[†]	1.5	15.6[†]	3.6[†]	2.7[†]	4.5	3.4	4.7
Feb	10.3	3.9	4.9	3.2	14.7	4.6	0.4	4.2	2.8	3.4

1 The above table of 20 industries was first published in the Monthly Digest in May 2002 (as table 18.11). The new set of 20 industry sectors was introduced as it better reflects the current state of the economy. Data are available in two formats: excluding bonus and including bonus, with each available as an index value and as an annual percentage change. An article covering the reasons for change can be found on our website: www.statistics.gov.uk/labour.

2 Users should note that the data contained in the previous set of 26 industry sectors are not comparable with the new set of 20 industry sectors.

Source: Office for National Statistics: 01633 819024

18.16 Average earnings index[1]: main industrial sectors
Great Britain

2000 = 100

	Whole economy				Public sector				Private sector			
	Actual	Seasonally adjusted	Single month[2]	3 month average[2]	Actual	Seasonally adjusted	Single month[2]	3 month average[2]	Actual	Seasonally adjusted	Single month[2]	3 month average[2]
SIC 1992												
	LNMM	LNMQ	LNMU	LNNC	LNNI	LNNJ	LNKW	LNNE	LNKX	LNKY	LNKZ	LNND
1997	86.8	86.8	..	..	89.7	89.6	..	..	86.2	86.2	..	..
1998	91.3	91.3	..	..	92.6	92.5	..	..	90.9	91.0	..	..
1999	95.7	95.7	..	..	96.4	96.4	..	..	95.5	95.5	..	..
2000	100.0	100.0	..	..	100.0	100.0	..	..	100.0	100.0	..	..
2001	104.4	104.5	..	..	105.1	105.0	..	..	104.2	104.3	..	..
2002	108.1	108.2	..	..	109.6	109.3	..	..	107.8	107.9	..	..
2003	111.7	111.9	..	..	115.0	114.8	..	..	111.0	111.3	..	..
2004	116.7	116.8	..	..	120.4	119.8	..	..	115.9	116.0	..	..
2005	121.4	121.5	..	..	125.9	125.4	..	..	120.4	120.6	..	..
2006	126.4	126.5	..	..	130.6	129.9	..	..	125.5	125.7	..	..
2003 Mar	116.8	110.7	4.2	3.3	112.2	113.3	5.1	5.2	117.9	110.0	3.9	2.9
Apr	110.0	110.7	2.5	3.1	114.6	113.9	5.1	5.2	109.0	110.0	1.9	2.7
May	110.0	111.3	3.1	3.3	114.5	113.9	4.7	5.0	109.0	110.9	2.9	2.9
Jun	111.2	111.6	3.2	3.0	115.7	114.7	5.4	5.1	110.2	111.0	2.7	2.5
Jul	111.8	112.5	3.7	3.4	116.7	115.6	5.3	5.1	110.7	111.9	3.3	3.0
Aug	110.2	112.5	3.5	3.5	117.2	115.6	6.0	5.5	108.5	111.8	3.0	3.0
Sep	110.4	113.2	3.9	3.7	116.0	116.1	5.5	5.6	109.0	112.6	3.5	3.3
Oct	110.9	113.5	3.9	3.8	115.8	116.1	4.7	5.4	109.7	113.0	3.7	3.4
Nov	111.2	113.8	3.3	3.7	116.6	116.3	4.2	4.8	110.0	113.2	3.1	3.4
Dec	114.7	114.2	4.4	3.9	117.8	116.9	4.2	4.4	114.0	113.9	4.9	3.9
2004 Jan	118.2	116.3	6.2	4.6	116.1	117.1	4.1	4.2	118.7	115.3	6.0	4.7
Feb	118.1	113.6	3.6	4.7	116.5	117.8	4.4	4.2	118.5	112.7	3.5	4.8
Mar	122.2	115.4	4.3	4.7	117.0	118.2	4.4	4.3	123.5	114.7	4.3	4.6
Apr	115.0	115.7	4.5	4.1	119.4	118.6	4.1	4.3	114.1	115.1	4.6	4.1
May	114.8	115.9	4.1	4.3	119.9	119.1	4.6	4.4	113.6	115.5	4.2	4.4
Jun	116.1	116.2	4.1	4.2	122.3	119.8	4.5	4.4	114.6	115.5	4.1	4.3
Jul	115.4	116.4	3.4	3.9	121.0	119.8	3.7	4.2	114.2	115.6	3.3	3.8
Aug	114.8	117.3	4.2	3.9	123.0	120.8	4.5	4.2	112.9	116.5	4.1	3.8
Sep	114.9	117.8	4.0	3.9	122.5	121.2	4.4	4.2	113.1	117.0	3.9	3.8
Oct	115.7	118.6	4.5	4.2	121.7	121.7	4.8	4.6	114.4	117.9	4.4	4.1
Nov	116.2	119.0	4.6	4.4	121.9	121.8	4.7	4.7	114.9	118.3	4.5	4.3
Dec	119.5	119.0	4.2	4.4	123.3	122.0	4.4	4.6	118.6	118.4	3.9	4.3
2005 Jan	123.3	120.9	4.0	4.2	122.1	122.7	4.8	4.6	123.7	119.8	3.9	4.1
Feb	124.9	119.8	5.4	4.5	122.2	123.2	4.6	4.6	125.6	119.1	5.7	4.5
Mar	127.5	120.0	4.0	4.5	123.0	123.1	4.1	4.5	128.6	119.2	3.9	4.5
Apr	119.9	120.6	4.2	4.5	125.6	124.5	5.0	4.6	118.6	119.7	4.0	4.5
May	119.2	120.6	4.1	4.1	128.9	128.4	7.7	5.6	117.0	119.4	3.4	3.7
Jun	120.4	120.6	3.8	4.0	126.9	124.9	4.3	5.7	119.0	119.9	3.8	3.7
Jul	120.5	121.7	4.6	4.2	125.9	124.9	4.3	5.4	119.3	120.9	4.6	3.9
Aug	119.0	122.1	4.1	4.2	126.8	125.9	4.3	4.3	117.2	121.2	4.1	4.2
Sep	118.8	122.3	3.8	4.2	126.2	126.1	4.0	4.2	117.1	121.3	3.7	4.1
Oct	119.1	122.5	3.2	3.7	126.5	126.6	4.1	4.1	117.4	121.5	3.0	3.6
Nov	119.9	123.3	3.6	3.5	127.0	127.2	4.5	4.2	118.3	122.3	3.4	3.4
Dec	124.6	124.2†	4.3	3.7	129.2	127.7	4.7	4.4	123.5	123.3†	4.1	3.5
2006 Jan	127.2	124.4	2.9†	3.6†	126.8	127.8	4.1†	4.4	127.4	123.3	2.9†	3.5†
Feb	131.6	125.7	4.9	4.0	128.5	128.3†	4.2	4.3	132.5	125.1	5.0	4.0
Mar	133.2	125.3	4.4	4.1	128.0	128.5	4.3	4.2	134.6	124.4	4.4	4.1
Apr	124.1	124.8	3.5	4.3	129.3	128.1	2.9	3.8	122.8	124.1	3.7	4.4
May	124.5	125.9	4.4	4.1	133.8	133.1	3.7	3.6	122.3	125.0	4.7	4.2
Jun	126.4	126.6	4.9	4.3	131.3	129.5	3.7	3.4	125.3	126.2	5.3	4.5
Jul	125.2	126.5	3.9	4.4	131.7	130.0	4.1	3.8	123.6	125.5	3.8	4.6
Aug	123.5	126.8	3.8	4.2	131.1	129.9	3.2	3.6	121.7	126.0	3.9	4.3
Sep	123.7	127.3	4.1	3.9	130.7	130.4	3.4	3.5	122.1	126.5	4.3	4.0
Oct	123.9	127.6	4.2	4.1	130.7	130.8	3.3	3.3	122.3	126.9	4.4	4.2
Nov	124.6	128.2	4.0	4.1	131.5	131.2	3.1	3.2	123.0	127.4	4.1	4.3
Dec	129.4	129.0	3.9	4.0	134.2	131.9	3.3	3.2	128.3	128.3	4.1	4.2
2007 Jan	133.3†	130.2	4.7	4.2	131.1†	132.0	3.3	3.2	134.0†	129.6	5.1	4.5
Feb	138.5	132.1	5.1	4.6	131.6	132.1	2.9	3.2	140.3	132.1	5.6	4.9

18.16 Average earnings index[1]: main industrial sectors
Great Britain
continued

2000 = 100

	Production industries				Manufacturing industries				Service industries				of which Private sector services			
	Actual	Seasonally adjusted	Single month[2]	3 month average[2]	Actual	Seasonally adjusted	Single month[2]	3 month average[2]	Actual	Seasonally adjusted	Single month[2]	3 month average[2]	Actual	Seasonally adjusted	Single month[2]	3 month average[2]
SIC 1992																
	LNMO	LNMS	LNMW	LNNF	LNMN	LNMR	LNMV	LNNG	LNMP	LNMT	LNMX	LNNH	JJGF	JJGH	JJGI	JJGJ
1997	88.3	88.4	..	..	87.8	87.9	..	..	86.6	86.6	..	..	85.5	85.5	..	..
1998	92.2	92.3	..	..	91.8	91.9	..	..	91.1	91.1	..	..	90.6	90.6	..	..
1999	95.8	95.9	..	..	95.6	95.6	..	..	95.7	95.7	..	..	95.4	95.4	..	..
2000	100.0	100.0	..	..	100.0	100.0	..	..	100.0	100.0	..	..	100.0	100.0	..	..
2001	104.2	104.2	..	..	104.2	104.3	..	..	104.4	104.4	..	..	104.1	104.2	..	..
2002	107.8	107.9	..	..	107.9	108.0	..	..	108.1	108.1	..	..	107.6	107.8	..	..
2003	111.6	111.7	..	..	111.7	111.9	..	..	111.7	112.0	..	..	110.6	111.0	..	..
2004	115.8	115.8	..	..	115.9	116.0	..	..	116.8	116.8	..	..	115.5	115.7	..	..
2005	120.0	120.0	..	..	120.1	120.2	..	..	121.6	121.7	..	..	120.1	120.4	..	..
2006	126.0	126.0	..	..	126.2	126.4	..	..	126.5	126.6	..	..	125.2	125.5	..	..
2003 Mar	118.2	110.7	3.4	3.8	117.9	110.7	3.6	3.9	116.3	110.3	3.8	3.0	117.5	109.1	3.3	2.3
Apr	110.7	110.2	3.1	3.6	110.5	110.4	3.1	3.7	109.9	110.7	2.6	2.9	108.2	109.6	1.7	2.1
May	110.4	111.3	3.5	3.3	110.5	111.4	3.5	3.4	110.0	111.5	3.3	3.2	108.5	110.8	2.9	2.6
Jun	110.9	111.5	3.2	3.3	110.4	111.5	3.2	3.3	111.3	111.7	3.3	3.1	109.8	110.8	2.6	2.4
Jul	111.6	111.9	3.4	3.4	111.8	111.9	3.4	3.4	111.9	112.9	4.0	3.5	110.3	111.9	3.5	3.0
Aug	109.7	112.4	3.4	3.4	109.8	112.4	3.4	3.3	110.4	112.7	3.8	3.7	108.1	111.7	3.1	3.1
Sep	110.4	112.7	3.6	3.5	110.6	112.8	3.6	3.5	110.1	113.3	4.0	4.0	108.1	112.3	3.5	3.4
Oct	111.2	113.0	3.5	3.5	111.5	113.1	3.4	3.5	110.6	113.6	4.0	4.0	108.8	112.7	3.7	3.4
Nov	112.0	113.6	3.9	3.6	112.3	113.9	4.0	3.7	110.7	113.9	3.3	3.8	108.7	112.9	2.9	3.4
Dec	114.9	113.4	3.3	3.6	115.4	113.7	3.4	3.6	114.3	114.6	5.1	4.1	113.0	113.4	4.9	3.8
2004 Jan	112.6	114.1	3.9	3.7	112.8	114.3	3.9	3.8	119.8	116.1	6.4	4.9	121.0	116.4	7.7	5.2
Feb	115.1	114.2	3.5	3.6	114.9	114.3	3.4	3.6	119.0	113.2	3.4	5.0	119.7	111.5	3.1	5.2
Mar	122.1	114.5	3.4	3.6	122.1	114.7	3.6	3.7	122.0	115.5	4.7	4.8	123.7	114.4	4.8	5.2
Apr	115.9	115.2	4.5	3.8	115.6	115.3	4.5	3.8	114.7	115.5	4.4	4.2	113.1	114.5	4.4	4.1
May	115.2	116.1	4.3	4.1	115.5	116.4	4.5	4.2	114.4	115.7	3.7	4.3	112.6	114.8	3.6	4.3
Jun	115.3	115.9	4.0	4.3	114.9	116.1	4.1	4.3	116.1	116.1	3.9	4.0	114.0	114.9	3.7	3.9
Jul	115.7	116.0	3.7	4.0	116.1	116.2	3.8	4.1	115.1	116.3	3.0	3.5	113.1	114.9	2.7	3.3
Aug	113.4	115.9	3.2	3.6	113.6	116.1	3.3	3.7	115.0	117.4	4.1	3.7	112.3	116.1	4.0	3.5
Sep	113.9	116.2	3.1	3.3	114.2	116.4	3.2	3.4	114.8	118.0	4.1	3.7	112.2	116.9	4.0	3.6
Oct	115.4	116.8	3.3	3.2	115.4	116.9	3.4	3.3	115.6	118.9	4.7	4.3	113.5	117.9	4.6	4.2
Nov	115.6	117.0	3.0	3.1	115.7	117.3	2.9	3.2	115.7	119.2	4.7	4.5	113.6	118.1	4.7	4.5
Dec	119.5	117.5	3.6	3.3	119.8	117.9	3.7	3.3	119.1	119.3	4.2	4.5	117.6	118.2	4.3	4.5
2005 Jan	116.3	117.7	3.2	3.2	116.3	117.8	3.0	3.2	125.0	120.9	4.1	4.3	125.9	120.7	3.7	4.2
Feb	119.6	118.4	3.7	3.5	119.2	118.4	3.6	3.4	126.4	120.1	6.1	4.8	127.8	118.8	6.5	4.8
Mar	126.6	118.6	3.6	3.5	126.6	119.2	3.9	3.5	127.6	120.2	4.1	4.8	129.1	119.0	4.0	4.7
Apr	120.2	118.8	3.1	3.4	120.0	119.0	3.2	3.5	119.8	120.8	4.6	4.9	117.9	119.5	4.4	5.0
May	117.4	118.5	2.0	2.9	117.5	118.7	2.0	3.0	119.4	121.0	4.6	4.4	116.3	119.2	3.8	4.1
Jun	118.5	119.1	2.7	2.6	118.2	119.4	2.8	2.7	120.7	120.9	4.1	4.4	118.7	119.5	4.0	4.1
Jul	119.6	120.0	3.5	2.7	119.9	120.3	3.5	2.8	120.5	122.0	4.9	4.5	118.8	120.8	5.1	4.3
Aug	117.9	120.7	4.1	3.4	118.1	121.0	4.3	3.5	119.2	122.2	4.1	4.4	116.7	121.0	4.2	4.4
Sep	118.9	121.2	4.3	4.0	119.2	121.5	4.4	4.1	118.3	122.2	3.5	4.2	115.7	120.9	3.4	4.2
Oct	120.1	121.7	4.2	4.2	120.4	122.0	4.3	4.3	118.5	122.4	2.9	3.5	115.9	120.9	2.6	3.4
Nov	120.1	121.7	4.0	4.2	120.5	122.3	4.3	4.4	119.4	123.4	3.6	3.3	116.9	122.0	3.3	3.1
Dec	125.3	123.5[†]	5.1[†]	4.4	125.1	123.1	4.5	4.4	123.8	124.1	4.0	3.5	122.1	122.9[†]	3.9	3.3[†]
2006 Jan	121.7	123.5	4.9	4.7	121.9	123.8	5.1	4.6	128.6	124.3[†]	2.9[†]	3.5[†]	129.2	123.2	2.1[†]	3.1
Feb	125.2	124.1	4.8	4.9	125.5	124.6[†]	5.3[†]	5.0[†]	133.4	125.9	4.9	3.9	135.1	125.0	5.3	3.8
Mar	133.0	124.4	4.9	4.9	133.0	124.9	4.8	5.1	133.5	125.5	4.4	4.0	135.3	124.4	4.5	3.9
Apr	126.9	125.7	5.8	5.2[†]	126.8	126.0	5.9	5.3	123.5	124.7	3.2	4.1	121.5	123.4	3.3	4.4
May	124.1	125.4	5.8	5.5	124.1	125.5	5.7	5.5	124.6	126.1	4.2	3.9	121.6	124.8	4.7	4.2
Jun	125.6	126.1	5.9	5.9	125.2	126.4	5.9	5.9	126.6	126.7	4.8	4.1	125.1	125.8	5.3	4.4
Jul	125.3	125.9	4.8	5.5	125.5	126.1	4.8	5.5	125.1	126.6	3.8	4.3	123.0	125.3	3.7	4.6
Aug	124.0	127.0	5.2	5.3	124.4	127.4	5.3	5.3	123.5	126.7	3.7	4.1	121.0	125.6	3.8	4.3
Sep	125.2	127.6	5.3	5.1	125.6	128.0	5.4	5.2	123.3	127.3	4.2	3.9	120.8	126.3	4.5	4.0
Oct	126.0	127.7	5.0	5.2	126.5	128.2	5.1	5.2	123.4	127.7	4.4	4.1	121.0	126.7	4.7	4.4
Nov	125.9	127.6	4.9	5.0	126.1	128.0	4.7	5.0	124.2	128.4	4.1	4.2	121.7	127.4	4.4	4.5
Dec	129.4	127.5	3.2	4.4	130.0	128.0	3.9	4.6	129.1	129.4	4.2	4.2	127.3	128.5	4.6	4.6
2007 Jan	125.7[†]	127.6	3.3	3.8	125.9[†]	128.1	3.4	4.0	135.3	130.7	5.1	4.5	136.7[†]	130.2	5.6	4.9
Feb	129.0	127.9	3.0	3.2	129.3	128.3	3.0	3.4	140.9	132.9	5.5	5.0	144.0	132.9	6.3	5.5

1 The most recent month's data is subject to revision.
2 Single month and 3-month averages show the percentage change year on year.

Source: Office for National Statistics: 01633 819024

19 Leisure

19.1 Television licences

Thousands

	Television licences current				Television licences current	
	End of period				End of period	
	Monochrome	Colour			Monochrome	Colour
	BTAA	BTAB		Aug	69	23 994
1999	232	22 205		Sep	68	23 984
2000	169	22 373		Oct	67	24 051
2001	124	22 896		Nov	63	23 926
2002	98	23 191		Dec	62	23 948
2003	79	23 523				
				2005 Jan	61	23 977
2004	62	23 948		Feb	60	24 026
2005	51	24 213		Mar	58	24 103
2006	42	24 364		Apr	58	24 130
				May	57	24 144
2002 Oct	107	23 377		Jun	56	24 170
Nov	100	23 146				
Dec	98	23 191		Jul	56	24 173
				Aug	55	24 202
2003 Jan	96	23 244		Sep	55	24 249
Feb	95	23 308		Oct	54	24 300
Mar	94	23 392		Nov	52	24 168
Apr	91	23 400		Dec	51	24 213
May	90	23 430				
Jun	89	23 443		2006 Jan	50	24 247
				Feb	50	24 297
Jul	88	23 483		Mar	49	24 370
Aug	86	23 490		Apr	49	24 377
Sep	85	23 550		May	48	24 410
Oct	84	23 626		Jun	47	24 442
Nov	80	23 465				
Dec	79	23 523		Jul	47	24 460
				Aug	46	24 462
2004 Jan	78	23 601		Sep	44	24 506
Feb	77	23 685		Oct	44	24 506
Mar	75	23 824		Nov	42	24 373
Apr	74	23 875		Dec	42	24 364
May	73	23 897				
Jun	71	23 934		2007 Jan	41	24 404
				Feb	41	24 440
Jul	70	23 951				

Source: Capita Business Services Ltd.: 0117 3021003

19.2 UK cinema statistics[1,2]

	Sites (number)	Screens (number)	Total number of admissions (millions)	Gross box office takings (£ million)	Revenue per admission (£)	Revenue per screen (£ thousand)
	JMHX	JMHY	JMHZ	JMIA	JMIB	JMIC
1997	747	2 383	138.9	486.2	3.50	204.0
1998	761	2 638	135.2	504.9	3.73	191.4
1999	751	2 825	139.1	549.7	3.95	194.6
2000	754	3 017	142.5	572.8	4.02	189.9
2001	766	3 248	155.9	645.0	4.14	198.6
2002	775	3 402	175.9	755.3	4.29	222.0
2003	776	3 433	167.3	742.0	4.44	216.1
2004	773	3 475	171.3	769.6	4.49	221.4
2005	771	3 486	164.7	770.3	4.68	221.0
2006	783	3 569	156.6	762.1	4.87	213.5

1 Includes Isle of Man and the Channel Islands.
2 Admissions are based on all cinemas taking advertising.

Source: CAA/Gallup/Nielsen EDI

19.3 Average issue readership of national daily newspapers
rolling 12 months' periods ending

Thousands

		2004 Mar	2004 Jun	2004 Sep	2004 Dec	2005 Mar	2005 Jun	2005 Sep	2005 Dec	2006 Mar	2006 Jun	2006 Sep	2006 Dec
The Sun	WSDV	8 897	9 056	8 872	8 825	8 584	8 185	8 157	8 138	8 059	8 071	7 874	7 716
Daily Mail	WSEI	5 647	5 681	5 666	5 740	5 818	5 686	5 682	5 635	5 456	5 455	5 364	5 302
Daily Mirror/Daily Record	WSEH	6 008	6 190	6 026	5 913	5 813	5 455	5 435	5 322	5 138	4 980	4 945	4 935
Daily Mirror	WSEM	4 657	4 827	4 737	4 657	4 587	4 274	4 214	4 148	3 956	3 857	3 825	3 803
The Daily Telegraph	WSEN	2 141	2 202	2 217	2 181	2 227	2 170	2 156	2 159	2 081	2 033	2 140	2 147
The Times	WSES	1 636	1 643	1 628	1 655	1 681	1 738	1 781	1 811	1 853	1 791	1 772	1 740
Daily Express	WSEP	2 076	2 088	2 088	2 132	2 114	2 063	2 064	1 977	1 876	1 838	1 751	1 720
Daily Star	WSEQ	1 767	1 824	1 936	1 965	1 941	1 848	1 825	1 778	1 682	1 617	1 533	1 557
The Guardian	WSET	1 172	1 095	1 072	1 068	1 132	1 175	1 217	1 222	1 175	1 189	1 190	1 248
The Independent	WSEU	611	605	627	643	606	617	672	705	731	766	741	763
Financial Times	WSEY	436	447	494	453	485	444	394	391	348	346	384	390
Any national morning	WSEZ	23 613	23 916	23 789	23 680	23 200	22 917	23 085	23 068	22 686	22 411	22 007	21 724

Source: National Readership Surveys Ltd.

19.4 Overseas travel and tourism

Not seasonally adjusted

	Visits by overseas visitors to the UK (thousands)	Expenditure by overseas visitors to the UK (£ million)	Visits by UK residents abroad (thousands)	Expenditure by UK residents abroad (£ million)	Net earnings in UK (£ million)
	GMAA	GMAK	GMAF	GMAM	GMAO
2001	22 835	11 306	58 281	25 332	−14 026
2002	24 180	11 737	59 377	26 962	−15 225
2003	24 715	11 855	61 424	28 550	−16 695
2004	27 755	13 047	64 194	30 285	−17 238
2005	29 970	14 248	66 441	32 154	−17 906
2006	32 170	15 400	68 410	33 385	−17 985
2001 Q1	4 863	2 406	10 842	4 888	−2 481
Q2	6 279	2 815	15 662	6 574	−3 760
Q3	7 100	3 819	19 652	8 921	−5 102
Q4	4 593	2 266	12 125	4 949	−2 683
2002 Q1	4 525	2 025	10 943	5 047	−3 022
Q2	6 375	2 885	15 611	6 945	−4 060
Q3	7 555	4 002	19 729	9 254	−5 251
Q4	5 724	2 825	13 094	5 717	−2 892
2003 Q1	4 944	2 150	11 506	5 446	−3 296
Q2	6 073	2 744	16 297	7 086	−4 342
Q3	7 534	4 041	20 330	10 018	−5 977
Q4	6 165	2 919	13 291	5 999	−3 080
2004 Q1	5 449	2 229	11 817	5 729	−3 500
Q2	7 022	3 231	16 911	7 602	−4 370
Q3	8 501	4 390	21 273	10 437	−6 047
Q4	6 783	3 196	14 194	6 517	−3 321
2005 Q1	6 172	2 644	12 821	6 411	−3 767
Q2	7 868	3 562	17 417	8 110	−4 548
Q3	8 858	4 474	21 767	10 912	−6 438
Q4	7 072	3 568	14 436	6 722	−3 154
2006 Q1	6 369	2 753	13 121	6 657	−3 904
Q2	8 371	3 928	18 589	8 663	−4 735
Q3	9 970	5 050	21 952	11 215	−6 165
Q4	7 460	3 670	14 740	6 850	−3 180

Source: International Passenger Survey, Office for National Statistics

20 Weather

20.1 District summary[1] for September 2006

| | Air temperature (degrees celsius) | | | | | Difference from average | | Percent of average | | |
| | | | Difference from average | | | Mean 30cm soil temperature (degrees celsius) | Raindays[3] | Rainfall | Sunshine | Sunshine (hours) |
	Highest maximum[2]	Lowest minimum[2]	Maximum	Minimum	Mean					
September 2006										
District:										
0 Scotland N	23.8	0.0	3.4	2.5	2.9	2.0	-2	87	120	108.5
1 Scotland E	25.4	-0.1	3.2	2.5	2.8	2.1	1	116	116	121.6
2 England E & NE	28.2	1.3	3.4	3.1	3.3	2.5	1	117	129	162.3
3 East Anglia	29.7	4.9	3.5	3.7	3.6	2.7	0	112	118	169.6
4 Midlands	29.0	3.6	3.5	3.1	3.3	2.4	1	114	120	155.1
5 England SE	30.0	4.4	3.2	3.5	3.4	2.3	1	106	111	164.4
6 Scotland W	24.8	2.5	2.7	2.5	2.6	2.0	3	116	106	107.2
7 England NW & N Wales	27.6	2.2	3.2	2.8	3.0	2.2	0	84	128	149.6
8 England SW & S Wales	26.4	3.8	2.9	2.8	2.8	1.9	0	70	110	150.3
N Ireland	23.0	0.7	2.3	2.3	2.3	1.9	3	136	101	108.3
Scotland	25.4	-0.1	3.1	2.5	2.8	2.0	1	103	114	112.2
England	30.0	1.3	3.3	3.2	3.3	2.4	1	103	119	158.9
Wales	26.7	2.9	3.0	2.6	2.8	1.9	1	68	120	148.8
England & Wales	30.0	1.3	3.3	3.1	3.2	2.3	1	96	119	157.5

Anomalies are with respect to the 1961-90 averaging period.

Sept. 2006 - Mean temperatures were exceptionally above average, with all district and regional climate areas having their warmest September (using areal series back to 1914). Heathrow recorded a temperature of 30.2 degrees C on 11th. Northern Ireland was one of the wettest areas compared to average, with gusts of 60 to 70 m.p.h. late on the 21st causing widespread tree damage and over 100,000 homes lost power.

1 District values for each element are computed using all available climate stations, excluding rooftop sites for minimum air temperature. The values in the table may not be compatible with other time series (eg. Central England Temperature, England and Wales Rainfall).
2 Highest maximum and lowest minimum air temperatures for each district are determined by calculating 95 percentiles.
3 Raindays are the number of days during which the total precipitation is at least 0.2mm.

Source: Met Office

20.2 UK Annual Summary

| | Max Temp | | Min Temp | | Mean Temp | | Sunshine | | Rainfall | |
	Actual (degrees celsius)	Anomaly (degrees celsius)	Actual (degrees celsius)	Anomaly (degrees celsius)	Actual (degrees celsius)	Anomaly (degrees celsius)	Actual (hours/ day)	Anomaly (%)	Actual (mm)	Anomaly (%)
	WLRL	WLRM	WLRO	WLRP	WLRR	WLRS	WLRX	WLRY	WLSH	WLSI
1985	11.3	−0.6	4.4	−0.4	7.8	−0.5	1 276.1	95.4	1 072.7	97.6
1986	11.2	−0.6	4.2	−0.6	7.7	−0.6	1 361.5	101.8	1 182.9	107.6
1987	11.4	−0.4	4.7	−0.2	8.1	−0.3	1 249.5	93.4	1 034.6	94.1
1988	12.2	0.3	5.4	0.6	8.8	0.5	1 324.3	99.0	1 131.2	102.9
1989	13.1	1.2	5.5	0.7	9.3	1.0	1 563.8	116.9	1 018.5	92.6
1990	13.1	1.2	5.8	0.9	9.4	1.1	1 490.7	111.4	1 172.8	106.7
1991	12.1	0.3	5.1	0.2	8.6	0.3	1 302.0	97.3	998.2	90.8
1992	12.3	0.4	5.2	0.4	8.7	0.4	1 290.8	96.5	1 186.8	107.9
1993	11.8	−0.1	5.0	0.1	8.4	..	1 218.6	91.1	1 121.1	102.0
1994	12.4	0.5	5.5	0.6	8.9	0.6	1 366.9	102.2	1 184.7	107.7
1995	13.0	1.1	5.4	0.6	9.2	0.9	1 588.5	118.7	1 023.7	93.1
1996	11.7	−0.1	4.7	−0.1	8.2	−0.2	1 403.5	104.9	916.6	83.4
1997	13.1	1.3	5.8	1.0	9.4	1.1	1 430.3	106.9	1 024.0	93.1
1998	12.6	0.8	5.8	1.0	9.1	0.8	1 268.4	94.8	1 265.1	115.1
1999	13.0	1.1	5.9	1.0	9.4	1.1	1 419.4	106.1	1 237.2	112.5
2000	12.7	0.8	5.6	0.8	9.1	0.8	1 367.5	102.2	1 335.6	121.5
2001	12.4	0.6	5.3	0.5	8.8	0.5	1 411.9	105.5	1 049.9	95.5
2002	13.0	1.1	6.0	1.2	9.5	1.2	1 304.0	97.5	1 280.5	116.5
2003	13.5	1.6	5.6	0.7	9.5	1.2	1 587.4	118.7	901.5	82.0
2004	13.0	1.2	6.0	1.2	9.5	1.2	1 361.4	101.8	1 210.1	110.1
2005	13.1	1.2	5.9	1.1	9.5	1.1	1 399.2	104.6	1 083.0	98.4

Anomalies are with respect to the 1961-90 averaging period.

Source: Met Office

Index - figures indicate tables numbers

Index